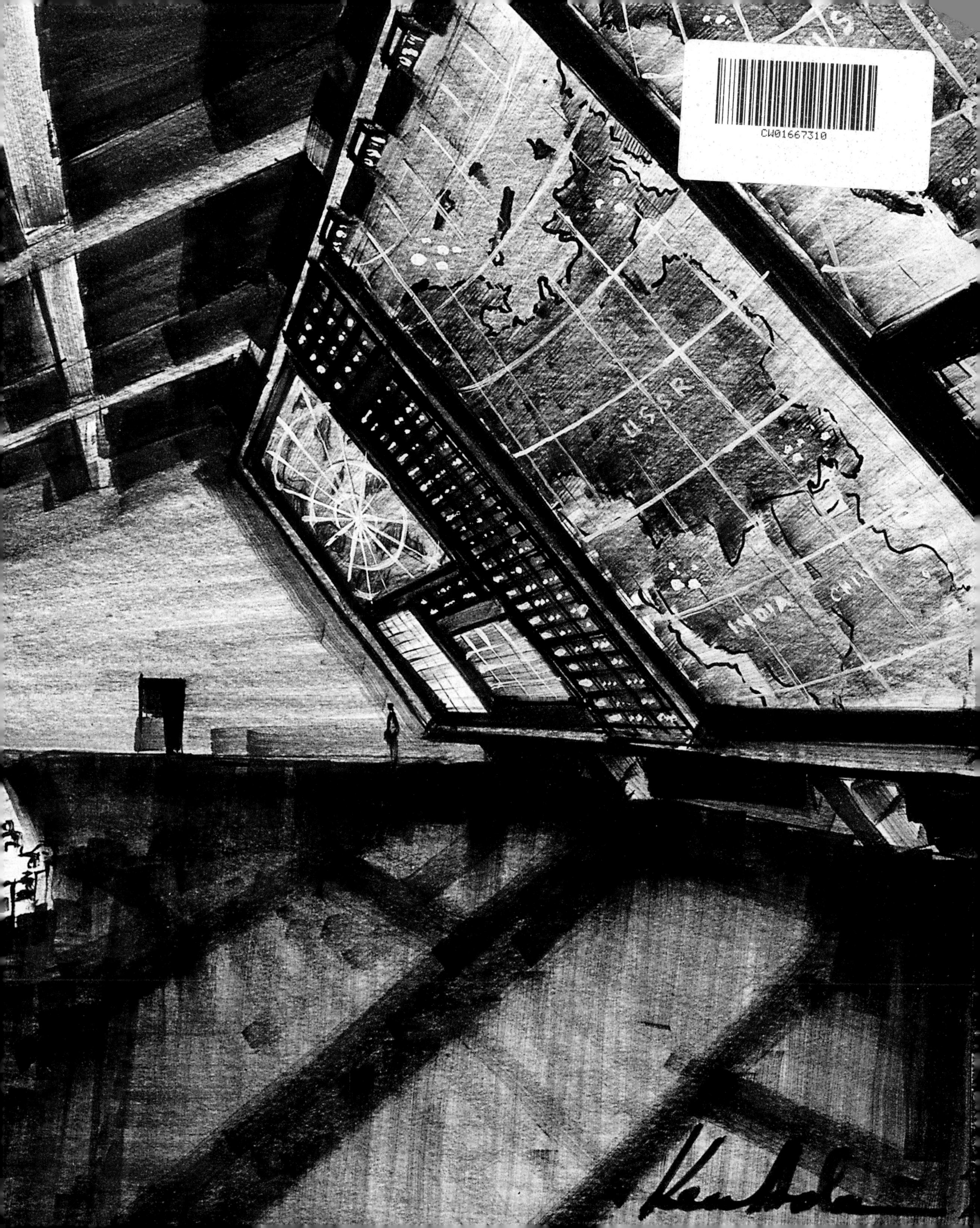
USSR
INDIA

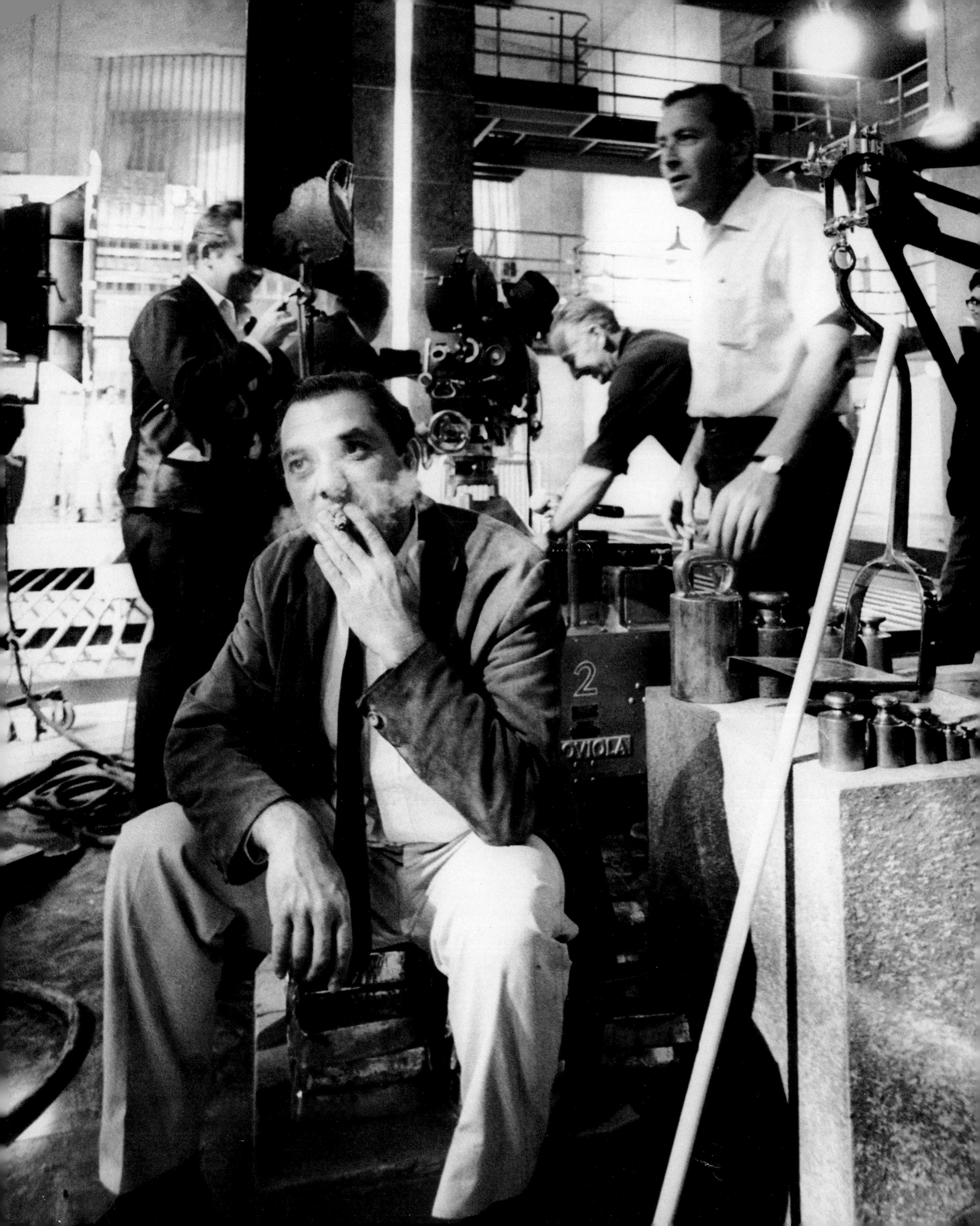
2
OVIOLA

David Sylvester

Moonraker, Strangelove and other celluloid dreams: the visionary art of Ken Adam

With texts by

Philip French

Christopher Frayling

Ken Adam

Serpentine Gallery, London 1999

This catalogue is published to accompany the exhibition

Moonraker, Strangelove and other celluloid dreams: the visionary art of Ken Adam

17 November 1999 – 9 January 2000

Curator and Editor: David Sylvester

For the Serpentine Gallery:
Director: Julia Peyton-Jones
Exhibition Organiser and Associate Editor: Leigh Markopoulos
Gallery Manager: Michael Gaughan

Sponsored by

INSINGER TOWNSLEY

In association with

Time Out London's Living Guide.

The Serpentine Gallery is supported by the Arts Council of England and the Westminster City Council

Prepared and published by the Serpentine Gallery, London 1999

Designed by Herman Lelie
Typeset by Stefania Bonelli
Production co-ordinated by Uwe Kraus GmbH
Printed in Italy

ISBN 18 70814 274

Serpentine Gallery
Kensington Gardens, London W2 3XA
Telephone: + 44 (0)171 402 6075
Fax: +44 (0) 171 402 4103

Funded by THE ARTS COUNCIL OF ENGLAND

SUPPORTED BY CITY OF WESTMINSTER

Photographic credits

© Bibliotheque nationale de France, Paris
The Cabinet of Dr Caligari Nicholson Collection/Decla-Bioscop
Cabiria Nicholson Collection/Itala
Edward Hopper, *Nighthawks* © 1999, The Art Institute of Chicago. All rights reserved.
The James Bond International Fan Club Archive
Knight without Armour/BFI Films: Stills, Posters and Designs/London Film/Carlton UK
Metropolis/The Ronald Grant Archive/UFA
© The New Yorker Collection 1946 Charles Addams from cartoonban.com. All rights reserved.
Dr No, *Goldfinger*, *Thunderball*, *You Only Live Twice*, *Diamonds are Forever*, *The Spy Who Loved Me*, *Moonraker* © 1962, 1964, 1965, 1967, 1971, 1977, 1979 Danjaq, LLC and United Artists Corporation. All rights reserved.
The Queen of Spades Nicholson Collection/Canal Plus
Stephen White

Contents

Sponsor's Foreword

Insinger Townsley is delighted to be associated with the Serpentine Gallery's exhibition of the works of Ken Adam, curated by David Sylvester.

It is fitting that this exhibition spans the two millennia. As we move from one century of innovation to another, Ken Adam's pioneering work stands as a tribute to the creativity and dynamism of the late 20th century.

This is the first arts sponsorship for the recently merged Insinger Townsley, a specialist stockbroking and financial advisory business. As part of the Insinger de Beaufort private banking and trust group, Insinger Townsley shares the same vision and values of its parent – creativity, dynamism and sustained innovation form the cornerstones of the group's business ethic. It is this common thread with the work of Ken Adam that drew us to supporting the exhibition.

From *Dr Strangelove* to *Moonraker*, from *The Ipcress File* to *The Madness of King George*, Ken Adam has made an indelible mark on the history and development of film and art. This exhibition is a celebration of Ken Adam's contribution to influential 20th century visual culture and is bound to leave you not shaken, but stirred.

INSINGER TOWNSLEY

Insinger de Beaufort and Townsley & Co are regulated by the Securities and Futures Authority.

Director's Foreword

David Sylvester has had a long association with the Serpentine Gallery, both as a curator of landmark exhibitions and as a Trustee. He has seen the exhibition programme develop in response to the changing demands of artists and a public increasingly interested in modern and contemporary art. When we invited him to propose an exhibition for the Serpentine that would span the millennium, we had anticipated – mistakenly, as it turned out – the direction in which his thoughts might turn. We envisaged a proposal focusing on an artist, or group of artists, whom he has long championed, for example the masters of Minimalism. His response, that an exhibition of the work of Ken Adam would not only be timely but long overdue, took us by surprise, although its relevance was more inspired than we fully appreciated at the time. It soon became clear that not only would this be a 'first' – there has never been a presentation in Britain, in a publicly funded art gallery, devoted solely to a film production designer – but that the richness, diversity and sheer virtuosity of Ken Adam's extraordinary contribution would make a compelling exhibition.

Ken Adam is hailed as the world's greatest living production designer, having worked on no fewer than eighty-eight film projects, seventy-five of which have been realised. It was his vision that placed Blofeld's lair inside a volcano, resulting in the largest set ever built in Europe (*You Only Live Twice*); that created the *Liparus* supertanker on the world's largest soundstage (*The Spy Who Loved Me*), and that transformed existing locations to recreate eighteenth-century England (*The Madness of King George*). In a time of ever more sophisticated computer technology, Ken Adam's preferred means of expression – the Flowmaster pen – has unleashed an array of extraordinarily diverse and original designs that have captured the imagination of successive generations. In recognition of his formidable achievements, Ken Adam has been consistently nominated for international film awards. He was presented with an Academy Award for both *Barry Lyndon* and *The Madness of King George* and received British Academy of Film and Television Awards (BAFTA) for *Dr Strangelove* and *The Ipcress File*. He has also been the subject of an exhibition organised for the Forum der Technik at the Deutsches Museum in 1994 which, after its showing in Munich, toured internationally for four years.

Ken Adam's exhibition at the Serpentine Gallery focuses on twenty-nine projects, concentrating almost exclusively on his designs for the cinema, with the exception of two great operas, namely Puccini's *La Fanciulla del West* and Alban Berg's *Wozzeck*. Central to this presentation is a compilation of film extracts that have been selected for their tremendous visual impact. However, the entrance to the exhibition already immerses us in Ken Adam's world. It was his idea that the South Rooms should give visitors a real sense of one of his most remarkable film-set designs. By extending his original drawing for the *Dr Strangelove* War Room so that its proportions matched the Gallery's when it was enlarged from floor to ceiling, and by surrounding it with enlarged photographic stills of the set, he has created a Pentagon-on-the-Park.

Ken Adam's commitment to the exhibition has been extraordinary. Both he and his wife, Letizia, have contributed many valuable ideas about its shape, and they have also undertaken the considerable labour of guiding us through the wealth of material in their archive, for which we are enormously indebted to them. They have joined David Sylvester, Leigh Markopoulos, the Serpentine Gallery's exhibition organiser, and myself, to work very much as a team on every aspect of this challenging project.

This catalogue, the first publication in English about Ken Adam, is edited, and includes an introductory essay, by David Sylvester, who was active as a film critic and documentary filmmaker in the 1950s and 1960s. Ken Adam's importance as a production designer is discussed by Philip French, the *Observer* film critic, who has long been one of our leading commentators on film. Christopher Frayling, Rector of the Royal College of Art, London, and cultural historian, focuses on the significance of Ken Adam's work. The publication also benefits from the inclusion of Ken Adam's own words, to describe those projects which are the subject of this exhibition, and from Cathy Surowiec's filmography, the first fully comprehensive version in print. Herman Lelie has designed a book that is as handsome as it is informative, and his sensitivity to the subject matter is greatly appreciated.

Through Insinger Townsley's sponsorship of the exhibition, it has been possible for the Serpentine to present Ken Adam's work to the highest standard. We are indebted to Barry Townsley and Graham Davin for recognising the benefit to their company of collaborating with the Gallery on this important occasion, and also wish to thank Michelle Kline-Bethlehem for coordinating all practical aspects of this association.

We are delighted that Barbara Broccoli and Michael G. Wilson of Eon Productions also wish to be associated with this landmark presentation, and we thank them for their invaluable support. Once again, we are fortunate to be working with *Time Out*, the media sponsor of this exhibition, and in particular with Tony Elliot and Christine Cort, who both appreciate and endorse our desire that a wide public is made aware of the exhibition and Ken Adam's work. David Jeffers and Michael Elson of the Moving Picture Company were quick to offer their company's impressive resources to edit the compilation film and to advise us on the technical aspects of the exhibition. Without them we would have struggled hard to meet the high standards required for such a film presentation and we cannot thank them enough for sharing their expertise.

Ken and Letizia Adam's wide circle of admirers, including Alvaro Maccioni of La Famiglia, Lawrence A. Mirisch of the Mirish Agency, Lois Sieff, Selim K. Zilka and other individuals, who wish to remain anonymous, have made donations in support of the exhibition. Stephen Evans of Renaissance Films, a colleague and admirer of Ken Adam's, has masterminded a small group to join him in generously sponsoring the Serpentine Winter Party, held on the occasion of this exhibition, and for this we are indebted to them.

The distributors of the films included in the exhibition graciously agreed to waive their standard licensing fees, thereby enabling us to show important film footage that is essential for a real understanding of Ken Adam's oeuvre. We are very much indebted to Columbia Tristar Motion Picture Group, FilmFour Ltd, Metro-Goldwyn-Mayer, Twentieth Century-Fox and Warner Brothers for their cooperation. We would especially like to thank Rick Senat and Julian Senior of Warner Brothers, Meg Simmonds and Anne Bennett of Eon Productions, Beverly Starr of Columbia Tristar Motion Picture Group, and Judy Franks of British Actors Equity for their endeavours on our behalf.

Among the many individuals and organisations who have made this exhibition possible, we would particularly like to acknowledge Jonathan Cameron, to whom we turned for advice on numerous occasions and who was unfailing in his response, and Gillian Gordon, who was instrumental in identifying sources for the specialist help we often needed. Additional thanks are due also to Peter Ettedgui, David Parfitt, John Woodward and his colleagues at the British Film Institute.

The Serpentine team have sprung into action once again to meet the challenge of organising this exhibition whose deadlines seemed imminent from the moment we began. Their sterling work and steadfast commitment has been remarkable.

The most important debt of gratitude is, of course, owed to Ken Adam. We could never have embarked upon this project without his support and constant encouragement, and also that of his wife, Letizia. This exhibition testifies to the immense respect and esteem that Ken's contribution to the world of film has earned him. We thank them both.

Julia Peyton-Jones
Serpentine Gallery

Curator's Foreword

I was at prep school with Ken Adam in the mid-1930s. He was emphatically handsome, splendidly foreign, charismatic, gifted at art, rather arrogant and the class wit. Thirty years on, I'd see him *chez* Stanley Kubrick, whom both of us had worked for, he in a famous position on *Dr Strangelove*, myself in an obscure one in connection with *Lolita*. I don't think I saw him again till the day in 1995 when he was awarded an Honorary Doctorate at the Royal College of Art and Christopher Frayling's oration in his honour brought home to me that no one had been more important for the popular arts in Britain in our time. Over lunch in the Senior Common Room I asked Ken whether there had ever been an exhibition of his work. 'Not in this country.' he said, and I inwardly resolved to put that right.

I am deeply grateful to Julia Peyton-Jones for enabling that to happen, undeterred by the complexity and novelty of the enterprise. The speed at which we have needed to work has meant that I have had to depend on her to take time out from running a gallery in order to share a great many curatorial decisions. By the same token, the urgency has made horrific demands on the energy and efficiency of Leigh Markopoulos, that ideal associate. And I am greatly indebted to Mike Gaughan, the Gallery Manager and my partner in the installation of the show, a task which in this case included making the final choice of drawings. All of the hundreds, or even thousands, of decisions involved were joint decisions.

Above all, of course, I have to thank Ken and Letizia Adam. Naturally the Director's Foreword has already described the nature and extent of their contribution. I would like to lay special emphasis on my gratitude to Ken for composing an overture to the show and to both of them for a wonderfully argumentative, exhilarating and affectionate collaboration.

David Sylvester

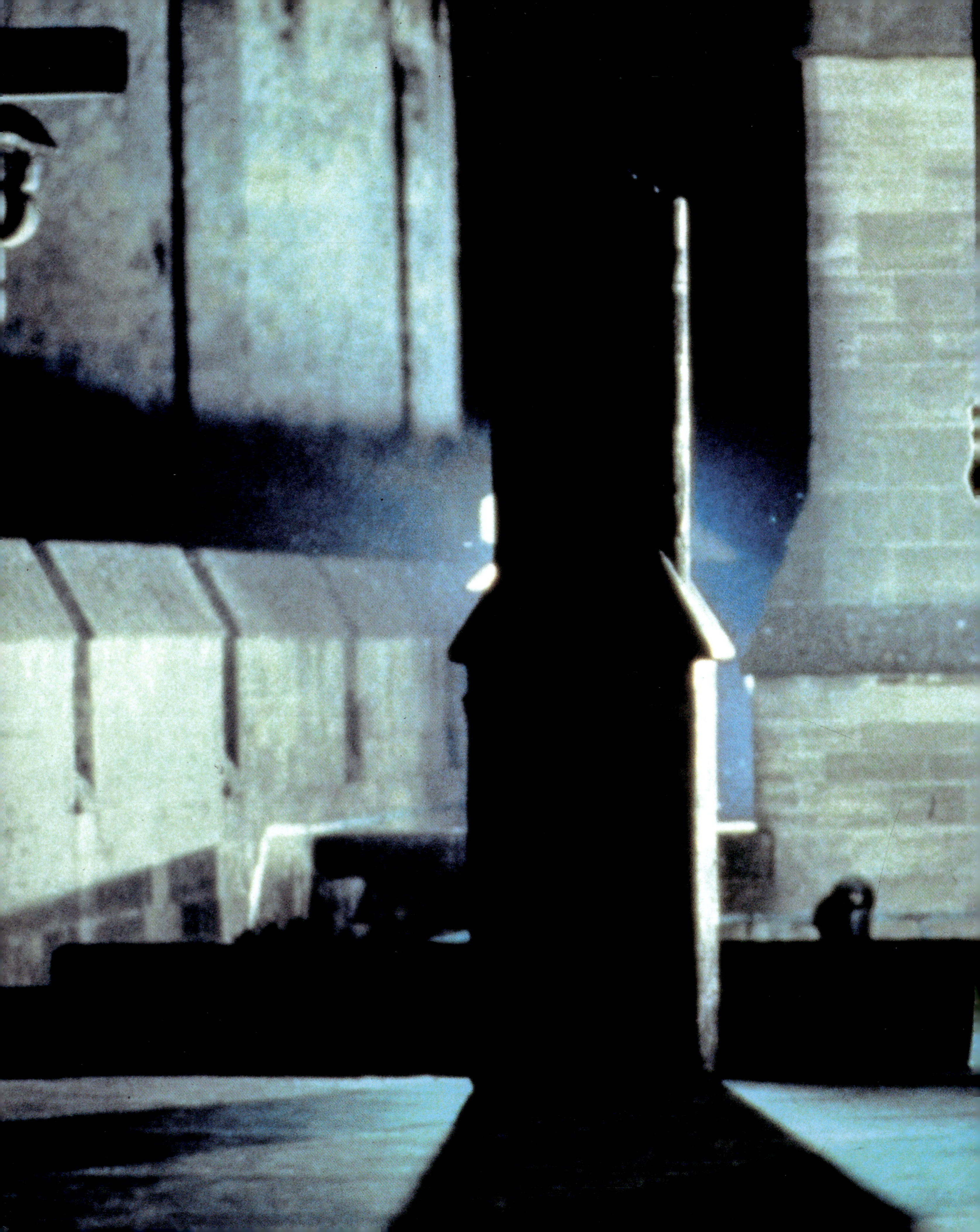

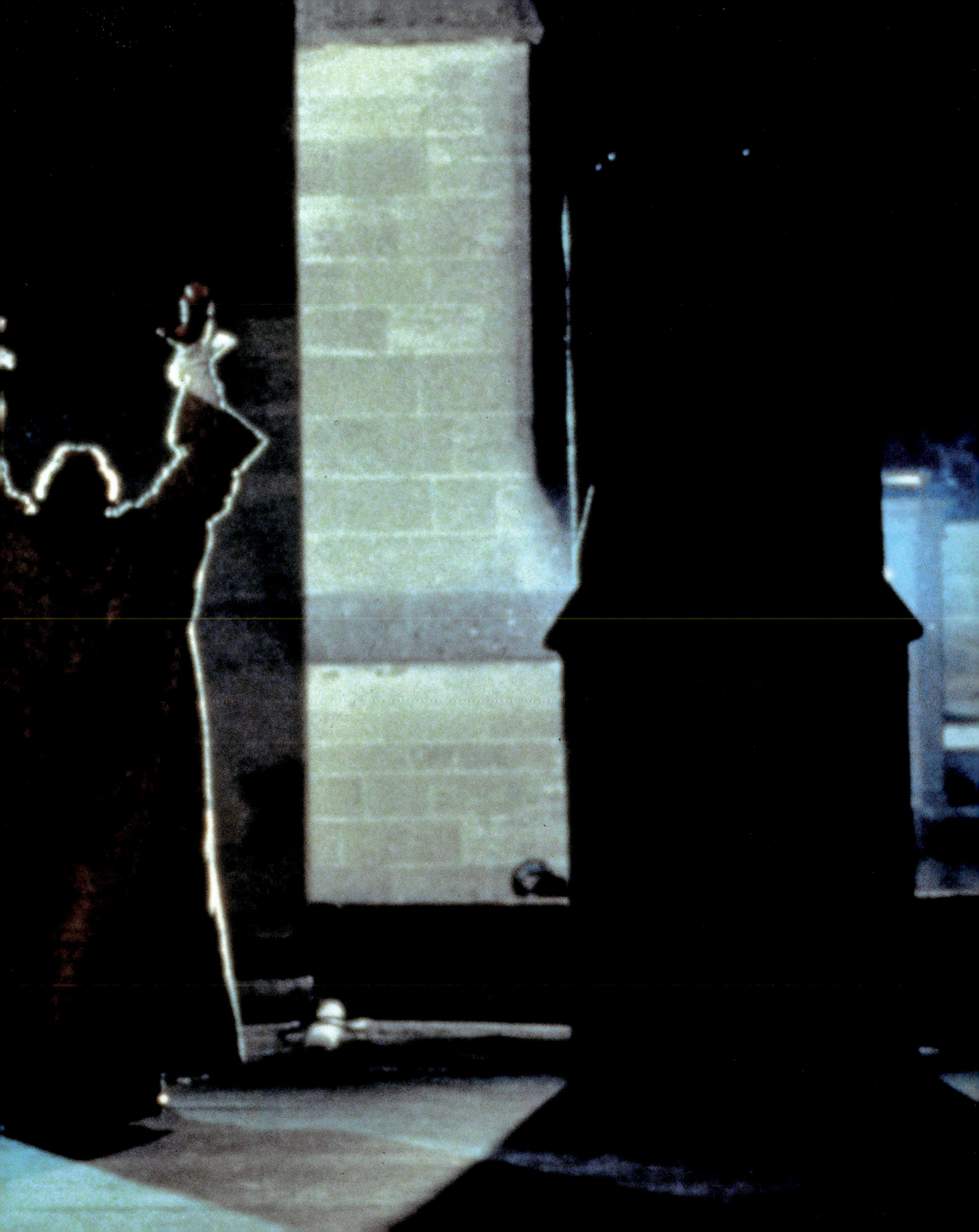

David Sylvester

Ken Adam, Production Designer: An Introductory Note

There are moments in film where the set is more magnetic than the actors, the dialogue, the editing, the music. Some of the unforgettable sets are real places: the Odessa Steps, Monument Valley, the rolling streets of San Francisco. Some are made up: 'Tara' in *Gone With the Wind*, the 'Silver Sandal' nitery in *Swingtime*, 'Xanadu' in *Citizen Kane*, the Pentagon War Room in *Dr Strangelove*. (Perhaps the last-named locus too should have been designated inside quotation marks: it's said that when Ronald Reagan came to Washington as the newly elected president, he asked to be taken to see the Pentagon War Room he had seen in the film, a holy-of-holies he wanted to view in the round, being innocent – despite his long experience as a movie actor – of the fact that it had never existed outside Shepperton Studios.) But who were the individuals who dreamed up the architecture of such sets? We can read quite informative histories of the cinema without coming upon their names, though some of them have left a mark on the medium as individual and as deep as those of great actors, directors, writers or cinematographers. But they somehow tend to share the anonymity of the designers of legendary monuments: Grand Central Station, Wembley Stadium, the Sacré Coeur, the White House.

Film designers are generally known as 'art directors'; for some time it was 'unit art directors', in distinction to 'supervising art directors', the ones who ran the studio art departments and received the prizes won by their subordinates. The creator of the room Reagan wanted to see, Ken Adam, was credited as 'art director' on his early films as the principal designer; since 1957, 'production designer' has been his usual credit. It is a term which seems to have been invented by David O. Selznick when producing *Gone With the Wind*. In a famous memorandum written in 1937 on the subject of the use he wanted to make of William Cameron Menzies – that great cinematic figure who was not only a designer but had directed such films as *Things to Come* – he contended that *G.W.T.W.* needed someone of Menzies's talent and experience so that the film could be prepared almost down to the last camera angle before shooting started. The whole physical side of the film should be personally handled by one man who had little or nothing else to do. Menzies's participation would therefore be 'a lot greater in scope than is normally associated with the term "art direction". Accordingly I would probably give him some such credit as "Production Designed by William Cameron Menzies" ...'

Previous page:
The Madness of King George (Nicholas Hytner, 1994)

Giving this amount of responsibility to the designer of a film was not a total break with the past, more a difference of degree: traditionally the job of art director could be purely architectural or could include involvement in creating storyboards and suggesting camera angles; there was always a tendency for the art director to do some directing of the action. At the same time, the job of the 'production designer' is not often as comprehensive as Menzies's was on *G.W.T.W.* That is to say, this credit is like all credits for collaborative work in that its precise meaning tends to vary from one project to another. (In one of the projects in which Adam was involved in an especially personal way, *Pennies from Heaven*, his role in designing the production got an odd pair of credits: 'associate producer' and 'visual consultant'.)

As it happens, William Cameron Menzies (pronounced as it is spelt) was to play a critical role in Adam's career. By the time they met, Adam, born in 1921, had worked in England or Italy on such films as *The Queen of Spades* (1948, directed by Thorold Dickinson), *Captain Horatio Hornblower R.N.* (1951, Raoul Walsh), *The Crimson Pirate* (1952, Robert Siodmak) and *Helen of Troy* (1955, Robert Wise). At this point Mike Todd invited him to work on *Around the World in Eighty Days* (1956, Michael Anderson) as one of two art directors operating under the command of Menzies. Not surprisingly, the great man became a mentor and an ongoing source of inspiration. Adam was assigned the sets for the film's European loci, and among those he created were his first masterpieces – Lloyds of London, with its challenging use of black and white, and the employment bureau, with its chorus of candidates for jobs placed in a very straight line while John Gielgud bickers with a bewigged Noël Coward. There is no knowing how far this surge of inventiveness and wit was due to Menzies's influence, how far to a simple process of maturation, how far to the spur of Todd's outrageous tycoonery. But it is certain that Adam had now made it clear that he was already the most brilliant and masterly designer in British films.

This meant that he got invited to work under several top American directors when they came over to make a film in Britain. He worked under John Ford on *Gideon's Day* (perhaps the worst of all Ford's bad films), under Robert Aldrich on *Ten Seconds to Hell*, *The Angry Hills* and *Sodom and Gomorrah*, and under Jacques Tourneur on *Night of the Demon*, aka *Curse of the Demon* (1957). This is a gem of a horror film by a master of the genre, based on a story by another, M. R. James. Sadly, it was left flawed by the interference of thick-headed producers who demanded blatancy where Tourneur and Adam would have preferred suggestion: thus, whereas the director and still more the designer wanted the demon to be manifest only in glimpses of its great steaming footprints, the producers insisted on two appearances of the monster in person and Adam had to come up with a toothy cousin of King Kong's.

The next major step in Adam's progress was constrained in another way: *The Trials of Oscar Wilde* (1960, Ken Hughes) had an extremely limited budget, but Adam contrived to make a shining aesthetic virtue out of practical necessity. The *réclame* won for this film did much to get him the job that made him a star: designing the first of the James Bond films, again on a small budget, *Dr No* (1962, Terence Young). And this triumph in turn induced Stanley Kubrick to hire him for *Dr Strangelove or:*

How I Learned to Stop Worrying and Love the Bomb (1963). This was undoubtedly the finest film he was ever to work on. But he did work on at least one other black comedy that was outstandingly well scripted and well acted, *Sleuth* (1972), made by another top American director, Joseph L. Mankiewicz, and the two films are perfect models of antithetic ways in which the settings and scripts in black comedies can interact. In *Strangelove* the War-Room set, while preposterous in its extravagance, is also seriously imposing and reflects the awesomeness of the tragic plot; the absurdity and subversiveness of the dialogue are a hysterically funny foil to the sense of doom. *Sleuth*, on the other hand, is a drawing-room comedy in which the situations, although they deal in life and death, are essentially flip, and the sets are a continuous active ingredient in the fun.

Strangelove and *Sleuth* are also complementary in that one represents Adam as a designer on a heroic scale, the other as a designer on a domestic scale. Others among his more intimate works are the interiors in *Agnes of God* (1985, Norman Jewison), which recall Vermeer in their sober, silent greys and blacks and whites and the severe rectangles of the doorways and corridors and grilles, and the aborted recent project for a stage production of Alban Berg's opera *Wozzeck*.

But it was, of course, the epic architecture that Adam created in the 1960s and 1970s for *Strangelove* and the Bond films that made his reputation. Among his seven Bond films, his finest achievements seem to me to be *You Only Live Twice* (1967), *The Spy Who Loved Me* (1977) and *Moonraker* (1979). It may or may not be relevant that these were the three Bond films that were directed by Lewis Gilbert. It is certainly relevant that two of them were the last two of the seven. In the course of an interview at the time of *Moonraker*'s release, Adam told Eliot Wald:

> The producers no longer really use the Ian Fleming novels. We start with a general story-line, which is almost always the same lately. Then we go location scouting, looking for places that haven't been seen in the movies too much. On the trip, the director, the writer and I begin putting together concrete ideas ... The Bond films are done so loosely that the script isn't the Bible that it is in most films. It changes all the time and the whole process of writing it is like some democratic debating society.

This was really Adam's modest and diplomatic way of telling the truth that what really mattered in these films was what he contributed: what are probably the most amazing and enthralling pieces of fantastic architecture in the history of talking pictures. They might even have been surpassed if the sketches he made in the late 1970s for a proposed but aborted translation to the cinema of *Star Trek* had been realised: these extraordinary visions, incidentally, sometimes seem to anticipate the architecture of Daniel Libeskind.

This brief note is not the place for serious investigation of possible origins or antecedents for Adam's architectural imaginings, but I would offer one suggestion. Adam is an avowed fan of Piranesi, and it is easy to see an affection for the *Carceri*, especially (for example see pages 86–87), in a number of his sketches. But Piranesi's vision tends to be hairy and Adam's to be bald, Piranesi's to be Roman and Adam's to be Egyptian, and I suspect that among Piranesi's heirs in France there was one visionary architect with whom Adam has a closer while surely unconscious affinity: Etienne-Louis Boullée (1728–99). One of the significant features that Adam's work shares with Boullée's is its awesome use of vast spheres, sublime incarnations of the form of which Boullée wrote:

> From whatever side we look at this shape, no trick of perspective can alter the magnificence of its perfect form ... Of all bodies, it offers the largest surface to the eye, and this lends it majesty. It has the utmost simplicity because that surface is flawless and endless. Besides these qualities, we must speak of a grace that owes its being to an outline that is as soft and as flowing as it is possible to imagine.

Boullée's *Newton's Cenotaph*, for example, or his *Conical Cenotaph*, its apex truncated, cypresses around its base and a huge hemisphere within, present a world very close to Adam's.

The failure of the Bond and *Strangelove* designs to win a single Oscar would be astonishing were it not for the fact that Academy Awards have always been aberrant: after all, John Wayne himself failed to get one for *Red River* or *Hondo* or *The Searchers* and had to wait till, with one foot in the grave, he had one kindly conferred upon him for *True Grit*. By the same token, Adam's only Oscars were awarded in 1975 and

Etienne-Louis Boullée
Newton's Cenotaph, exterior by night 1784
Ink and wash

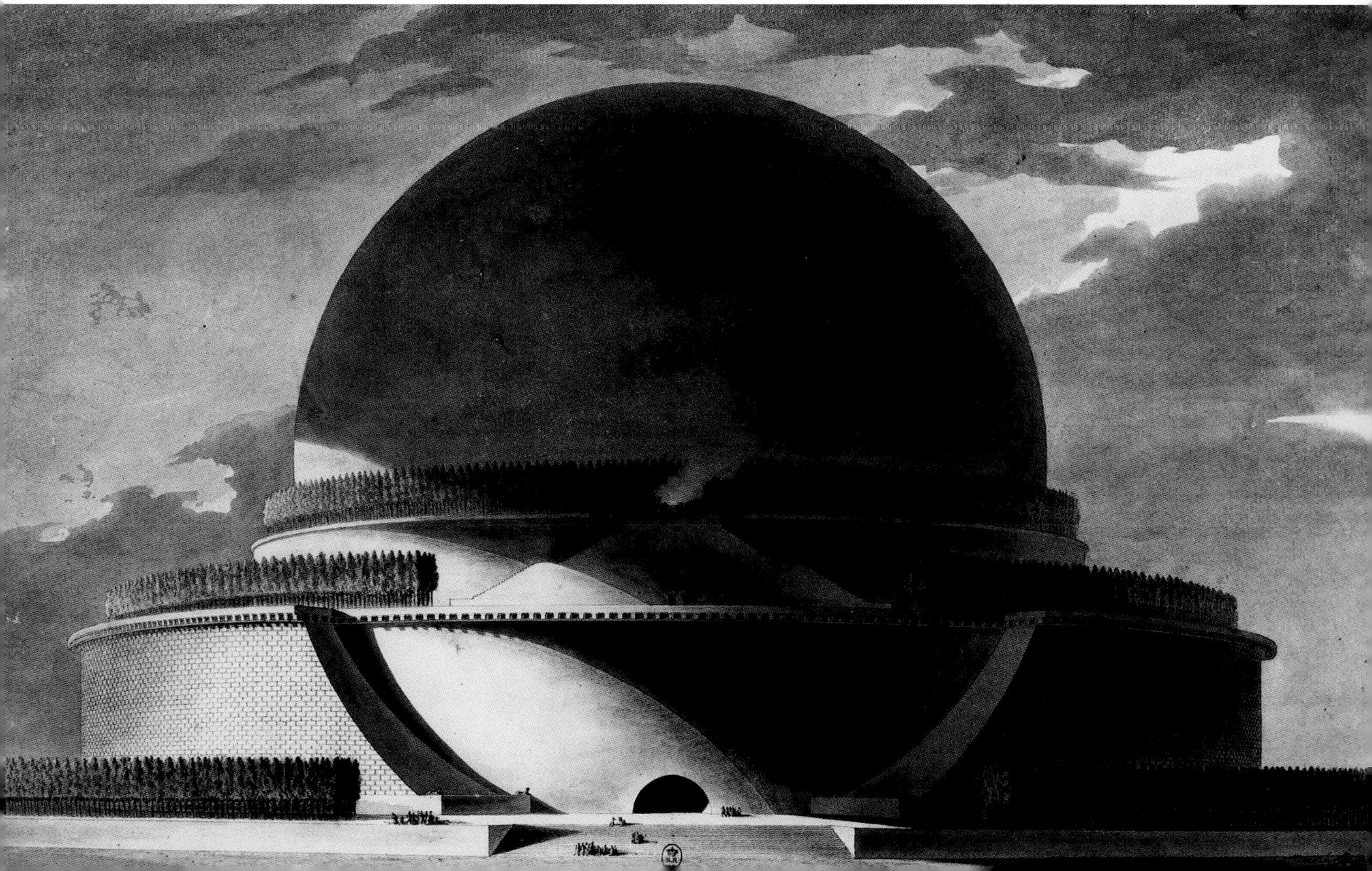

1994, both for atypical work, on *Barry Lyndon* and *The Madness of King George*, costume dramas which exhibit all his marvellous talent for pastiching or quoting historic architecture but not his more important talent for inventing fantastic architecture. Nevertheless, *King George* is a wonderful film, and Adam's contribution to it is wonderfully resourceful and convincing in the ways it mixes existing and constructed sets – as in the series of scenes in which the King hijacks the harpsichord at an orchestral concert, wrestles the Prince of Wales to the ground, and flees with his young children up a stone spiral staircase to escape the delusory threat of rising floods. Totally constructed interiors are interspersed with the Painted Room at Greenwich, a staircase in St Paul's, and part of a roof at Arundel Castle where Adam, finding tall stone chimneys whose resemblance to classical columns hinted at the tragic, proceeded to multiply their number to heighten that effect.

Adam's brilliance in both appropriating and pastiching bits of the eighteenth century is almost matched when he is dealing with biblical times, as in *King David* (1985), or with yesterday, as in *Pennies from Heaven* (1981), the musical scripted by Dennis Potter and directed by Herbert Ross, a close friend of Adam's with whom he has worked on seven films. Here the evocation of Chicago in the 1930s is entirely fabricated, using no photography of real places (with the notable exception of a long road across a flat landscape which bears a striking resemblance to the road where Cary Grant was ambushed by an aeroplane in *North by Northwest* – and is indeed that very road, near Los Angeles). By the same token, while the songs, including their performances, are lifted from period recordings, the dances are pastiches subtle enough to contain comment as well as imitation – which is what makes this a postmodernist musical. Thus the dazzling parody of a Busby Berkeley number is not just a re-creation but an updating, so that there is suddenly a passage where the chorus and its reflection at a lower level anticipates the layered horizontal rhythms of photographs taken in the 1990s by Andreas Gursky.

Pennies from Heaven may provide a key to the essential nature of Adam's more spectacular designs: that in spirit they are designs for musicals. In *Around the World in Eighty Days* the row of job candidates in the employment bureau has the look of a chorus line. In *Goldfinger* the fight to the death in Fort Knox between Bond and the Korean hired assassin, Oddjob, is as balletic as it is violent. If *Salon Kitty* is one of the few films ever made in which orgiastic scenes are not unintentionally comic, it is because of the choreographic art with which nude and semi-nude figures disport themselves among Nazi banners. In *The Madness of King George* there are frequent surging movements of human figures – sometimes a small group, sometimes a crowd, as when the court has assembled for the concert – which are highly balletic. And again and again in the Bond films there are choruses of rapt figures moving like dancers, above all in the scenes in *Moonraker* in which the beautiful young couples who are to be the progenitors of a master race are parading through the halls and corridors of a space station like the chorines of the great Hollywood musicals of the 1930s, films which, hardly less than the UFA productions of Ken Adam's native country, must have formed a large part of his early boyhood intake of celluloid dreams.

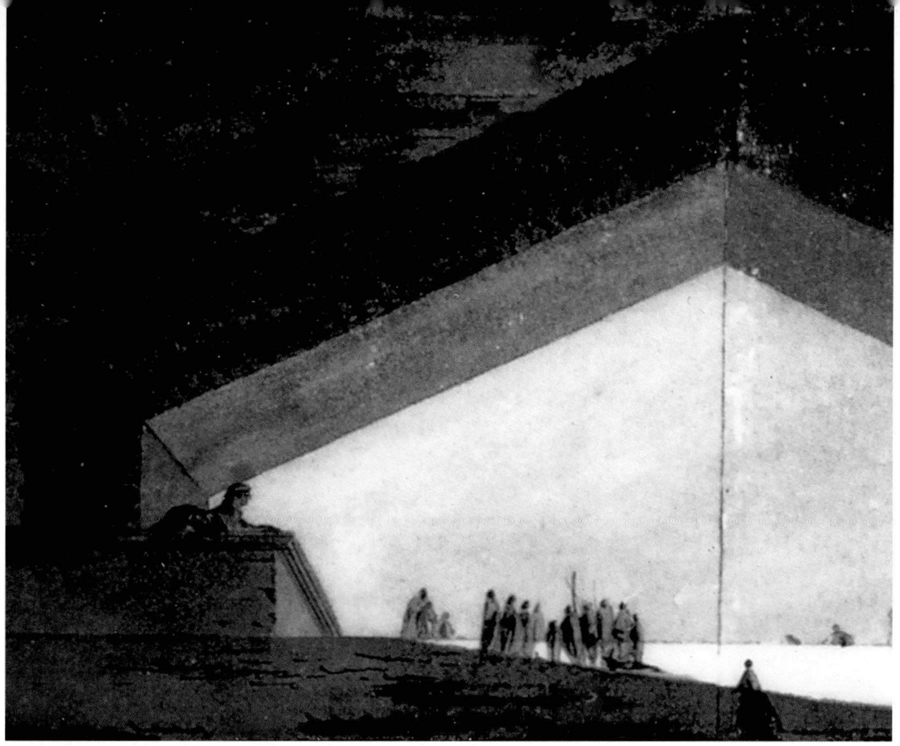

Below:
Etienne-Louis Boullée
Entrance to a Cemetery
undated
Ink and wash

Left:
Detail

Etienne-Louis Boullée
Cross-section of the Conical Cenotaph
undated
Ink and wash

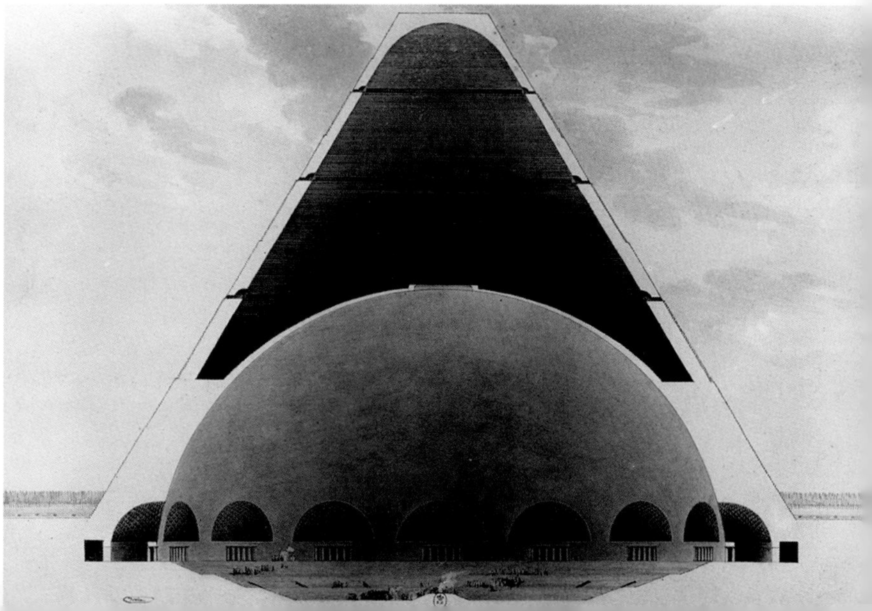

Philip French

The Designer as Collaborator and Auteur

Behind the proscenium arch is an empty box with bare walls. So when the curtain parts in the theatre we know that the sitting room, the landscape, or whatever confronts us on the stage, has been wholly created by someone to fill the vacant space. What is projected onto a cinema screen is altogether different. Is it someone's real sitting room we are looking at, or an exact copy of a real one, or a purely imaginary place? We can rarely be absolutely sure. This is the crucial distinction René Clair notes in his Foreword to Léon Barsacq's history of film design, *Le Décor de film*, the only book of consequence on the role of the production designer.[1]

Barry Lyndon
(Stanley Kubrick, 1975)

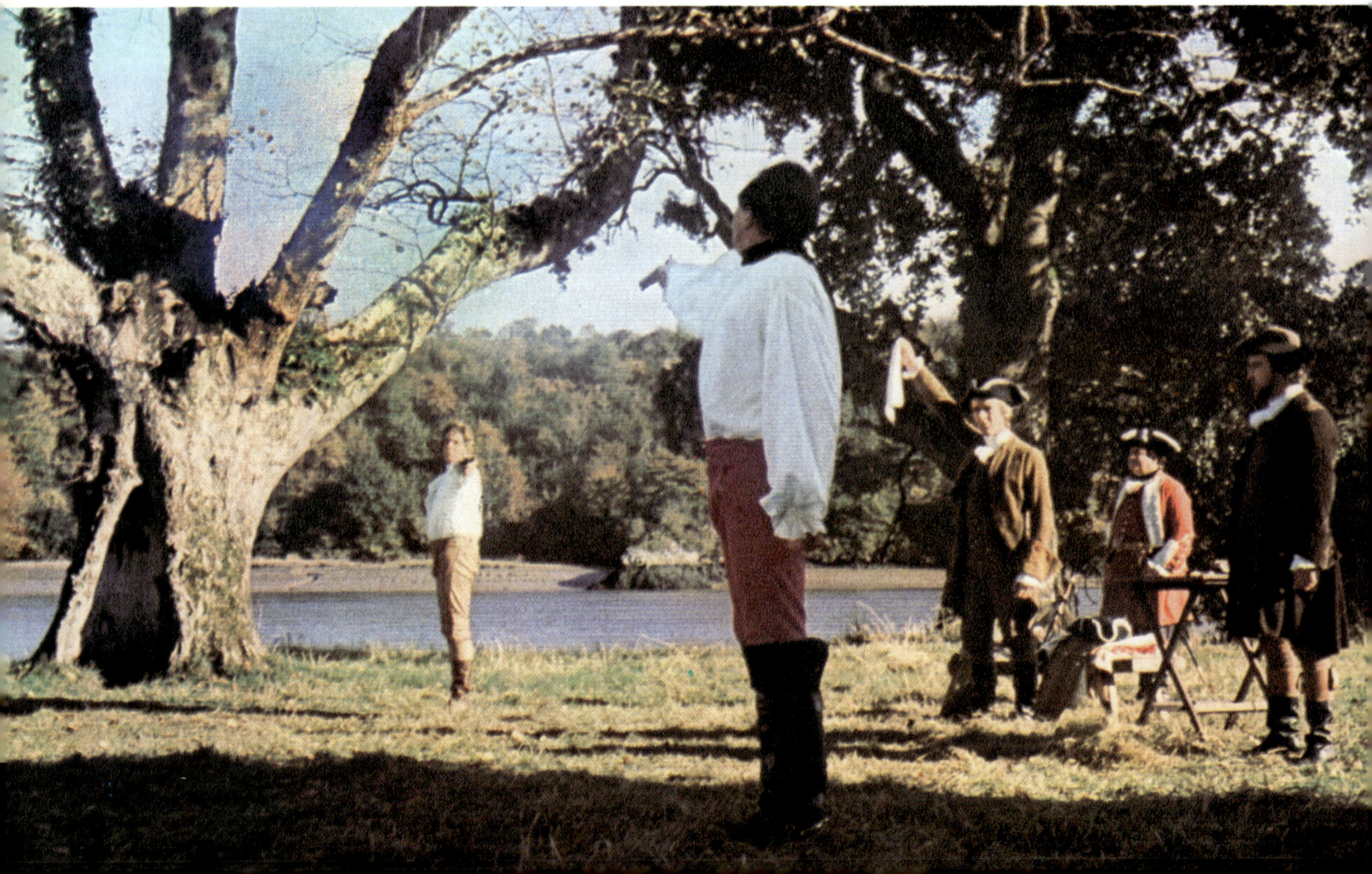

Obviously in a Bond movie we know that the villain's fantastic lair has come out of someone's imagination, though a good many viewers of Patrick McGoohan's TV series *The Prisoner* thought that its sinister setting – Clough Williams-Ellis's visionary Portmeirion built in North Wales between the wars – had been constructed in a studio. In the opening shot of *Barry Lyndon*, though we know that the duellists and their seconds are actors in eighteenth-century costume, we suppose that we are looking at a real Irish field. Yet did someone build the stone wall that provides depth to the composition and offsets the figures, and did someone colour the grass, and is that lowering sky real or painted on glass? Nobody not intimately associated with the production of a movie can ever know who did precisely what. As the years pass, as egos become inflated and memories distorted, claims are made, blame is laid, legends grow. The only reliable evidence about the making of a picture is the contemporary memorandum, dictated at the time and filed in the studio archives. But even this can be self-serving, a hedge against posterity.

Ken Adam will be talking for himself elsewhere in this catalogue, and for the purpose of this essay I have deliberately not spoken with him or tracked down interviews he has given, though over the years I have read a few. Most memorably a feature in *Sight and Sound* which appeared at an impressionable time for me and thus permanently impressed itself on my mind to the extent that thereafter seeing a new film bearing Adam's name or seeing an earlier one on which he is credited caused me to look at the sets. There are many things I would like to ask him, about his concepts and his collaborators, but I have restricted myself here to the facts provided in the reference books and to films he has worked on as they appear on the screen and (just as important) *when* they appeared on the screen. I have recently looked again at a good many, at least twenty, and several of my favourites are pictures I saw before being aware of his role. I was delighted to discover, while perusing a list of Adam's non-theatrical undertakings, that in 1953 he had designed the Harlequin Coffee Bar in Oxford, a fashionable rendezvous of my student days.

If we reckon on the cinema beginning with the Lumière Brothers' show to the first paying audience at the Grand Café on the Boulevard des Capucines in Paris on 28 December 1895, then Ken Adam's first movie job came exactly at the midpoint of its history so far, in 1947. Of course the Lumières had no use for an art director or indeed anyone other than a man to point and crank the camera as workers left the Lumière factory in Lyon or a train arrived at a station on the Côte d'Azur. The first audiences were sufficiently amazed to see the world recorded and the Lumières sent photographers to the four corners to film its wonders. But meanwhile, Georges Méliès, the cinema's first artist, created his own little studio to explore the new medium's magical properties and create fantasies like his 1902 *A Trip to the Moon*. Over the next century the pendulum has seemed to swing back and forth between documentary and fiction, between what was thought of as the honest simplicity of the Lumières and the clever artifice of Méliès. But this begs the question about the nature of realism, what it consists in and where it is to be found. Michael Balcon hired the great documentarist Alberto Cavalcanti to introduce gritty realism into

Ealing Studio productions early in World War II. But once ensconced, Cavalcanti made melodramas and elegantly designed costume pictures like *Went the Day Well?*, *Champagne Charlie*, *Dead of Night* and *Nicholas Nickleby*, all shot on sound stages.

Architecturally trained set constructors and theatre-based designers began to establish their presence in the cinema early in the century, the former most significantly in Italy, the latter in France. The grandiose sets of Italian spectaculars like *Brutus* (1910), *Quo Vadis?* (1912) and *Cabiria* (1914) inspired a generation of future art directors. Unquestionably they became a seminal influence on Hollywood through the effect *Cabiria* had on D. W. Griffith. He made a quantum leap from the detailed, reconstructed realism of *Birth of a Nation* (1915), in which intertitles insist on the historical accuracy of his *tableaux vivants*, to the gigantic sets for *Intolerance* (1916) which remain unsurpassed to this day. Paolo and Vittorio Taviani made a whole movie, *Good Morning Babylon* (1987), about the influence of *Cabiria* on Griffith and how a pair of Italian artisans, recruited from the 1914 San Francisco Exposition, shaped his masterpiece. Sadly, their film needed a designer with larger resources.

World War I threw cinema into confusion; the coming of sound in 1927 created an aesthetic crisis to accompany the worldwide Depression that followed the Wall Street crash of 1929; the ascent of the Nazis in 1933 initiated a diaspora of talent that started in Germany, continued through Austria and France, and permanently

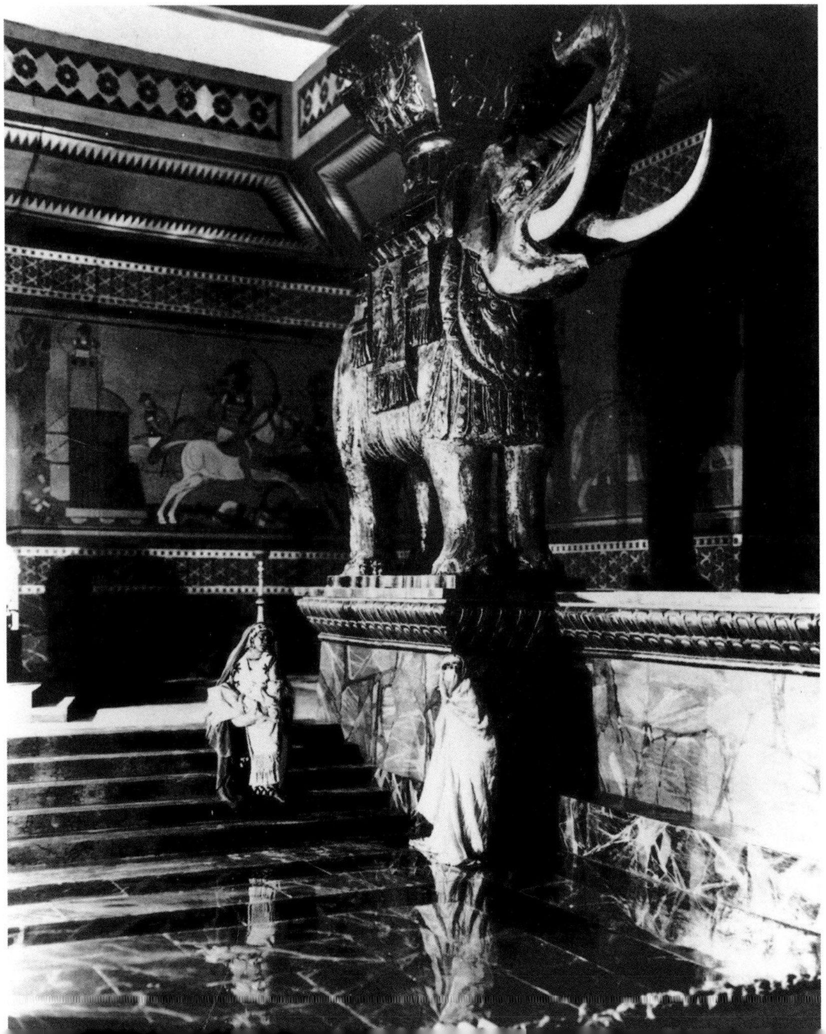

Cabiria
(Giovanni Pastrone, 1914)

altered the ecology of world cinema; the experimental era of Soviet cinema came to an end as the enlightened cultural commissar Lunacharsky was replaced by the Stalinist proponent of socialist realism, Zhdanov. At the UFA studio in Berlin, Europe's largest and most sophisticated film complex, a succession of ambitious, imaginatively designed pictures had been made in a style described as expressionist, directed by Robert Wiene, Fritz Lang, F. W. Murnau and others, designed by artists like Hermann Warm, Walter Röhrig, Walter Reiman, Otto Hunte, and photographed by Karl Freund, say, or Eugen Schüfftan. All had gone into exile by 1934, the year the thirteen-year-old Ken Adam left his native Berlin, where he had studied at Le Collège Français, to continue his education in Edinburgh and at London's St Paul's School.

During this period – which started around the time of Adam's birth in 1921 – the studio system had taken shape in Hollywood and art direction had become an economic determinant in the movie-making business. In the 1920s eight major companies arose to dominate the production, distribution and exhibition of films: Paramount, RKO, Warner Brothers, Universal, Columbia, Twentieth Century Fox, MGM, United Artists. Each of them (except UA, which was primarily a releasing organisation) had its own style, which derived from the personalities of the studio heads (e.g. the sentimental, social-climbing Louis B. Mayer of MGM, the abrasive Harry Cohn of Columbia, the strutting Jack Warner of Warner Brothers), the actors they hired, and the technicians they put under contract. Cedric Gibbons (1893–1960), who claimed

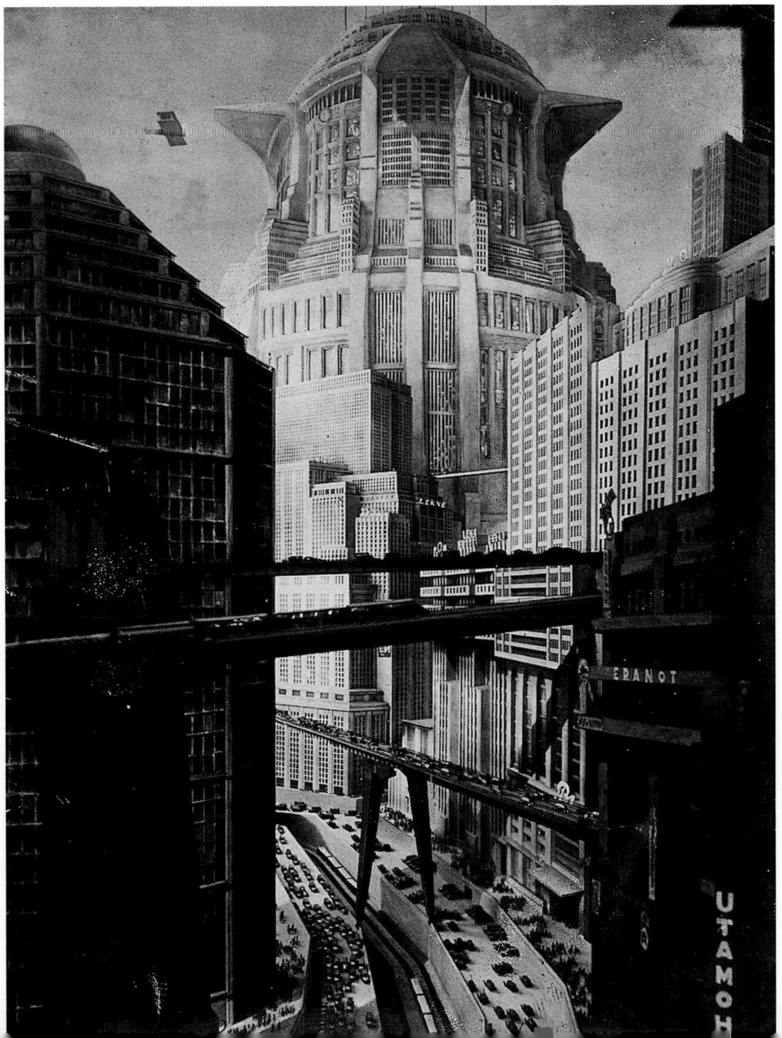

Metropolis
(Fritz Lang, 1926)

to have got rid of two-dimensional painted sets from the Edison Studio in 1915, became head of the art department at MGM in 1924. His own Art Deco house is a landmark (it figures in Robert Benton's 1998 thriller *Twilight*), his opulent ideas about public and domestic architecture informed the MGM ethos, and his name appears on every picture the company produced for the next thirty-two years whether he designed it or (more regularly) cast his eye over an underling's work.

An example of the cultural exodus produced by Nazism is to be seen in the credits of *The Man Who Knew Too Much* (1934), the British thriller that confirmed Alfred Hitchcock's reputation as 'the master of suspense'. Hitchcock entered films as a jack-of-all-trades and became a designer before graduating to director, working initially in Germany, where he became enamoured of the expressionist style. *The Man Who Knew Too Much* is very English in its class tensions and understated attitudes to family life, but it is formally a highly Germanic movie, due to the contributions of the expatriate designer Alfred Junge (who would subsequently be a major collaborator of Michael Powell and Emeric Pressburger), the refugee cinematographer Curt Courant, and the exiled actor Peter Lorre, making his first appearance in an English-speaking film.

The film industry withdrew into the studio and the so-called real world was abandoned to John Grierson, Robert Flaherty and the self-proclaimed documentary purists. But while the feature-film producers were making reality in the studios, the documentarians were faking it on location. It took the author of great fiction, Graham Greene, in his capacity as movie critic of *The Spectator*, to compare Flaherty's 'bogus and sentimental' *Man of Aran* unfavourably with a low-budget British drama, *Turn of the Tide*, and the expensive MGM production *The Good Earth*.[2] Control was the issue. The big studios wanted to keep their employees under daily observation; directors wanted a controlled environment of light, sound, camera movement. In her study of German expressionist cinema, *The Haunted Screen*, Lotte Eisner uses the term 'landscape imbued with soul' (*Landschaft mit Seele*) to describe the aim of the sets used in films of the 1920s and writes that 'according to Rudolf Kurtz [author of *Expressionismus und Film*] only when a director builds his own landscape can he give it soul and make it play an active part in the plot'.[3]

So art and commerce combined in creating the world on sound stages in Los Angeles with a few locations within driving distance and exotic backgrounds filmed by second units for back projections or featuring stand-ins for the stars. Each Hollywood studio had a backlot where standing sets of city streets, Western towns, Oriental villages, *mittel*-European communities, jungles and middle-class American suburbs stood ready to be adapted and decorated for a new film. The streets on the Paramount and Warner Brothers lots have survived fortune and fires for over sixty years. The UFA studio in Berlin maintained generic sets for a while, as did Cinecittà in Rome, but the general European practice has been the creation of ad hoc sets film by film, and even sequence by sequence, which created a problem for postproduction retakes and pick-ups. When Hitchcock was shooting *The Lady Vanishes* (1938) in the minute Islington Studio, the sets were constantly being dismantled in readiness for the next scene.

In the interwar years there developed legendary associations between directors, performers, writers, cinematographers and designers, though most of these collaborations were known only to people within the business and to cinéphiles. There were no readily accessible journals of record or reference books then that included filmographies (a term not recorded in English-speaking dictionaries until the 1950s). Jean Renoir and Eugène Lourié; Marcel Carné and Alexandre Trauner; John Ford and James Bashevi – for several years the relationships between these directors and designers were as crucial as those between comic duos. But these designers, unsung heroes all, worked with others too: Lourié directed astounding low-budget horror flicks like *The Beast from 20,000 Fathoms* (1953), and designed Chaplin's *Limelight* (1953) and Samuel Fuller's *Shock Corridor* (1963); Trauner worked with Orson Welles on *Othello* (1954) and *The Trial* (1964) and on numerous Billy Wilder films; Bashevi created the earthquake in *San Francisco* (1935), the Yorkshire of Wyler's *Wuthering Heights* (1939) and the turn-of-the-century California of Kazan's *East of Eden* (1955).

Directors rail against producers, writers rail against directors, and a vast library of indignation has been produced. There's Scott Fitzgerald's letter to Joseph L. Mankiewicz over the script of *Three Comrades* (1938): 'I feel like a good many writers must have felt in the past. I gave you a drawing and you simply took a box of chalk and touched it up'; Raymond Chandler's unsent letter to Hitchcock about his script for *Strangers on a Train* (1951): 'Regardless of whether or no my name appears on the screen among the credits, I'm not afraid that anyone will think I wrote this stuff'; most recently Frederic Raphael's *Eyes Wide Open*, a book-length account of Stanley Kubrick's failure to respect his literary input into *Eyes Wide Shut*. Film designers do not have this kind of exaggerated *amour propre*. They need to command a vast area of technical and historical knowledge (the history of architecture as well as its practice), and to combine this with the skills of a quantity surveyor and an accountant. They are in on the project from the moment it begins to move from speculation to realisation. They may be proud and ambitious, but they accept their role as collaborators engaged to help realise someone else's vision. And their success is judged precisely through the way they have taken a producer's or director's concept and turned it from words on paper or in discussion into an expressive environment by designing sets in studios and transforming or subtly adjusting the existing world. Some designers have turned to direction to pursue their own visions, and a number have met with a certain success, though perhaps the only two to become great directors are Alfred Hitchcock, whose design career was fairly modest, and Vincente Minnelli, whose work as a designer was largely confined to the stage.

In 1938, when Ken Adam was studying at St Paul's School in London, David O. Selznick sent a memorandum to John Hay Whitney and John Wharton, respectively the chairman and treasurer of Selznick International Pictures, that is a milestone in the development of the role of the designer. *Gone With the Wind* was in preproduction, though neither Clark Gable nor Vivien Leigh was yet cast, and Selznick was concerned about the crucial role of William Cameron Menzies. The previous year Menzies had directed the most visually impressive picture to have emerged up to that time from a British studio, *Things to Come* (1936), and back in 1928 had won the first Academy Award for Best Art Direction (or 'Interior Decoration' as it was then called). Selznick wrote:

> I feel that we need a man of Menzies's talent and enormous experience on the sets of this picture, and on its physical production. I hope to have *Gone With the Wind* prepared almost down to the last camera angle before we start shooting, because on this picture really thorough preparation will save hundreds of thousands of dollars. Accordingly, if we do go ahead with Menzies, he will start on the *Wind* sets directly he finishes his work on the cave sequence of *Tom Sawyer* ... While our script is not completed, and we are not yet certain of what we will have to cut, we know that there are half a dozen things ... such as Tara, the Wilkes home, Miss Pittypat's home, the ball at Atlanta ... that must of necessity stay in, as well as the streets of Atlanta for the news of Gettysburg and the big evacuation scene which involves great physical problems and which will more than utilise all of Menzies's time until we can give him a complete script. When he gets the complete script, he can then do all the sets, set sketches, and plans during my absence, for presentation upon my return, and can start on what I want on this picture and what has only been done a few times in picture history (and these times mostly by Menzies) – a complete script in sketch form, showing actual camera setups, lighting etc. This is a mammoth job that Menzies will have to work on closely with Cukor [the film's initial director]. There is also the job of the montage sequences, which I plan on having Menzies not merely design and lay out but also, in large degree, actually direct. In short, it is my plan to have the whole physical side of this picture, with many phases that I have not dealt with in this paragraph (such as the handling of the process shots) ... personally handled by one man who has little or nothing else to do – and that man Menzies. Menzies may turn out to be one of the most valuable factors in properly producing this picture. One of the minor problems in connection with this arrangement is the matter of Menzies's credit. Menzies is terribly anxious not to get back to art direction as such, and of course his work on this picture, as I see it, will be a lot greater in scope than is normally associated with the term 'art direction'. Accordingly I would probably give him some such credit as 'Production Designed by William Cameron Menzies' or 'Assistant to the Producer'.[4]

In the event the credit on *Gone With the Wind* reads 'This Production Designed by William Cameron Menzies', and as Selznick was an independent producer he was able to bestow it. Had *Gone With the Wind* been an MGM production, rather than made in association with that studio, the credit would have gone to Cedric Gibbons with a mention for Menzies underneath. It is significant therefore that this particular designation should have been made by a pioneering independent, because the role of the production designer came into its own with the decline of the studio system and the studio's roster of contract artists and artisans. This process was underway in the 1950s as Ken Adam was getting his first credits for art direction, and it was on Mike Todd's *Around the World in Eighty Days*, the biggest independent production of the decade, that he received his first Academy Award nomination.

Adam entered the cinema shortly after his World War II service in the RAF, working as a draughtsman on *This Was a Woman* (1948), a stage adaptation directed by the journeyman Tim Whelan, an American who had worked regularly in Britain in the 1930s. His first assignment as assistant designer came the following year when he worked under Oliver Messel, the most prestigious British stage designer of the time (his sets were frequently applauded by West End audiences), on *Queen of Spades*, an adaptation of Pushkin's novel directed by Thorold Dickinson, one of the most admired filmmakers of postwar Britain. In an ecstatic *Sunday Times* review Dilys Powell wrote:

> The English have made plenty of films in fancy dress and a few (Lean's films of Dickens, Olivier's Shakespearian films, Carol Reed's *Kipps*) in which costume serves the purpose of drama or comedy, but the evocation of the romantic atmosphere in period has not been the strong point of our cinema ... The adapters ... have realised that Pushkin's austere narrative is untranslatable as it stands and must take on some sombre richness of decoration in its passage to the screen ... Oliver Messel's settings and costumes are among the most beautiful I can remember seeing on the British screen.[5]

Queen of Spades, Adam's first costume picture, was in career terms a major work for a tyro to be associated with. Thereafter, between routine chores on forgotten British movies, Adam served a valuable eight-year apprenticeship working with visiting Americans, drawn to Europe by frozen US currency and international co-productions.

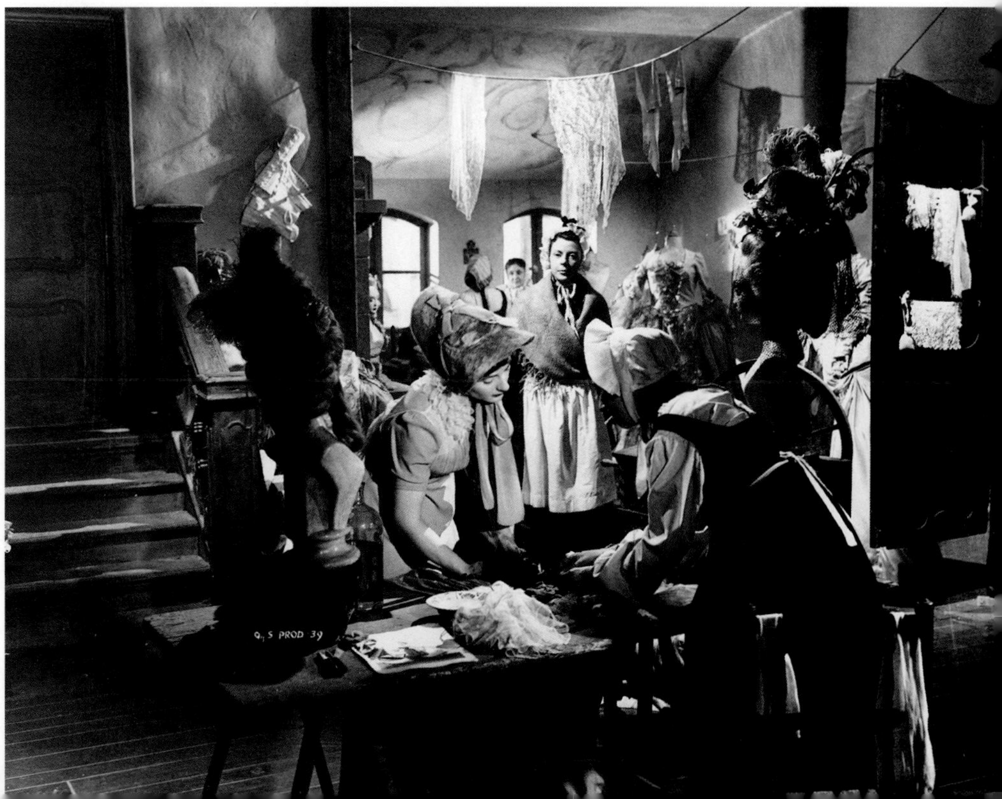

The Queen of Spades
(Thorold Dickinson, 1948)

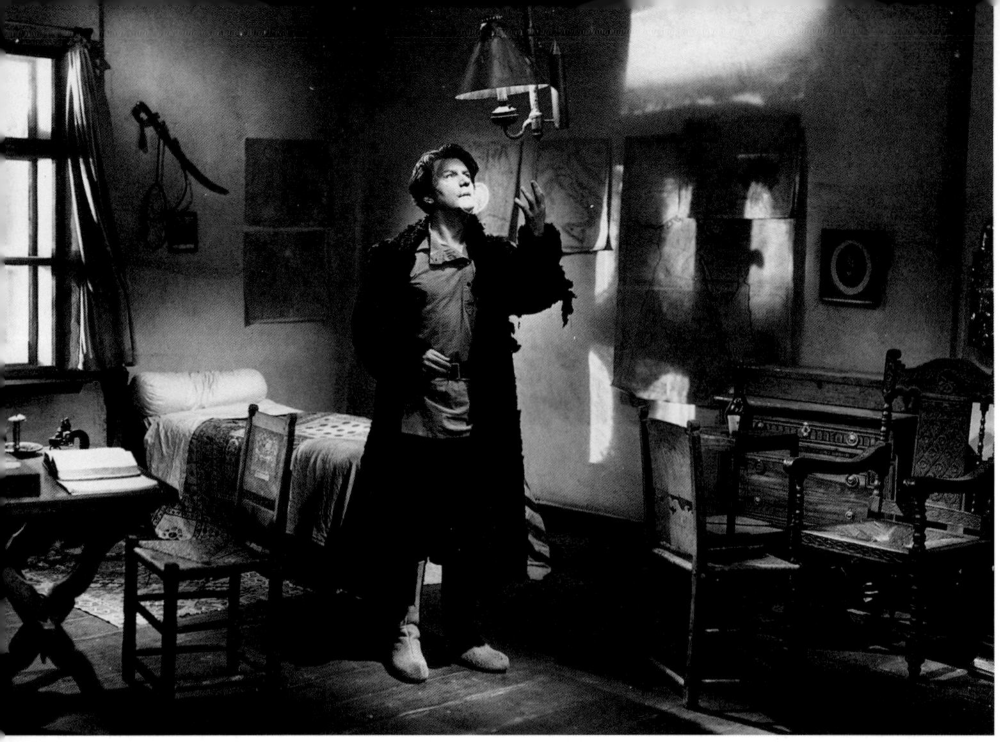

The Queen of Spades
(Thorold Dickinson, 1948)

The first of these projects was *Obsession* (1949), directed by Edward Dmytryk, a master of the *noir* thriller and, as one of the 'Hollywood Ten', to be jailed for defying the House Un-American Activities Committee. In that dark melodrama, a cuckolded doctor (Robert Newton) keeps his wife's lover imprisoned in a cellar beneath a postwar London bomb site; it is the first instance of a characteristic Adam setting, the windowless bunker with an oppressive concrete ceiling.

In 1950 he was assistant art director on *Captain Horatio Hornblower R.N.*, a vigorous action movie directed by the Hollywood veteran Raoul Walsh, who played the presidential assassin John Wilkes Booth in D. W. Griffith's *The Birth of a Nation* (1915). On *Hornblower* Adam assisted Tom Morahan, who worked on Hitchcock's last British movie, *Jamaica Inn* (1939), as well as two of his postwar pictures (*The Paradine Case*, *Under Capricorn*), and designed many notable films at Ealing. Immediately afterwards, on *The Crimson Pirate* (1952), Adam assisted Paul Sherriff, an illustrious British stage designer most famous in the cinema for his innovative sets for Olivier's *Henry V*. It was directed by Robert Siodmak, who had begun his career as an editor in Berlin and made his directorial debut working with Edgar Ulmer, Fred Zinnemann, Billy Wilder and Eugen Schüfftan on *People on Sunday* (1929), the silent classic that anticipated neo-realism. Working with Walsh and Siodmak put Adam in touch with film history.

Burt Lancaster had become a star in his first film, Robert Siodmak's *noir* thriller *The Killers*. This costume adventure romp was an enterprise of an altogether different order. To save money *The Crimson Pirate* used the ship built for *Horatio Hornblower* and became increasingly tongue-in-cheek as the picture progressed. The script (originally the work of blacklisted writers) was rewritten day to day on location in Ischia.[6] As a result Adam was constantly having to devise new contraptions, mostly attributed to the pawky eighteenth-century professor played by James Hayter, including a flame-throwing tank, a hot-air balloon and a rowing boat that becomes a submarine. Here we have the origins of the technical gimmickry of the Bond movies and *Chitty Chitty Bang Bang*, some of it deriving from the tradition of invention pioneered by Leonardo da Vinci and turned into comic eccentricity by Heath Robinson and Roland Emmett.

Adam was to work again with Siodmak as art director on *The Rough and the Smooth* (1959), a sinister depiction of louche London life that preceded, indeed anticipated, Joseph Losey's *The Servant* (1963); both were based on novels by Robin Maugham. It was the second of five pictures he made with the veteran cinematographer Otto Heller, another fugitive from Nazi Germany.

Before becoming a fully fledged art director, first on a pair of minor British productions in 1956, then on *Around the World in Eighty Days* (1957), Adam had a further useful assignment on the spectacular but rather dull *Helen of Troy* (1955), directed by Robert Wise, who had edited *Citizen Kane* and cut his directorial teeth on the elegant, low-budget horror films produced by Val Lewton's unit at RKO. Here Adam was assisting Edward Carrere, who designed the futuristic buildings for King Vidor's *The Fountainhead* (1949), a visually stunning movie about a visionary architect modelled on Frank Lloyd Wright, and was later to create the authentic Texas border town for Sam Peckinpah's *The Wild Bunch* (1969).

Around the World in Eighty Days was part of Hollywood's attempt to counter the challenge of television with colourful movies of a sort too large and expensive for the small screen. This need to provide something of which TV is incapable, because of its scale, style or content, has been an important consideration ever since, and *Around the World in Eighty Days* is what came to be called an 'event movie'. It is essentially a producer's picture, a pet project of the showman Mike Todd, a man of the theatre rather than the cinema, who replaced the director John Farrow on the first day of shooting. The film, like Jules Verne's novel, depends on stereotyped characters and scenes – the Victorian gentleman Phileas Fogg and the places he visited had to fulfil Todd's and the audience's simple expectations, and in designing the European part of the film Adam perfectly executed his brief. Fogg's apartment, the Reform Club where the journey begins and ends, and the Lloyds offices, were re-created in the studio, a little brighter, more polished than life, as elegant as Orchardson paintings, as heightened as Spy's flattering caricatures. Various streets were dressed in the finery of the 1870s, none more so than the Place Vendôme and environs for the big crowd scene when Fogg and his valet visit Paris. Adam was not to work with so lavish a budget for nearly a decade, not until *Goldfinger* in 1964. *Around the World in Eighty Days* and the two relatively modest, but infinitely superior, monochrome pictures he made immediately afterwards determined the two streams of his work, which one might call the decorative and the plain, the fantastic and the mundane, the imaginary and the realistic, though at times they intermingle.

The two late 1950s works I refer to were directed by Hollywood *petits maîtres*, *Night of the Demon* (1957) and *Ten Seconds to Hell* (1959). The first is a horror movie adapted from M. R. James's tale 'Casting the Runes', about a sceptical American

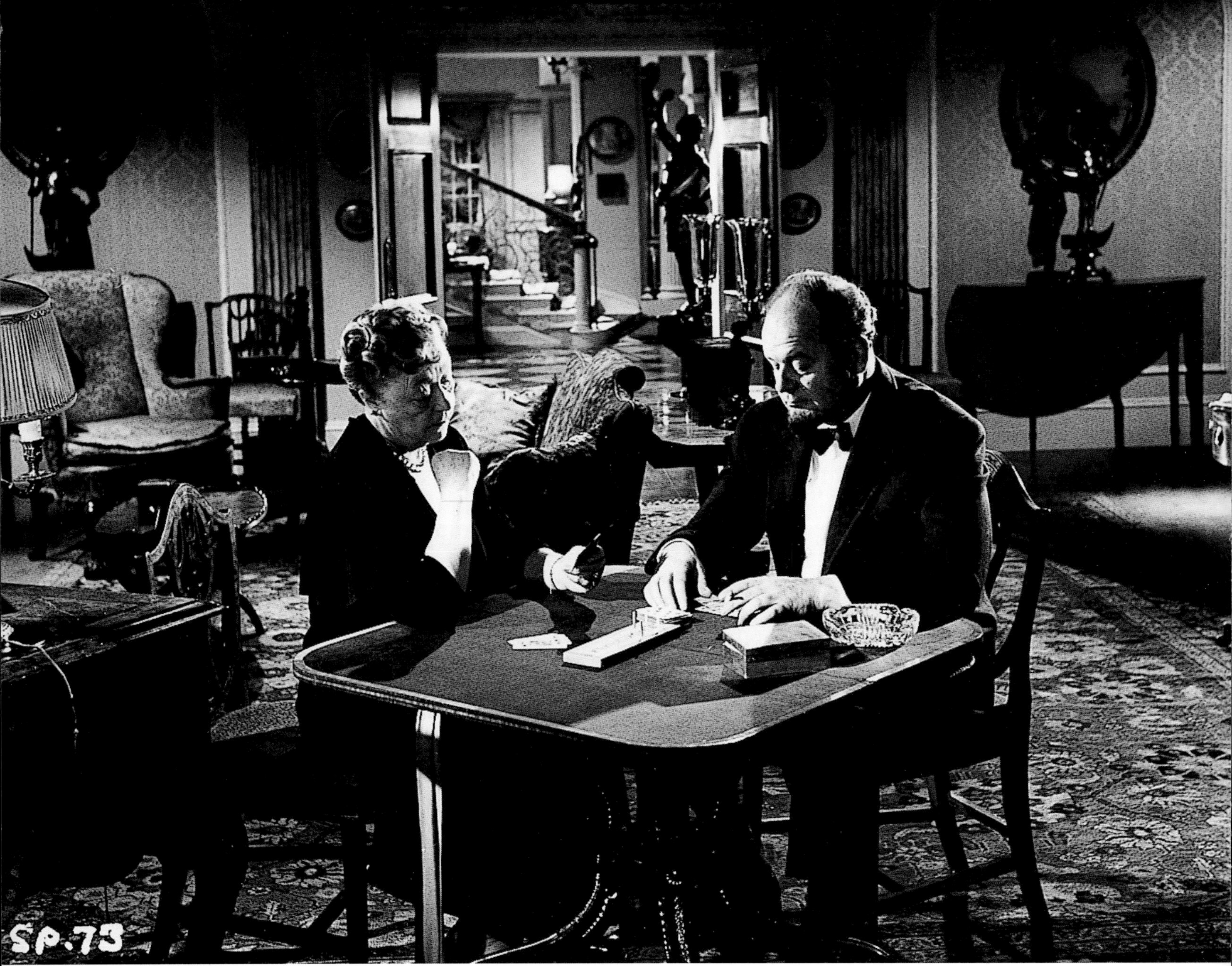

Curse of the Demon
aka *Night of the Demon*
(Jacques Tourneur, 1957)

scientist challenging an English diabolist, directed by Jacques Tourneur, the most gifted protégé of Val Lewton. Except for an unfortunate manifestation of the demon at two points (something Lewton would not have countenanced), the film is a marvel of understated terror. It is difficult to tell what is real and what created in the studio, but the film charges the British Museum Reading Room, Stonehenge, the charismatic villain's country mansion, a windblown copse, a railway line at night and a lower-middle-class parlour, with low-key menace. *Ten Seconds to Hell* (the first and best of Adam's three collaborations with Robert Aldrich) is less good, but in some ways more interesting in the context of Adam's career. The movie centres on a team of ex-Wehrmacht soldiers involved in the suicidal task of disposing of bombs in 1945

Berlin and was made almost in its entirety on the vast sound stages at the UFA studio, where Lang's *Metropolis*, a film that must have impressed the juvenile Adam, was shot. It has only two interior sets – a flat in a shattered, once elegant apartment block and the team's office – and the rubble-covered bomb sites on which they work. The film finds Adam returning to his native city, then in the process of rising from the ashes as a result of the German miracle and American subventions, and depicting it as a hellish wilderness. The engineers' operations room is an oppressive low-ceilinged bunker lit by naked bulbs under cheap shades. The traumatised hero (played by Jack Palance) is an anti-Nazi architect, his career interrupted by the war, who has seen his buildings destroyed and wonders whether he can pick up the pieces again. Adam must have found him a sympathetic figure.

In 1959 Adam worked for the first of the three uncontestably great movie-makers he has been associated with, but the result was hugely disappointing. *Gideon's Day* (aka *Gideon of the Yard*) is the low point of John Ford's postwar work, a routine pre-*Z-Cars* police-procedural movie scripted by Ealing Studio's T.E.B. Clarke, who wrote *The Blue Lamp*. Set in a London that is by turns touristic and redolent of TV commercials, it was photographed by Freddie Young in a naturalistic (though not very natural) colour, but released in the USA in black and white.

Adam began the 1960s by returning to the late Victorian era with Ken Hughes's *The Trials of Oscar Wilde*. But this was uncharacteristic of the work he would be doing during the most significant decade of his career, in which he continued to collaborate with North American producers and directors. For Albert Broccoli and Harry Saltzman he designed the first of his seven films based on Ian Fleming's James Bond novels, as well as two counter-Bond thrillers based on the novels of Len Deighton, and the period musical *Chitty Chitty Bang Bang* from Fleming's children's book. He worked with Stanley Kubrick on *Dr Strangelove*, one of the key pictures of the decade, and in 1969 he began a seven-picture partnership with Herbert Ross with the musical *Goodbye, Mr Chips*.

That Adam significantly raised the profile of the production designer and drew audiences' attention to the visual aspect of movies is beyond question. But he came to maturity after a valuable and varied period of apprenticeship at a time when the visual was taking ascendancy over the literary in our culture. This was at the point when the gritty *Picture Post* (itself the creation of European émigré photojournalists) went out of existence to be replaced by fashion-conscious journals like *Queen*, *Town* and the colour magazines of the *Sunday Times* and the *Observer*, which boldly experimented with new layouts and typography. After a decade that celebrated abstract art, figurative work drawing on the iconography of popular culture emerged in the form of Pop. Television made viewers design-conscious, as did a new generation of designers, and the sleeves of long-playing records became a new terrain for graphic design. Saul Bass emerged as a cult figure for his credit titles and poster designs for films by Preminger and Hitchcock, as did a little later Maurice Binder for the credits of the Bond pictures. Richard Chopping's *trompe l'oeil* gothic dustjackets for Fleming's novels became collector's items (the wrapper for *Thunderball* depicting

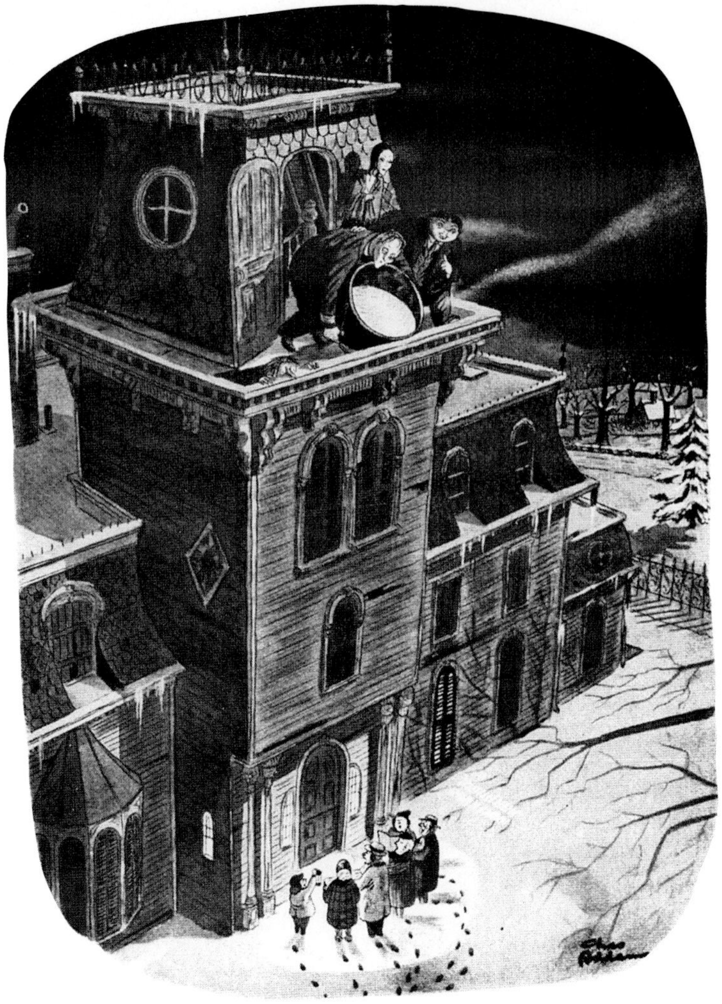

Charles Addams
The Addams Family 1946

a switchblade knife impaling a black ace and a red queen through the outstretched hand of a skeleton is a masterpiece of dread), as did the clean black-and-white photomontage jackets that Raymond Hawkey (design consultant for the *Observer*) devised for Len Deighton's first novels. One of the most celebrated figures in London was the ingenious stage designer Sean Kenny, whose sets dominated the West End productions of *Oliver!* (1960) and *Blitz!* (1962). Of the latter Kenneth Tynan observed in the *Observer*: 'I have a fearful premonition of the next show Mr Kenny designs. As soon as the curtain rises, the sets will advance in a phalanx on the audience and summarily expel it from the theatre. After that the next step is clear: Mr Kenny will invent sets that applaud.'[7] Joseph Losey, the most revered London-based director of the 1960s, always acknowledged in his frequent interviews the importance to his films of Richard MacDonald, who, because he could not join a craft union, had to be credited as 'design consultant'. Interestingly, Macdonald designed *The Addams Family* (1991) and Ken Adam designed the sequel, *Addams Family Values*.

People started to notice and talk about Ken Adam in 1964 when *Dr Strangelove* opened (widely previewed in October–November 1963, it had been postponed owing to the assassination of President Kennedy) and was soon followed by the third Bond

Ken Adam
The Addams House 1992
Pen and ink wash on paper
(*Addams Family Values*, Barry Sonnenfeld, 1993)

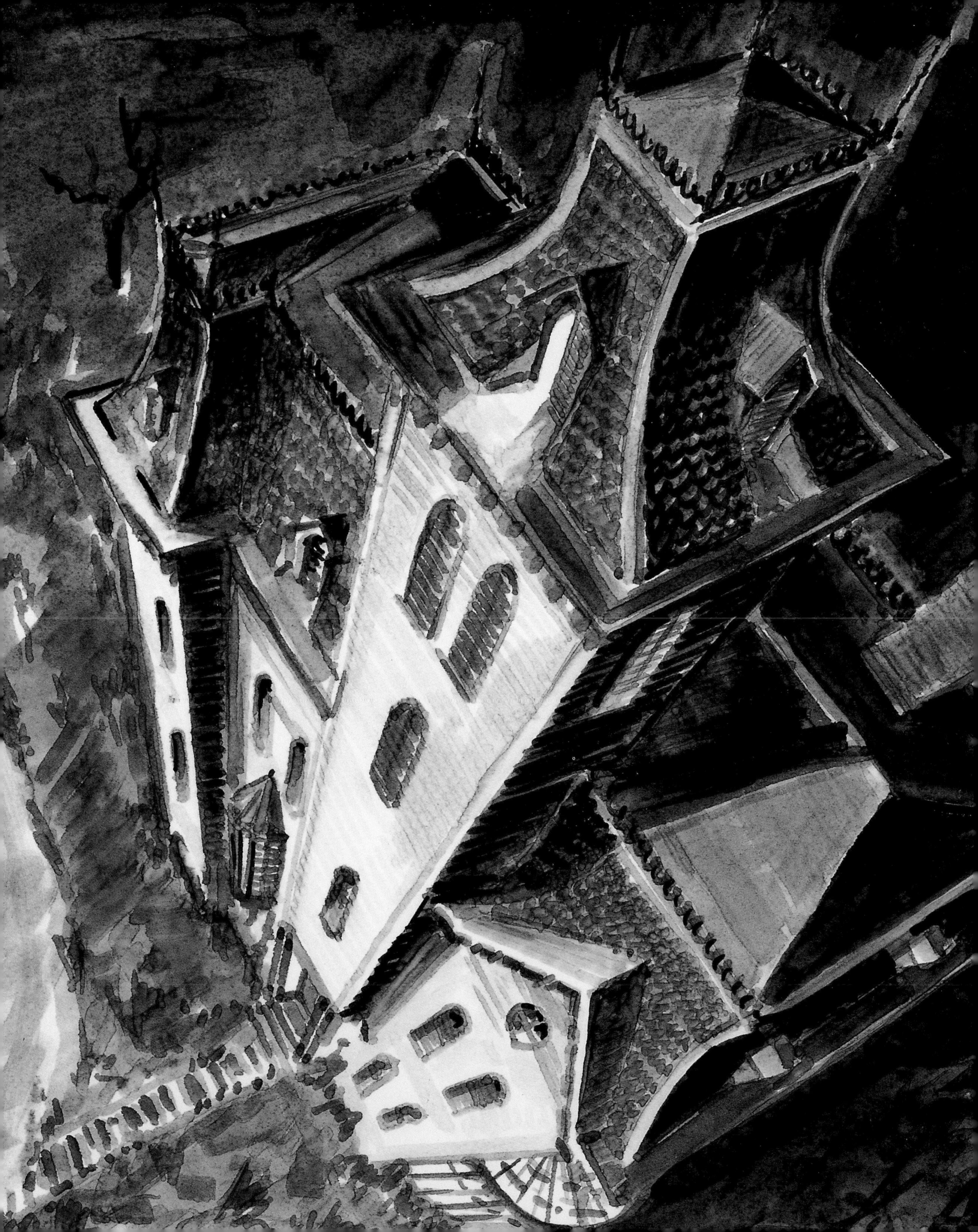

movie, *Goldfinger*. A check list of his credits was published in the January 1965 issue of the British Film Institute's *Monthly Film Bulletin* to coincide with an article in the BFI's sister publication *Sight and Sound* by Roger Hudson that featured Adam along with Richard MacDonald and Edward Marshall (designer of *Saturday Night and Sunday Morning* and *The Charge of the Light Brigade*) and included his sketches for the War Room in *Dr Strangelove* and the rumpus room in *Goldfinger*.[8]

Dr No and *Dr Strangelove* – their names evoke the megalomaniac world of Dr Caligari and Dr Mabuse, the sinister underground geniuses of the expressionist cinema of the 1920s, that is supposed to have prefigured Hitler and Nazism. Hitler had his Wagnerian lair at Berchtesgaden and died in a bunker beneath Berlin. The general public both of Germany and of the nations the Luftwaffe tyrannised cowered for much of World War II in dank, low-roofed shelters. Fifteen years after the end of that war the Cold War intensified. The Berlin Wall went up, North America and the USSR were dotted with silos containing intercontinental ballistic missiles, the rich and powerful built nuclear shelters from which the less privileged were excluded, and the Cuban missile crisis brought Kennedy and Khrushchev 'eyeball to eyeball'. We all returned to the World War II above-ground/underground dichotomy.

Adam had explored this world in *Obsession* and *Ten Seconds to Hell*, realistic films of cellar life in a blitzed postwar Europe. In the 1960s the subterranean world became for him an elegant metaphor for power and the hubristic belief of the privileged that they might survive the horrors that their madness – whether criminal or political – would bring about. From the War Room President Muffley can despatch nuclear weapons, from Crab Key in the Caribbean Dr No can capture American missiles and hold the world to ransom. They're different sides of the same Cold War laissez-faire capitalism coin, and their extravagance derives from their being comedies.

Dr No, the first and the least expensive of the 37-year-long Bond cycle, begins simply enough with Bond's superior 'M' in his office of pale wood-panelled walls and Bond himself living in a Chelsea flat of conservative good taste. The picture takes on a sinister visual note when the shifty villain, the Professor, comes to Crab Key, where he is given an audience by the unseen Dr No in a large, sparsely furnished white room illuminated only by a circular, barred skylight. A cross between a chapel and an abattoir, the room exudes pitiless terror, and the only living thing it contains is a tarantula that the Professor must place in Bond's hotel room. We don't meet Dr No until Bond and the girl Honeychile Rider have entered his inner sanctum from the sea and become his prisoners. No's underground lair is a curious mixture of the ultra-modern and the traditional, and it established a pattern for the grandiloquent inner sanctums that Adam was to design for future 007 adversaries. The high-tech aspect – the lifts, the gantries, the banks of gleaming equipment, the rockets ready for lift-off – is the necessary prerequisite for advancing their plans of world domination. But the villains' actual living quarters with their baronial stone walls, old master paintings and tapestries, large open fires with antique andirons, vast dining tables, reveal that they see themselves, or Adams sees them, as Renaissance princes, the Medici, the Visconti, the Sforzas. None affects conventional twentieth-

Dr No
(Terence Young, 1962)

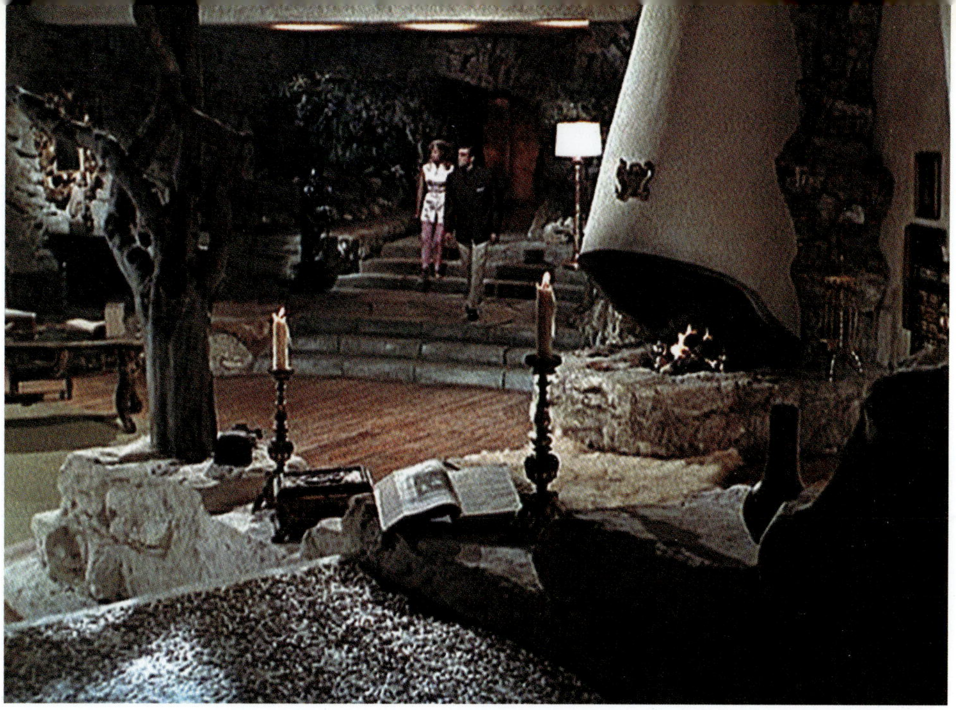

Dr No
(Terence Young, 1962)

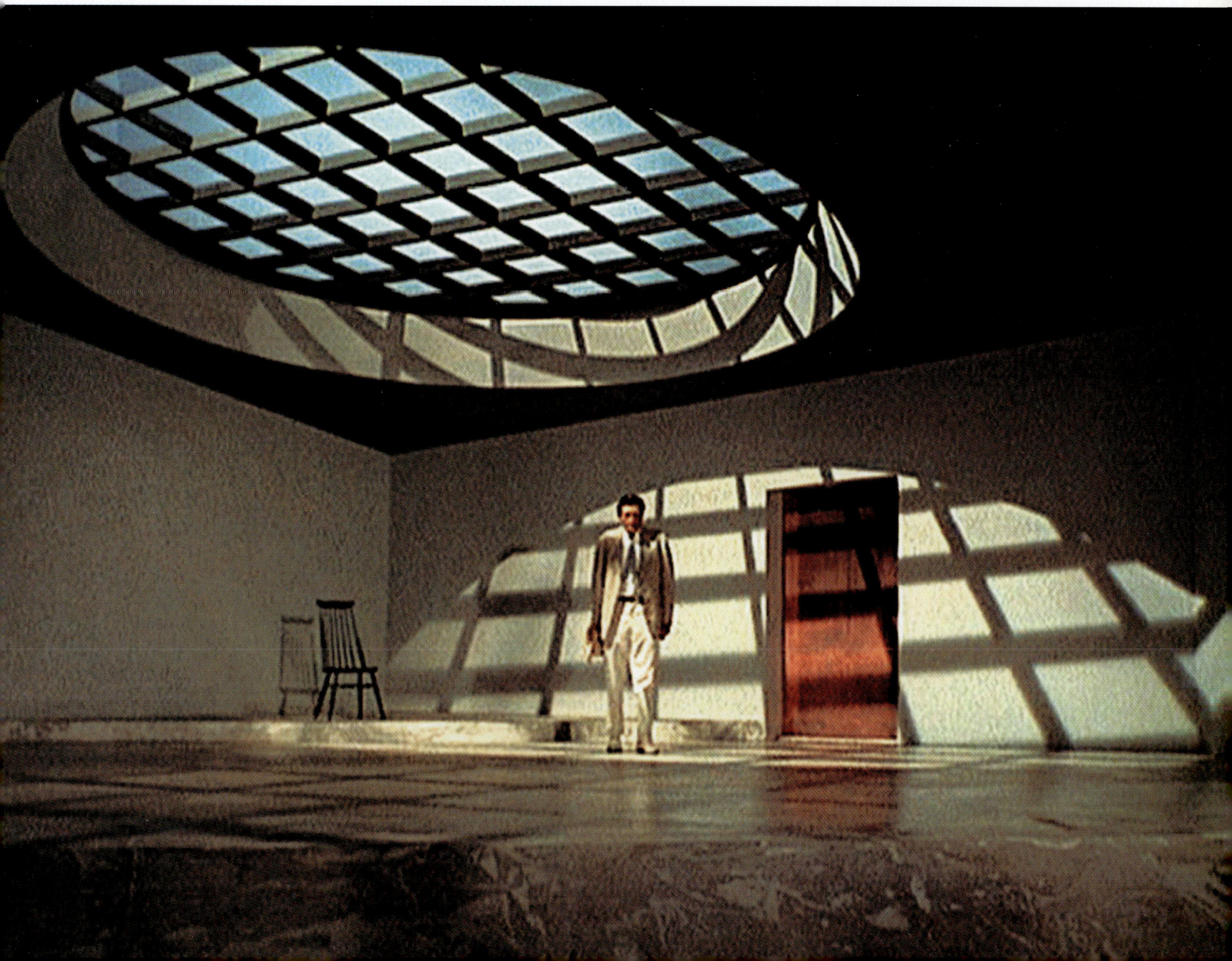

century dress. The extreme case is that of Hugo Drax, the villain of *Moonraker*, the last Bond movie Adam designed, who has a vast industrial complex outside Los Angeles manufacturing advanced missiles, but lives beside it in a grandiloquent eighteenth-century château that he had transported brick by brick from the Loire to southern California.

Well before *Moonraker* the Bond movies had become more formally rigid than the haiku 007 writes in the novel of *You Only Live Twice*. The formula crystallised, one sees in retrospect, with *Goldfinger*, the third movie in the series and the second that Adam designed. The producers knew they had struck gold and they rarely deviated from this linear narrative progression: self-contained pre-credit sequence with jokes and stunts; Bond assigned to pursue super-villain; Bond meets aggressive heroine

Dr Strangelove or: How I Learned to Stop Worrying and Love the Bomb (Stanley Kubrick, 1963)

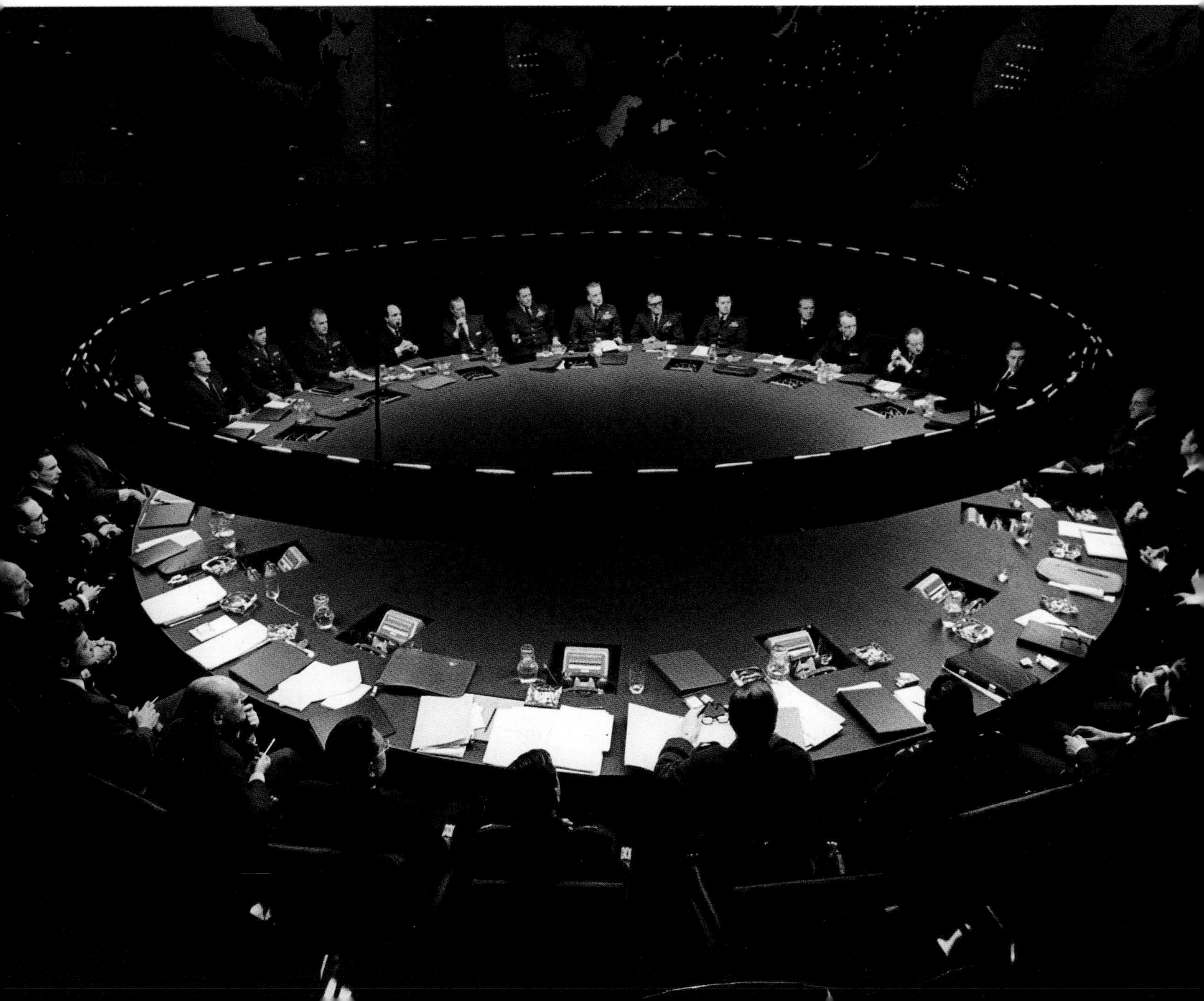

who becomes his partner; Bond penetrates the villain's lair, is captured, but escapes to frustrate his nefarious schemes, destroys the subterranean headquarters and saves the Western world as we know it. The plot mechanism was oiled by casually punning jokes about death, double-entendres and sex (invariably cutting from foreplay to Bond awakening from post-coital sleep to find his partner dead or fled). The real wit of the films, however, is to be found in the sets and the decor, and the funniest moment in *Dr No* (though it needs explaining to moviegoers not around in the 1960s) is Bond's double-take on seeing on an easel in No's parlour Goya's portrait of the Duke of Wellington which had been stolen the previous year from the National Gallery. In *Goldfinger*, the exasperated figure of 'Q' (played throughout the series by Desmond Llewellyn), the intelligence service's chief of secret weapons, first appeared to provide Bond with a range of ingenious devices, most especially the Aston Martin equipped with protective shields, radar and oil-spreading jets. If the villains' lairs have a precedent in the classic Ernest Shoedsack melodrama *The Most Dangerous Game* (aka *The Hounds of Zaroff*, 1933), the origins of Bond's secret equipment are to be found in American comic strips such as *Dick Tracy* and *Batman*, the custom-built Aston Martin anticipated by Bob Kane's Batmobile. Fancifully one might identify Ken Adam with the character of 'Q', undervalued, constantly raising the ante, always providing the instruments of survival. In the way that Tynan saw Sean Kenny's sets possessing London's theatre, Adam's designs came to dominate the Bond pictures. The films fed on clichés about the various cultures in which the 007 series were set (e.g. Brazil is the Sugar Loaf Mountain, Rio's garish festival, the impenetrable Mato Grosso), but Adam's sets made them surreal by having 'M', 'Q' and Moneypenny turn up – cool, unperturbed, ready for action – in Egyptian pyramids and submarines. The Bond pictures – partly through the imaginative persuasion of Adam's designs – created and sustained the ludicrous idea that Britain was a major player in world politics. One of the cinema's most memorable sets (it secured Adam his second BAFTA nomination) is the interior of Fort Knox in *Goldfinger*, a visionary creation of the Aladdin's cave of Western capitalism, an American holy of holies saved by a British hero.

The cataclysmic explosions wrought in the final moments of every Bond films save the world from annihilation. The greatest picture Adam has designed ends with the destruction of the world by a nuclear holocaust to the strains of Vera Lynn, 'the Forces' Sweetheart' of World War II, singing 'We'll Meet Again'. *Dr Strangelove* has three main centres of action – a humdrum US Air Force base besieged after its insane commander has launched a pre-emptive strike against the Soviet Union; an American nuclear bomber on its way to a predetermined target in Russia; the War Room at the Pentagon. The first two are realistic, and serve both to set off and to validate the third, which is among the most memorable creations in the history of cinema. Basically it's a windowless, triangular shed, the longer side of the roof being of concrete with heavy beams, the shorter side covered with vast screens showing the dispositions of the Strategic Air Command's aeroplanes and their intended targets. In the midst of this vast underground space is an enormous circular table where the President meets with his political and military advisers to evaluate the crisis and attempt to resolve it. Above the table, but some way beneath the ceiling, is a suspended hoop of harsh fluorescent tubing, the room's only apparent light source. The shadows outside the table reach away into infinity, the circular light suggests the mushroom of a nuclear explosion, the screens on the wall express the way the world has been reduced to a strategic map that excludes the human factor, the spartan, undecorated character of the room tells us that this is a world of warriors engaged in manly activities (there is no woman at this table). The height of the ceiling justifies the acoustics – a combination of boomy sonorousness and conspiratorial whisper. This War Room also exudes a madness of the sort found in the architecture of the Third Reich, and eventually in the final section of the movie we meet Dr Strangelove, a former adviser to the Nazis and now a key policymaker at the Pentagon. Almost everyone in the film is disturbed in some way. But Strangelove, who like Dr No has a deformed hand covered with a glove, is truly mad. He's a figure out of German expressionist cinema and, depending on what aspect of the war room most impresses you, is at the apex of the film's pyramid of insanity or at the centre of the circle of malign power in a world threatened by darkness.

The War Room is the American power elite's equivalent of the eyries inhabited by the Bond villains, and in effect the rumpus room that lies behind the Palladian portico of Goldfinger's Kentucky farm is a smaller, wood-panelled version of it. When the windows are sealed and the maps and models appear for Goldfinger to brief his gangland associates, the initially attractive, Lloyd Wright-tinged interior has become the villain's own war room. Immediately following *Goldfinger* and the fourth 007 film, *Thunderball*, Adam – working with the same producers and production team, though with a different director – made a film that set out to turn the world of James Bond on its head. Instead of Lieutenant-Commander Bond, loyal servant of the Establishment, *The Ipcress File* (based on Len Deighton's novel where the narrator remains anonymous) centres on Sergeant Harry Palmer, a bolshie soldier on secondment to British intelligence.

Dr Strangelove was Adam's last black-and-white movie, but *The Ipcress File* is virtually monochrome. The only flashes of red are signs of danger, indications of a world of decadent tradition inimical to the hero (such as Guardsmen in scarlet tunics parading in London streets) or double-decker buses, a device that pays off at a crucial climactic point to establish that the setting is not, as we suppose, Albania but England. The settings are deliberately drab with no excursions to exotic foreign climes. Palmer's superiors work in offices that 'M' would be ashamed of; Palmer's flat is a mess, except for the kitchen where he pursues his gastronomic hobby; the villains are dull figures loitering in the Science Museum library. The largest set is an empty warehouse, a place both ordinary and faintly menacing, used by the heavies to brainwash their victims, and there are ironic echoes here of the War Room and the inner sanctums of the Bond pictures. Among the dark, apparently commonplace settings is an underground car park where a brutal shootout takes place. This is one of the first uses of a location which was to become an emblematic rendezvous

Dr Strangelove or: How I Learned to Stop Worrying and Love the Bomb
(Stanley Kubrick, 1963)

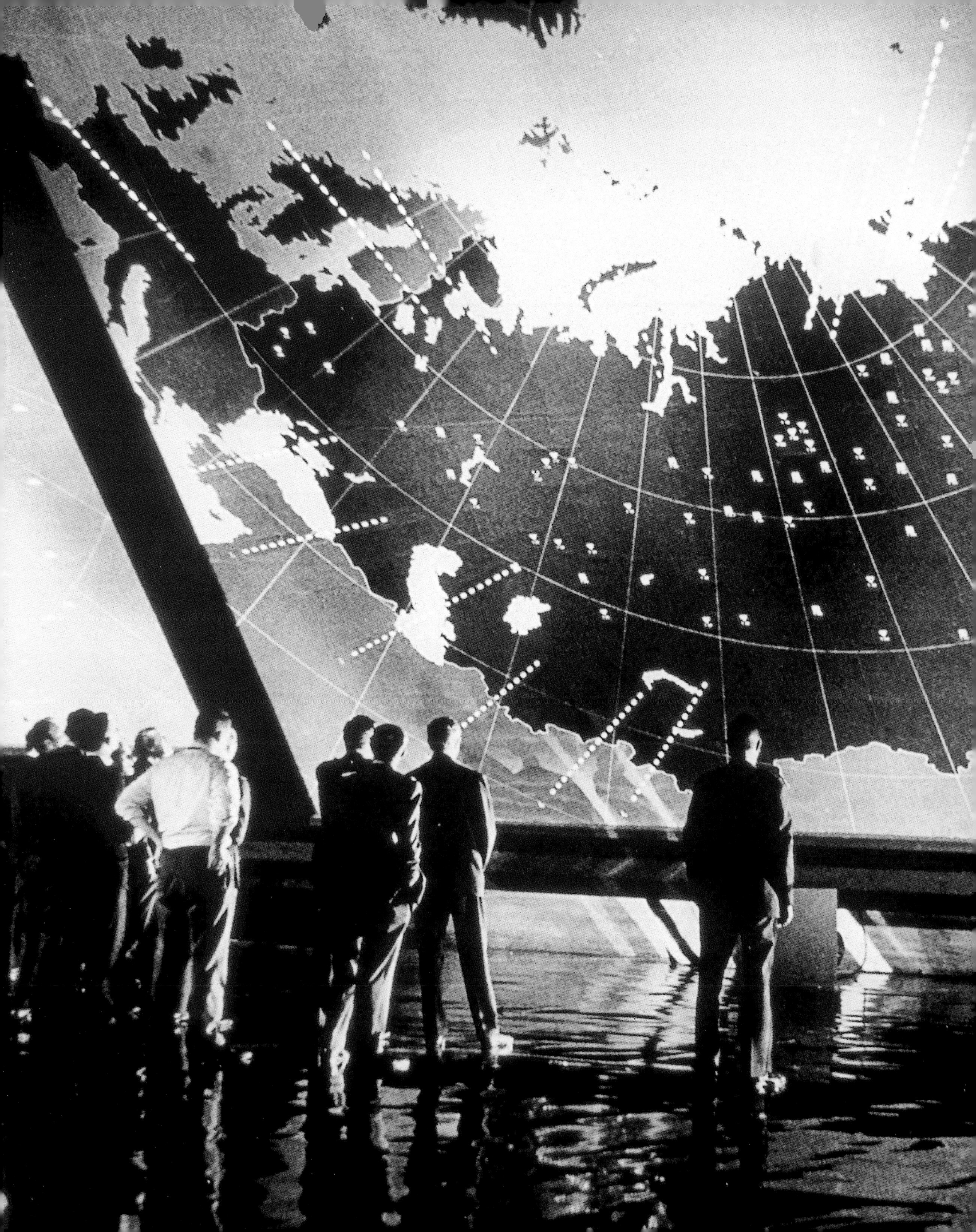

in the 1970s. It is where Robert Redford as Bob Woodward meets Deep Throat in *All the President's Men* (1975) and where Ryan O'Neal encounters his antagonists in Walter Hill's *The Driver* (1978). There is, however, throughout *The Ipcress File* a conflict between Ken Adam's insistently bleak decor and the self-conscious, obtrusive direction by Sidney J. Furie with the camera invariably observing the characters from bizarre angles.

At the end of the 1960s and in the early 1970s Adam worked with two American directors whose roots lay in the theatre, designing the first film of the choreographer Herbert J. Ross, the musical *Goodbye, Mr Chips* (1969) and the final movie of the veteran Joseph L. Mankiewicz, a screen version of Anthony Shaffer's *Sleuth* (1972). Both were stories of snobbery and class-consciousness in Britain – the former the nostalgic romance of a public schoolmaster's love for a working-class music-hall entertainer, the latter a comedy thriller about a sadistic author of snobbish detective stories humiliating his wife's lower-class lover. The characters' backgrounds are established through the settings and decor, deliberately heightened for foreign audiences, and much of the films' appeal resides in the charm, grace and wit of Adam's design. *Sleuth* is a two-character stage play of great artifice in which Mankiewicz sticks to his source as closely as he did when filming his 1953 *Julius Caesar*. But to a greater extent than in any previous film by this most literate of directors, the furnishings and garden of the obsessively ludic writer match the wit and insight of the text.

Goodbye, Mr Chips is less interesting, but it was the beginning of a seven-film partnership (there may be more films to come) that took Adam to the USA, and it led to another collaboration – with the writer and director Nicholas Meyer. Unquestionably the two best pictures Adam has designed for Ross are *The Seven-Per-Cent Solution* (1976) and *Pennies from Heaven* (1981). *The Seven-Per-Cent Solution*, adapted by Nicholas Meyer from his own novel, is pastiche Conan Doyle, one of numerous post-modern works of the 1970s and later in which fictional characters meet historical figures. In this case Dr Watson lures Sherlock Holmes to Vienna to be psychoanalysed by his fan Sigmund Freud and get over his obsession with Professor Moriarty. The film allows Adam to indulge his passion for *fin-de-siècle* Europe with superb sets for the Watsons' cosy Arts and Crafts home in London, Moriarty's tasteless basement flat, and Art Nouveau Austria. He must have been aware that he was competing with the great Alexandre Trauner, who designed Billy Wilder's similarly affectionate invasion of Baker Street, *The Private Life of Sherlock Holmes* (1970). As in all movies Adam has worked on there are dazzling sets for brief dramatic sequences – in this case a sombre real-tennis court in which Freud confronts an anti-Semitic aristocrat and a claustrophobic aren*a where Freud and Holmes narrowly a*void being trampled to death by a troupe of Lipizzaner horses in Vienna's Spanish Riding School. The triumphant design aspect of *The Seven-Per-Cent Solution*, however, comes when Holmes (Nicol Williamson) impresses Freud (Alan Arkin) by reading his life and career from what is to be found on the walls of his consulting room – including the blank spaces. This witty scene comments on and deconstructs the designer's art.

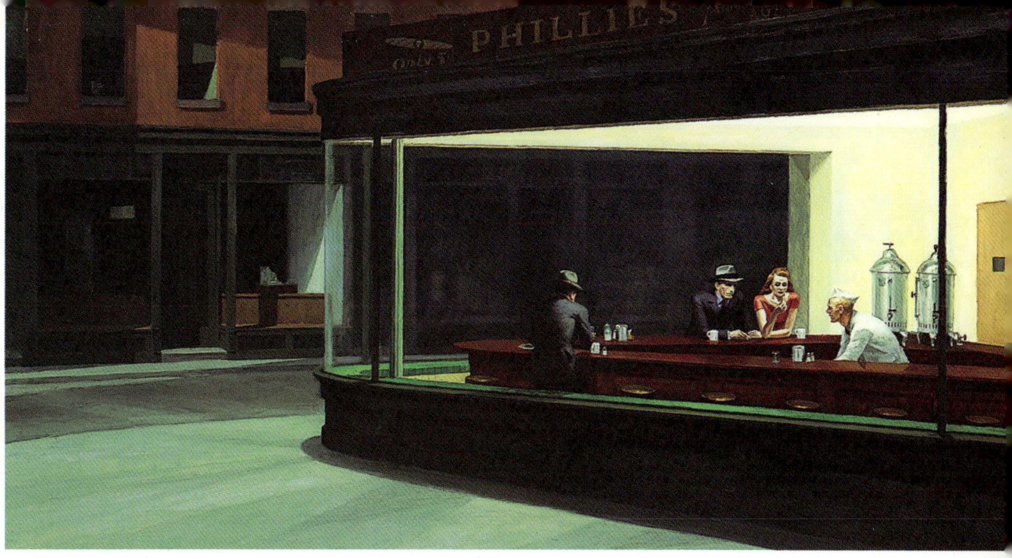

Edward Hopper
Nighthawks 1942
Oil on canvas

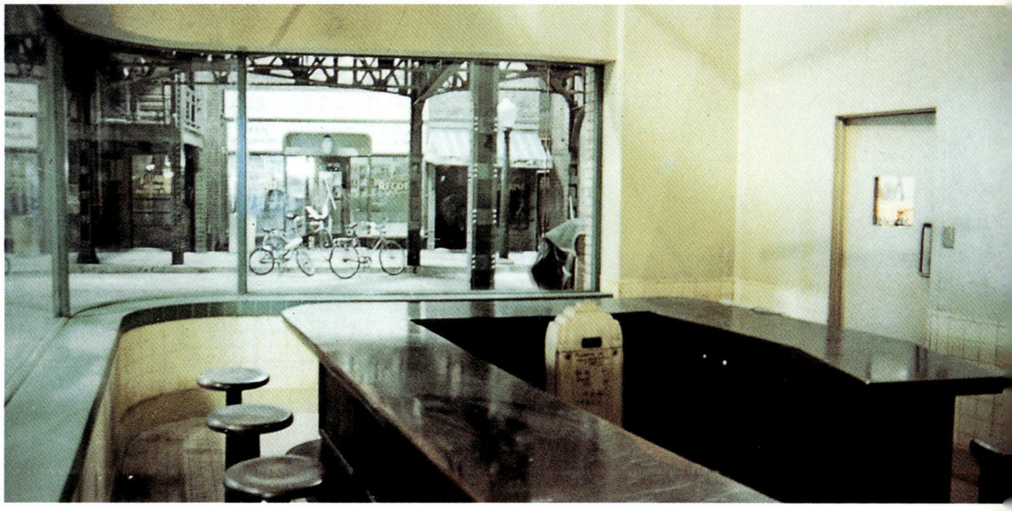

The Nighthawks bar
Pennies from Heaven
(Herbert Ross, 1981)

Pennies from Heaven, transposes Dennis Potter's celebrated eight-hour BBC TV serial of 1978 from 1930s Britain to Depression Chicago. It is the high point of Adam's association with Herbert Ross, though in this instance he is credited as associate producer and visual consultant, not as production designer. The film retains Potter's device of the characters miming to popular songs of the 1930s, but the dour tale of the doomed cockney sheet-music salesman travelling southern England has been reduced to less than a quarter of the length of the TV original and turned into an extremely glamorous production. The latter probably accounts for the film being critically undervalued, and the fact that much of the harshness, tragedy and religious mysticism of Potter's vision has been retained could explain why the picture flopped at the box office. With Potter doing his own adaptation, the movie has in fact been thoroughly rethought in American terms. The song-and-dance numbers evoke the Warner musicals of Busby Berkeley and the RKO films of Astaire and Rogers elaborate tableaux are based on the Edward Hopper painting *Nighthawks* and Reginald Marsh's *A Movie Theater*, and there is a set modelled on Walker Evans's *Atlanta, Georgia*, a 1936 photograph of peeling posters for Hollywood movies on a fence beneath two dilapidated frame houses. But the film's elegance is ironic. It exists to show the role Hollywood glamour and romance play in expressing and shaping the dreams and aspirations of the socially deprived characters.

There are interesting and attractive aspects to most of Adam's work in North America. One thinks of the chill, spartan look that he and the cinematographer Sven Nykvist give to the convent and its wintry Quebec setting in Norman Jewison's *Agnes of God* (1985) that make it a companion piece to Hitchcock's *I Confess*; the radiant, futuristic, inhuman hospital where William Hurt works and where he himself becomes a patient in *The Doctor* (1991); the loving tribute to his near namesake Charles in *Addams Family Values* (1993); the evocation of an idyllic Midwestern community, a latter-day version of Andy Hardy's hometown, for the outing of a gay schoolteacher in Frank Oz's gentle comedy *In and Out* (1997). *Addams Family Values* reminds us that the names of John Adam, Charles Addams and Ken Adam have attached themselves in the popular mind to distinctive styles of architecture. But although it was nominated for an Oscar (as was the positively rococo 1977 Bond picture *The Spy Who Loved Me*), it was for two prestigious costume movies – Stanley Kubrick's *Barry Lyndon* (1975) and Nicholas Hytner's *The Madness of King George* (1994) – that Adam received his two Academy Awards.

Both are films of distinction set in the eighteenth century of George III, but neither is especially characteristic of Adam's work. With little or no use of studio sound stages, they're shot largely on authentic locations which are skilfully decorated and, where several buildings are merged into one, beautifully matched. Stylistically they're quite different. Kubrick wanted *Barry Lyndon* to have a documentary look, as if it had been made in the eighteenth century, with interiors lit by candles. There are stunning sequences like the British army in red advancing across a green field towards the French army in white, and the scene on the top of the German castle, a study in grey, white and dark blue, when Lyndon is rewarded for bravery in the service of the Prussians. The movie draws for its effects on contemporary painters, and there are several unforgettable moments, especially the fatal riding accident of Lyndon's son, where the massive rearing horse is based on Stubbs's *Whistlejacket*, and the confrontation between the drunken Lyndon and his stepson Bullingdon, where Lyndon's decadent companions are arranged and lit like figures out of Hogarth.

Barry Lyndon is a dark, quietly observant movie about an antihero, an essentially passive man at the mercy of fate and fortune. *The Madness of King George* is about a sympathetic monarch going insane in an agitated fashion, descending from lightness into dark and ascending again. The lighting and decor follow this progression, and a blue-tinted spiral staircase that King George rushes up becomes a vortex transporting him into madness. When he is handed over to be cured by the uncompromising therapist Dr Willis, the mansion in which he is detained has dark rooms from which the paintings have been removed, the blank spaces on the walls resembling lost memories. The film's setting is historical, its theme of madness as a condition induced by systems of deference and self-deception is a modern one, and the film's payoff in which the royal family put on a show of unity on the steps of St Paul's is intended as a satirical comment on the monarchy today. But the picture avoids obvious anachronisms, and Adam and the film's costume designer, Mark Thompson, have worked at creating a sense of heightened reality which reflects an absurdity that involves everyone but the servants. It is an altogether brighter, more sanitised world than that of *Barry Lyndon*.

One suspects that Adam was honoured by his peers in the Academy of Motion Picture Arts and Sciences for the classy and classic look of *Barry Lyndon* and *The Madness of King George*, and they are fine films. But however admirably the designs serve the authors' intentions (which is after all the art director's aim), they are altogether less arresting than the Old Testament worlds that Adam conjured up from almost nowhere to provide visual authenticity for Robert Aldrich's *Sodom and Gomorrah*, (1963) and Bruce Beresford's *King David* (1985). And they pale beside the War Room in *Dr Strangelove*, Ernst Stavro Blofeld's headquarters beneath a false lake in the crater of an extinct volcano in *You Only Live Twice* (1967), and the black-and-white confectionery factory in *Chitty Chitty Bang Bang* where only the sweets are coloured. These are imaginative creations of a high order in their own right.

Notes:

1
Published in Paris in 1970, Léon Barsacq's *Le Décor de film* has been translated by Michael Bullock and revised and edited by Elliott Stein as *Caligari's Cabinet and Other Grand Illusions: A History of Film Design* (Boston, 1976). Among Stein's valuable additions is an appendix containing the filmographies of 243 designers. Barsacq (1906–1969) designed Renoir's *La Marseillaise* (1938) and most of René Clair's postwar pictures.

2
The Pleasure Dome: The Collected Film Criticism of Graham Greene, edited by John Russell Taylor (London, 1972), p. 29, p. 146.

3
The Haunted Screen by Lotte Eisner, translated by Roger Greaves (London, 1969), p. 153.

4
A Memo from David O. Selznick, edited by Rudy Behlmer (New York, 1972), pp. 151–2.

5
The Golden Screen: 50 Years of Film by Dilys Powell, edited by George Perry (London, 1989), p. 82.

6
Robert Siodmak: Le maître du film noir by Hervé Dumont (Paris, 1981), pp. 243–4.

7
A View of the English Stage 1944–63 by Kenneth Tynan (London, 1975), p. 243.

8
Monthly Film Bulletin January 1965, pp. 15–16; *Sight and Sound* Winter 1964/65, p. 26 f.

Christopher Frayling

The Theatre of the Real[1]

At an American Film Institute seminar, the film director George Roy Hill of *Butch Cassidy and the Sundance Kid* fame was once informed by a member of the audience that there were no llamas in Bolivia. His reply was brief and to the point: 'Well, there are now.' There is something about the medium of film that enables it to implant images in the mind that are more real than the real world; to stage-manage our perception of the facts of everyday life. Southern plantation houses look like Tara; airports look like the last scene of *Casablanca*; motels look like the Bates family establishment, albeit without the gingerbread gothic house on the hill; the post-modern city centre has come increasingly to resemble the retrofitted chaos of *Bladerunner*. Several of Ken Adam's production designs – especially of secret places the public cannot enter and see for themselves – are classic examples of this. The gigantic War Room in *Dr Strangelove*, one part concrete bombshelter, one part oval light-ring illuminating a global poker game, one part animated map or scoreboard showing the flight paths of nuclear weapons, three parts paranoia, has since 1963 been everyone's idea of the inner sanctum of the Pentagon. Of Fort Knox's main vault in *Goldfinger*, Adam recalls:

> In reality, no vault would ever look like that, because you would never stack gold more than a couple of feet high. I had seen that for myself at the Bank of England. The gold would be much too difficult to move about. But I decided that to stack the gold up, forty feet high, would look interesting for the biggest gold depository in the world. After all, the public wanted to see gold! You have to convince people about your visual ideas. I showed a sketch to the producer. 'It looks like a prison,' he said. 'What are you trying to do? You can't do that.' I replied, 'The gold is behind bars and we look at it from the outside, which makes us immediately aware of it,' and he bought that. The strange thing is, after the film came out, United Artists received something like 300 letters which said, 'Why is it that the Bond crew were allowed inside Fort Knox when the President of the United States hasn't got that permission?' Everyone is now convinced Fort Knox looks like that. As a film designer you can create a reality which is more acceptable to the public than the actual thing. I'm sure the inside of Fort Knox is very dull, with low vaults and a few trolleys travelling around.

Other Bond films contained variations on the theme of the laboratory or the operations room which were always 'slightly ahead of contemporary'. The early ones were linear;

Top:
One of the drawings of the final concept for the interior of Fort Knox in *Goldfinger*, 1963
Felt-tip pen on paper

Bottom:
Goldfinger
(Guy Hamilton, 1964)

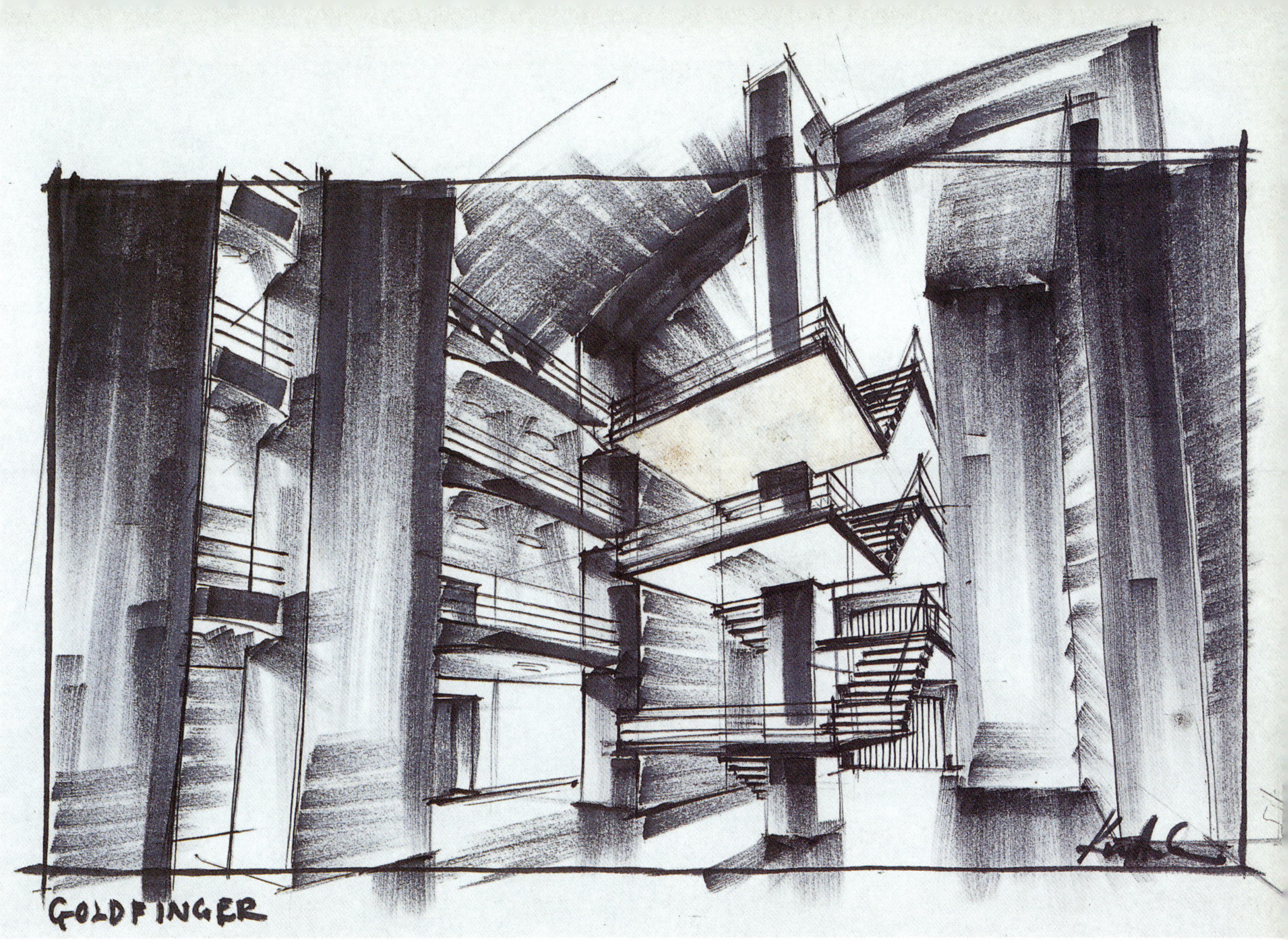

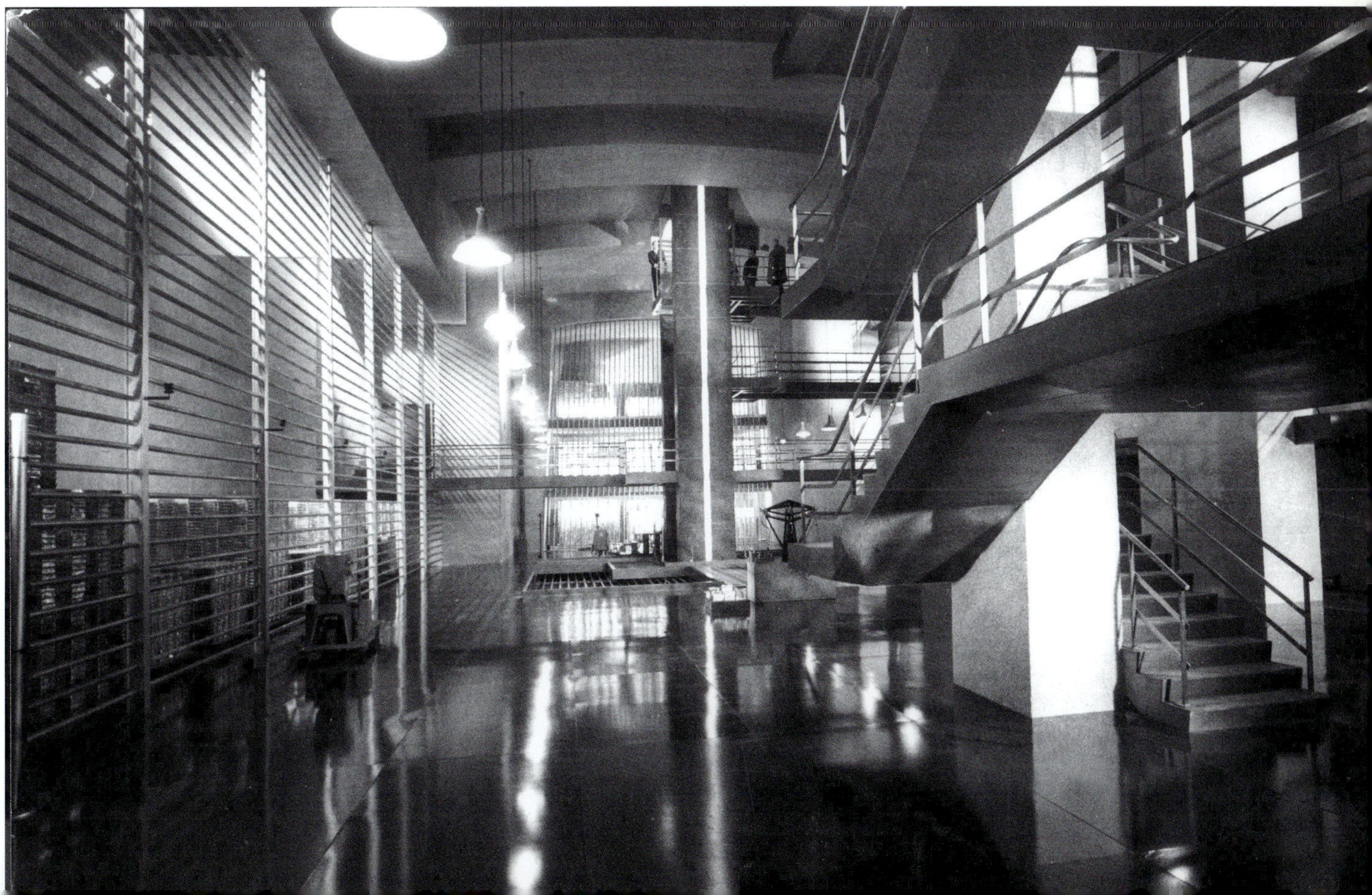

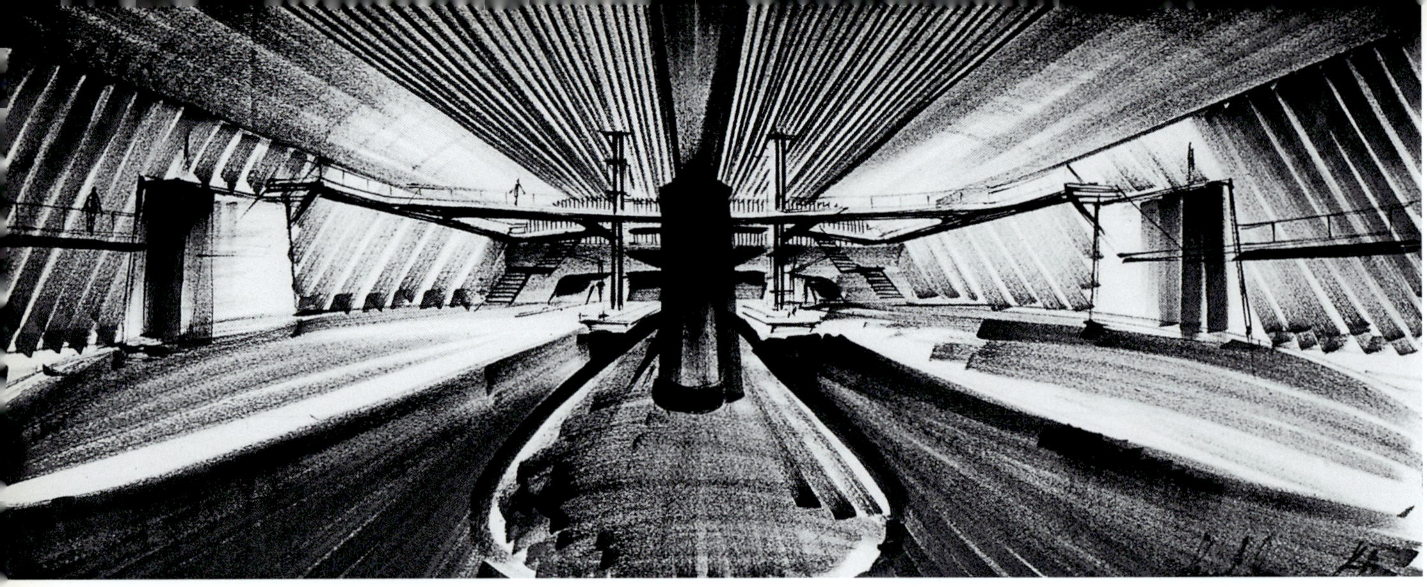

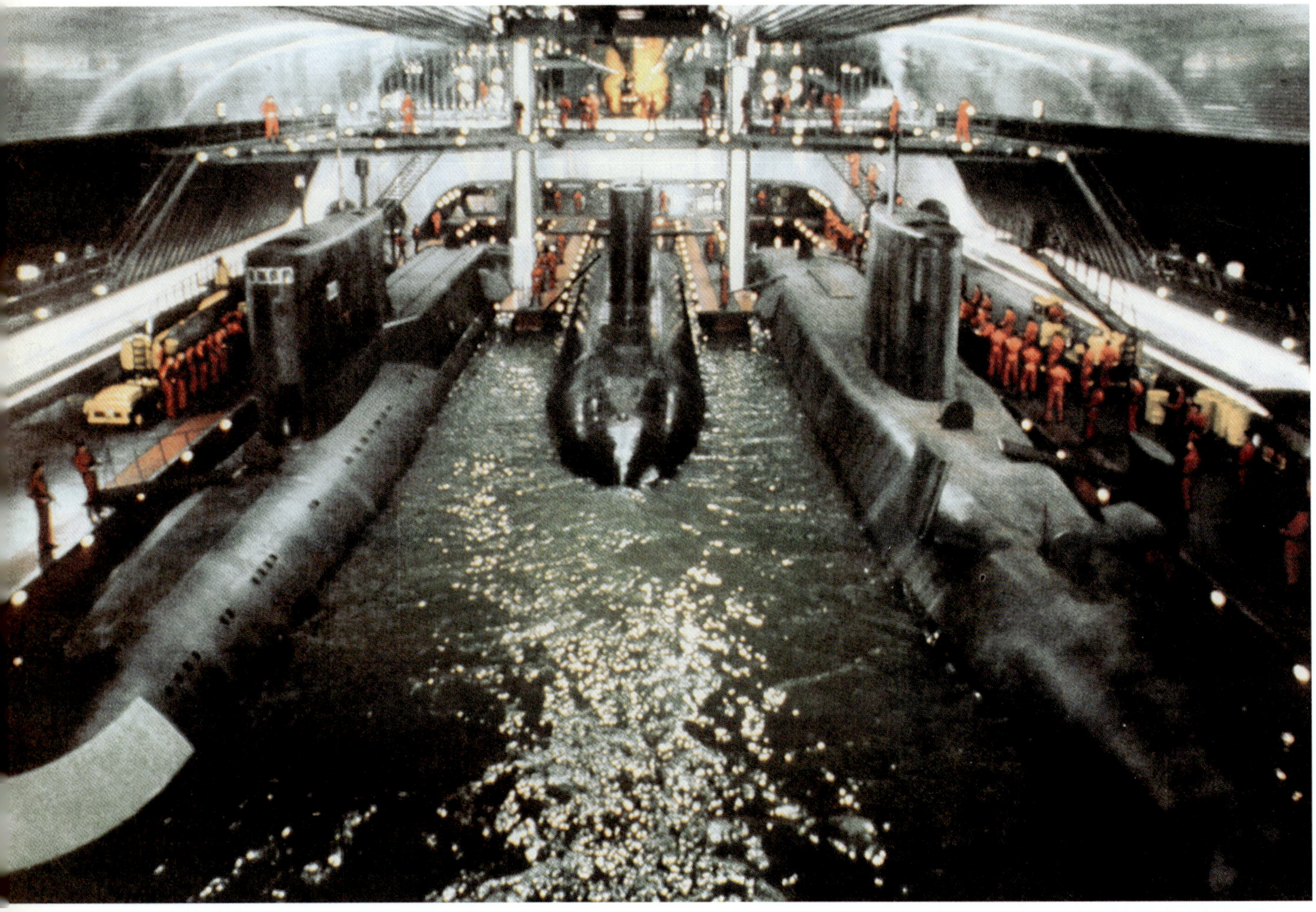

Top:
One of the drawings for the final concept of the *Liparus* supertanker interior in *The Spy Who Loved Me*, 1976
Felt-tip pen on paper

Bottom:
The Spy Who Loved Me (Lewis Gilbert, 1977)

for the later ones Adam says he 'started fooling around with circles'. These sets make real-life laboratories, computer clusters and even corporate boardrooms, usually kitted out with anonymous contract furniture and fittings, seem very low-rent indeed. And how about the missile launchers inside the Japanese volcano in *You Only Live Twice*, which absorbed 700 tons of structural steel and enough tubing to stretch twice from London to Edinburgh; or the mammoth supertanker which digests into a single compartment three nuclear submarines in *The Spy Who Loved Me*? So much more acceptable than the scrapyard-and-breezeblock look of the real things. To put it another way, as the director Ernst Lubitsch observed of the interwar era of Hollywood studios, with their armies of in-house designers and art direction as a branch of corporate imaging, 'There is Paramount Paris and MGM Paris and RKO Paris and Universal Paris and of course the real Paris' – but Paramount Paris was the most Parisian of them all. To continue the Parisian theme, on one famous occasion Cedric Gibbons, the supervising art director at MGM, complained to his boss Irving Thalberg when he was asked to come up with 'a moonlit ocean in Paris'. Thalberg instantly replied, 'Whatever you put there, they'll believe it!'

In some ways, it is strange that Ken Adam's most celebrated sets should have proved 'more acceptable than the actual thing', because his trademark as a designer has always been a form of architectural stylisation which has been called 'theatrical realism', 'exaggerated practicality' and – most recently – 'hyper-reality by design'. He has even been called, by the architectural historian Donald Albrecht, 'the Frank Lloyd Wright of *décor noir*'. In his first published article, 'Designing Sets for Action' (*Films and Filming*, August 1956), Adam already defined his brand of stylisation as the creation of an atmosphere or an impression by dramatically communicating the *idea* of a place while making it seem 'apparently real'. In a 1991 dialogue on film at the AFI, he added: 'I'm always hoping there will be a return to the studio environment, because I think one can give more of a heightened reality to a scene in a studio environment than by shooting actual locations.' However outlandish his environments might seem, he always managed to make them look as though they might actually work.

Adam's apprenticeship in the film business coincided with the Italian neo-realists shooting film on the streets of Rome and Milan, and Hollywood exposé thrillers using the subways, neon-lit alleys and railyards of actual cities. But it also coincided with most of the critical accolades, at least in Britain, going to arty art directors who had emerged from a theatrical tradition and who tended to design flamboyantly, in a painterly backdrop style: visualisers such as Hein Heckroth (who worked with Michael Powell on *The Red Shoes* and *The Tales of Hoffman*) and Oliver Messel (for whom Adam drew sketches on *Queen of Spades*). Meanwhile, in Hollywood, the grand old men of art direction and production design had spent their professional careers working indoors or on studio backlots. Léon Barsacq, in his important study of the history of film design, concluded that in the battle between these two traditions – the street and the studio – the moment real-life exteriors became fashionable and feasible, 'the future of the film set was virtually decided'. He was wrong. Ken Adam, who has by his own admission 'always had the ability to imagine what my sketches will look like in three dimensions' and who combines a rich imagination with a feet-on-the-ground attitude towards how things function, made his name from the mid-1950s onwards by combining the two traditions. The 'new wave' did not, after all, wash away the magic realism of the sound stage: the movement may even have helped to enhance it. Ken Adam once chatted to François Truffaut about this, when he was in Nice for location work on *The Last of Sheila* and Truffaut was shooting *Day for Night* nearby. *Day for Night* was partly about the frustrations of working in the open air, and Truffaut expressed nostalgia for the days of the studio-bound movie, and the creative control which went with it. 'I think one can as an artist realise one's concepts more fully there,' he said. Fellini, after all, had had a career-long love affair with the big stages of Cinecittà in Rome, where his carnivalesque sketches could credibly come alive in a completely manipulable environment.

So it is doubly ironic that Ken Adam should have won his first Academy Award for *Barry Lyndon*, a film shot entirely on location, where the production designer's job was to move the furniture around in historic houses and try to make the settings and costumes resemble Kubrick's selection of Gainsborough, Hogarth, Reynolds, Rowlandson, Chardin, Watteau, Zoffany, Stubbs and Chodowiecki reproductions – as well as giving some visual coherence to the geography of Lady Lyndon's residence, made up of 'a combination of about ten or eleven stately homes in England [including Longleat, Wilton and Petworth]'. Ironic because Adam's forte was the present and the near future, not the historical past. Ironic, too, because he had begged Kubrick to shoot the film in a studio. The film was not a happy experience. 'It eventually became quite a costly exercise,' Adam recalls,

> because Stanley would never be satisfied with one house. And yet real locations were the only way he felt he could express a period in the past. So it was much more about reproduction than imagination, which was interesting in its way but not nearly so stimulating for me personally in terms of design. I scarcely touched a sheet of paper … I never received an Academy Award for the James Bond films where my contribution was far more important. James Bond is not regarded as art!

Ken Adam's first nomination had been for his work on *Around the World in Eighty Days*: the black and white Lloyd's of London, the green and black Reform Club, both contrasting with the very rich palette of the journey itself. His second Academy Award was for *The Madness of King George*, which was apparently 'much more the way I feel one should design a picture – a combination of customising and heightening the locations [such as Eton College for the Houses of Parliament] and sets. It was never intended to make this film a "documentary" of the period.' Both Academy Awards, though, were for uncharacteristic work.

His commitment to artifice rather than the literal – Ken Adam reckons – may go right back to his childhood in Berlin:

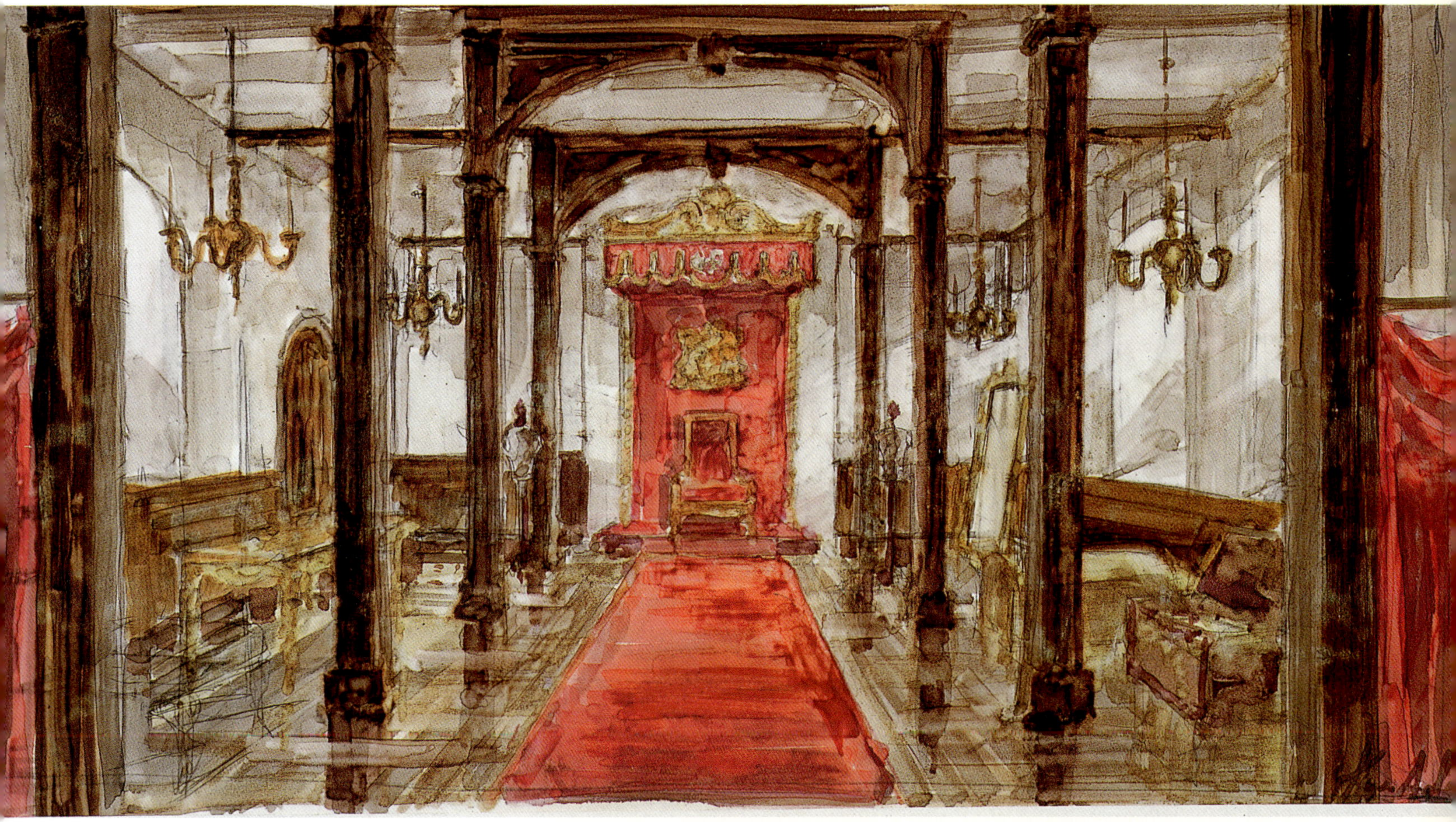

Ken Adam
The Robing Room 1994
Pen and watercolour on paper
(*The Madness of King George*,
Nicholas Hytner, 1994)

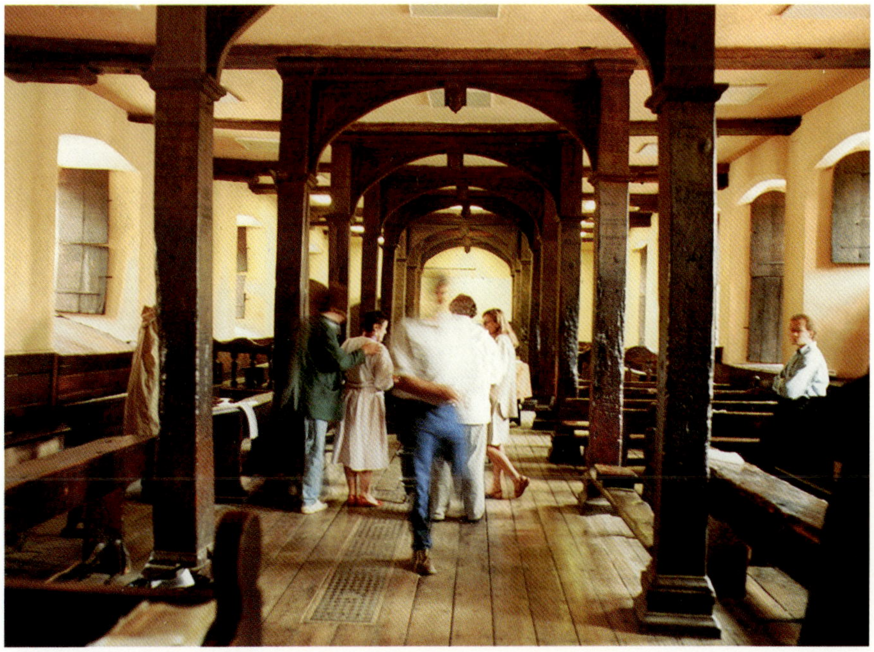

Eton College
pre-transformation

> The Berlin of the twenties formed the foundation of my future education … The Berlin of UFA studios, of Fritz Lang, Lubitsch and Erich Pommer. The Berlin of the architects Gropius, Mendelsohn and Mies van der Rohe [who designed a new building for his father's exclusive sports store on the corner of Leipziger and Friedrich streets, which was never built because of the Nazi boycott of Jewish firms and the consequent liquidation of the business]. The Berlin of the painters Max Liebermann, Grosz, Otto Dix, Klee and Kandinsky …

Ken Adam first saw *The Cabinet of Dr Caligari* (produced by Erich Pommer), *Dr Mabuse* and *Metropolis*, after his arrival in England as a refugee – with his family – in 1934. '*Caligari* I saw in 1934 in London, *Dr Mabuse* shortly afterwards, *Metropolis* much later.' *Caligari*, in particular, made a huge impression on him and he was to revisit the film at various stages in his subsequent professional career. It is tempting to relate Caligari's painted sets and matching costumes, diagonal lines and crazy expressionism – which Eisenstein, who didn't like the film, likened to a grotesque funfair – to Ken Adam's future aesthetic development. As the film's designers put it, they saw their job as creating a painted universe where 'drawings came to life'.

Donald Albrecht has speculated that 'while perfecting his craft as a production designer, Adam conjured a celluloid universe where he exorcised the evil spirits of his youth'. Not just in the overtly camp-expressionist *Addams Family Values*, or the cellar full of mechanical dolls and automata in *Sleuth* (all borrowed from a collector in Scarborough, as it happens) or Dr Strangelove's War Room – where Peter Sellers as the mad scientist seems in his element, a music-hall version of Fritz Lang's Dr Rottwang from *Metropolis*, with a black-gloved hand which inadvertently performs Nazi salutes – but also in the magnified Nazi-deco interiors of *Salon Kitty* and even the headquarters of successive Bond villains working for SMERSH and SPECTRE. Dr No's disembodied voice interrogates a henchman in a claustrophobic room where the

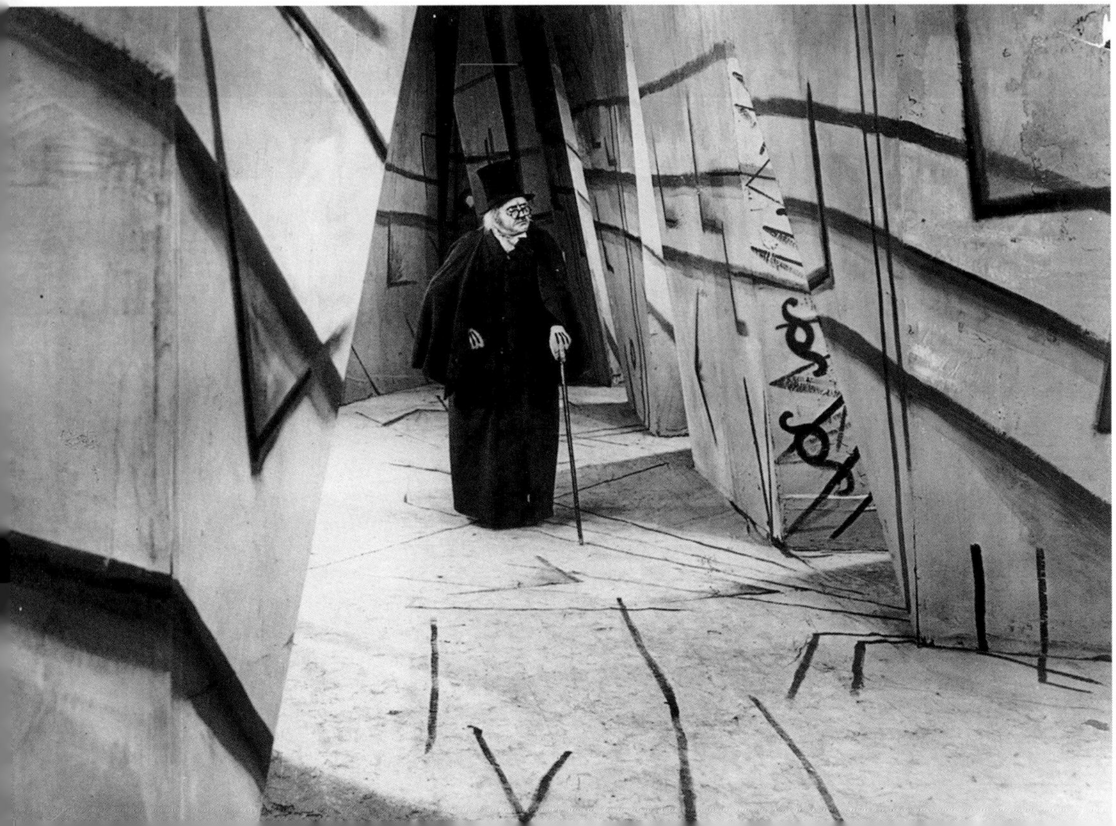

The Cabinet of Dr Caligari
(Robert Wiene, 1919)

skylight casts distorted spiderweb shadows; the henchman leaves with a tarantula in a cage. Gogol's office in *The Spy Who Loved Me* is Eisenstein to the power of ten, while Stromberg's submersible lair Atlantis looks just like a huge Meccano spider. Idyllic natural surroundings in exotic locales – filmed like pages from an upmarket tourist brochure – are often masks for nasty subterranean operations rooms where super-villains plot world domination, using elaborate weapons disguised as expensive consumer goodies. The skull beneath the sun-tanned skin. The Cabinet of Dr Adam seems sometimes to make the visual and thematic link – as did Siegfried Kracauer's controversial book *From Caligari to Hitler* – between the topsy-turvy world of German thrillers in the years following World War I, and the rise of the Third Reich.

This aspect of Ken Adam's work transforms his sets into larger-than-life characters in their own right, thus gloriously realising the ambition of the architect and film designer Robert Mallet-Stevens, who wrote in his pamphlet *Le décor moderne au cinéma* (1929): 'The set, in order to be a good set, must act. Whether realistic, expressionistic, modern or historical it must play its role ... The set must present the character before he appears, must indicate his position in society, his tastes, his habits, his lifestyle, his personality.' In Adam's case, the sets are often machines for tyrants to live in. But the closer you look, the more diminished the tyrants become – like the fish in Dr No's magnifying aquarium: 'Minnows pretending they are whales.' The aquarium tells you a lot about them.

Mallet-Stevens was one of the designers (with Fernand Léger) of the futurist film meditation on art and technology *L'Inhumaine*, made in 1924 and credited with being the first-ever feature film to use the latest in modern architecture: its laboratory sequences helped to inspire Fritz Lang's *Metropolis*. But when the seventeen-year-old Ken Adam enrolled as a part-time external student at the Bartlett School of Architecture, London, for 1937–39, he found that its syllabus was 'extremely conservative': rigid, tweedy and utterly innocent of modernism. 'I was always a bit of a rebel when I was there.' It is hardly surprising. Simultaneously, straight after leaving St Paul's School, he was articled with a firm of architects and civil engineers where the senior partner had been an assistant to Erich Mendelsohn and 'was very much into the Bauhaus'. This appealed to Adam much more, as did helping out a young MARS Group architect (short for Modern Architecture Research Group) 'when I had moments to spare'. The MARS Group, in north London, was a haven at that time for refugees from the Bauhaus and converts to the gospel of modernism. It was not because he wanted to be an architect that Adam was studying at the Bartlett or serving his apprenticeship. He already wanted to be a film or perhaps theatre designer, and a meeting with Vincent Korda at Denham Studios – where the huge Russian sets and monuments for *Knight Without Armour* were being built – had convinced him that an architectural education would provide the best foundation. This had been while he was still at St Paul's, and his entrée into the Korda empire came through a Hungarian painter-turned-cameraman who was lodging at his mother's boarding house. 'I was fascinated by the huge sets at Denham, and Vincent Korda definitely influenced my decision to become a film designer.'

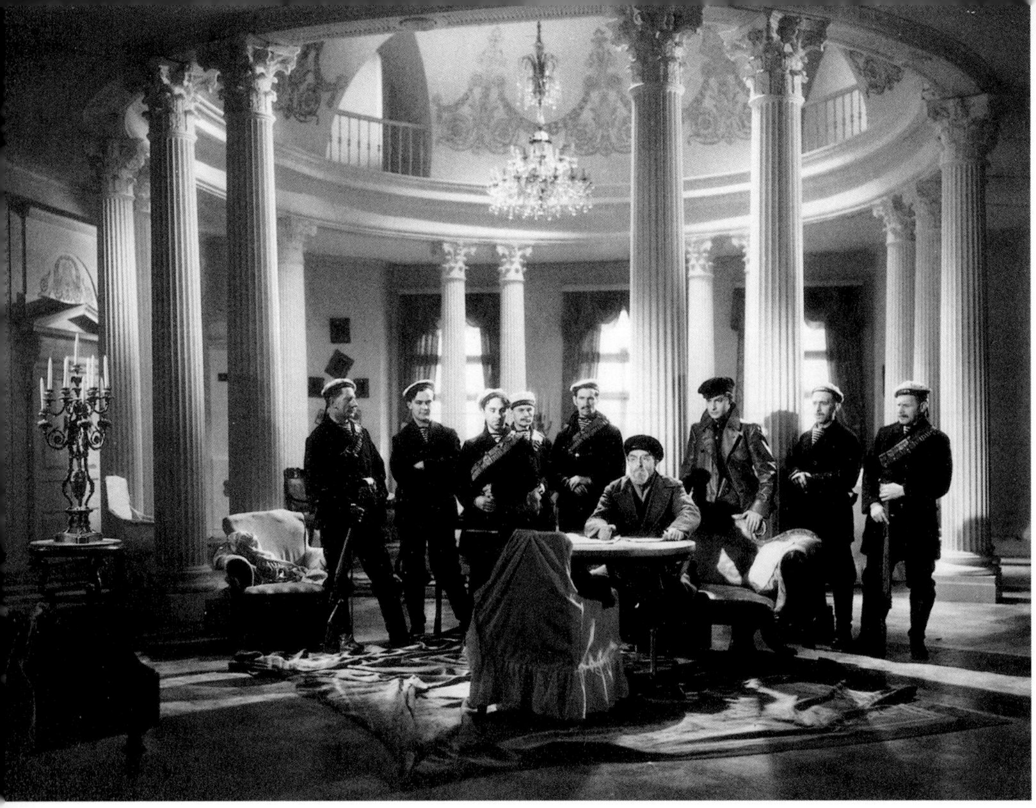

Knight Without Armour
(Jacques Feyder, 1936)

Korda himself had trained at Budapest's College of Industrial Art and Academy of Art before practising as a painter in Paris for twelve years. Although in the mid-1930s he would periodically turn up on the sets his brother Alexander had expensively financed, dressed in denims, espadrilles and a straw hat – a van Gogh among 'the applied artists' – he knew well how valuable an architectural education could be. Many of the most innovative post-silent movie Hollywood art directors attached to the big studios – Anton Grot at Warner Brothers, Hans Dreier at Paramount, Charles D. Hall at Universal – had studied and practised the subject, or else interior design, in Europe before chancing their arm in Hollywood. Grot and Dreier were Germans (they emigrated in 1909 and 1923 respectively) and Hall was English. Together, they created variations on the modern 'look' for their studios: at Warners, stylised expressionism for historical adventures; at Paramount, Art Deco; at Universal, a contemporary and highly exaggerated version of the gothic. And they all knew about the latest International style. The art history books assert that this style was introduced to America via *The International Style*, a seminal exhibition about modern architecture at the Museum of Modern Art, New York, in 1932. In fact, Hollywood had been deriving designs from pictures of modernist buildings and interiors – some of them by the very same architects who were to be exhibited at the MOMA show – for the past four years at least. The movie moguls who ran the studios often started out in the fashion business, and had strong intuitions about the added value that the latest styles could bring. With a few notable exceptions, curators and art historians, then as now, knew little about film, which was considered to be well below their visual threshold. The art directors and the cinema-going public were quicker to catch on.

Later, Ken Adam would observe that 'in a way the war helped me because it prevented me from studying more than three years. I might have become too rigid and too influenced by the practical applications of architecture.' In addition, he said, he was 'continually worried about becoming too academic'. What he had learned, though, both at the Bartlett and at the firm of C. W. Glover and Partners, was a visual lexicon of architectural history and above all how to develop his remarkable drawing abilities: a repertoire which came to extend from precise technical drawings to uninhibited freehand sketches done with powerful and confident strokes. By the mid-1950s, coinciding with his promotion to solo art director, he had 'altered my technique by using a felt pen [called a Flowmaster] with a wedge-shaped tip instead of pencil, conté or pen and ink. My sketches had more strength and allowed me to experiment with light and shade.' In order to heighten the chiaroscuro effect, he often drew in black and white – even when preparing a colour film. Some designers (such as John Box, who worked with David Lean) found it more useful to start with models. Ken Adam always started, and starts, with a sketch: this is 'very important for me, however rough the sketch, in visualising the eventual three-dimensional effect ... it is something to do with the way my mind works.' A long way from the precise and rigid delineation drummed into him as a student, and a distinctive way of communicating the effects he had created to the director and lighting cameraman. His fluency as a draughtsman was to stand him in very good stead when Stanley Kubrick suddenly changed his mind about the design of the War Room in *Dr Strangelove*, and stood over his production designer while he was expected to improvise a revised concept, the one used in the finished film. 'I must say, when Stanley asked for something different it really threw me at first: I had to get over the shock by walking in the gardens at Shepperton.' Kubrick was delighted with the result, once Adam had explained the reasoning behind it, but then proceeded to cut out the only shot in the film that revealed the whole of the set in all its glory.

During World War II, Ken Adam served in the Pioneer Corps – a specialised army unit open to refugees – and, after many applications, was transferred in 1941 to the RAF. He was the service's only fighter pilot who was born in Germany and still a German citizen, and he flew Hawker Typhoons – 'one of the fastest and most powerful fighters' – in support of Allied troops advancing across Europe after D-Day. To this, and to his childhood love for building detailed models of planes and ships in Berlin, he attributes the emphasis in his professional career on visionary, powerful and often nasty vehicles which actually seem to function. After his early experiences in the film industry on projects that combined a lot of studio work with a few location sequences (his first location film, made as late as 1965, was *The Ipcress File*, in which only the interior of the warehouse was a set), and the support he gave as draughtsman to a succession of theatrically inclined art directors, he became known in the trade – quite by accident – as a specialist in designing ships. 'Suddenly,' he says, 'I found myself described as a ship expert.' It began with *Captain Horatio Hornblower R. N.* in 1950, when he converted two beaten-up ships in the south of France – one of them had transported refugees from Palestine to Marseilles – into eighteenth-century men-of-war, following some research at the National Maritime Museum. On the Errol Flynn film *The Master of Ballantrae*, he did some similar makeovers in Sicily. Then he designed a Greek galley for *Helen of Troy* and had it hand-crafted 'by an old

Italian family of shipbuilders I'd found'; the other nine hundred and ninety-nine ships launched by Helen's face had, however, to be faked. But it was the ships in *The Crimson Pirate* that pointed towards the shape of things to come. For this romp (directed by Robert Siodmak and starring Burt Lancaster), shot on the island of Ischia in the Gulf of Naples, he had to design numerous historical gadgets 'because we were writing the script as we went along: suddenly they would ask me for an eighteenth-century submarine, to be invented almost overnight! In some ways it was like a historical Bond film.' While filming *Pirate* in Ischia, Ken Adam also met his future wife, Letizia, whom he married two weeks later.

Of the gadgets he was later to design for the Bond films, the best known – it turned out to be a pivotal moment in the development of the whole saga – was the silver-birch Aston Martin DB5 driven by Sean Connery in *Goldfinger*. In Ian Fleming's original novel, the DB3 with which James Bond was issued from the car pool – instead of his usual four-litre Bentley (the author's car, in fact) – had been a very, very different vehicle:

> The DB3 had the advantage of an inconspicuous colour – battleship grey – and certain extras which might or might not come in handy. These included switches to alter the type and colour of Bond's front and rear lights … reinforced steel bumpers, fore and aft, in case he needed a ram, a long-barrelled Colt. 45 in a trick compartment under the driver's seat, a radio pick-up turned to receive an apparatus called the Homer, and plenty of concealed space that would fox most customs men.

For the film, this inconspicuous DB3 was transformed by Ken Adam into a highly conspicuous DB5 with 'certain extras' which included bullet-proof windows, revolving number plates, ground radar system with dashboard reception, oil-slick squirter, wing-mounted machine guns, protruding wheel scythe (*Ben-Hur*-style, only this one can slice through the bodywork of a Ford Mustang like a tin can) and of course passenger ejector seat. As the man from Q Branch patiently explains these devices to Bond, he walks past – in a deliberate touch -– several other classics of British design: a parking meter, an anglepoise lamp, a Mini van in the background. The Aston Martin, with its hand-beaten aluminium body and hand-stitched leather upholstery, is presented as a distinguished new addition to the canon. *Goldfinger* was released at precisely the same time as Lord Snowdon's promotional mission to Council of Industrial Design exhibitions in Eastern Europe – motoring in an open-top Aston Martin DB5 Volante. Buy British! Many of Q Branch's modifications to the DB5 actually worked – powered by high-pressure hydraulics in the boot – and some extra ones were included, such as twin flame-throwers mounted behind the fog lights, which never made it into the finished film: the car had been customised at a cost of £25,000 before the screenplay was completed. Its combination of urbane, gentlemanly exterior and vicious interior was perfect for the part. Ken Adam was and is a 'sports-car freak' and, he has added enigmatically, 'all the gimmickry and gadgets were just what I would have wanted in my own car'.

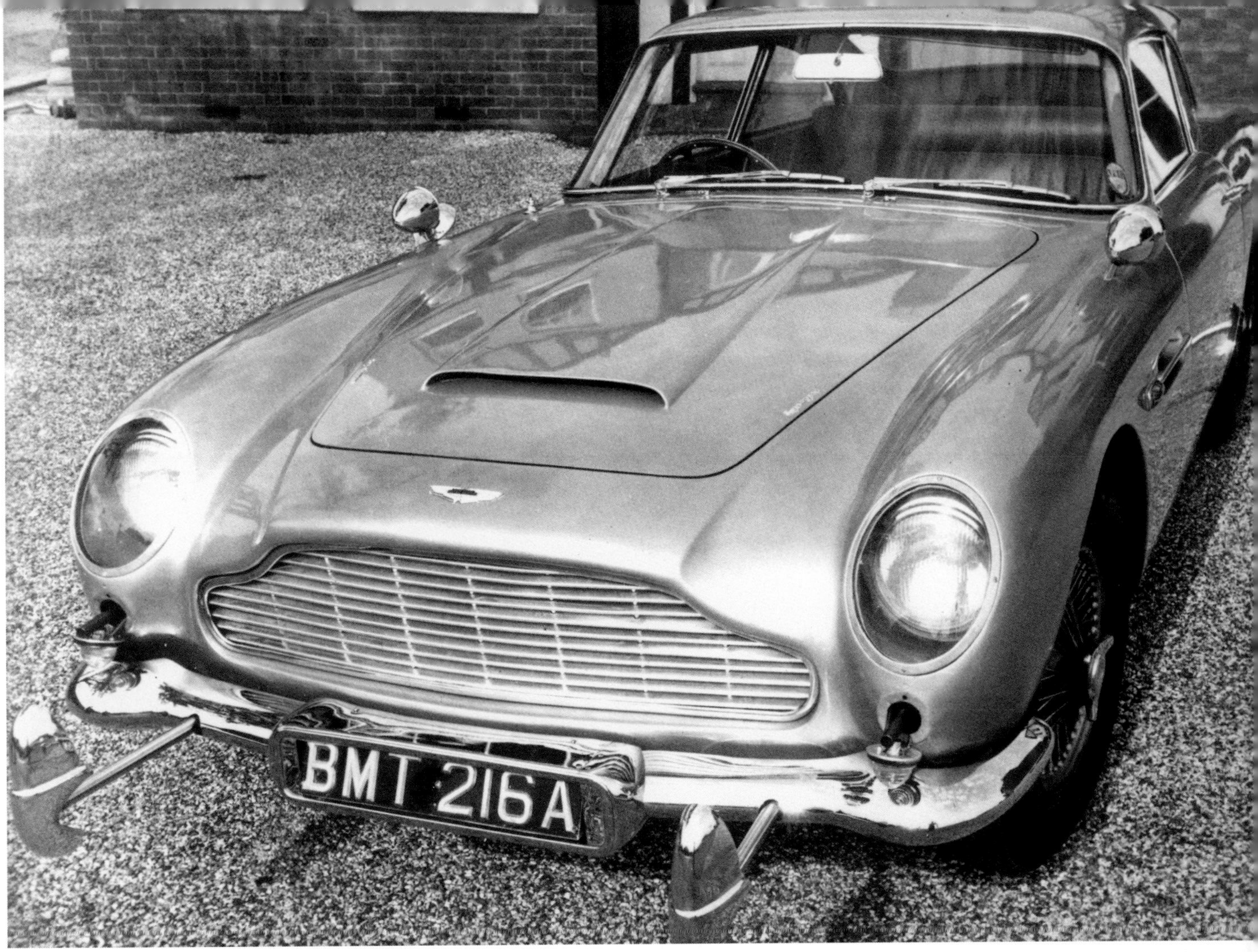

The Aston Martin DB5
Publicity still
(*Goldfinger*, Guy Hamilton, 1964)

The DB5 appeared on screen for a mere thirteen minutes, but it changed the tone of the whole Bond series. The scriptwriter Tom Mankiewicz rightly said, 'Once you added the Aston Martin in *Goldfinger*, you couldn't do a serious Bond again.' The gadgets in *Dr No* and *From Russia with Love* (a film not in fact designed by Ken Adam) – guns with screw-on silencers, a trick briefcase, a shoe with a knife in the sole – had been both mundane and in the spirit of the novels. But this was something very different, and it also ushered in the era of product placement after orders began to pour in to the plant at Newport Pagnell following the film's release. When asked to donate a car to the production, Aston Martin had at first been very reluctant indeed. It soon became apparent that unlike other screen cars – whether fantasy vehicles (television's Batmobile) or models available in the shops (the Mini Coopers in *The Italian Job*) or vintage cars (the farmboy Fords in *Bonnie and Clyde*) – this one could be seen in the local showroom *and* came with fantasy fitted not as an extra but as standard. After that realisation, product placement began in earnest. From then on, too, most of the big action sequences in Bond films would be written around the sets and props: Ken Adam would 'be sent an outline or a progression' and would be intimately involved in the development of the scripts. The multi-climax digital extravaganzas of Spielberg and Lucas start here: the sense that 'anything is possible', which up to then had been confined to the animated film. An industry one-liner went, 'Adam created James Bond, seven times over; Bond did not make Adam.' Another, in reply to the question 'Who is the real star of James Bond – Connery, Lazenby or Moore?', was: 'The real star is Ken Adam.' Quite right.

The idea of a very close collaboration between scriptwriter, director, cinematographer and designer, at all stages in the production, was one Adam had first seen at close quarters when working with the associate producer and production designer William Cameron Menzies on *Around the World in Eighty Days* in 1956. 'I was very influenced by him,' Adam has said, as they talked together about the advantages of sound stages, the attractions of stylised sets and colours, the need to loosen up drawing techniques – and the benefits of collaborative projects if the designer's presence was to be felt in the finished work. The experience liberated him from his inhibitions. He gained the confidence to see the production designer's role as 'to set a style and visual progression for the whole film and to physically realise it: ideally speaking, that means supervising everything that is visual'. Menzies, the man who invented storyboards and 'production design' – and who had directed his own films as well – was in this sense a key to Adam's career development over the next forty years. If Ken Adam had visited Denham Studios and Vincent Korda just one year before he did, in 1936, he would have seen Menzies hard at work on H. G. Wells's *Things to Come*, a spectacular science-fiction epic which was to modernism what *Bladerunner* is to postmodernism. And he might have played less safe from the late 1940s to the mid-1950s. As it transpired, his work from *The Trials of Oscar Wilde* onwards – in the words of one critic – 'contributed more to the success of British postwar cinema than anyone else, with a list of credits as a … designer and artistic director on feature films which is hardly credible.' At a time when 'art' in film design is too often associated with digital effects, landscape photography and historical set dressing, it is singularly appropriate that Ken Adam should at long last be having his own exhibition in a major British art gallery. The man himself is far too modest and sensible to admit it, but he is a key contributor to twentieth-century visual culture and a very influential one. The film world, and the cinema-going public, realised that years ago.

Note:

1
The sources I found most useful when preparing this essay were two supplements on production design in *Film Comment* (May–June 1978; January–February 1982); a long article on Ken Adam in *Positif* 191 (March 1977); Donald Albrecht's *Designing Dreams* (London, 1986) and the same author's introduction to the catalogue *Production Design: Ken Adam* (Munich, 1994); Michael Kirsch's Royal College of Art thesis *Aston Martins, Laser Beams and the Glint of Gold* (RCA/Industrial Design Engineering, London, 1993); my own *Things to Come* (BFI, London, 1995) and my Paul Reilly Lecture *Design and the Dream Factory in Britain* (Design Museum, London, 1990); a three-hour question-and-answer session with Ken Adam and design students at the RCA in January 1989; and conversations with Ken Adam – plus research into his archive.

Catalogue of the Exhibition

The South Galleries form an introductory section designed by Ken Adam. The images are drawings for and stills from *Moonraker* and *Dr Strangelove or: How I Learned to Stop Worrying and Love the Bomb*.

The North Gallery presents a showing of extracts from:

Curse of the Demon (aka *Night of the Demon*) 1957; *Dr No* 1962; *Dr. Srangelove or: How I Learned to Stop Worrying and Love the Bomb* 1963; *Goldfinger* 1964; *You Only Live Twice* 1967; *Sleuth* 1972; *Barry Lyndon* 1975; *The Spy Who Loved Me* 1977; *Moonraker* 1979; *Pennies from Heaven* 1981; *The Madness of King George* 1994.

The graphic works and stills in the East and West Galleries consists of material relating to twenty-eight films, three unrealised film projects, a multimedia project and two operas. Unless otherwise stated all works are executed in Flowmaster pen on paper, all measurements give height before width and are of the sheet size. Several of the illustrations in the catalogue are of works not in the exhibition.

The date ascribed to a film is that of its release; where no film resulted, the date given indicates when the work was done.

The synopses of the films are by Philip French. The remaining information is drawn from interviews with Ken Adam. The sources of the extracts are indicated by initials explained in the bibliographical key adjacent. Those previously published include a few minor revisions provided by Ken Adam in the interests of accuracy

GM
Geoffrey Macnab, *Sight & Sound*, vol. 9, no. 9, September (London 1999)

JB
Jürgen Berger, ed. *Production Design: Ken Adam* (Kulturreferat der Landeshauptstadt München). Translated from the German.

JD
James Delson, *Film Comment*, vol. 18, no. 1, January/February (Film Society of Lincoln Centre, New York 1982)

PE
Peter Ettedgui, ed., *Screencraft: Production Design and Art Direction* (RotoVision, Hove 2000)

SG
Interview conducted for this catalogue (London, September 1999)

VL
Vincent LoBrutto, ed., *By Design: Interviews with Film Production Designers* (Praeger, Westport CT. 1992)

1952

The Crimson Pirate

A homage to Douglas Fairbanks's silent *The Black Pirate*, this tongue-in-cheek swashbuckler, directed by Robert Siodmak, stars Burt Lancaster as an acrobatic freebooter battling oppressive tyrants on the Spanish Main with the aid of an eccentric inventor.

1956

Around the World in Eighty Days

In Mike Todd's spectacular costume comedy, directed by Michael Anderson, Victorian gentleman Phileas Fogg, accompanied by his manservant Passepartout, circles the globe to settle a wager and is pursued by a detective, Inspector Fix, who believes Fogg has robbed the Bank of England.

1958

Battle of the V-1

World War II action picture, directed by Vernon Sewell, about the Polish underground plotting to destroy the Nazi rocket centre at Peenemünde on the Baltic.

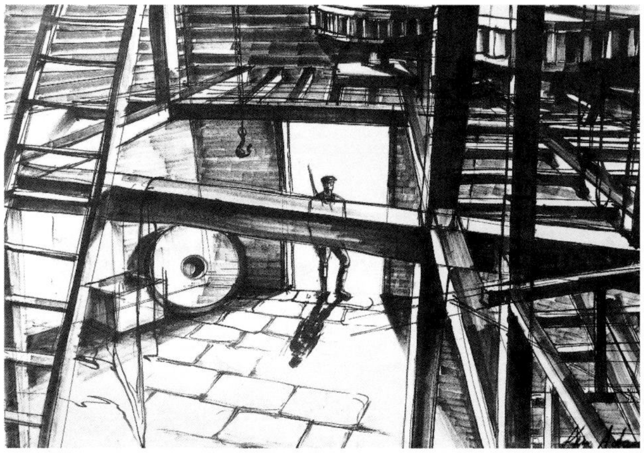

Freedom fighter 1957
Study
44 × 62 cm

1958

Gideon's Day

John Ford's police-procedural thriller follows twenty-four incident-packed hours in the private and professional life of Inspector George Gideon of Scotland Yard.

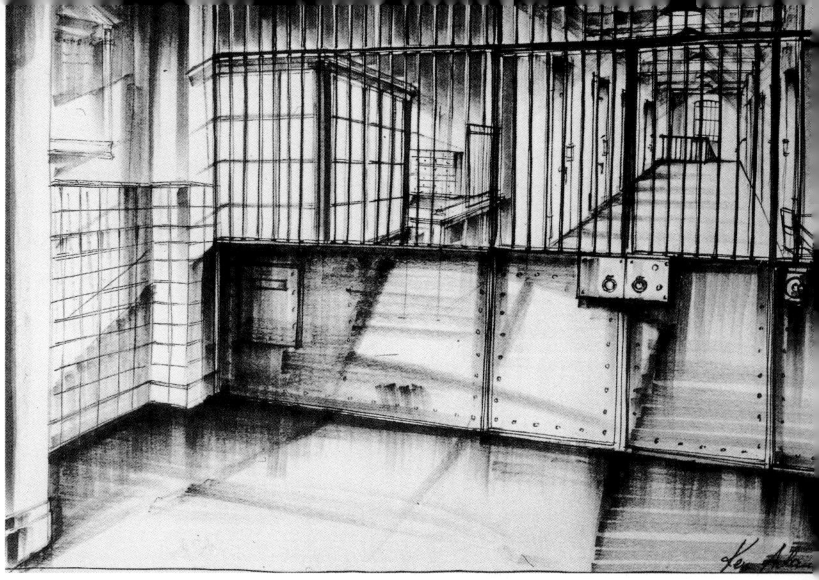

Entrance to the safe deposit 1957
Study
30 × 42 cm

1959

Ten Seconds to Hell

Robert Aldrich melodrama centring on a team of six German bomb-disposal experts, led by an anti-Nazi architect, who are killed one by one as they attempt to neutralise unexploded bombs in the devastated Berlin of 1945.

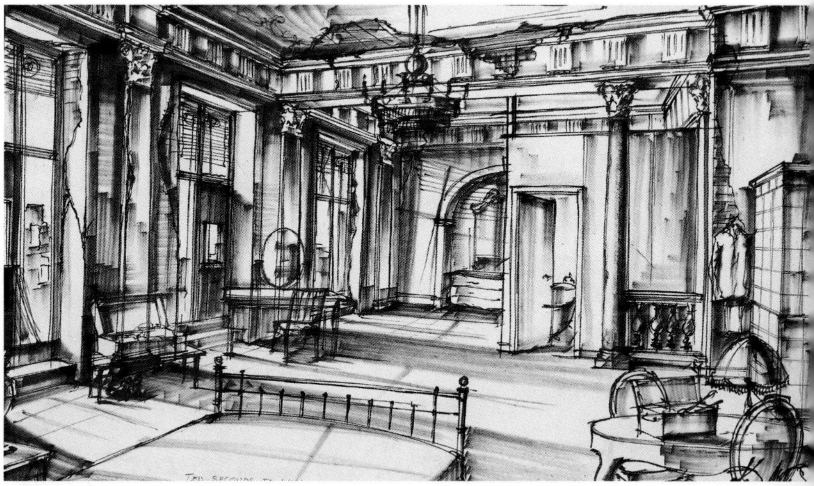

Martine Carol's Berlin apartment 1958
Final concept
37 × 64 cm

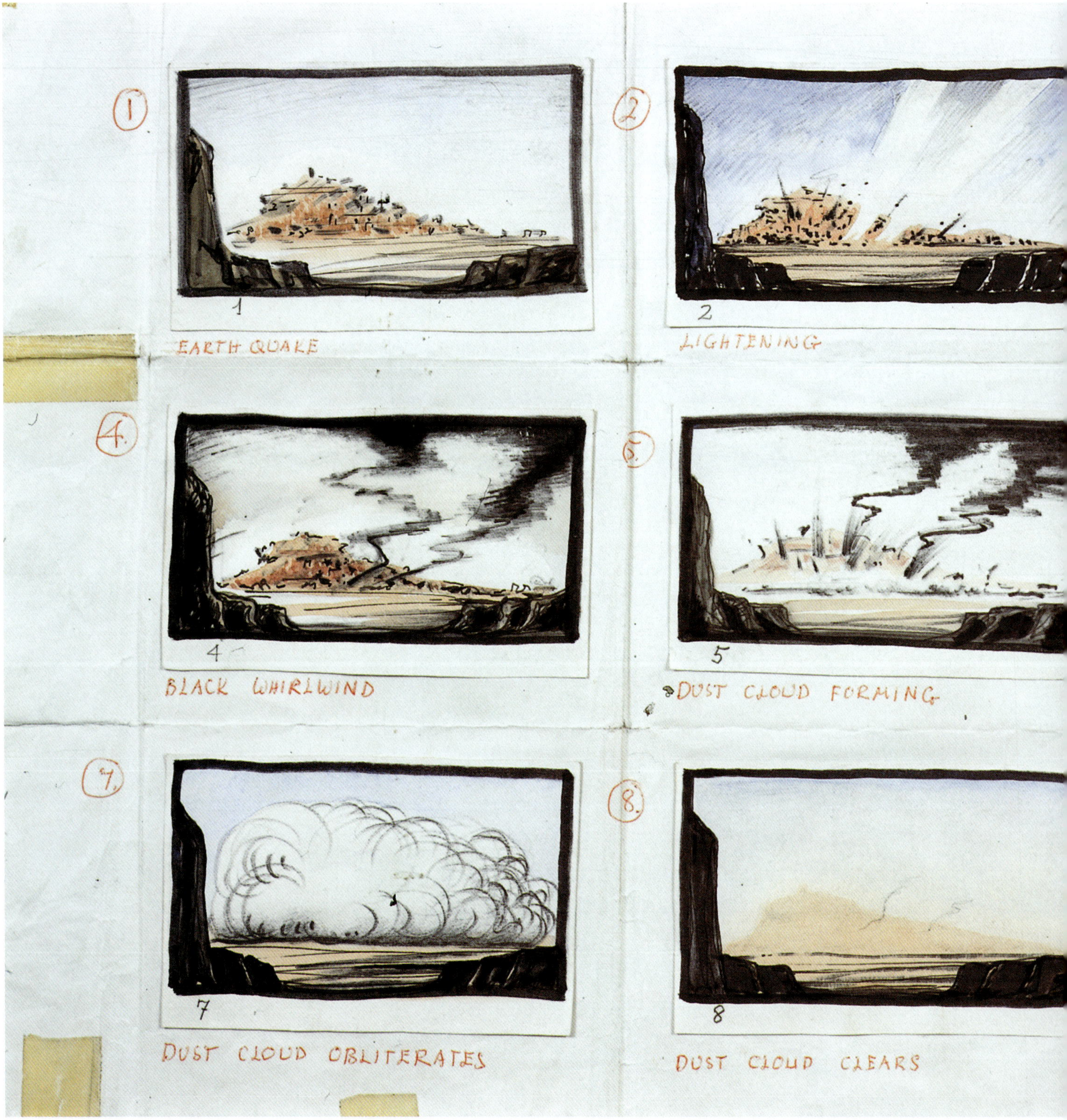

The destruction of Sodom 1960
Storyboard page
Felt-tip pen and watercolour on paper
34 × 47 cm

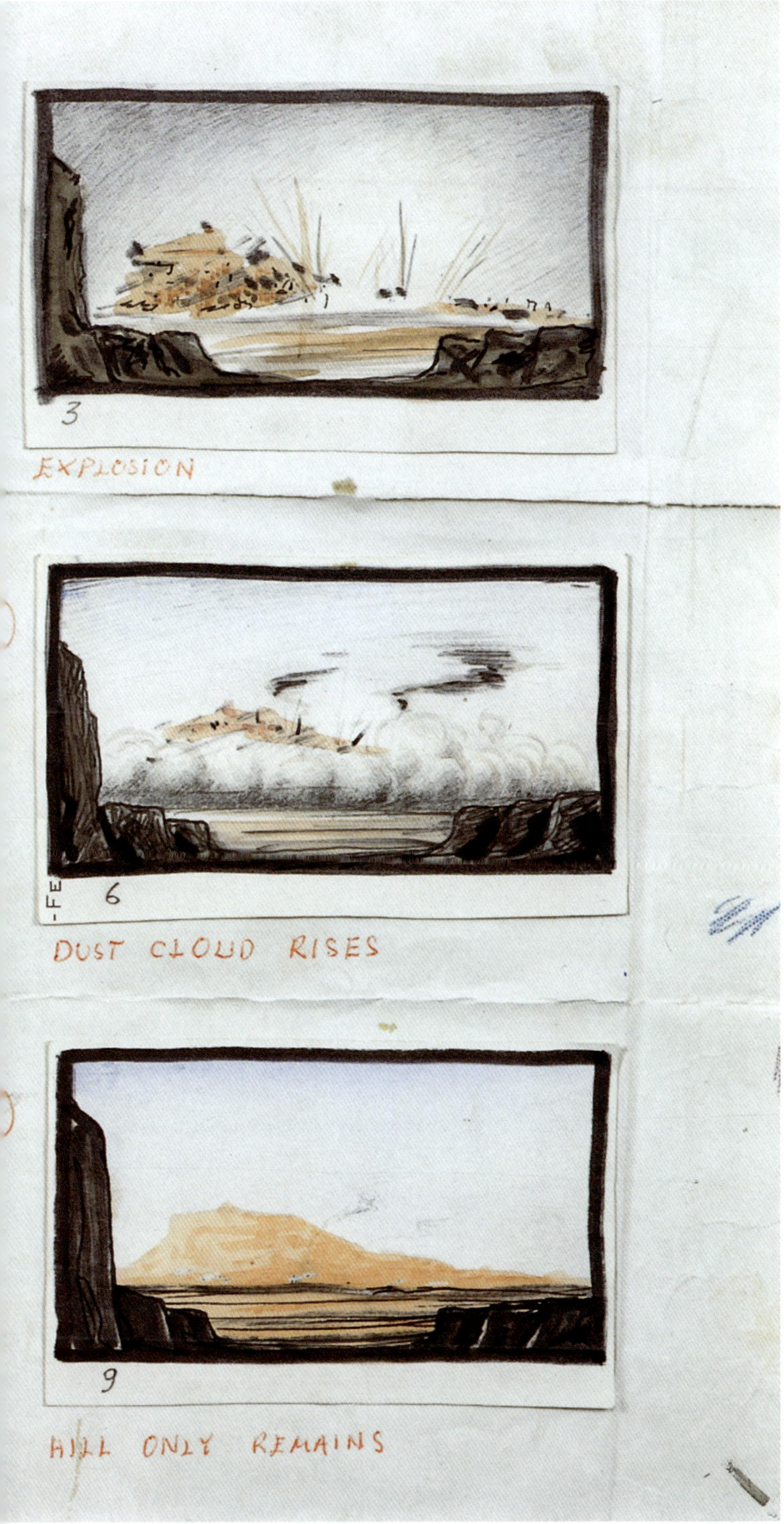

1961

Sodom and Gomorrah

In Robert Aldrich's Old Testament epic, a largely apocryphal Italian-American gloss on Genesis xix, the righteous Hebrew leader Lot becomes involved in the conflict between Queen Bera, ruler of the depraved Sodom and Gomorrah, and her evil brother.

1957

Curse of the Demon

Jacques Tourneur's low-key occult thriller, (aka *Night of the Demon*), an update of the classic M. R. James story, brings a sceptical American psychic researcher to England to challenge a brilliant British diabolist.

At what point in the making of the film did the producers insist on the introduction of the demon in person?

I think it was being discussed almost throughout the making of the film, and Jacques Tourneur and myself always hoped that by using the footprints of the monster we wouldn't have to design an actual monster. I felt that it should never be seen as a physical shape except for the steaming footprints it left when walking. I wanted more of an illusion or abstract effect, but the producers insisted and so I had no choice. I therefore designed the demon and then the effects department took over. I suppose nowadays I might have come up with something different and more original.

The exterior scenes were locations and all the interiors were studio sets. **SG**

Attic storeroom in Dr Karswell's house 1956
Final concept
Felt-tip pen on card
50 × 75 cm

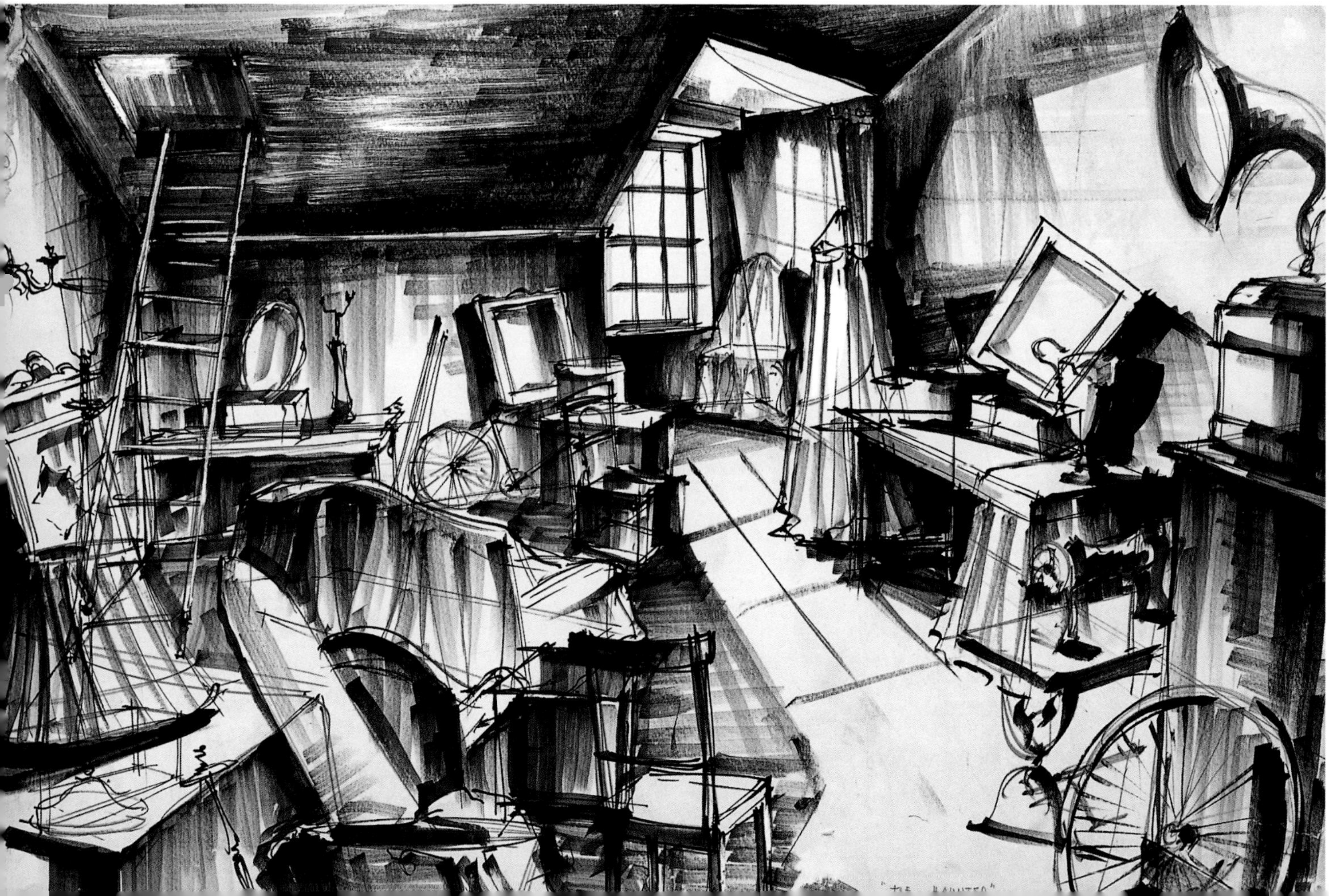

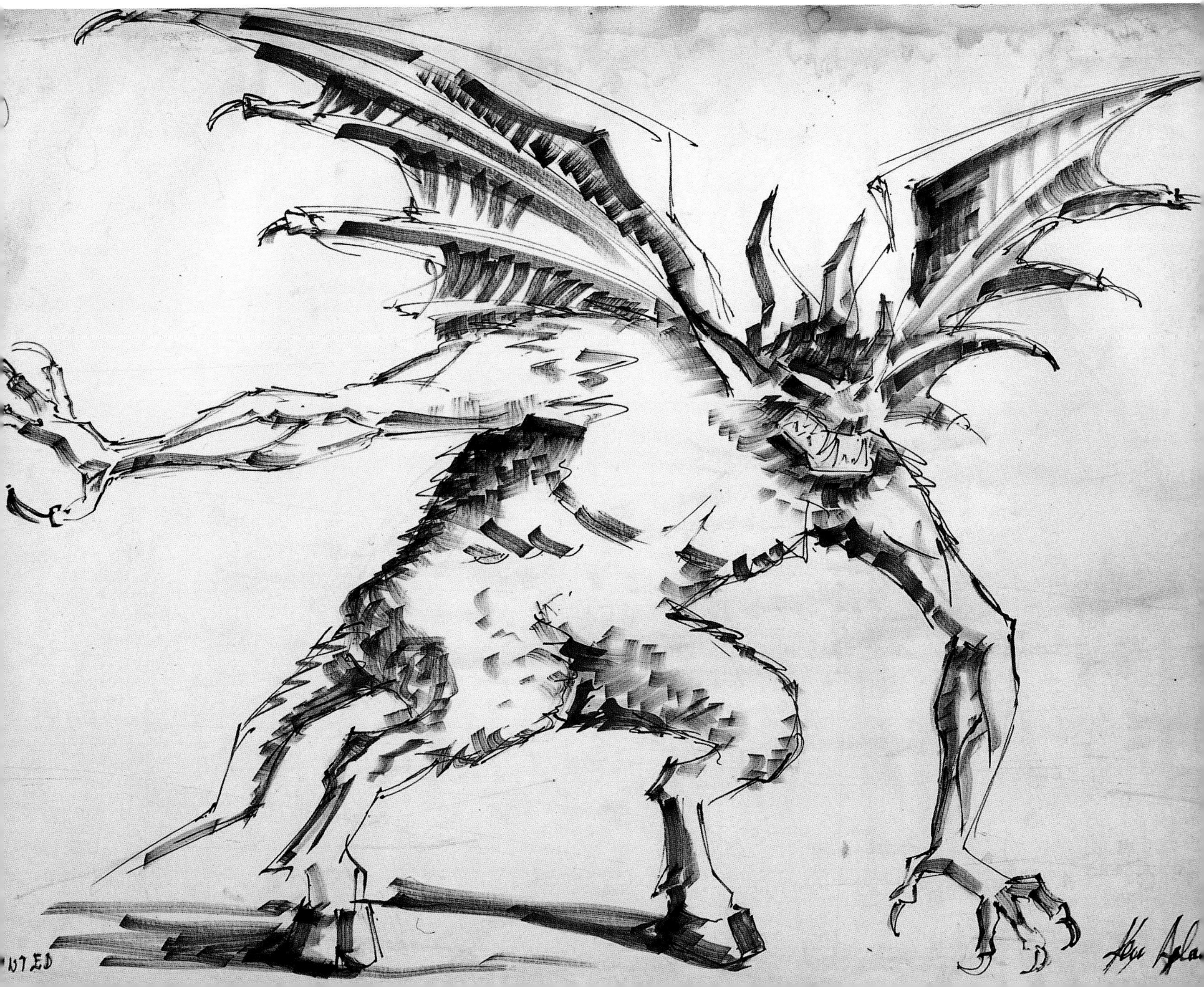

The monster 1956
Study
Felt-tip pen on card
55 × 72 cm

The Trials of Oscar Wilde

Written and directed by Ken Hughes, the film casts Peter Finch as the most fashionable author and playwright of the 1890s, who destroys himself by bringing a libel action against his lover's vindictive father, the Marquess of Queensberry, leading to his own prosecution and imprisonment.

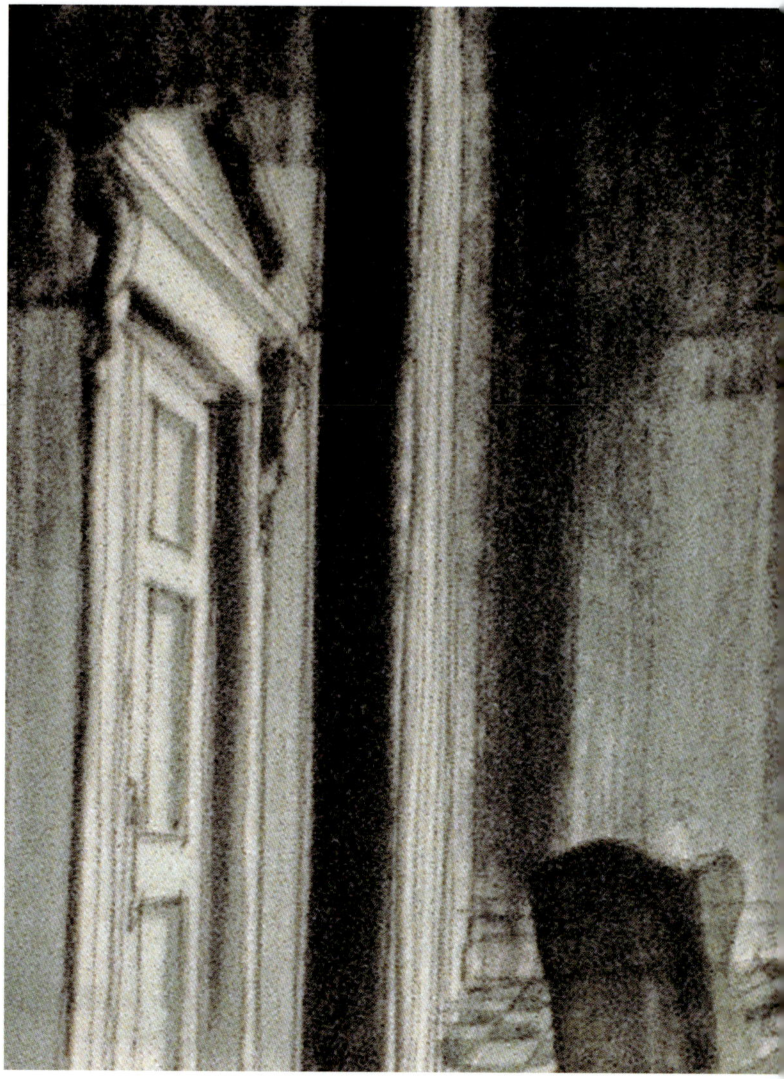

Kinmount House interior 1960
Final concept
Ink and watercolour on paper
12 × 25 cm

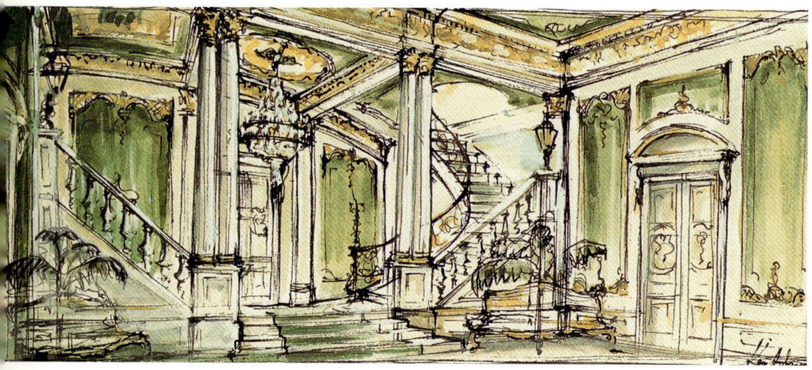

Foyer of the St James Theatre 1960
Final concept
Felt-tip pen and watercolour on paper
13.5 × 27cm

I was enormously lucky to work for a time during the 1940s and 50s with Georges Wakhévitch, the Russian designer. Although he had worked on films like *La Grande Illusion* for Renoir, he was perhaps better known for his work in opera and theatre. A stage designer has to create a self-sufficient universe within the proscenium arch and the dimensions of the stage. These limits mean that one cannot simply reproduce reality; one is much more dependent on imagination. I began to realise that this approach could be applied to film. I experimented with theatrical stylisation on *Around*

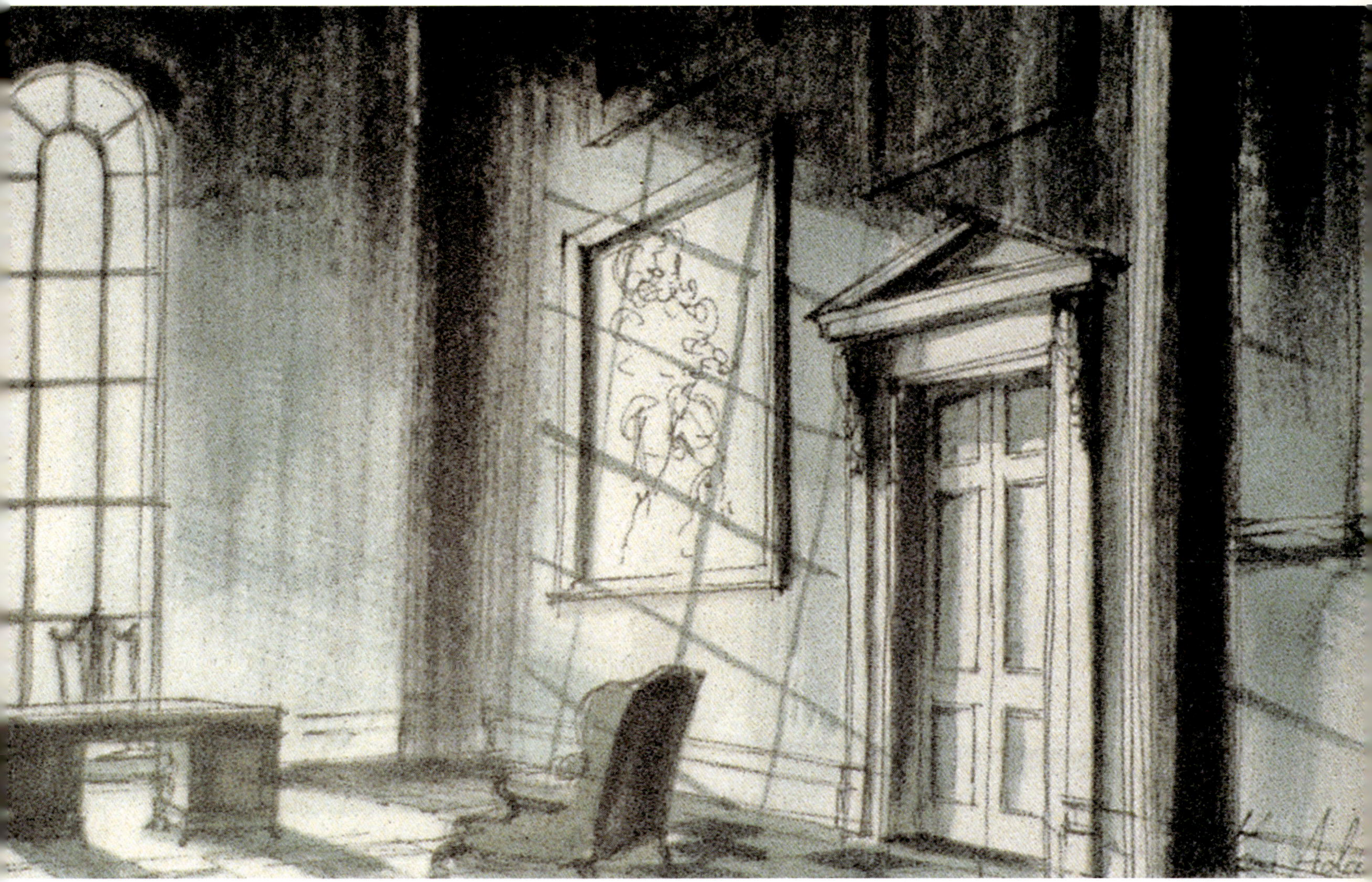

the World in 80 Days, whose associate producer was William Cameron Menzies, the father of modern production design. Menzies encouraged me to stylise, and he taught me not to be afraid to use colour in bold ways. But it was practical considerations as much as aesthetic ideals that forced me to apply these ideas to *The Trials of Oscar Wilde*. The low art department budget meant I could not have attempted authentic period reproductions even if I wanted to. I had to simplify the design – and this led to a stylisation for which I won critical recognition for the first time. **PE**

This was made primarily with studio sets; we even built the exterior of the St James Theatre. The only exterior locations that come to my mind were Oscar Wilde's house in Tite Street, and Woodrow Wyatt's house off Regent's Park. I don't think there were any location interiors, but perhaps we used some. **SG**

1962

Dr No

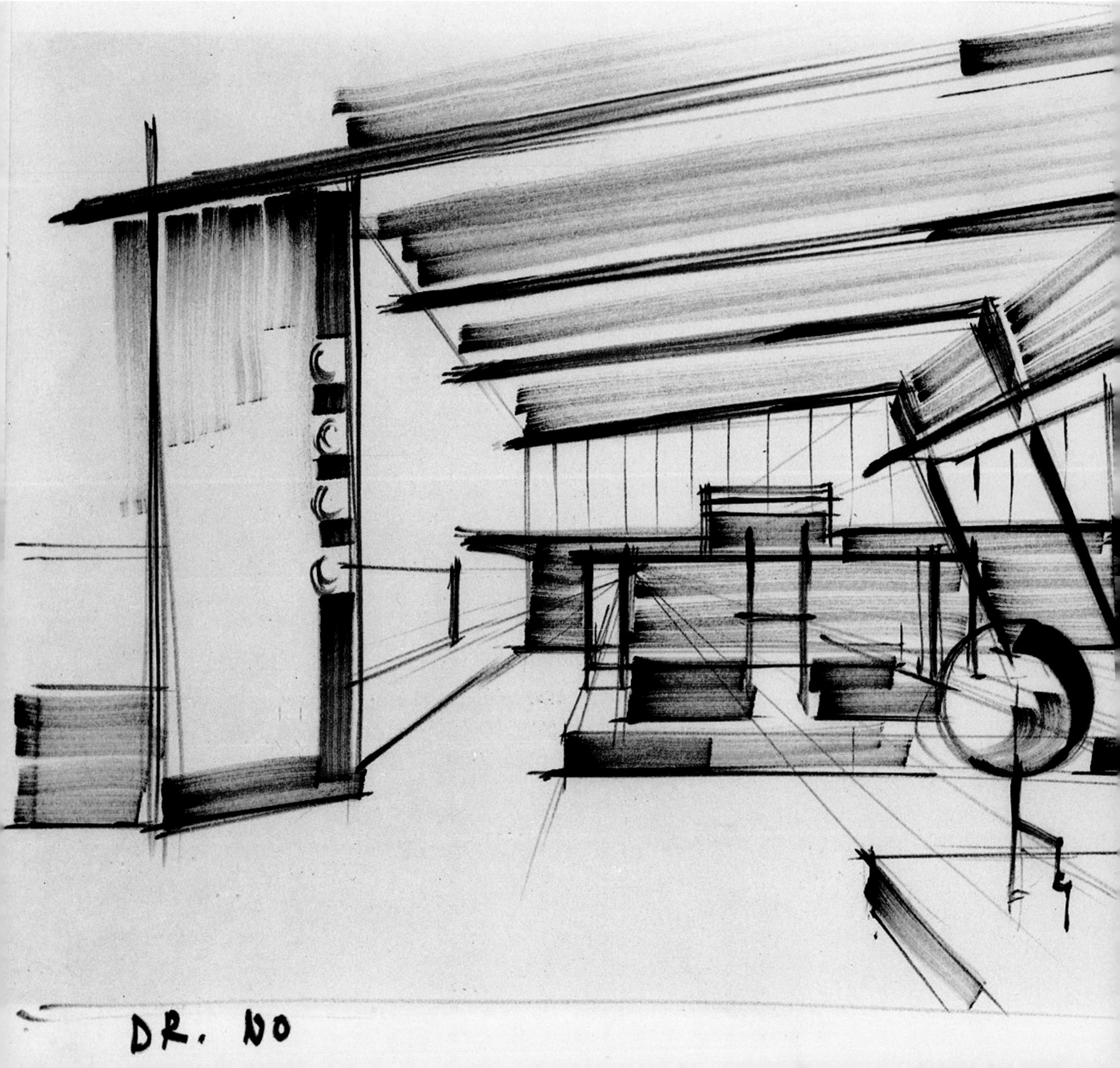

In the first James Bond thriller, directed by Terence Young, British secret agent 007 – assisted by the beautiful Honeychile Rider – investigates the nefarious activities of the eponymous megalomaniac master criminal who operates from a private island off the coast of Jamaica.

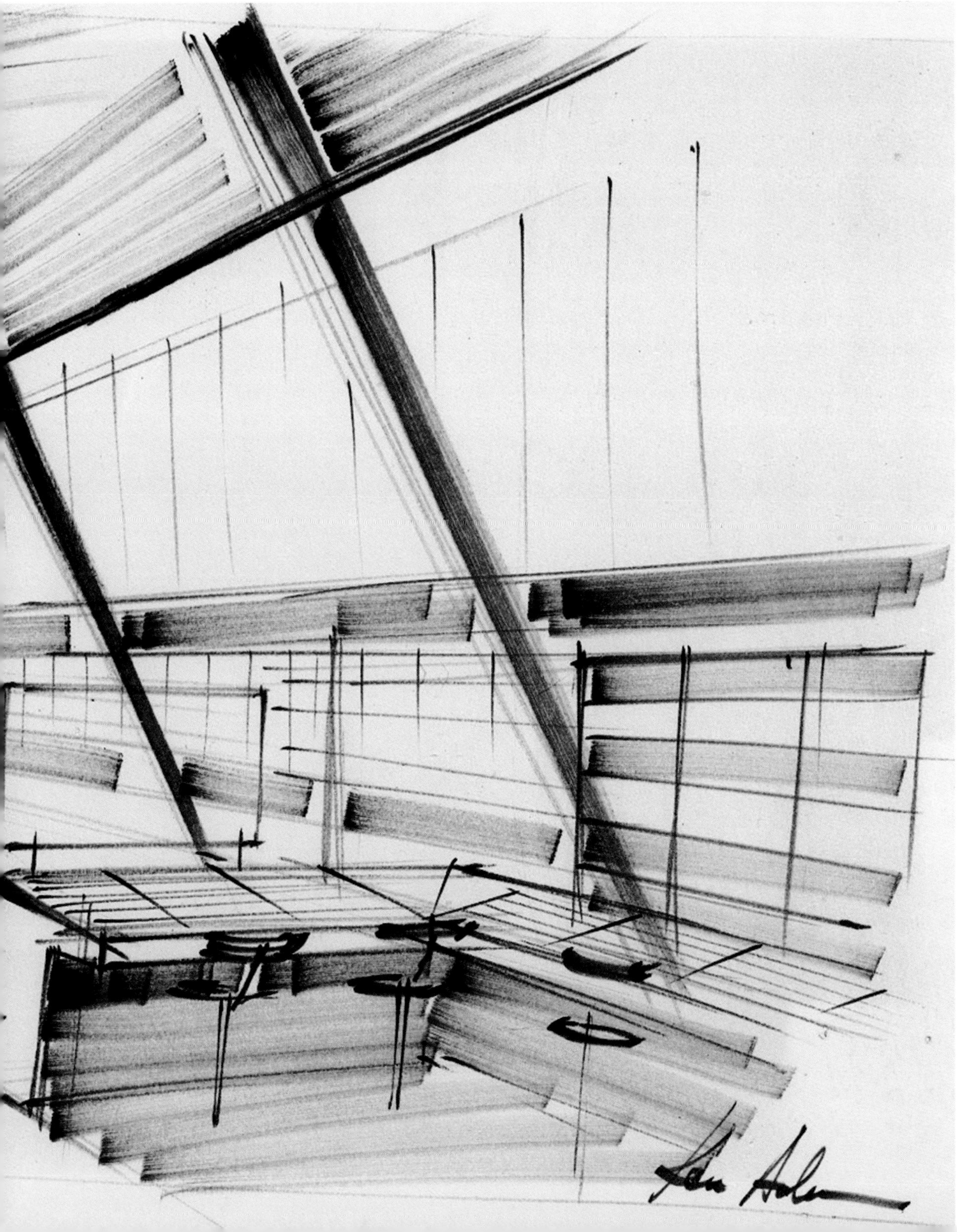

Dr No's nuclear reactor room 1961
Study
40.5 × 50.5 cm
Courtesy Eon Productions

In the first draft that I saw, Dr No was a monkey or an ape or something. It wasn't very good, and I had serious doubts about whether I should be involved with it or not. I had read some of the Fleming books, which I had liked. And Terence Young seemed to have a certain panache, identifying himself with Bond. Harry Saltzman was brought up as a showman and started talking in those terms, so it became rather an exciting undertaking.

From the first film, you manage to convey a futuristic feel to the villains' lairs. Did this arise out of the script? General discussions?

When shooting *Dr No* began in Jamaica, Terence and I had some preliminary discussions about how we visualised the film. He continued to shoot while I went back to Pinewood. Because we were short of time, I had to design and start to build four or five stages full of sets before the unit came back. So when they arrived they were really faced with a *fait accompli*. But Terence really liked them, and Harry and Cubby Broccoli agreed.

There seemed to be a lot of copper in Dr No's underground house. Stylistically, that carried over to the other Bonds as well.

We faked that with a process system, as well as a lot of other metal, which I'd never done before. I was trying for a slightly tongue-in-cheek, slightly ahead-of-contemporary concept, and when it worked it became more important from film to film.

Did you use existing reactor plans for your nuclear control room?

That was one of the biggest sets I had done to that point, so I used two technical advisers to be sure it was accurate. I also liked Dr No's underground apartment with the fish tank. But the set I was keenest on was the big tarantula room, with the circular opening in the ceiling. Simple, but ominous. **JD**

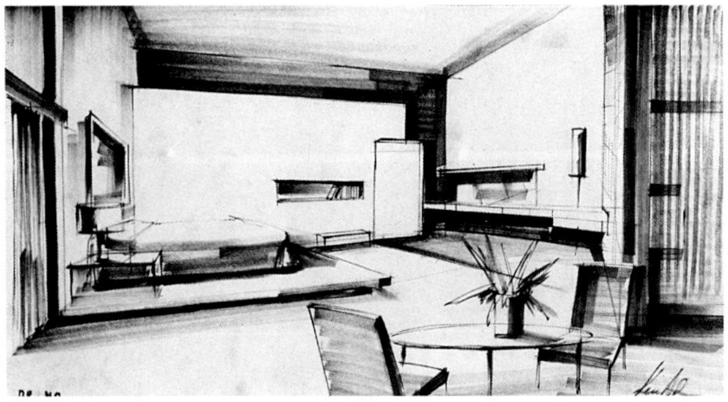

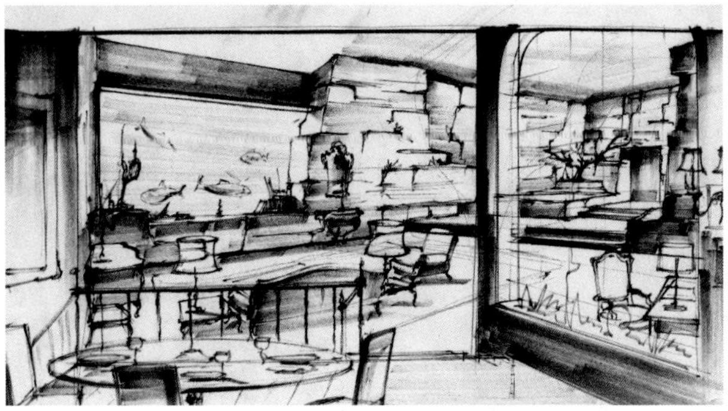

Top: *Dr No's underground living room* 1961
Study
28 × 52 cm

Bottom: *Dr No's underground guestroom* 1961
Study
23.5 × 43 cm

Dr No's underground apartment stimulated a lot of thought and ideas from everybody. Somebody said, 'This big villain has all of this antique furniture and a big aquarium. Maybe he should have some art treasure that has recently disappeared.' Someone came up with the idea of the Goya painting of the Duke of Wellington, which had been stolen from the National Gallery. Literally within forty-eight hours, I had to reproduce the stolen Goya painting. I think that started the tongue-in-cheek concept of Bond pictures, and it became more and more important as we made these films. **VL**

Dr Strangelove or: How I Learned to Stop Worrying and Love the Bomb

Stanley Kubrick's black comedy turns on the decision of an insane US Air Force general to launch a pre-emptive nuclear strike on the USSR. Despite the combined efforts of Washington and Moscow, one American bomber gets through and triggers the Soviets' latest secret creation, a Doomsday machine.

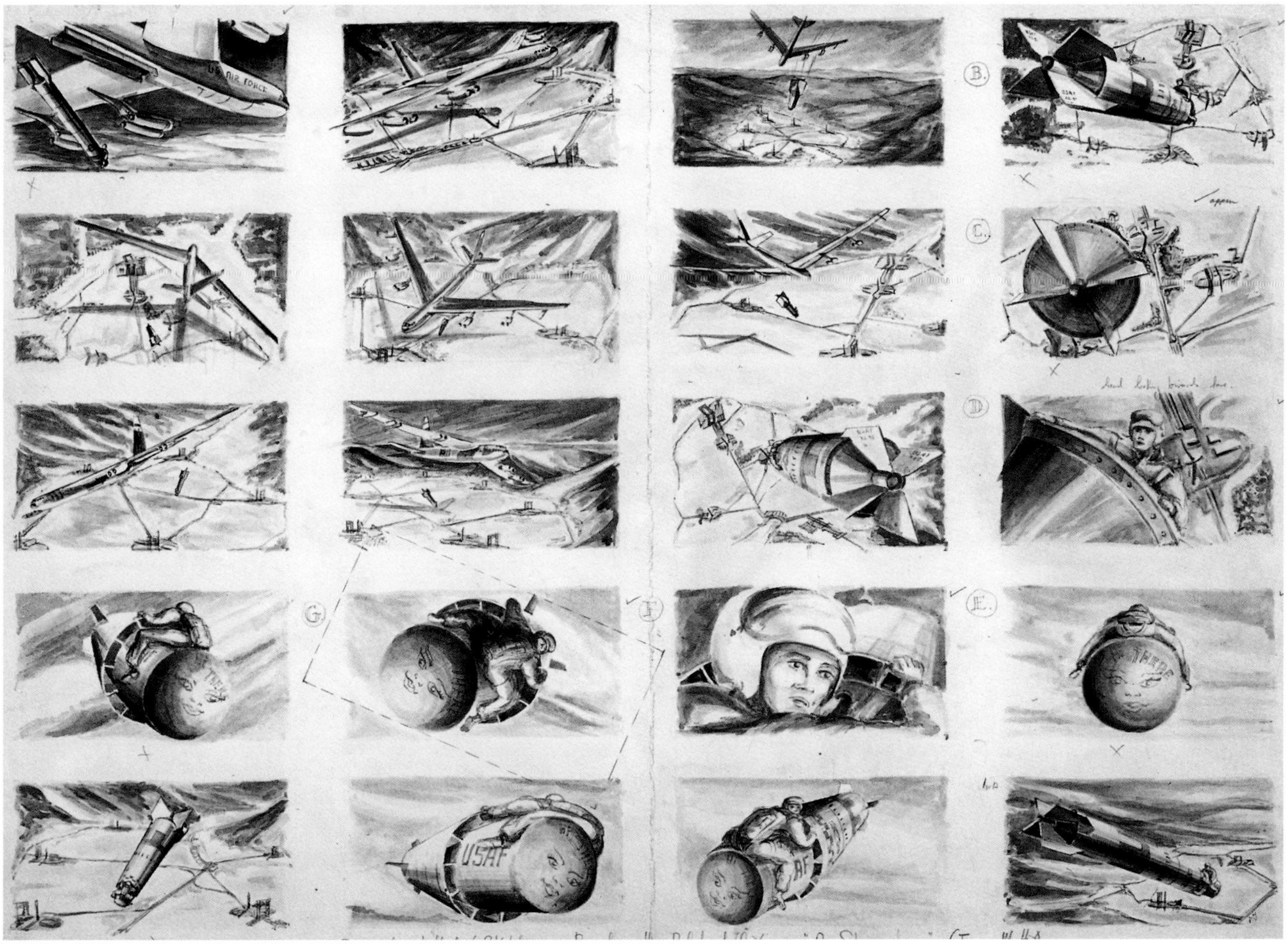

The bomb release sequence 1962
Storyboard
Ink and wash on paper
55 × 75 cm

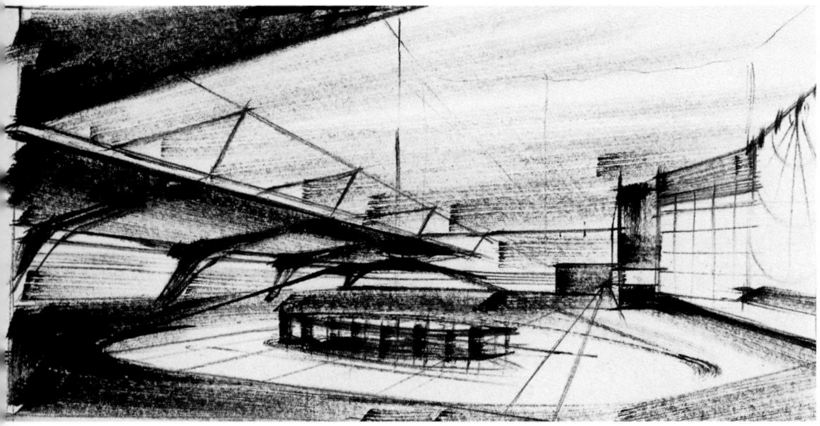

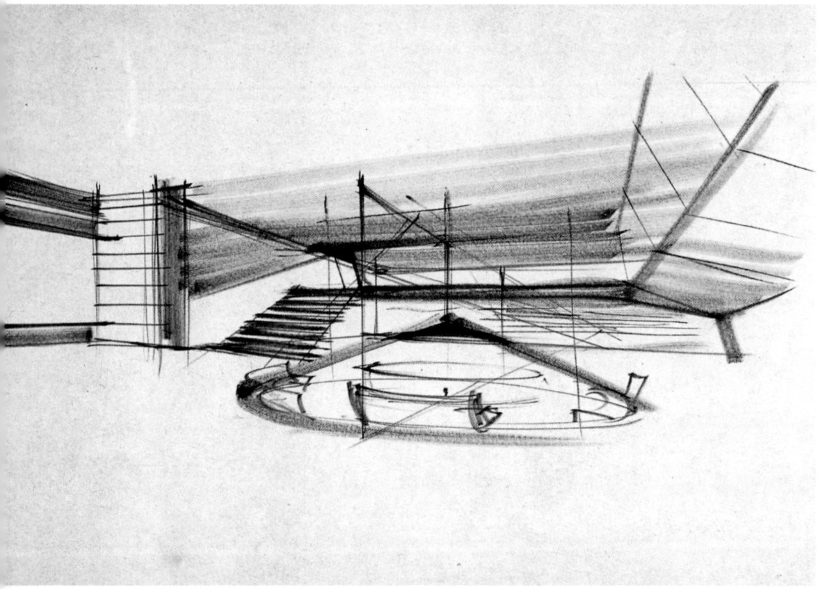

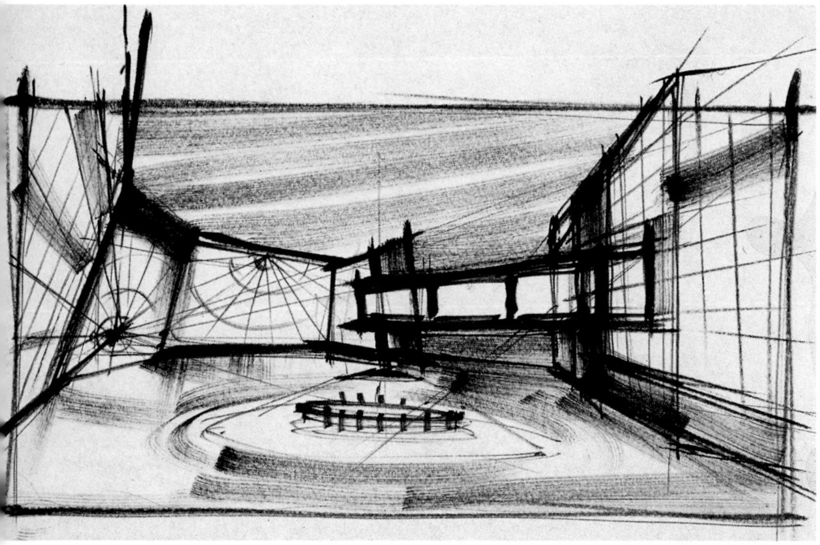

Kubrick was a brilliant visual director, and although we hit it off, he was extremely difficult and demanding to work for. When we met to discuss the War-Room set, I scribbled a two-level set which he immediately said he liked. I thought, well, that was easy; and the art department began to draw up plans and build models. One morning, three weeks later (when work on the set was well advanced), I was giving Stanley a lift to Shepperton, when he turned to me and said, 'About the War Room, Ken … I don't think the two-level concept will work; what am I going to do with the upper level? It's too costly to fill it with extras …' Well, this threw me. I went into tailspin. I walked around the garden at Shepperton for over an hour trying to calm myself down. Then I began scribbling again – with Stanley looking over my shoulder. I doodled various shapes before coming up with a triangular form. Stanley stopped me. 'Isn't the triangle the strongest form in geometry?' he asked. Me: 'You

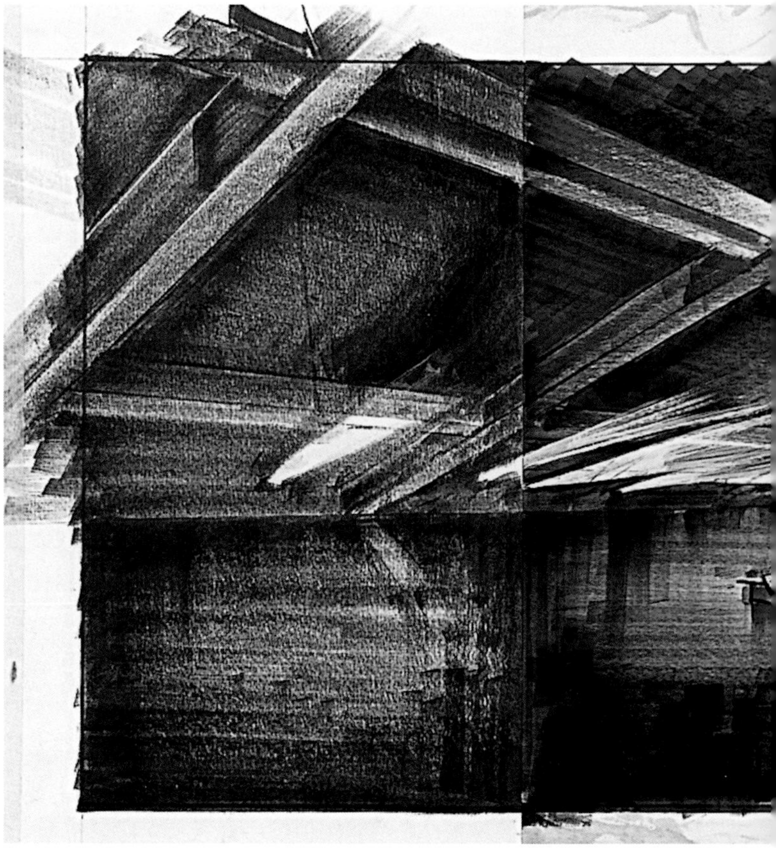

Bottom: *The two-tier War Room* 1962
Initial study
46 × 58.5 cm

Middle: *The two-tier War Room* 1962
Initial study
46 × 58.5 cm

Top: *The War Room* 1962
Initial study
44 × 66.5 cm

War Room 1962
Final concept (extended 1999)
Felt-tip pen on card
31.5 × 80 cm

may well be right.' Him: 'In other words, it would make for a good bomb shelter.' Me: 'Reinforced concrete.' Him: 'A huge, underground bomb shelter – fantastic.' I elaborated on the design with big maps and a circular table. Him: 'Green baize on the table, it's like the President and his generals all taking part in a gigantic poker game.' **PE**

The lighting of the War-Room set was dramatically effective. What was Kubrick's involvement with the cinematography of these sequences?

Stanley does it; he's a brilliant cameraman. He wanted only source lighting. I had designed a circular light fitting that could be suspended. We sat in my office and experimented with varying types of photofloods. I would sit in the chair, and he'd put up a photoflood at a certain distance to see how light would fall on my face. The lighting of all the personnel around the table was done through that circular light fitting.

Did you design the cockpit in the plane that carried the bomb?

Yes. We had no cooperation at all from the military; it was considered an anti-American picture. It was so

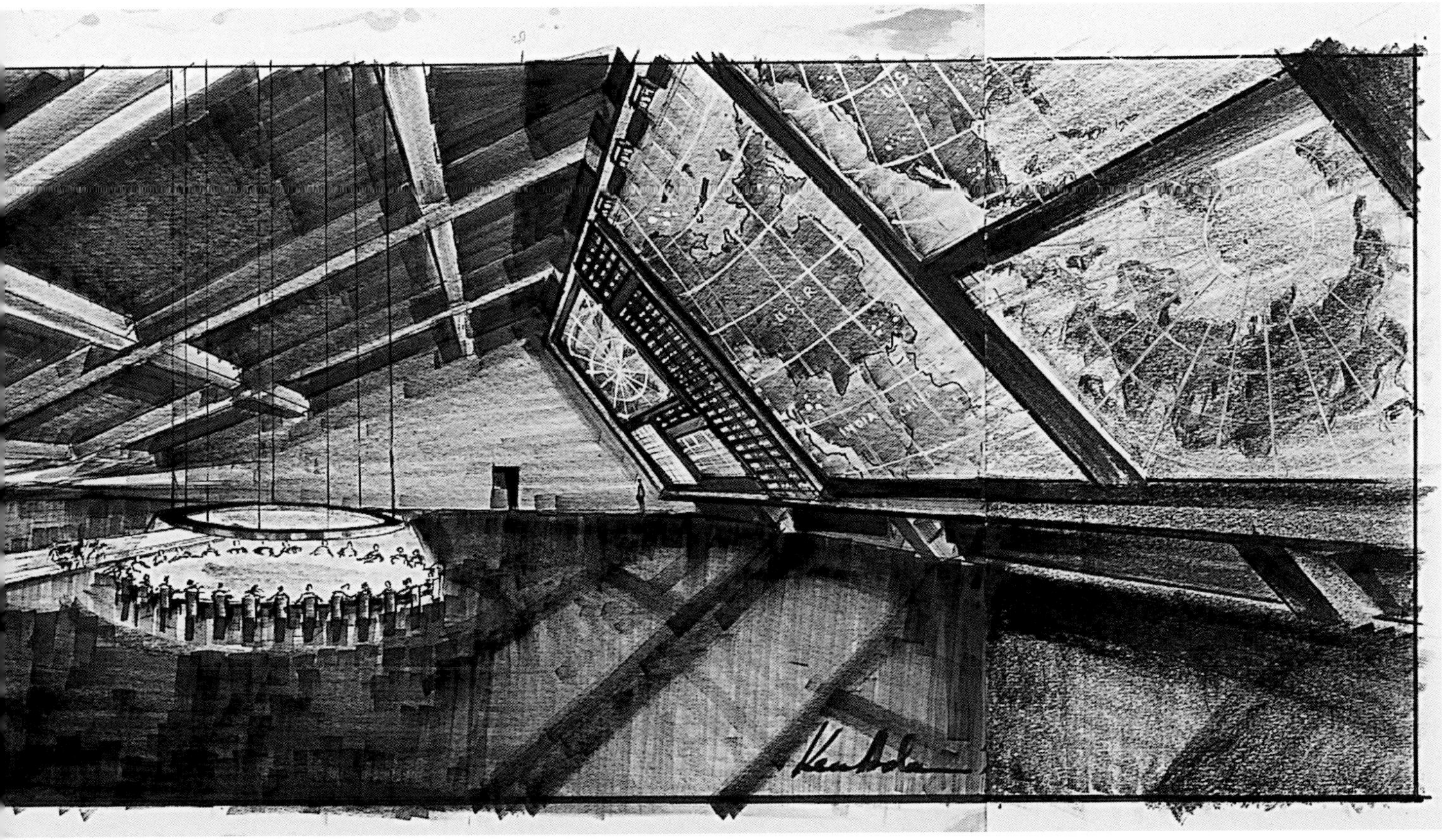

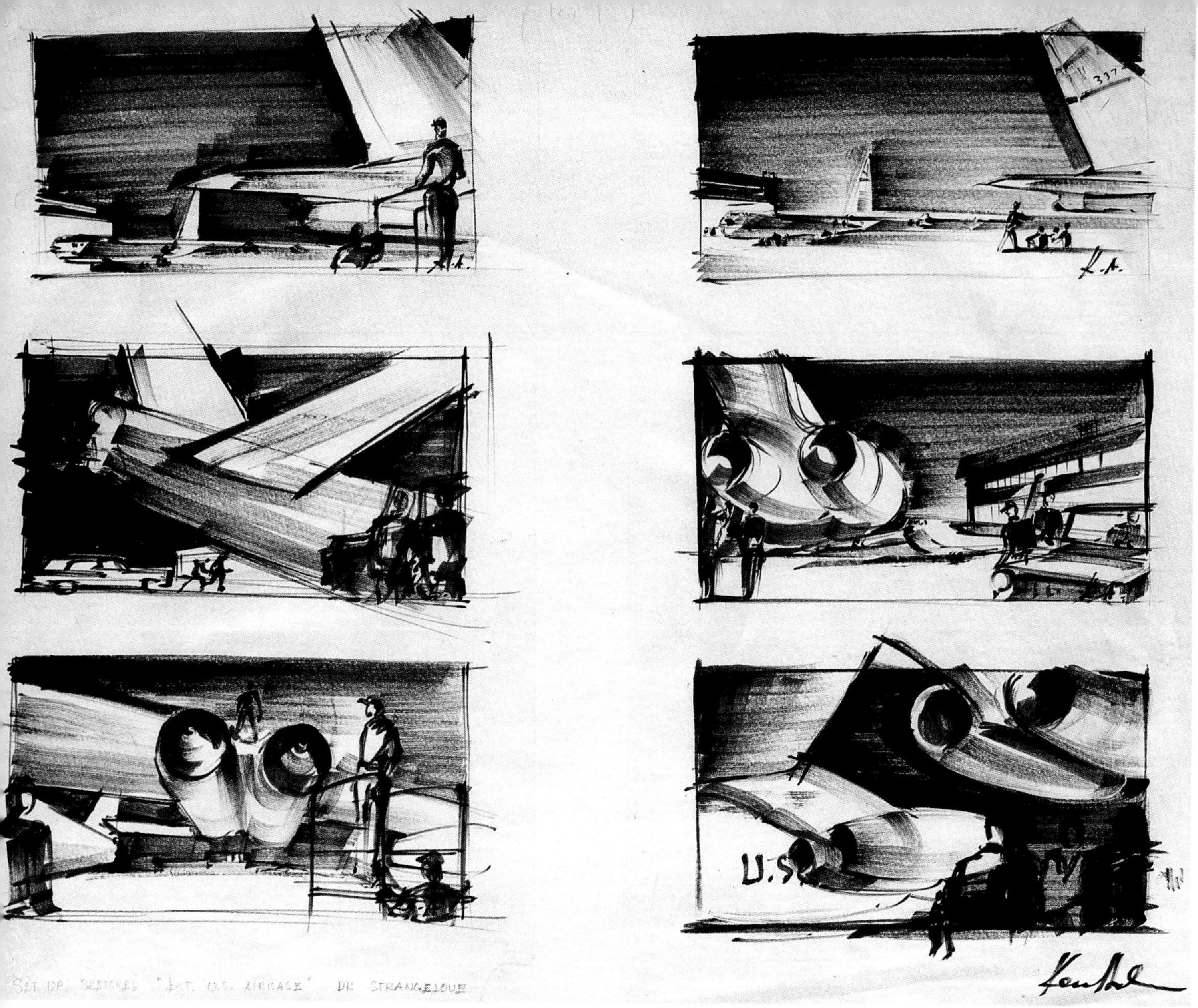

The B52 bomber base
1962
Studies
Felt-tip pen on card
45.5 × 52.5 cm

amazing that through technical flight magazines like *Janes* we could get all the information we wanted. So we had all of it at our fingertips and then copied the B-52. The only thing we were not sure about was that little box, the CRM, the fail-safe device. I came up with an idea, and during the shooting we invited some Air Force personnel to visit the set. They went white when they saw that CRM, so it must be pretty close. I got a memo from Stanley that said, 'You better find out where you got your research from because we could be investigated.' Basically, it was all from technical data in magazines. **VL**

Working with Stanley, I had to force myself to be more elastic. Through my architectural studies – and also maybe through my character – I was too pedantic and rigid in my approach to sketching. I started using a large felt nib called a Flowmaster. That forced me to express myself more dramatically and gave me an opportunity to use chiaroscuro to influence the atmosphere of the drawings. I kept that method of working for years to come. **GM**

All the interior sets were at Shepperton Studios. We used the exterior of the back lot there for Ripper's office and part of Heathrow Airport for the establishing shot of the American base. **SG**

1964

Goldfinger

Directed by Guy Hamilton, the third Bond movie (but only Adam's second) sets 007 on the trail of the gold-obsessed super-villain Auric Goldfinger, whose ultimate objective is to clean out the American bullion depository at Fort Knox.

The rumpus room conversion
1964
Study
30.5 × 52 cm

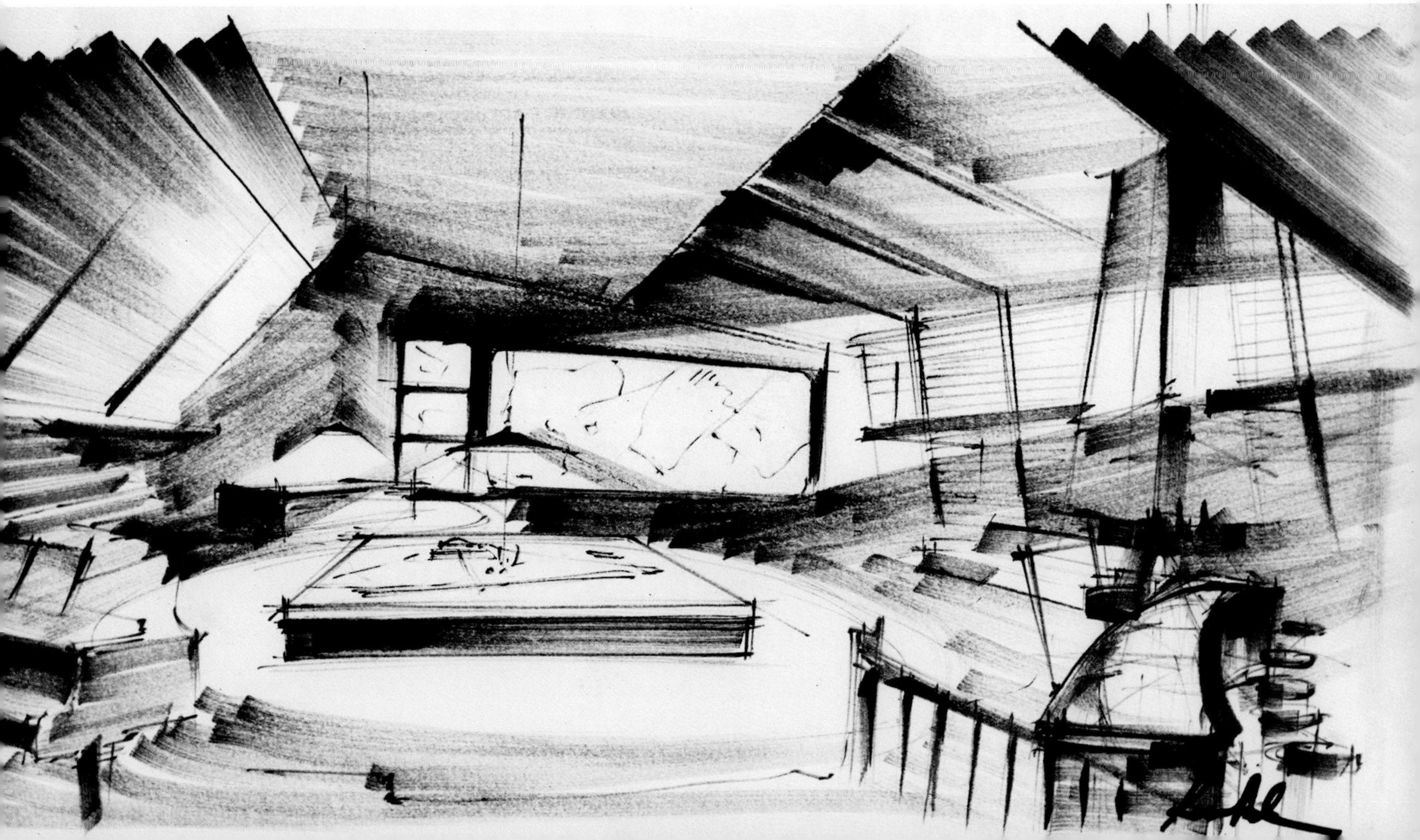

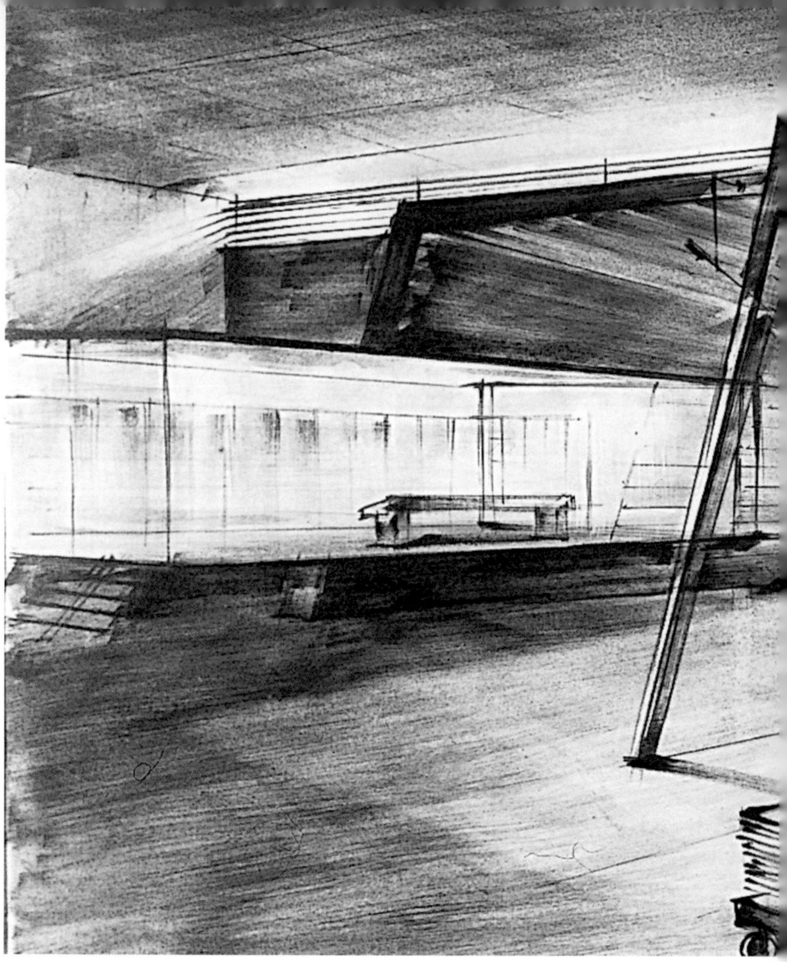

The laser room 1964
Final concept
30 × 59.5cm

All the interiors were built at Pinewood and we even built the exterior of the stud farm there. We had some locations in Switzerland and also did some second unit shooting outside Fort Knox and the Fountain Blue Hotel in Miami. **SG**

The rumpus room 1964
Final concept
Pen and colour ink wash
28 × 46.5 cm

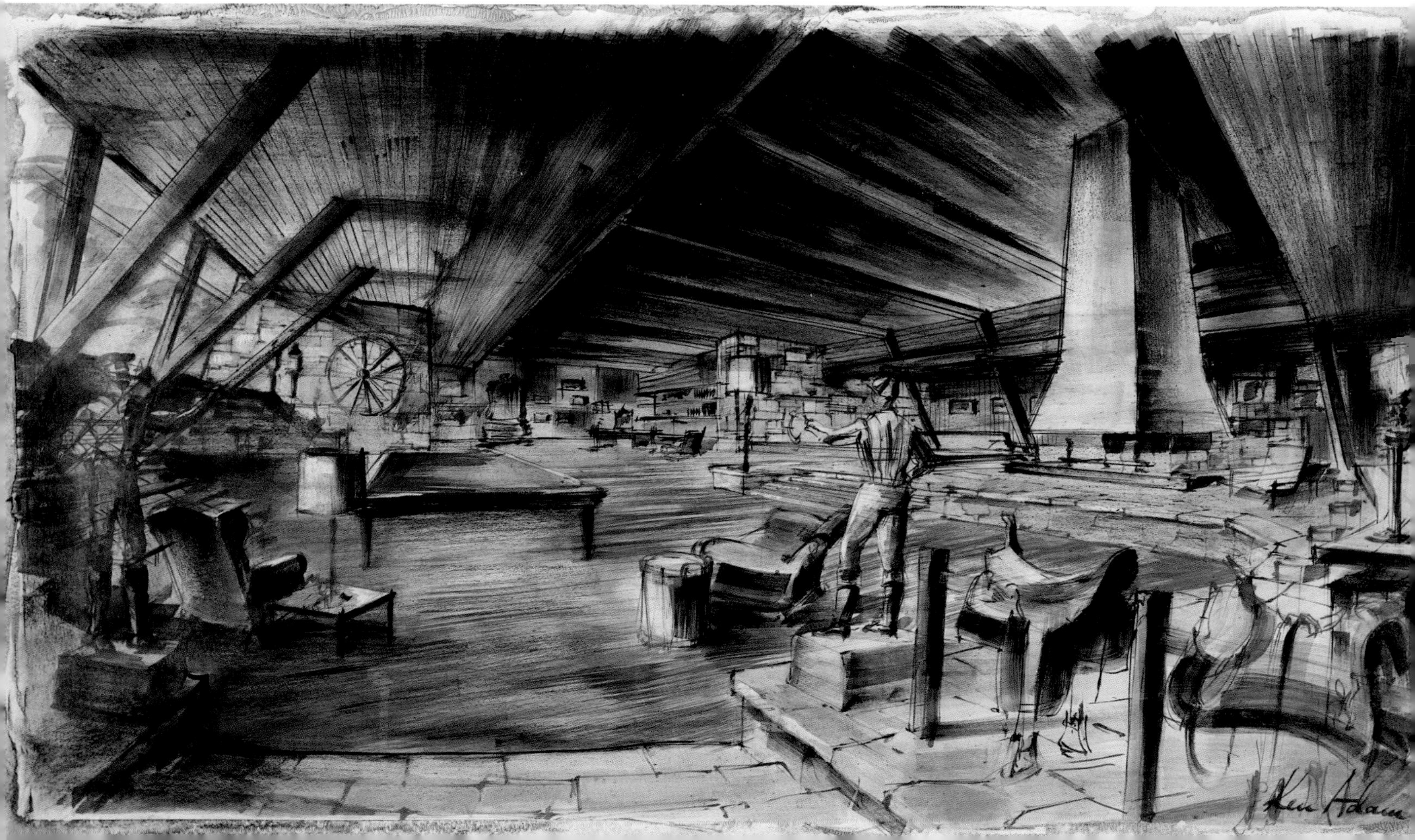

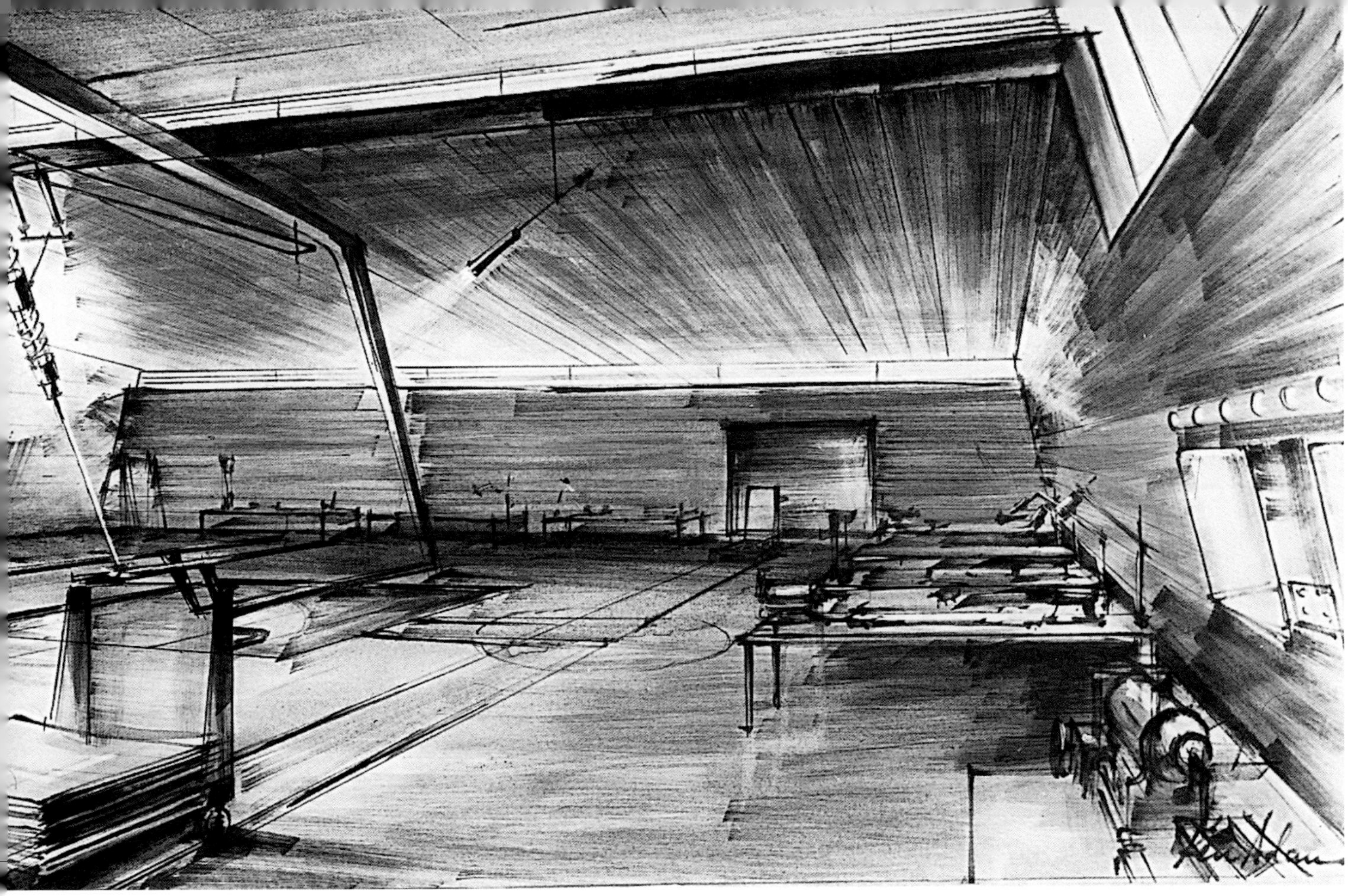

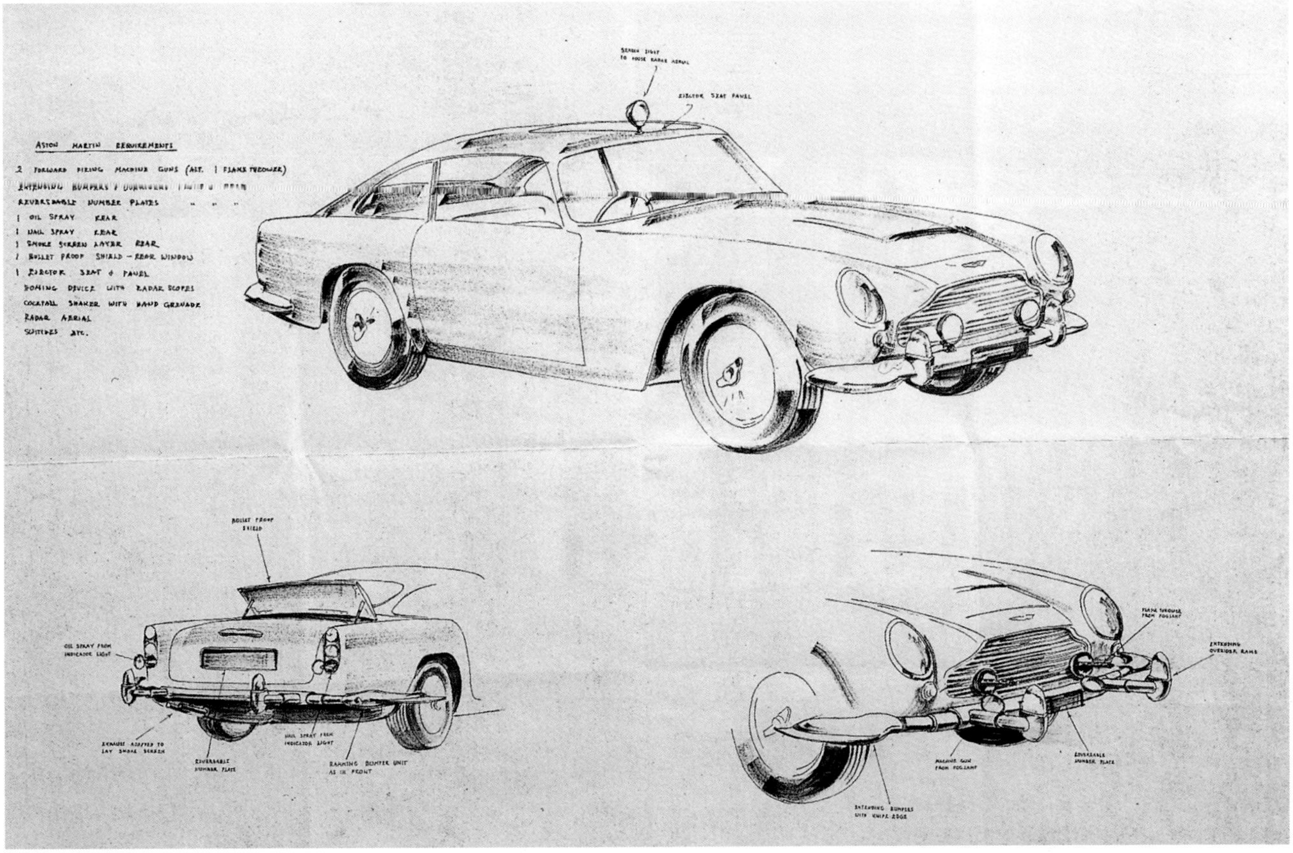

The Aston Martin DB5 1964
Final concept
49.5 × 75 cm
Courtesy Eon Productions

What research did you do to design the Fort Knox set for Goldfinger?

Up to a point, we had unbelievable cooperation because of Albert Broccoli's Washington contacts and the fact that the Kennedys loved the Ian Fleming books. I was allowed to fly over Fort Knox in a helicopter to look at the outside, which was incredible – nobody thought I would get permission. Everywhere around Fort Knox there were these strange loud speakers blaring out, 'You are now entering a restricted area.' That was quite dicey because on the roof of Fort Knox there were people with machine guns; it was really frightening. Of course, nobody allowed me inside. As you know, the President is not allowed inside of the place.

Is there any documentation of the interior of Fort Knox?

None, and if there was I wouldn't have looked at it. I was pleased again about having to invent a reality for the audience which I thought was more right, more visually acceptable, but one which was obviously theatrical. I knew that the gold vaults in the Bank of England were very low. They're a series a tunnels really; I didn't think that was interesting. Gold is never stacked very high because it is so heavy, but what if you could stack gold up to forty foot in height! That long, tall elevator going up and down could never have worked in reality. I did a complete replica of the exterior of Fort Knox; however, the interior was a complete invention. The amazing thing was the number of letters United Artists received when the film was released: 'How were you allowed inside Fort Knox?' So people accepted it completely. **VL**

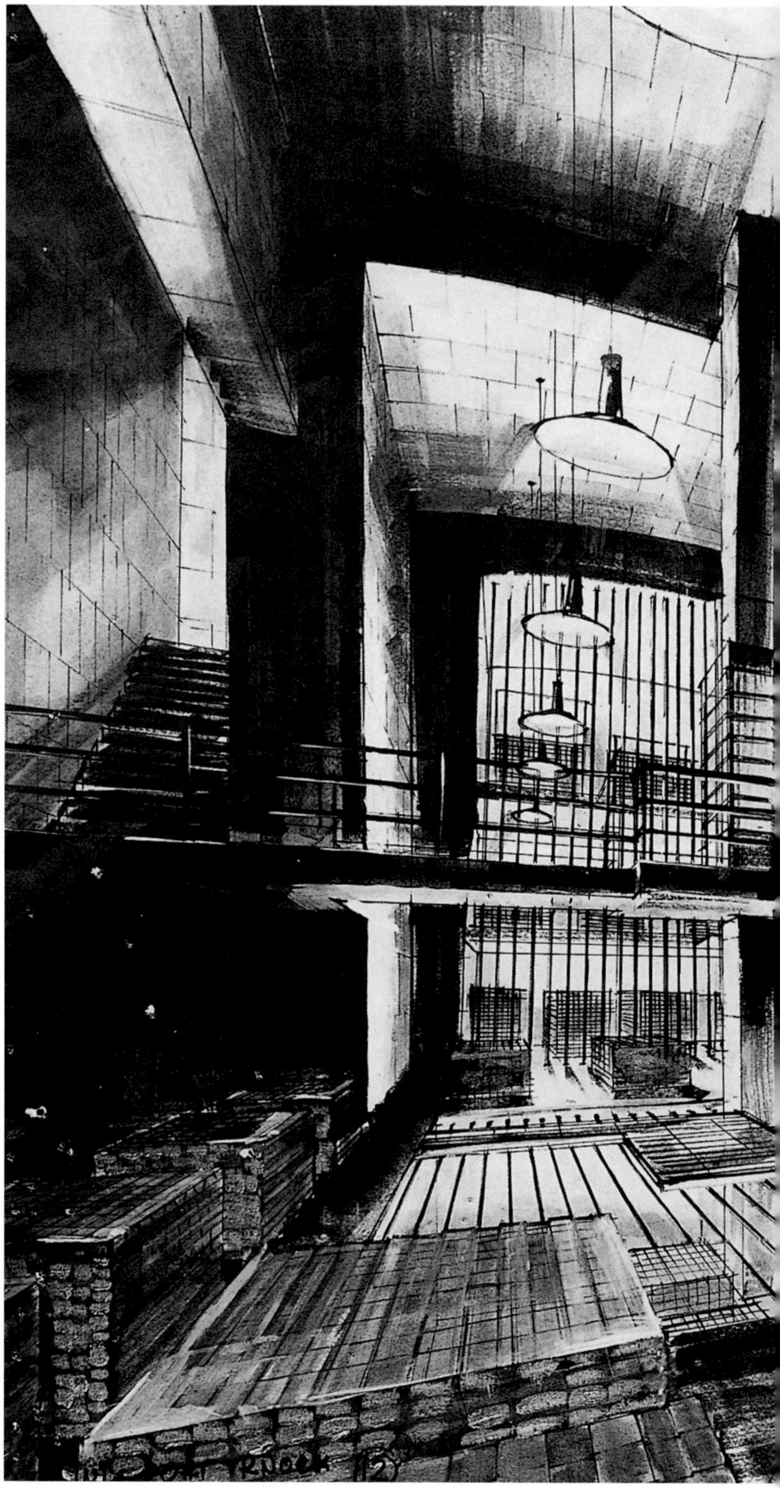

Fort Knox interior 1964
Final concept
30 × 59 cm
Courtesy Eon Productions

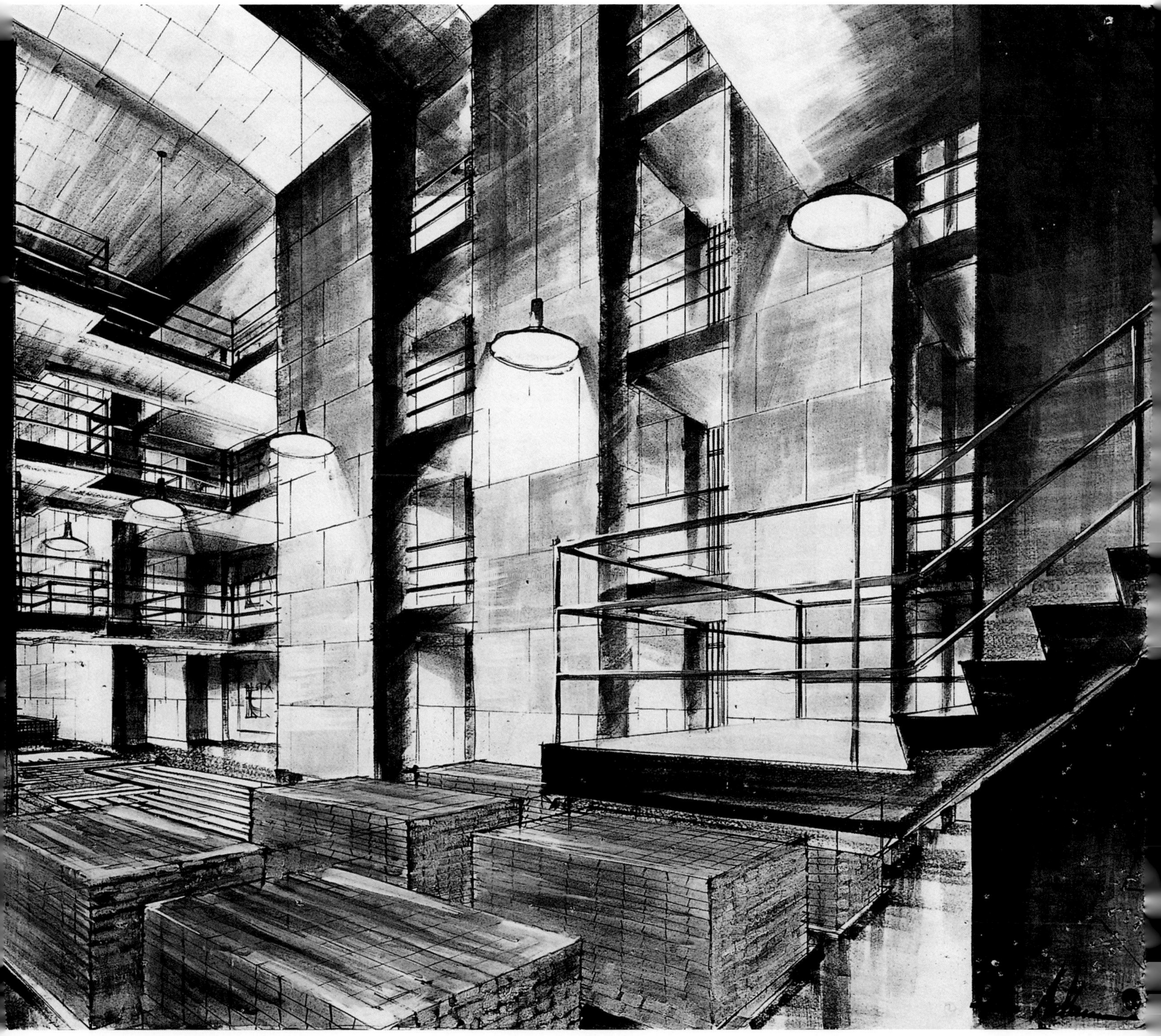

The Ipcress File

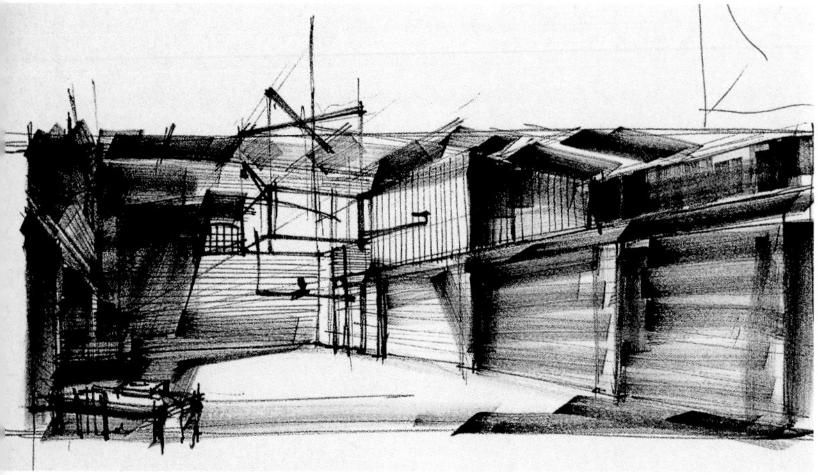

The brainwashing chamber 1964
Study
41 × 51 cm

Based on Len Deighton's first espionage thriller, a calculated riposte to Ian Fleming's Bond books, the film was directed by Sidney Furie and stars Michael Caine as a maverick working-class intelligence sergeant who discovers that one of his own superiors is working with the enemy.

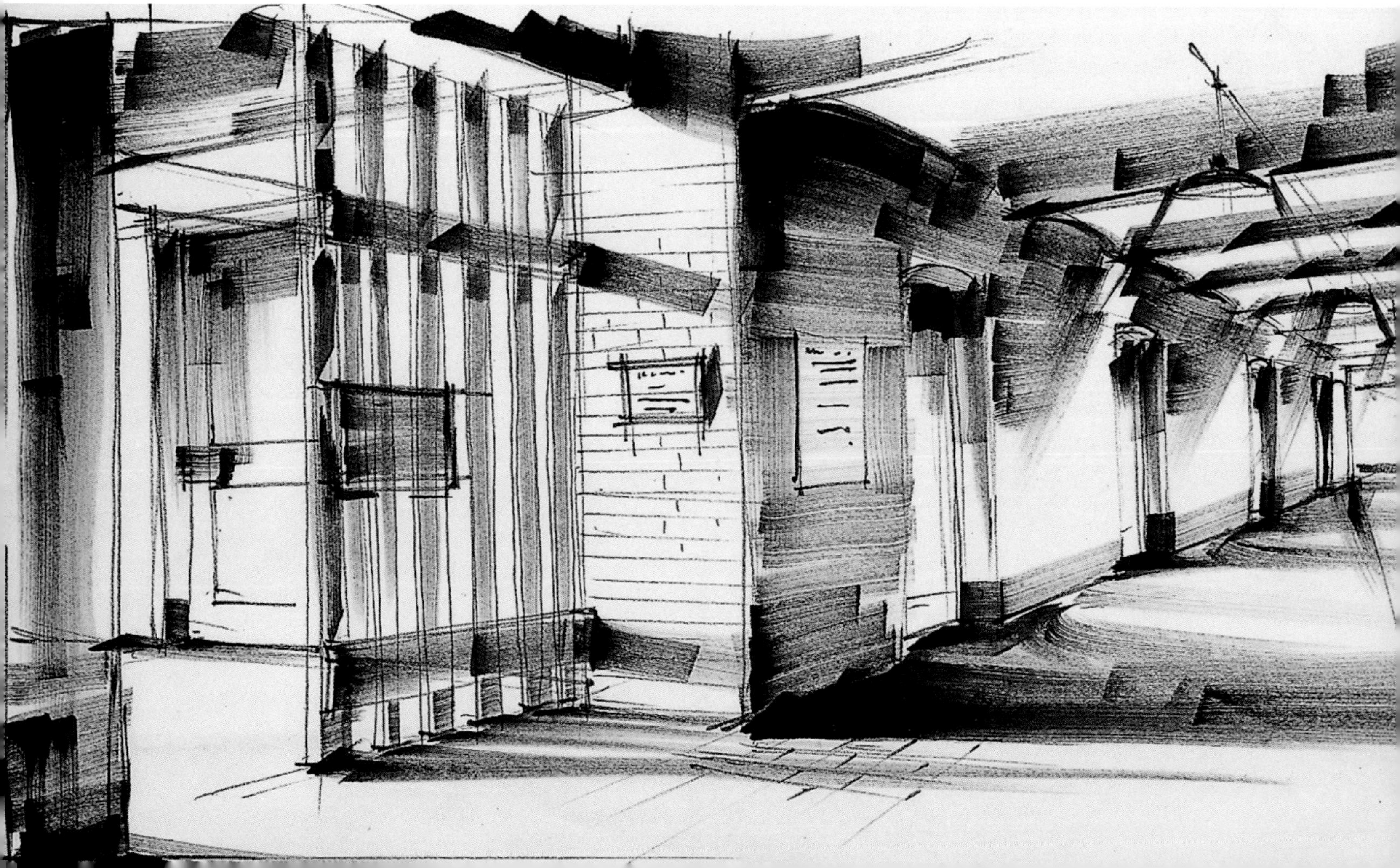

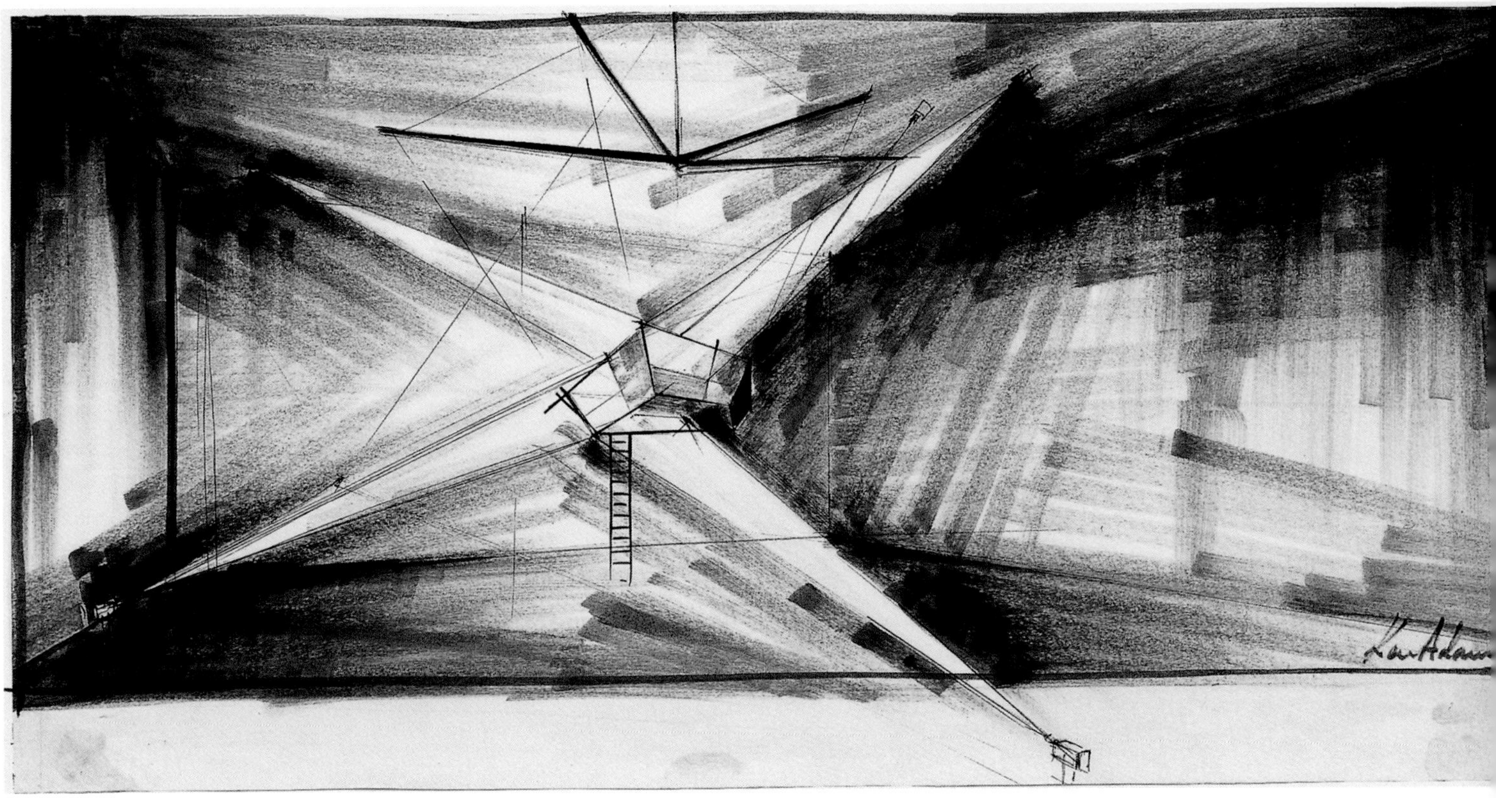

The brainwashing chamber 1964
Study
26 × 50 cm

In the preparatory stages of *The Ipcress File*, there was much discussion about how we should approach the film. The temptation to film it like Bond, even if only a poor-man's version, was great. In Len Deighton's novels, secret agent Harry Palmer is an underdog, an anti-hero, and thereby the exact counterpart to Ian Fleming's James Bond.

We eventually decided on a documentary approach. In other words, to film mainly on location and as little as possible in the studio, which was different from what I was used to. Director Sid Furie and I wanted to show London in shades of grey and brown, and I chose the locations accordingly.

With increased experience it has become ever more important for me to perfect my designs whilst ensuring that they are realised in the way I envisage them. Earlier on, I was often satisfied when the majority of the constructions accorded with my imagination, and I did not worry in depth about smaller things which I felt were less important. But it was precisely these minor details which made me blush when I saw the finished film. Every detail counts on the screen, and a poorly painted wall or door can completely destroy the illusion of reality in close-up. **JB**

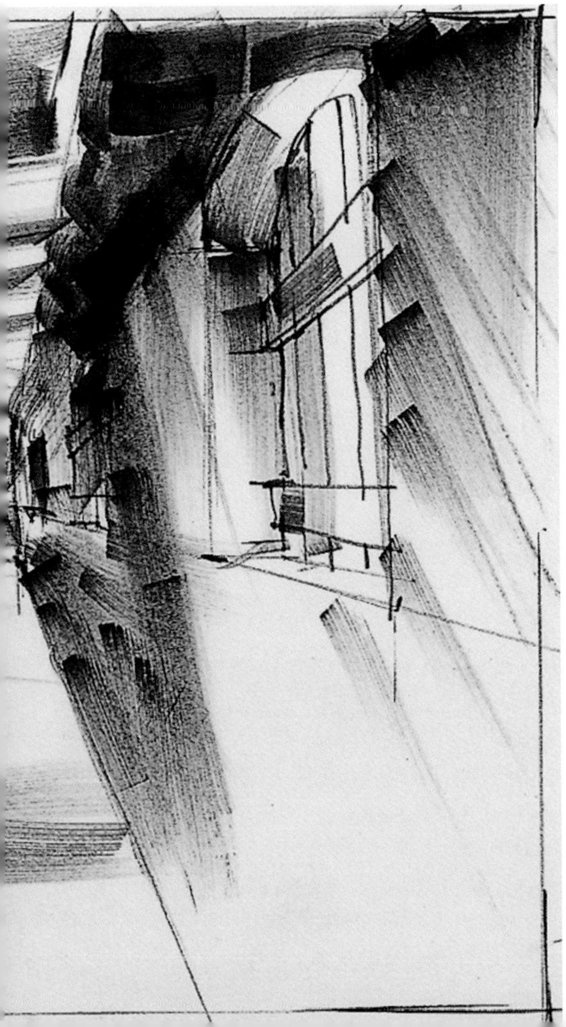

Prison corridor 1964
Study
29 × 48 cm

Thunderball

The villainous Largo hijacks nuclear bombs from the US Air Force to hold America to ransom, and James Bond, in his fourth screen outing, directed by Terence Young, tracks him to his Caribbean lair.

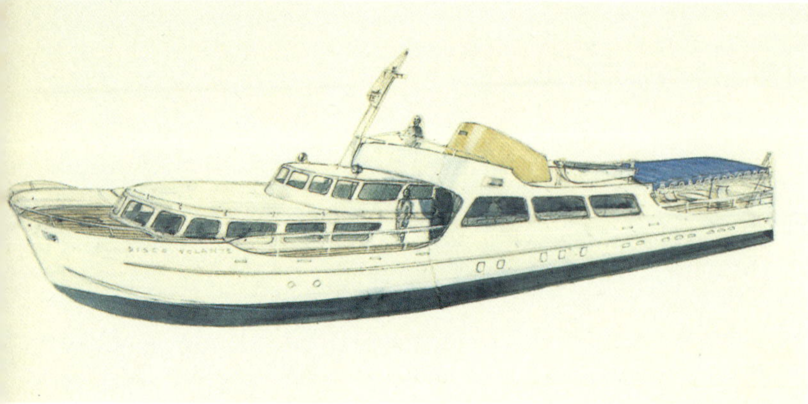

The Disco Volante 1965. Final concept. *c.* 30 × 58.8 cm

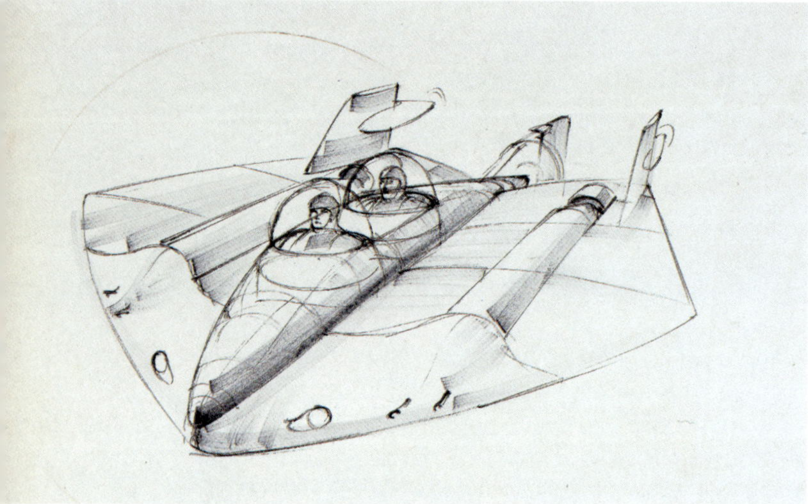

Underwater craft 1965. Initial concept. 50 × 42 cm

Underwater craft 1965
Final concept
35.5 × 63.5 cm
Courtesy Eon Productions

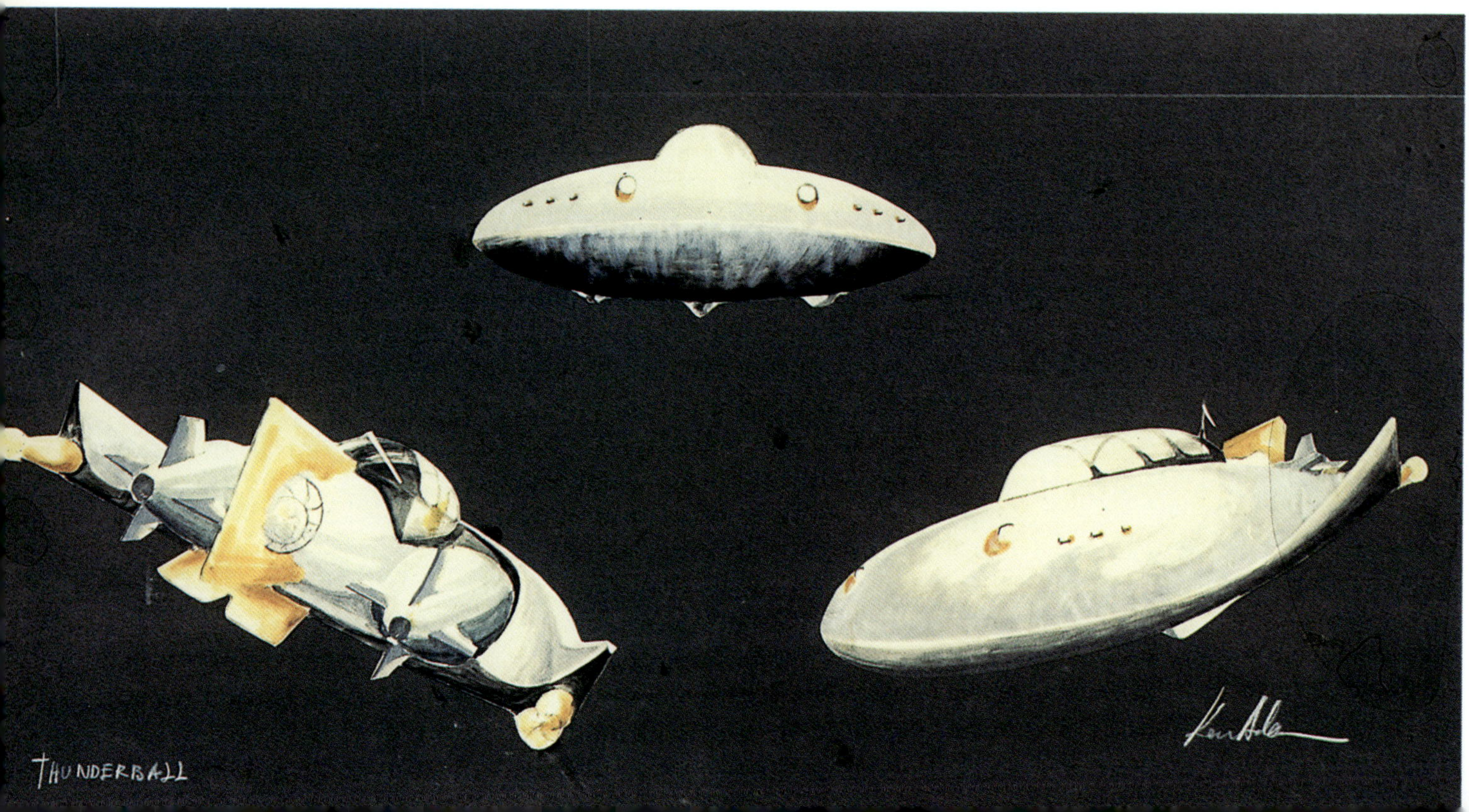

M's conference room 1965
Final concept
35 × 54.5 cm

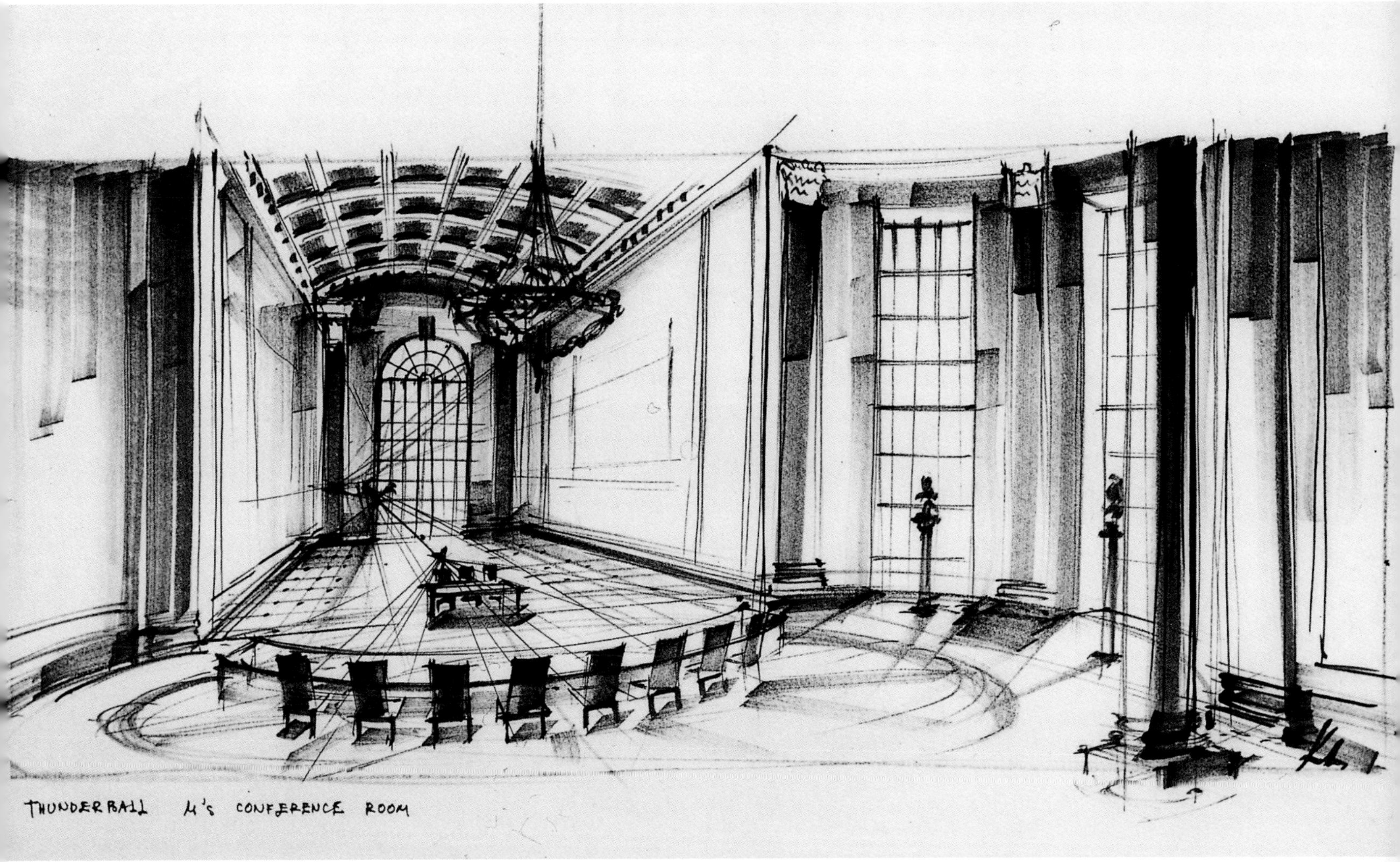

We needed many different types of underwater craft and I greatly enjoyed designing them. I drew the mini-submarine for the bomb transport as a type of flying saucer. On Nassau, in the Bahamas, I worked together with the First Unit, Model Unit and Underwater Unit to construct the Vulcan bomber to life size as well as the catamaran for the disguise of the hydrofoil, the *Disco Volante*.

I designed and built M's conference room in Pinewood as a huge neo-classical hall in which the wallpaper rolled up at the touch of a button to reveal maps, in so doing giving the Georgian ambience a functional military appearance.

A problem arises in all the Bond films: there is simply too much discussion about locations and having run out of ideas for SPECTRE HQ, I decided on designing a set. Instead of tables, I put hyper-modern, electrically fitted chairs in two facing rows. In order to kill an employee, Largo had only to press a button: the victim received a fatal electric shock and sank, chair and all, into the floor; after a while the chair emerged again, empty, of course.
JB

You only Live Twice

US space rockets are disappearing and Bond, on his fifth screen assignment, directed by Lewis Gilbert, tracks down the thief, SPECTRE boss Ernst Stavro Blofeld, to his headquarters inside an extinct volcano on a Japanese island.

Until this picture, we had stuck very close to the original Fleming stories. But when we went to Japan to scout locations he talked about, we couldn't find them. So we began to improvise, which became standard operating procedure ever afterwards – and which I sometimes regret. After covering two-thirds of Japan by helicopter, we found a volcano on Kyushu and thought, 'Wouldn't it be fun to have our villain inside a volcano?' So that became the most important and most expensive set we've ever had.

I'd always assumed it was an indoor set, aided by glass shots or mattes.

It was all real! Roughly 400 feet in diameter, 120 feet high, with a 70-foot diameter sliding lake set at an angle at the top. Too big for any sound stage in the world. So we built it free-standing, and waterproofed it as best we could. I suddenly broke out in eczema all over the place. All I could think was, Am I going crazy to take on a million-dollar set? I must have used 700 tons of structural steel. With that much effort we *should* have built a sound-stage and put the set inside it so it wouldn't have been such a total loss after the picture was finished. But it was so tall, and had such an odd shape, and it had never been done before. We built it to be shot from the inside only, except for exterior shots of the crater lake, with the steelwork following the contours of the set. I covered myself by calling in firms of structural engineers, but it was still experimental. When the real helicopter came through the roof door for the first time, neither the pilot nor we knew whether there might be updraft, downdrafts or something else to wreck him. It was nerve-racking, but ended up working extremely well.

Were most of the interiors for You Only Live Twice *shot at Pinewood?*

All but two, the sumo wrestling and the scene where Bond meets his bride-to-be. Two of the Pinewood sets – Osato's office and Tanaka's office, with its two copper television monitors – are among my personal favourites.
JD

Osato's offices
1966
Final concept
Colour felt-tip pen on paper
33.5 × 51 cm
Courtesy Eon Productions

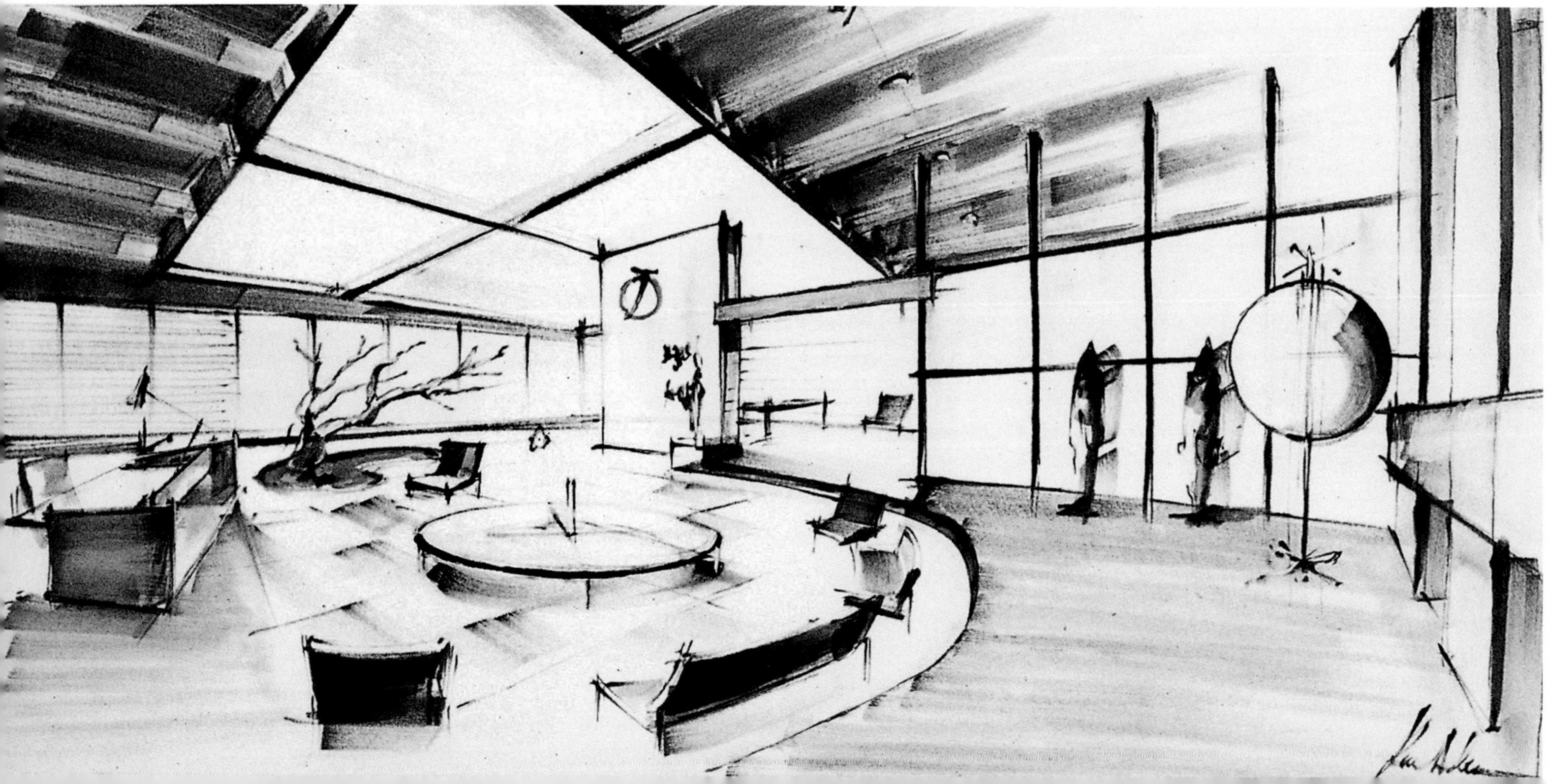

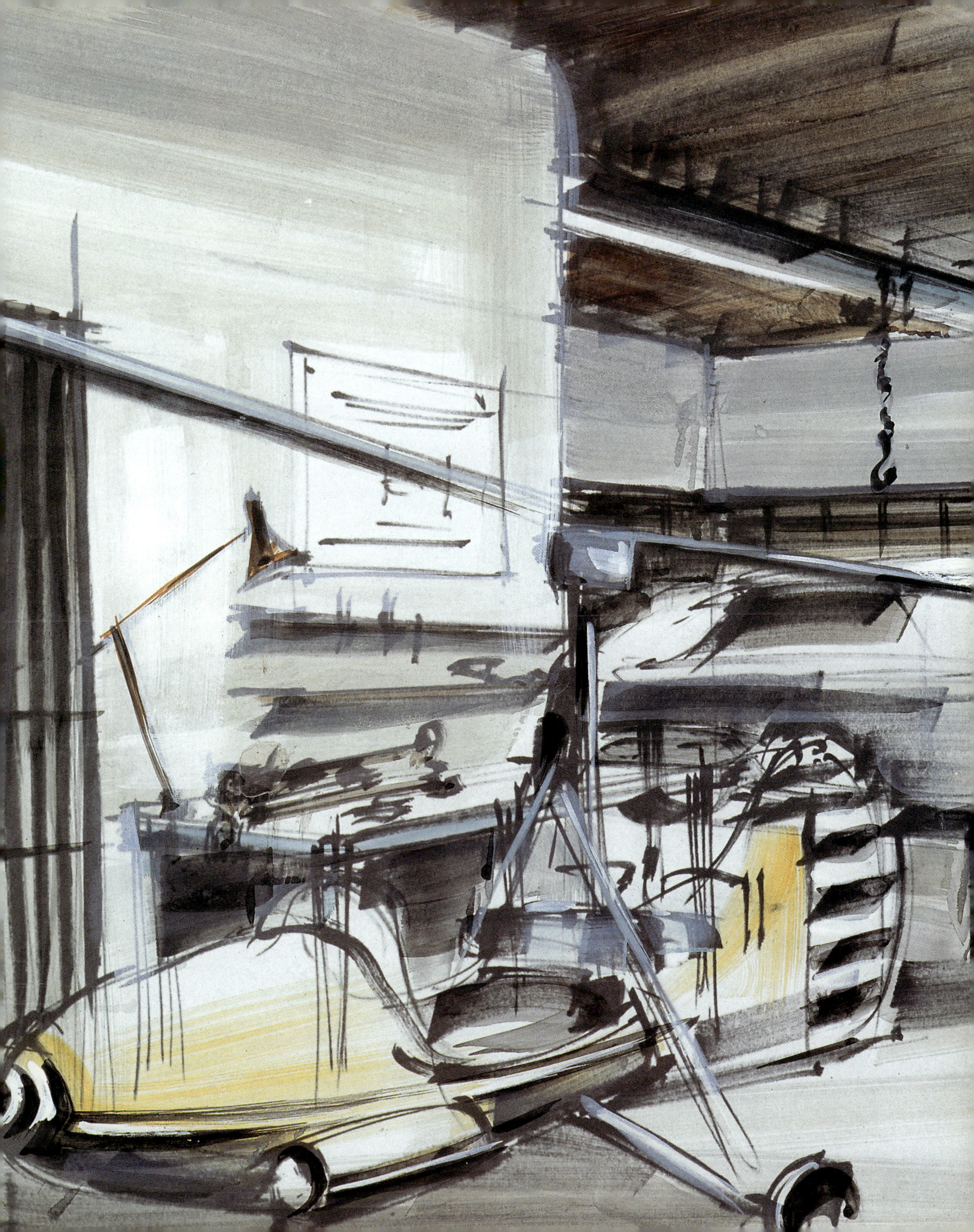

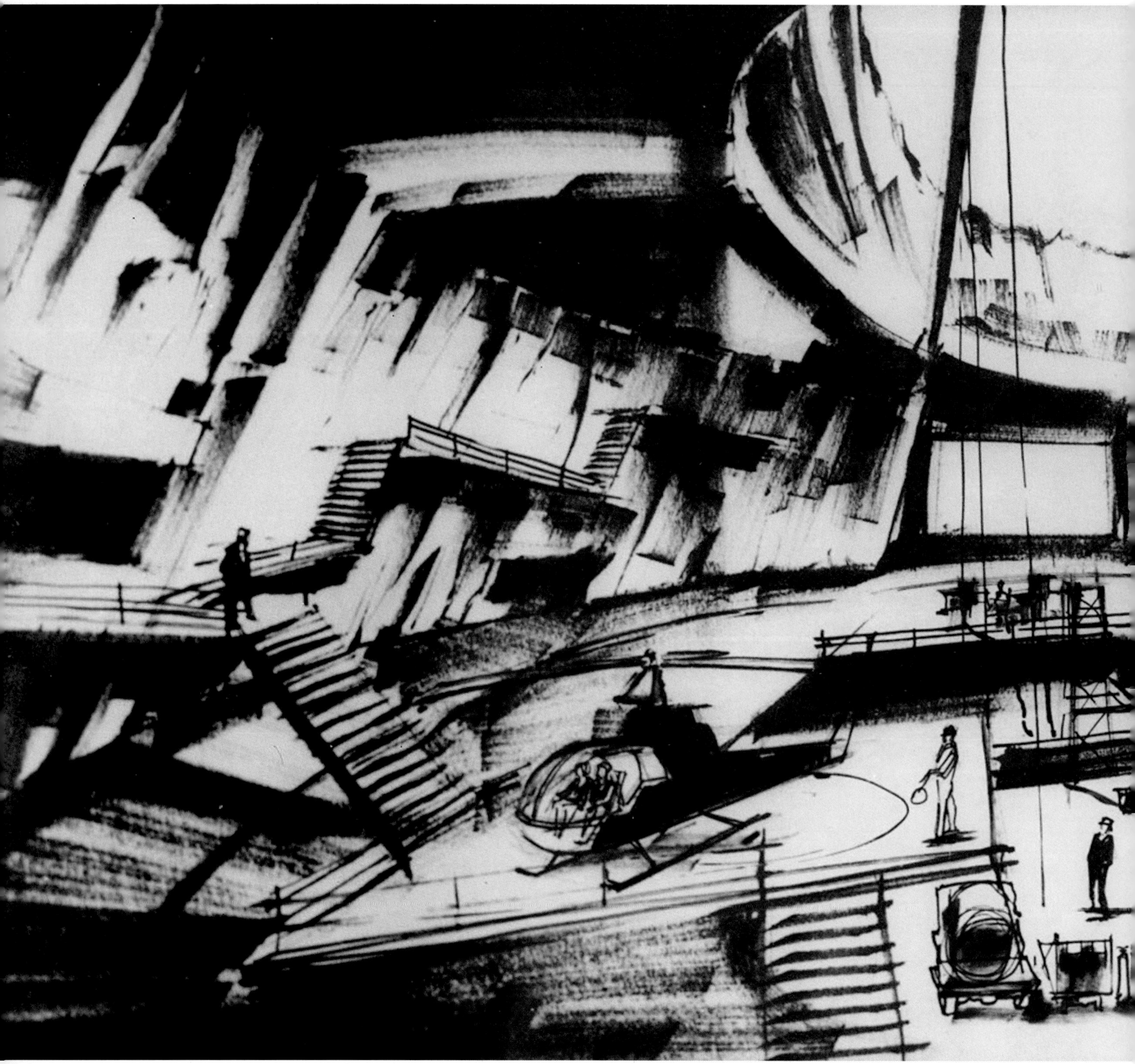

Previous page:
Q's workshop (detail) 1966
Final concept
Pencil and gouache on paper, 40 × 59 cm
Courtesy Eon Productions

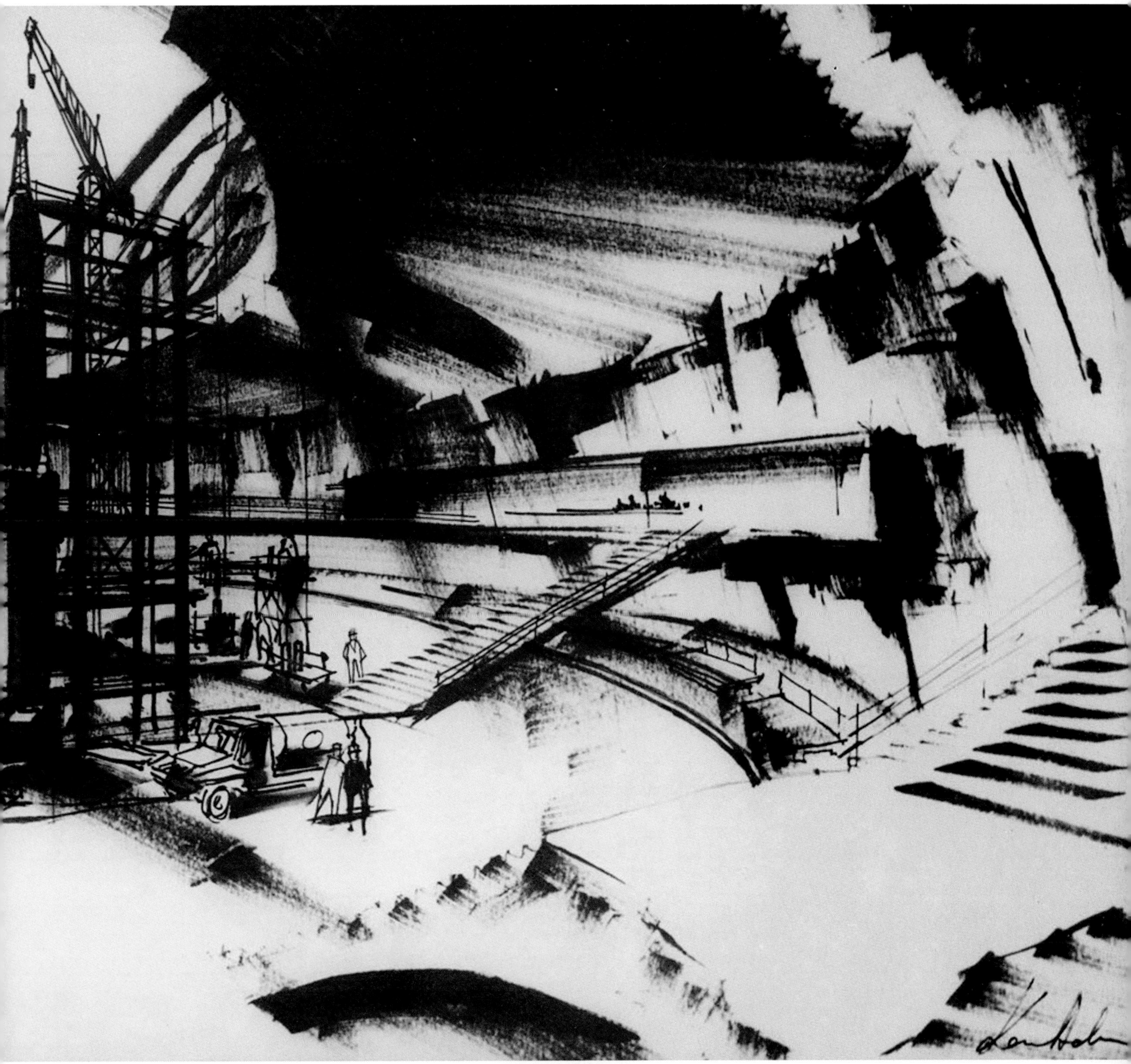

Volcano interior 1966
Final concept
31 × 61 cm

1968

Chitty Chitty Bang Bang

Mary Poppins meets James Bond in a Fleming-derived children's fantasy musical set in Edwardian England and directed by Ken Hughes. To please his children, an eccentric inventor, played by Dick Van Dyke (ex-Bert the Chimneysweep), restores an elegant racing car so that it can fly and float. The car is coveted by a villainous German prince played by Gert Fröbe (ex-Goldfinger).

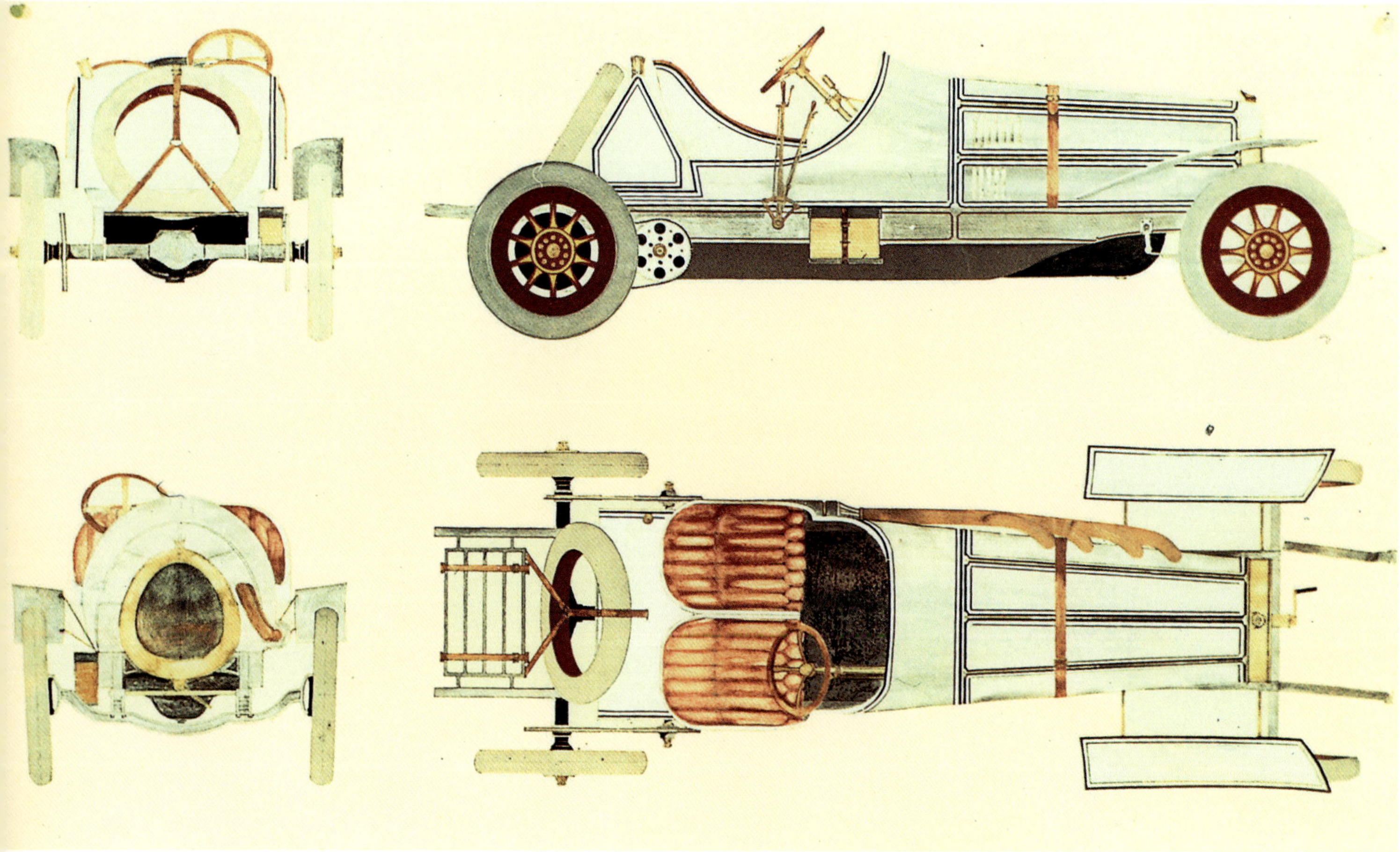

Racing car pre-conversion 1967
Final design
Colour felt-tip pen on paper
c. 34 × 65 cm

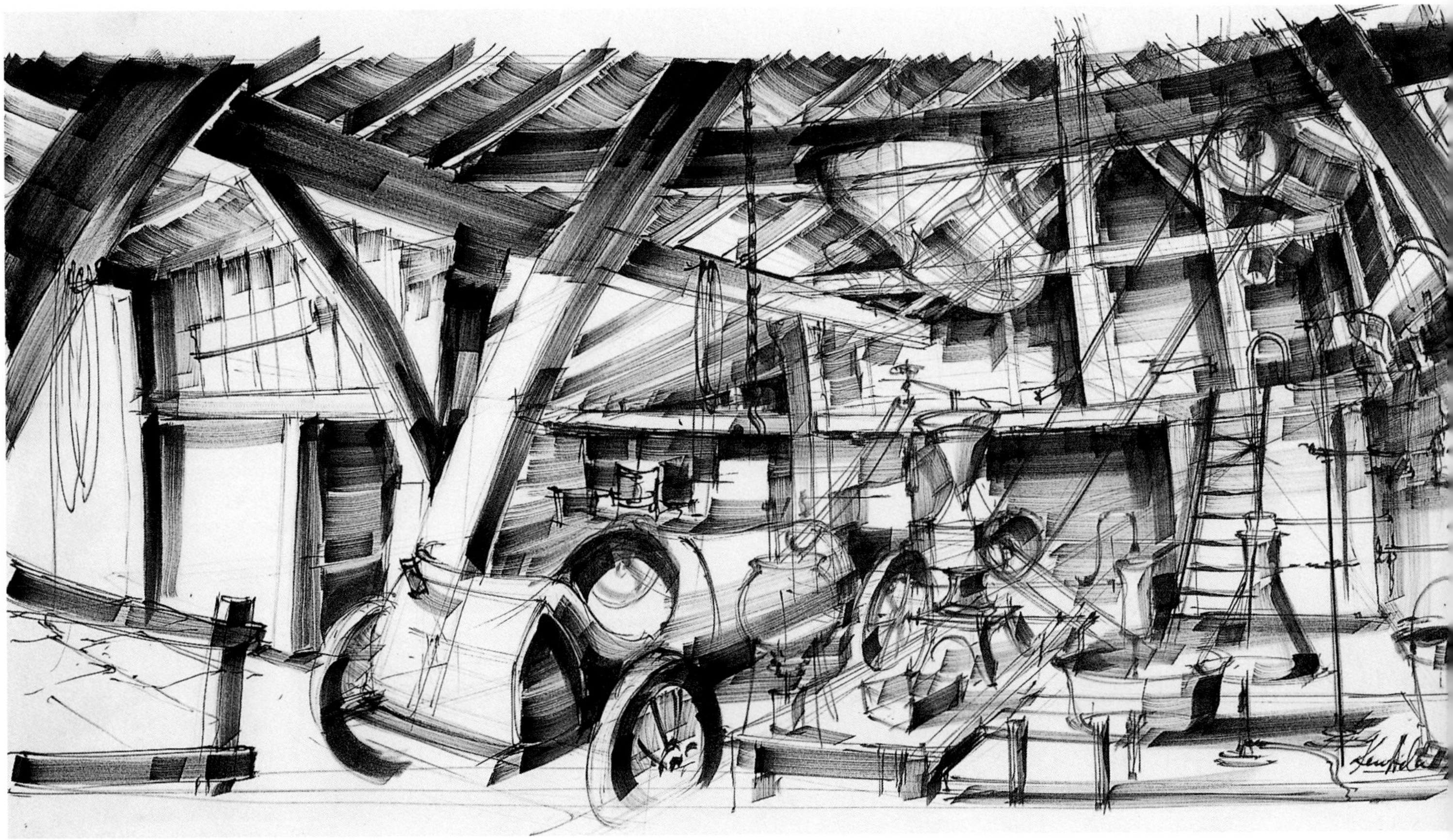

Caractacus Potts's work room 1967
Final concept
40.5 × 51 cm

The car laboratory in the dungeon of Baron Bomburst's Castle 1967
Initial concept
Felt-tip pen and watercolour on paper
38.5 × 60cm

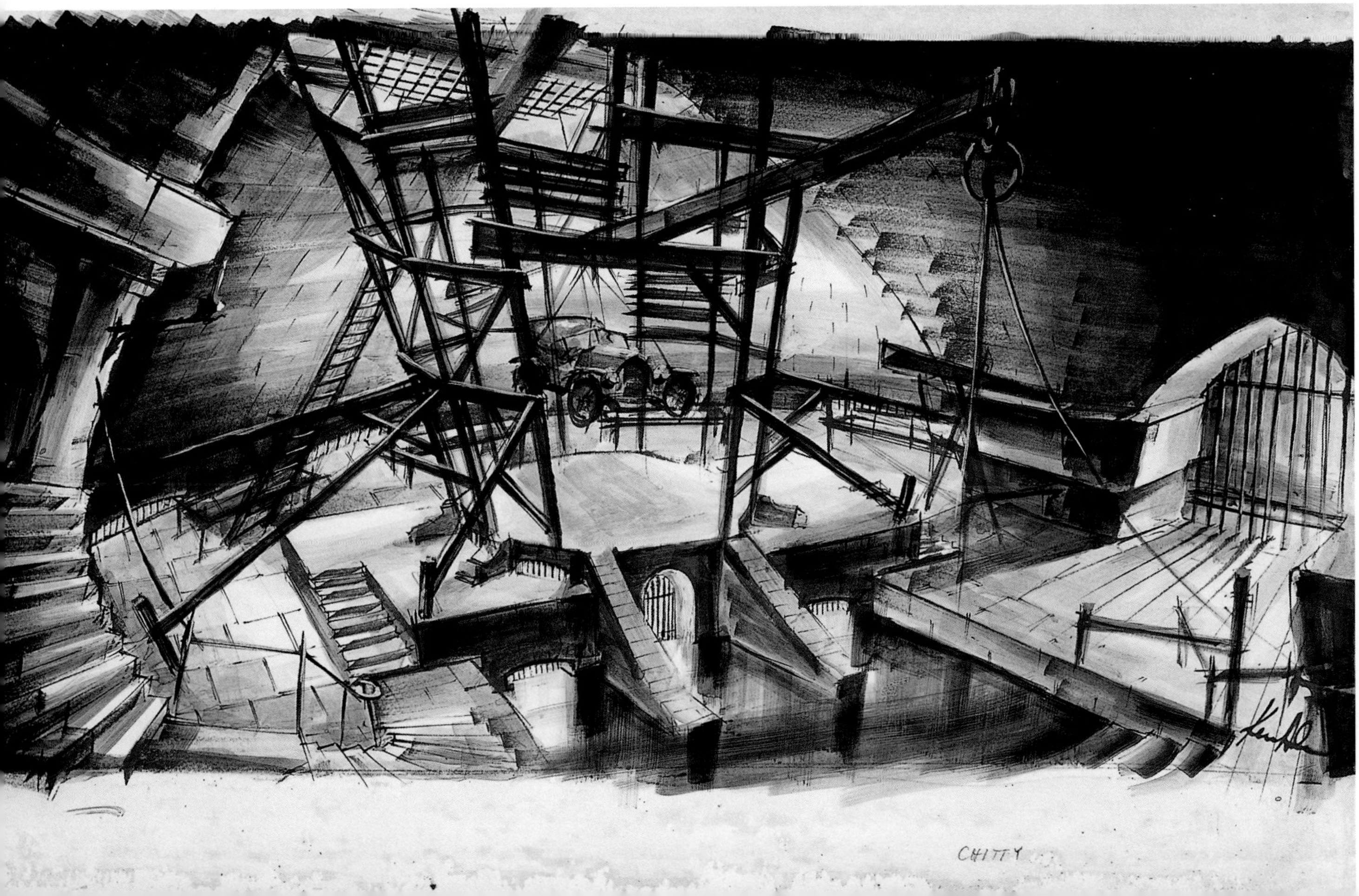

Several locations were used in England, France and Germany, but the sets were mainly constructed at Pinewood. The exterior scenes of Neuschwanstein Castle were partly shot on location, partly in the studio. **SG**

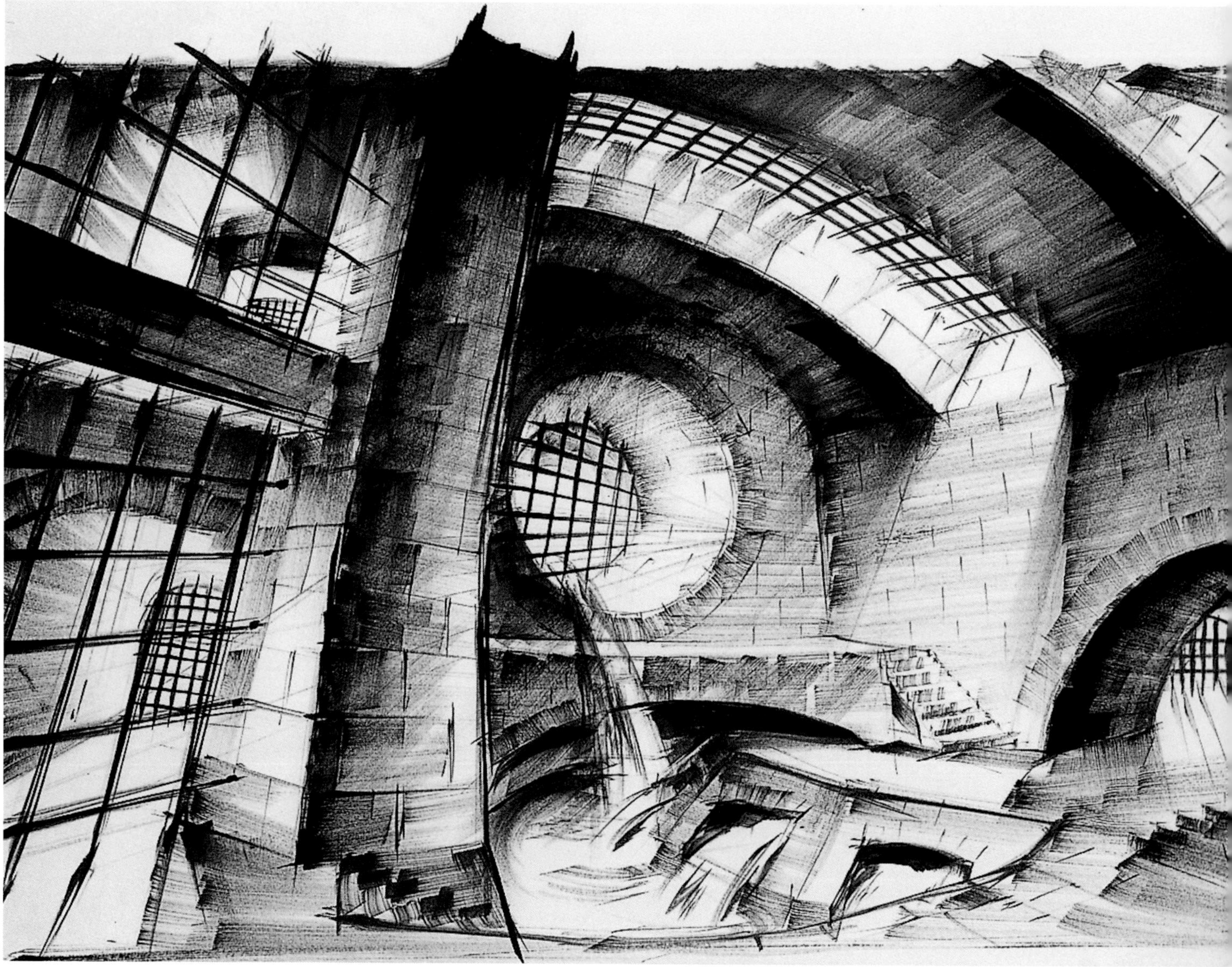

Design for the underground children's prison in Baron Bomburst's Castle 1967
Initial concept
38.5 × 51 cm

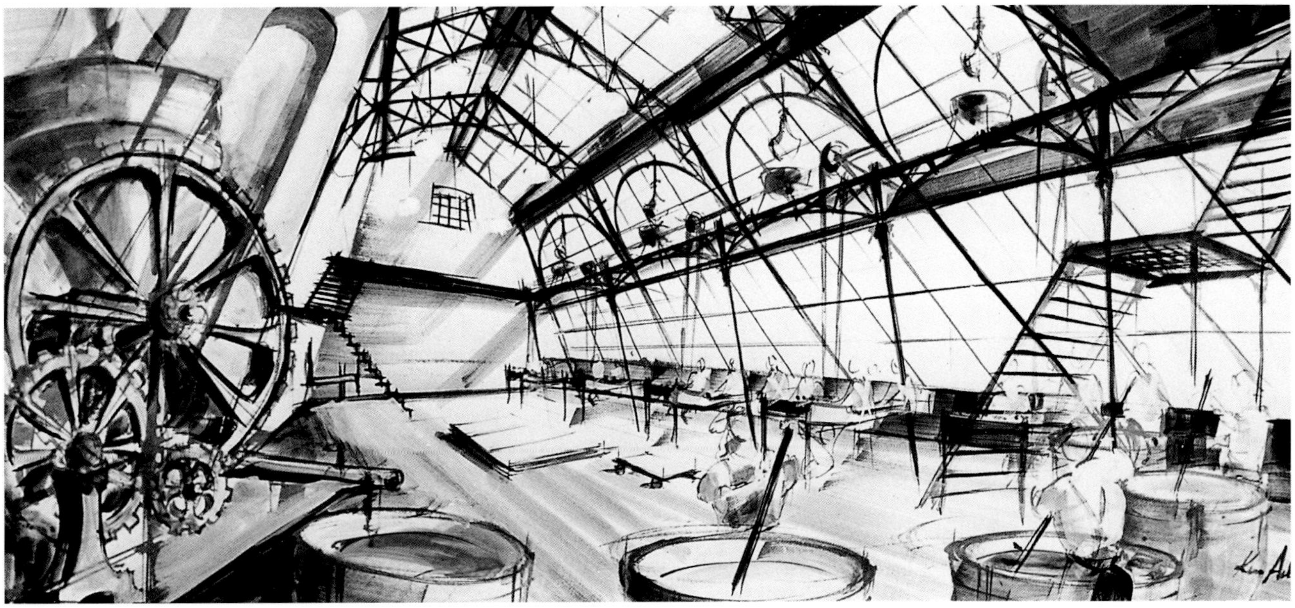

The sweet factory 1967
Final concept
40.5 × 51 cm

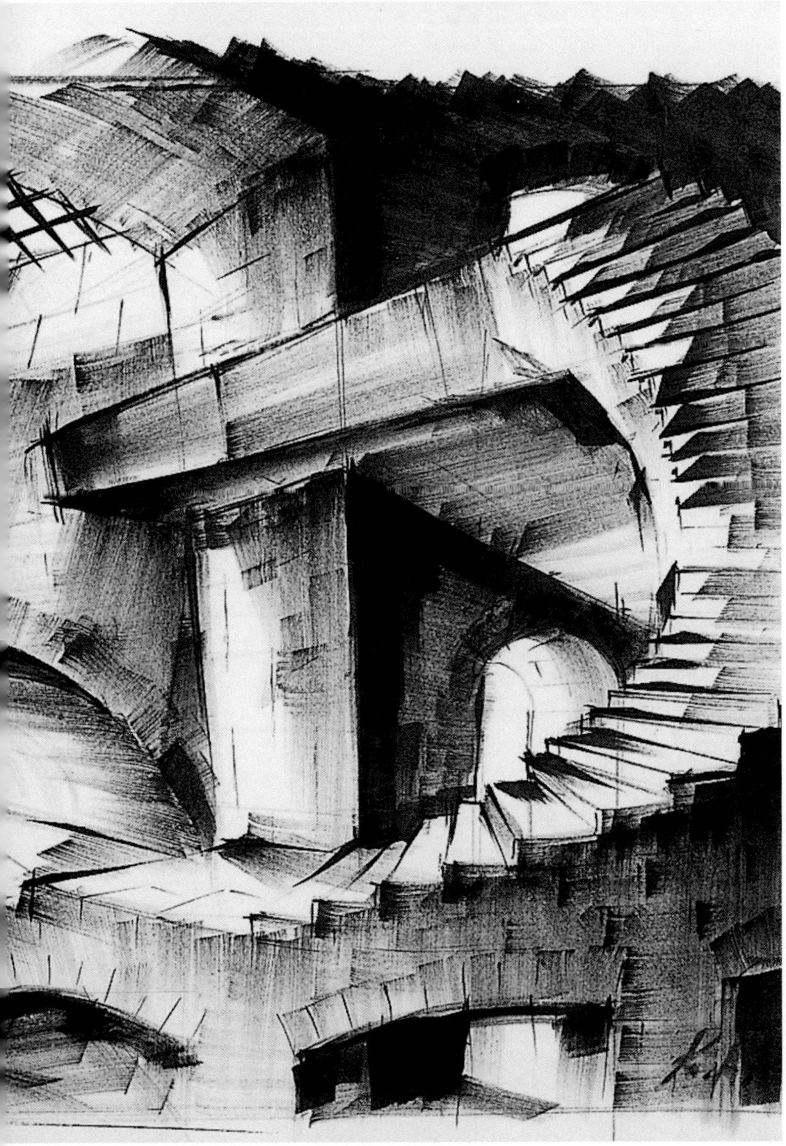

The only colour in the sweet factory was provided by the copper pots of brightly coloured sweets. Colour can comfort, cheer, soothe, excite; it can animate and destroy. I have very exact ideas about colour. One should always try to avoid colour on walls, it is best to leave them white, and use furniture, curtains and pictures to place colour accents.

At the beginning it is unimportant whether I develop ideas for a colour or a monochrome film. I always begin sketching in black and white. If it works in black and white it will also work in colour.

The sketch is a designer's most important tool and must make clear which light is needed, direct or diffuse. The cameraman should be able to draw ideas and stimulus for the lighting of the completed set from my sketch. Even when a design is based on only one or two lines, it is often the incompleteness of these rough sketches with their bold chiaroscuro contrasts out of which an interesting composition or exciting atmosphere grows. The rough sketch gives me an idea of the 3-D realisation. After that I draw more specific designs, the ground plan, the completed walls or models. **JB**

1969

Lord L

I formed a partnership in the sixties with a wonderful Italian writer called Ennio de Concini who had won an Academy Award for *Divorce Italian Style*. We decided it would be nice for me to produce and design a film for him to direct and he came up with this very revolutionary story called *Lord L* which was about God being fed up with what was happening on earth – it was the time of the hippies. The film became very political and included meetings with Marx and Freud and references to the Last Supper. United Artists wanted to do the film if the budget could be small, but as Concini spoke very little English, they wanted me to do it with another director, but I couldn't accept this. And so *Lord L* was never made. **SG**

The hangar 1969
Study
10 × 26.5 cm

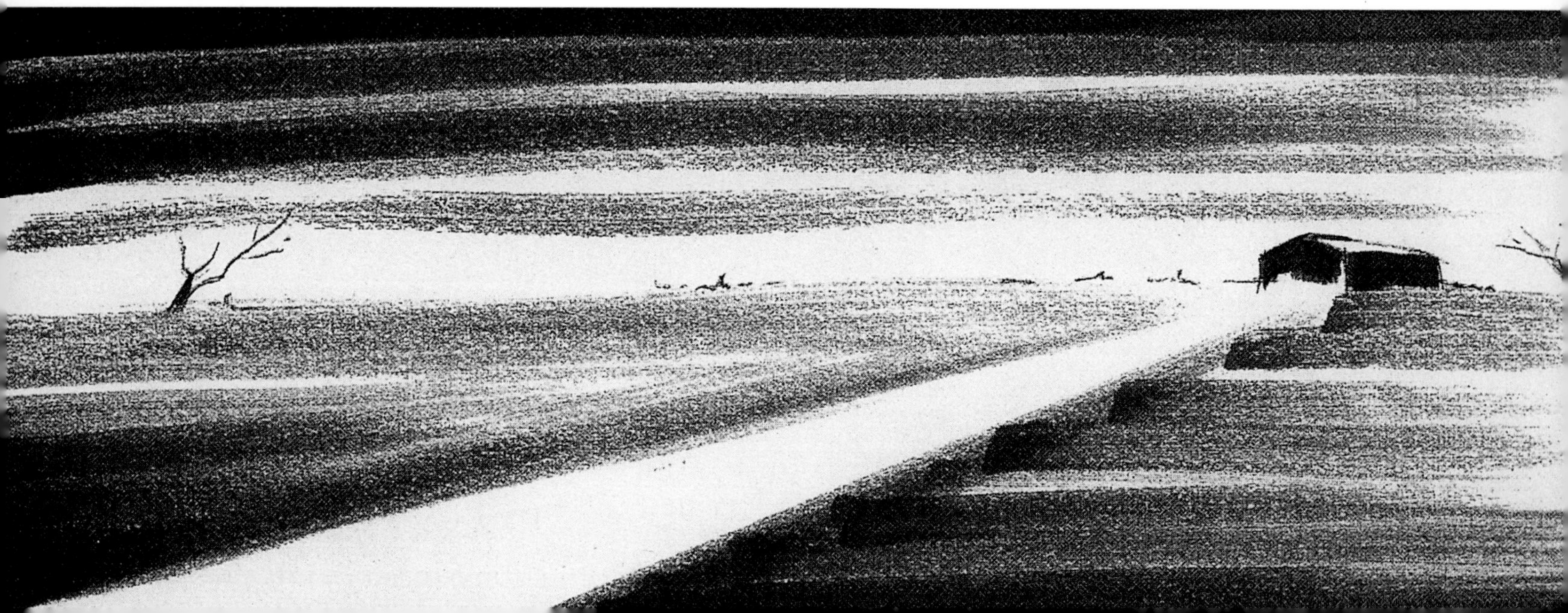

Diamonds Are Forever

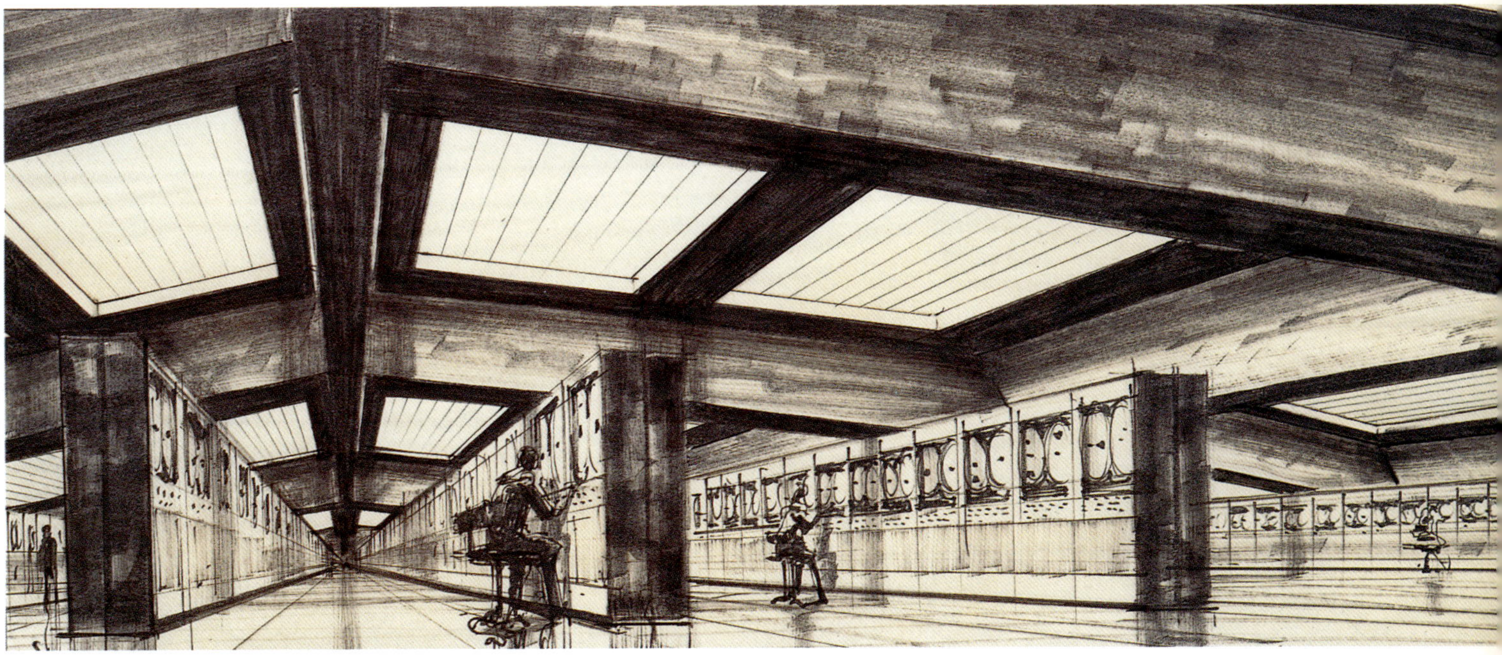

The interior of Willard Whyte's penthouse complex 1971
Final concept
Colour felt-tip pen on paper
21.5 × 50 cm

Following George Lazenby's impersonation of 007 in *On Her Majesty's Secret Service* (1979), Sean Connery returns in his sixth and final Bond movie, directed by Guy Hamilton. Bond's search for the perpetrators of a worldwide diamond conspiracy leads to Las Vegas, where a reclusive Howard Hughes-like billionaire is being held captive by the infamous Blofeld who has gems and space rockets on his mind.

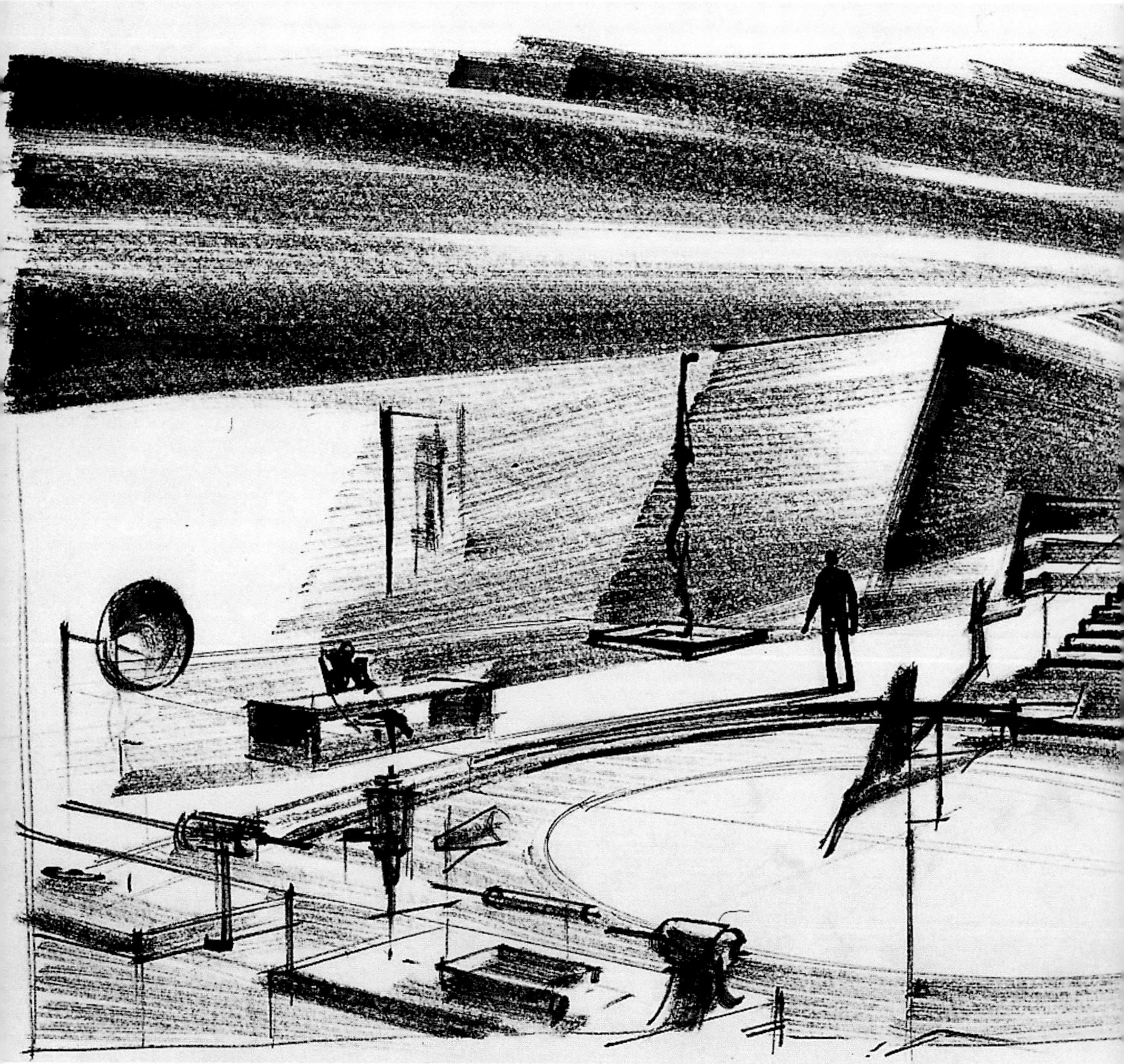

The interior of Willard Whyte's penthouse apartment 1971
Study
36 × 56.5 cm

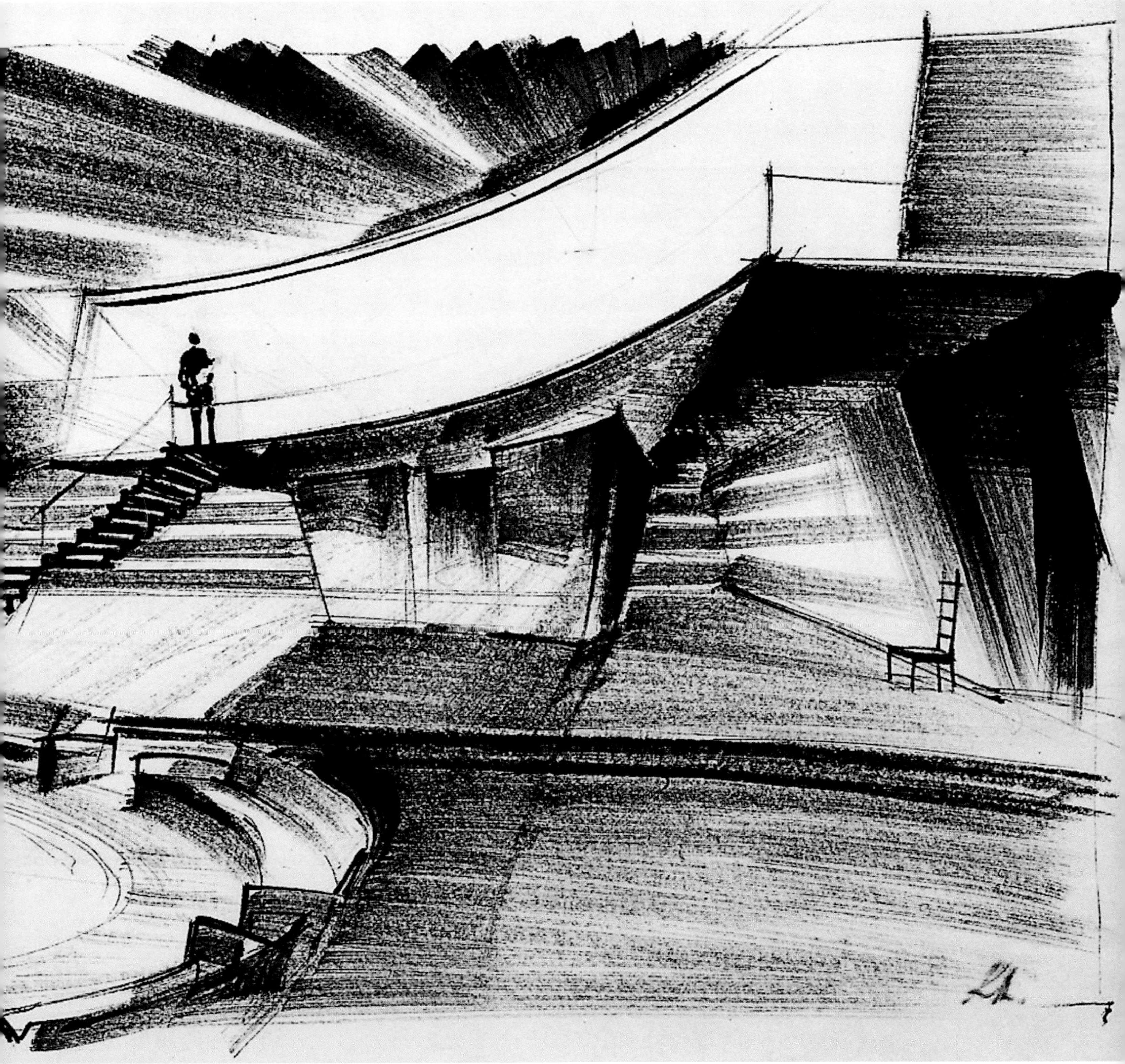

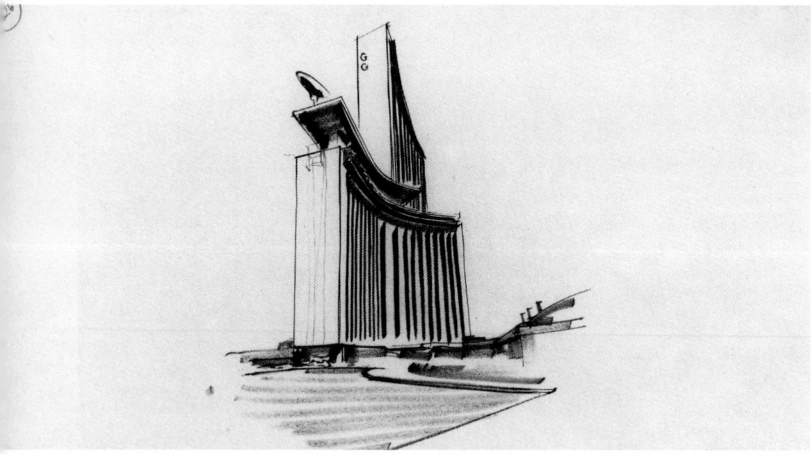

The exterior of Willard Whyte's penthouse complex 1971
Final concept
Felt-tip pen and pencil on paper
30 × 55.5 cm

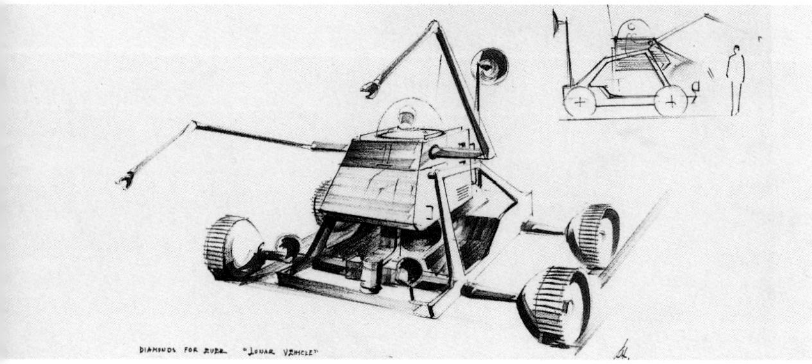

The moon buggy 1971
Final concept
Felt-tip pen and wash on paper
30 × 55 cm

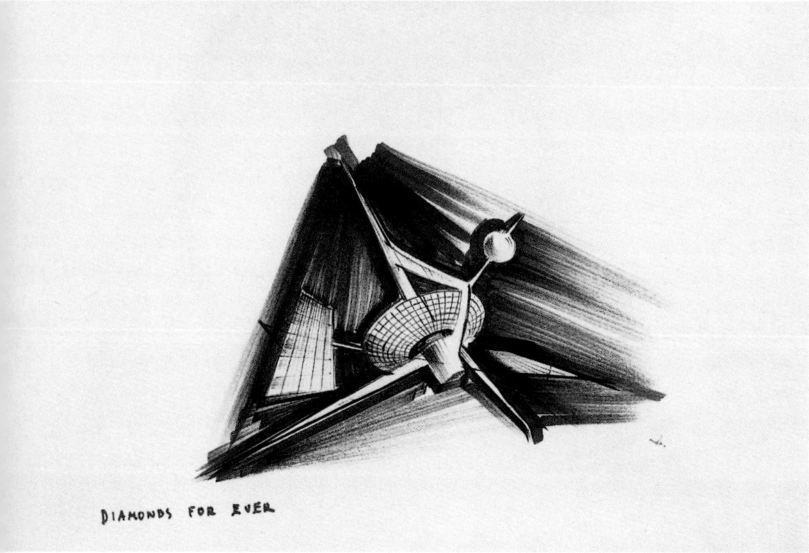

The satellite 1971
Final concept
39.5 × 57 cm

We intended to do the whole picture in the United States, and as Harry Saltzman had just bought Technicolor and had a very good relationship with Universal, I started designing the whole film at Universal Studios in Hollywood. They were planning to do it without Sean Connery, and finally decided on an actor called John Gavin, until David Chasman of United Artists suggested that we do it in England, because that would enable us to recover, as tax relief, the US $2million that Sean was going to cost at that time. So, not half, but certainly a quarter of the way through the film it was decided to go to Pinewood to do the rest of the picture, which was a gigantic problem for me. I had to get Peter Lamont, my assistant, over from England and see that we had the right liaison between Hollywood and England. We ended up shooting the oil rig in Santa Barbara, the moonbuggy sequence in a gypsum mine close to Las Vegas and a number of scenes at various places in Vegas. **SG**

Everything had become bigger than life, though still tongue-in-cheek. There was a *basis* in reality for a lot of what I did, for example, Willard Whyte's penthouse. Cubby Broccoli had been a friend of Howard Hughes, so I based the penthouse on his, but more operatic, less realistic. I was trying to carry a mood of absurdist reality in the moonscape and lunar-vehicle chase sequences – although I used NASA photographs for the moonscape. The diamond satellite I designed to look like a cross between a mobile and a radar dish, collapsible so it could be carried underwater. **JD**

Sleuth

Joseph L. Mankiewicz's last movie, a film about decor and decorum, was adapted by Anthony Shaffer from his two-character comedy thriller, a major success in the West End and on Broadway. Laurence Olivier, as a successful mystery writer, snobbish and ludic, plays vicious games to his ultimate disadvantage with his wife's hairdresser lover, Michael Caine.

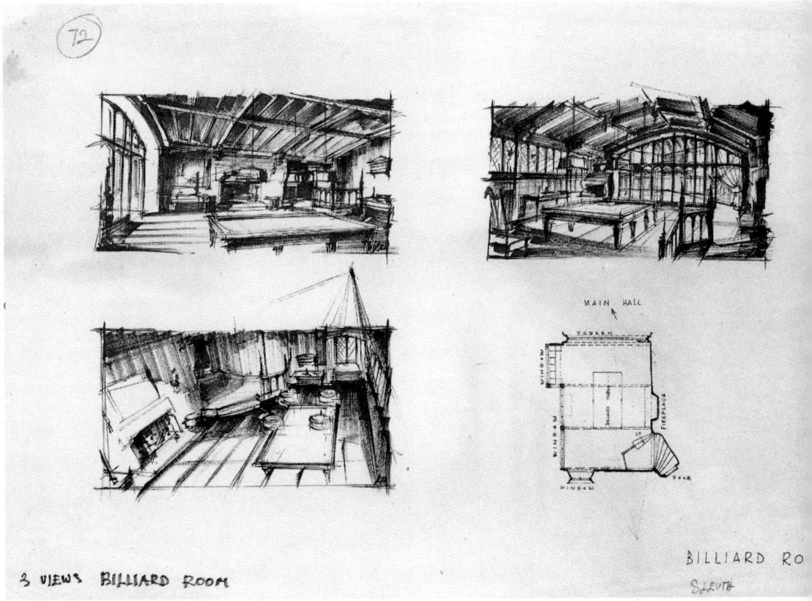

The Billiard Room 1972
Studies
42 × 59.5 cm

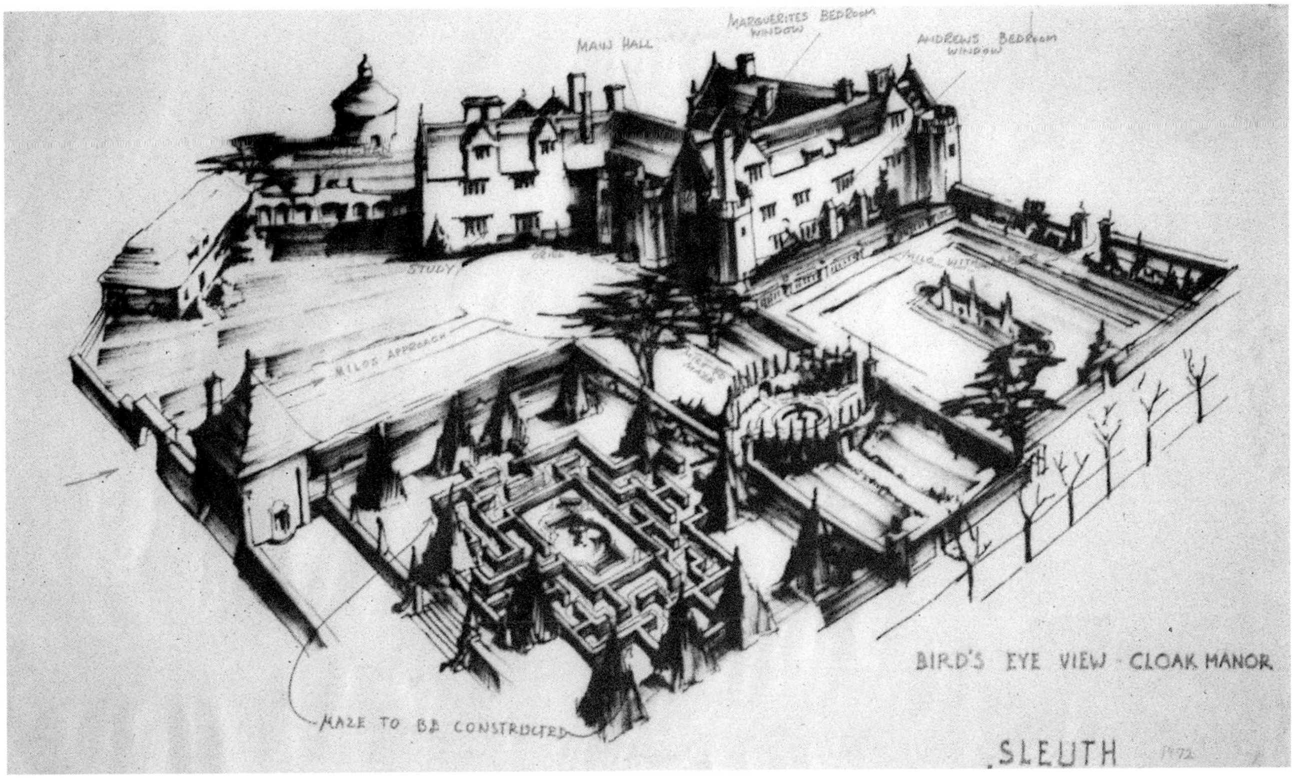

Cloak Manor and grounds 1972
Final concept
33 × 59 cm

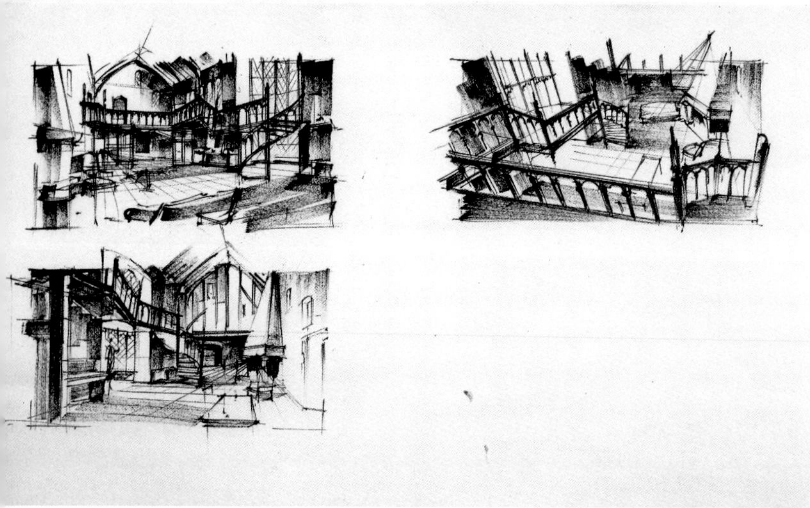

The Great Hall 1972
Studies
40 × 56 cm

The exterior of the house was a location, but we constructed the maze in the garden. The interiors and part of the exterior were built at Pinewood. **SG**

I had a meeting with the director, Joseph Mankiewicz, and he said, 'I want the set to be like the third actor in the film, and I want it theatrical. The whole thing should be like a game. They're playing a game, and the set should reflect that in some way.' We knew I would not be able to find such a place in reality. I had a concept in my mind which was a type of baronial hall in a medieval manor house. So I went all over southern England and the Midlands to look at possible exteriors and eventually came up with a place near Dorchester at Athelhampton. Joe liked the exterior. I flew to New York and showed him all my sketches and designs, and he went along with all of it. The interiors were built in the studio. I built the main entrance and the oriel window in the studio to match the exterior of the location house. **VL**

I was fortunate to work twice with Laurence Olivier, an actor who paid enormous attention to his props and how he interacted with his surroundings. I remember he decided to play an entire scene from a position by the fireplace I'd designed. As I watched him rehearse, my attention was distracted by three props on the mantle. I sneaked up and removed them. After we'd shot the scene, Olivier said to me, 'I'm glad you did that. I knew they wouldn't fit in.' I've probably been guilty of designing sets which overpower the actors on some of the Bonds, but ultimately I believe that the designer should think of a set as a frame for the actor to work in. **PE**

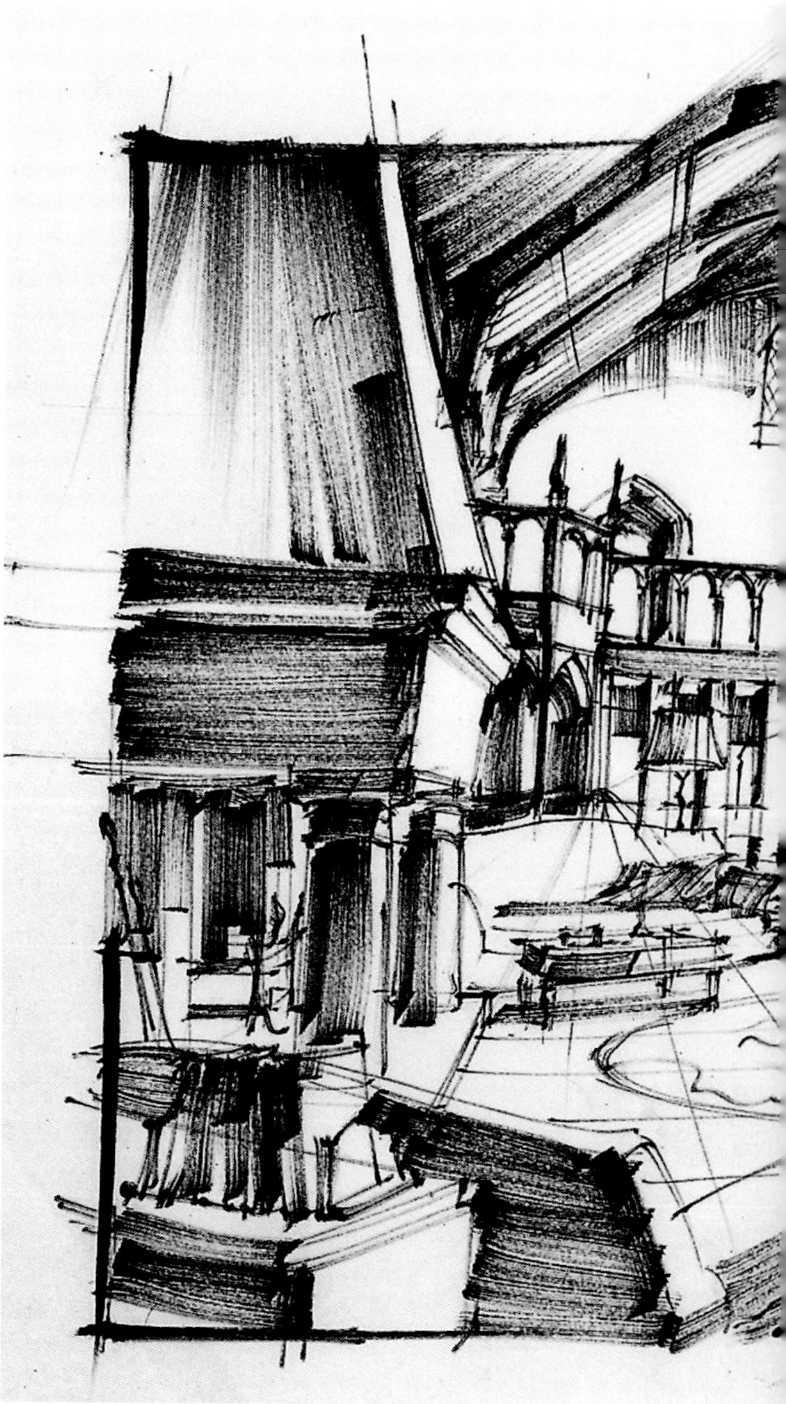

The Great Hall 1972
Final concept
42 × 59.5 cm

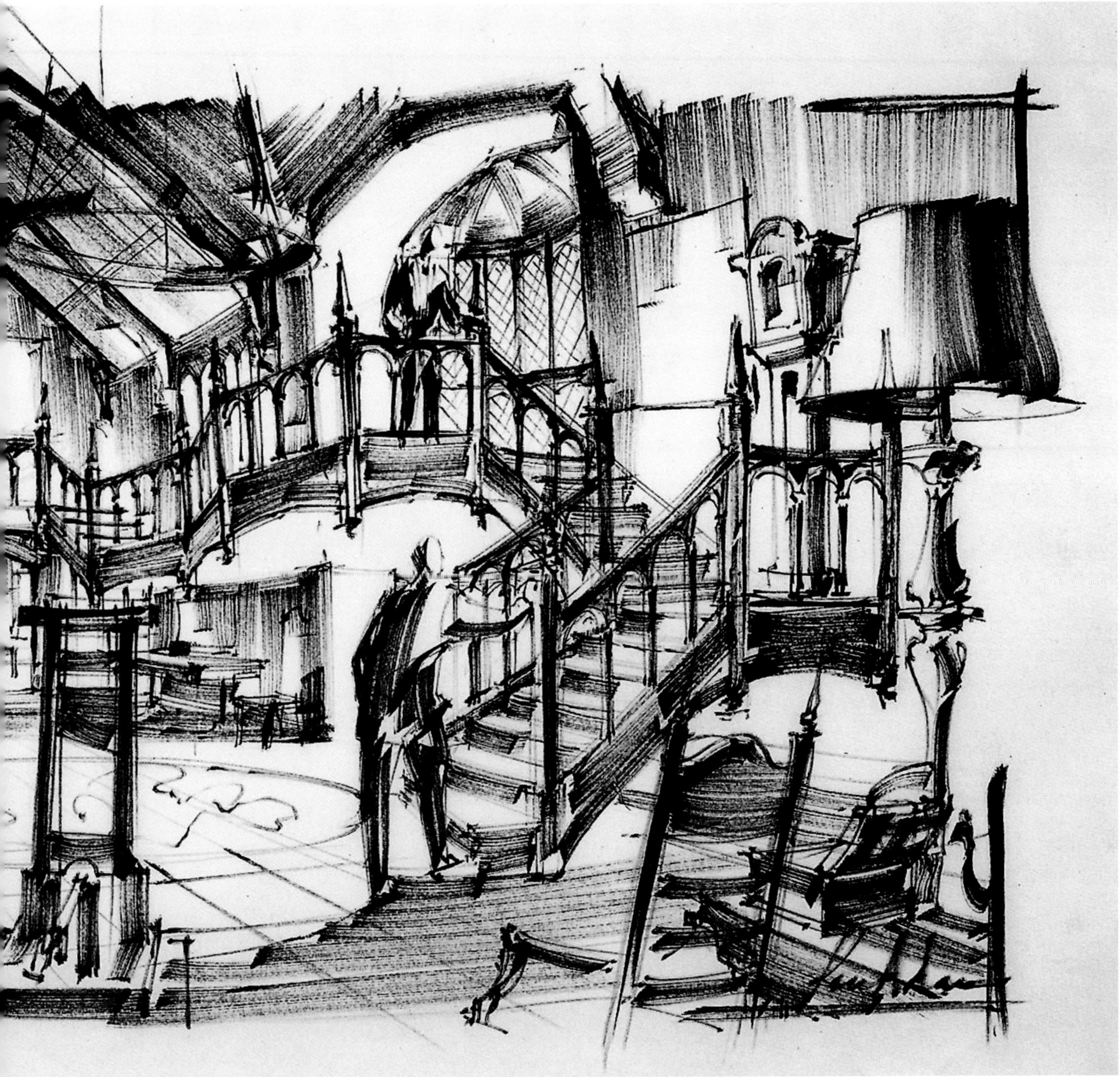

Barry Lyndon

Adapted from Thackeray's *The Luck of Barry Lyndon* by the director, Stanley Kubrick, the film recounts the picaresque adventures of an impetuous, penniless eighteenth-century Irish adventurer. He leaves home after a duel, serves in the Seven Years' War with both the English and the Prussian armies, becomes a spy and card-sharp, marries a rich widow, estranges her aristocratic son and is eventually cast into oblivion.

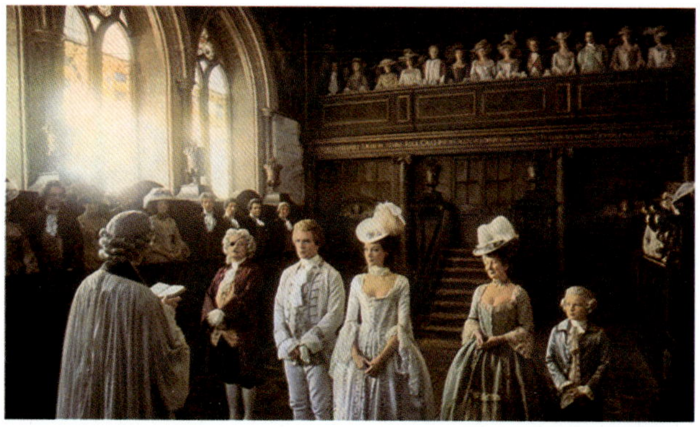

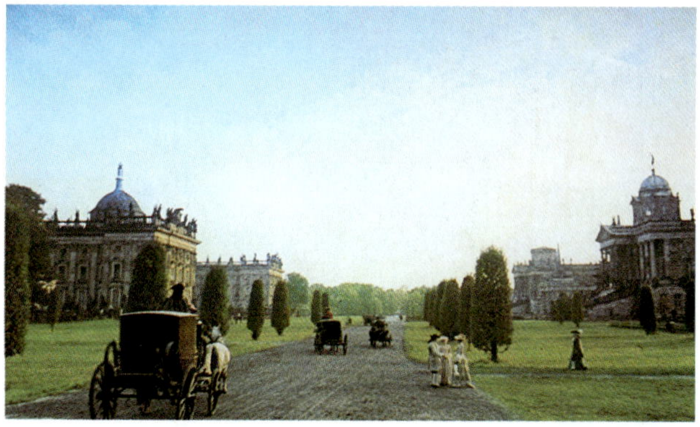

This was shot entirely on location, beginning in Ireland at Waterford and Kilkenny, and using interiors at Dublin Castle, Powers Court, Caher Castle and Huntingdon, then in England, at Wilton, Petworth, Longleat, Blenheim, Castle Howard and Corsham Court. In both countries we would use rooms from different houses to create an imaginary house. In Germany the second unit filmed locations in Potsdam which I chose from past knowledge.
SE

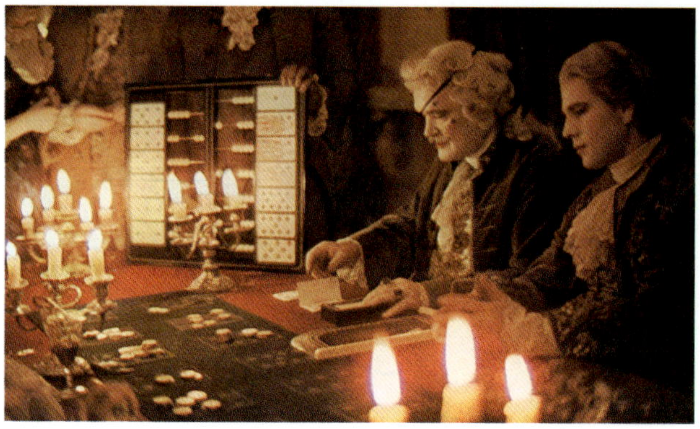

I had been used to designing and creating my sort of reality in a studio. Here we were using stately homes and actual places. Part of the picture took place in Germany, but we never went to Germany. Stanley refused to go until the bitter end, so we had to find the continental buildings in Ireland. Eventually towards the end of the picture, he sent the second unit to Potsdam and East Berlin to get some of the superb atmosphere of Germany in castles and streets of that period. The painstaking process of reproducing paintings of the period was a different challenge for me.

What painters were you and Kubrick inspired by during your research?

Of course we used the English painters like Gainsborough, Reynolds and Stubbs and Hogarth and Rowlandson, but we used also French painters like Watteau and Italians like Zoffany. We used the Polish artist Chodowiecki for some of the continental scenes.

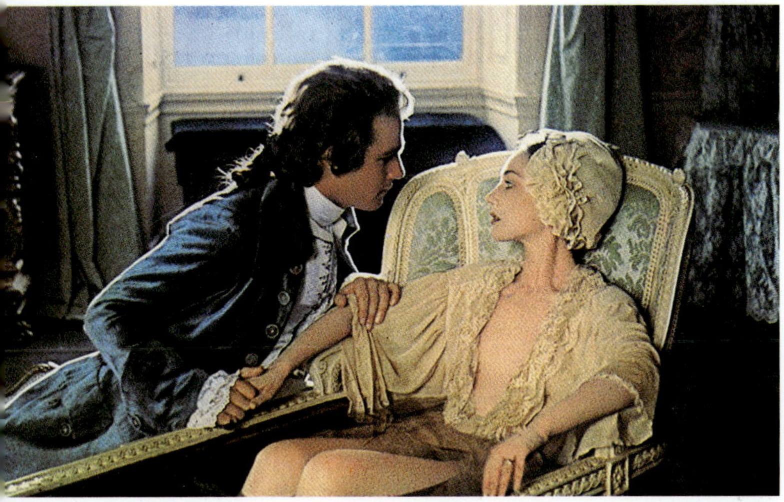

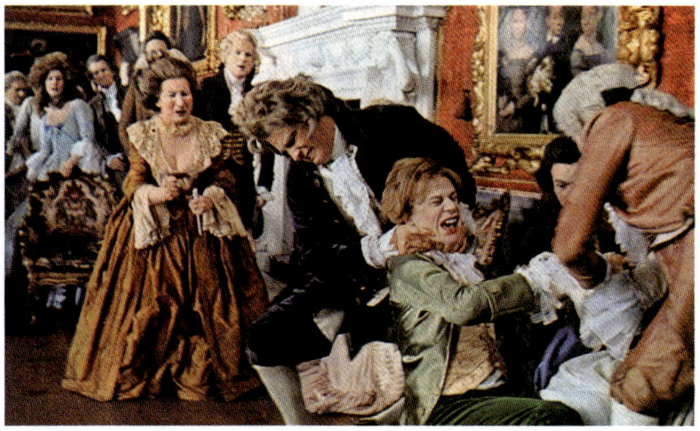

The film depicts the period so realistically, it almost makes the viewer feel transported back in time.

Yes, and that's what Stanley tried to do. He wanted to do it almost like a documentary of the period, but when we started researching and preparing the film, he knew very little about the period. Eventually, he got to know more and more, but we got into terrible arguments because he was more attracted to Victorian interiors than to the stark, more formal eighteenth-century interiors. We used to photograph every location and come back and analyse the photographs, and he would say, 'I like that wallpaper,' and I would say, 'Stanley, you can't use that wallpaper, that's Victorian.' Of course, in the end he knew more about that period than I or probably anybody else because of the amount of research he did about the living conditions of the people: the lice in their wigs, the toothbrushes they used, condoms. We went through everything to find out how those people lived. Right from the start, Stanley was insistent that the costumes should not be costumes but should be clothes. So we bought a lot of real eighteenth-century clothes, which one could still find in England. We found that they were all too small, because people were obviously smaller two hundred years ago. We set up our own factory at Radlett, opened up these clothes, and made new clothes in exactly the same patterns as the old clothes. The thing was to get the actors to wear them properly, to get used to them and walk properly in them. **VL**

The Seven-Per-Cent Solution

Based on Nicholas Meyer's 1975 novel, one of numerous Conan Doyle pastiches of the time, Herb Ross's film has Dr Watson luring cocaine-addicted Sherlock Homes to Vienna to be treated by his fellow detective Sigmund Freud and resolve his obsession with his mother's lover, Dr Moriarty.

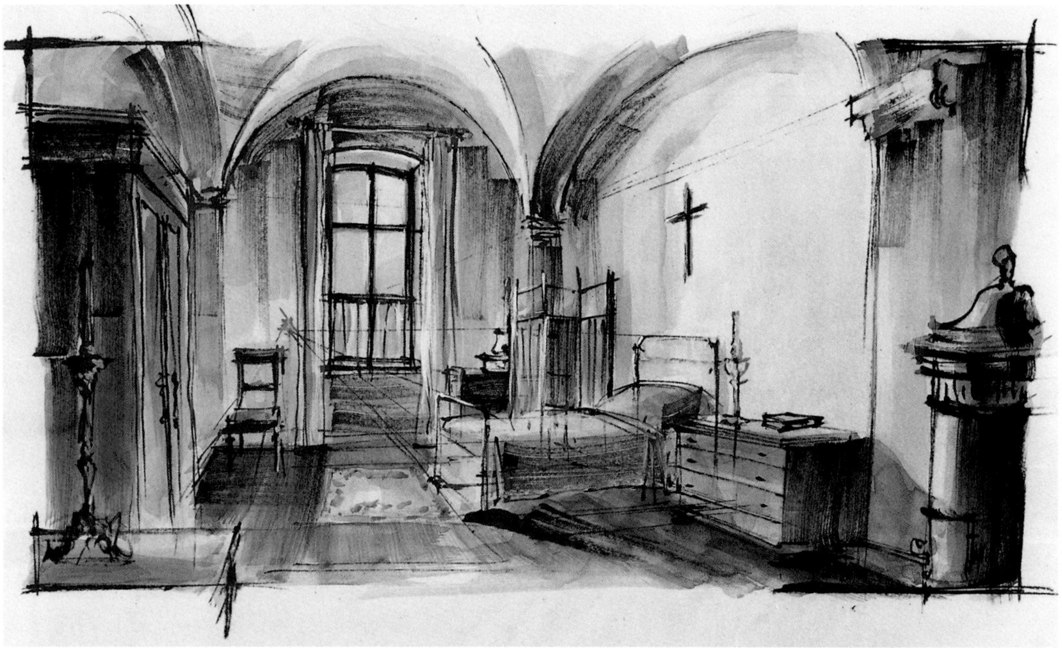

The convent hospital room 1975
Final concept
Felt-tip pen and watercolour on paper
32 × 43 cm

A number of locations were filmed in Vienna, but not the riding academy, which was one of the sets constructed at Pinewood along with the other interiors. The train sequence was shot in the Severn Valley where a group of enthusiasts run steam trains.

Because Holmes is a cocaine addict and I wanted to reflect this in the design of his apartment, I had the walls inclined, as though they were seen through the eyes of a drug addict, which in a way is a cheat, but Herb Ross thought it was a good idea except that once or twice I'd gone too far, so I calmed it down a little. **SG**

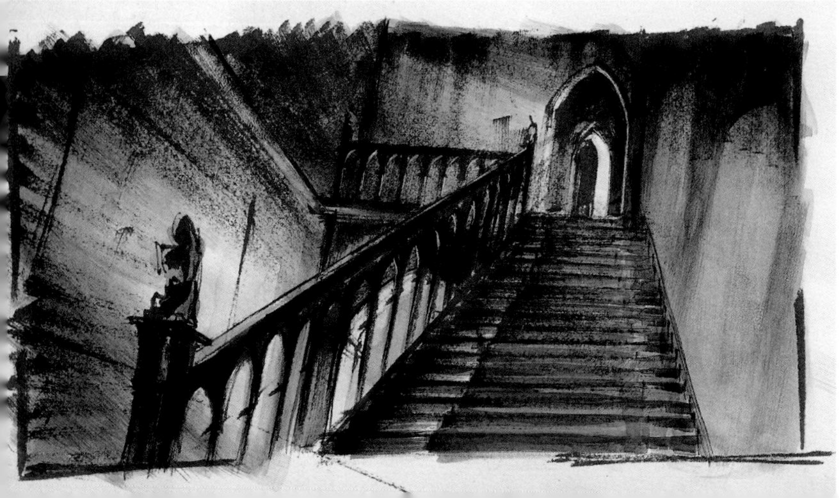

Stairway leading to Sherlock Holmes' Vienna apartment 1975
Final concept
Felt-tip pen and watercolour on paper
32 × 43 cm

The Spy Who Loved Me

In his will, Ian Fleming insisted that his 1961 novel should not be filmed. So the film, directed by Lewis Gilbert, uses just the title, and launches 007 Roger Moore into orbit to combat arch criminal Stromberg, who plans to hijack NATO nuclear submarines and control the world from his subterranean, Mediterranean headquarters.

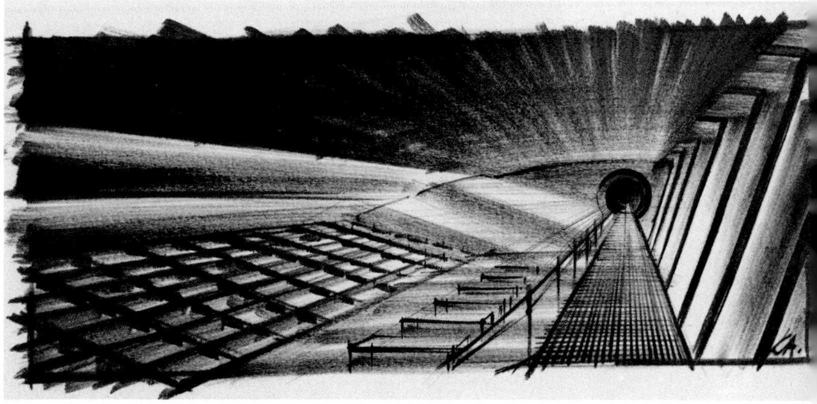

The brig on the Liparus *supertanker* 1976
Study
30 × 57 cm

The submarine docking bay in the Liparus *supertanker* 1976
Study
Felt-tip pen on paper
22 × 57 cm

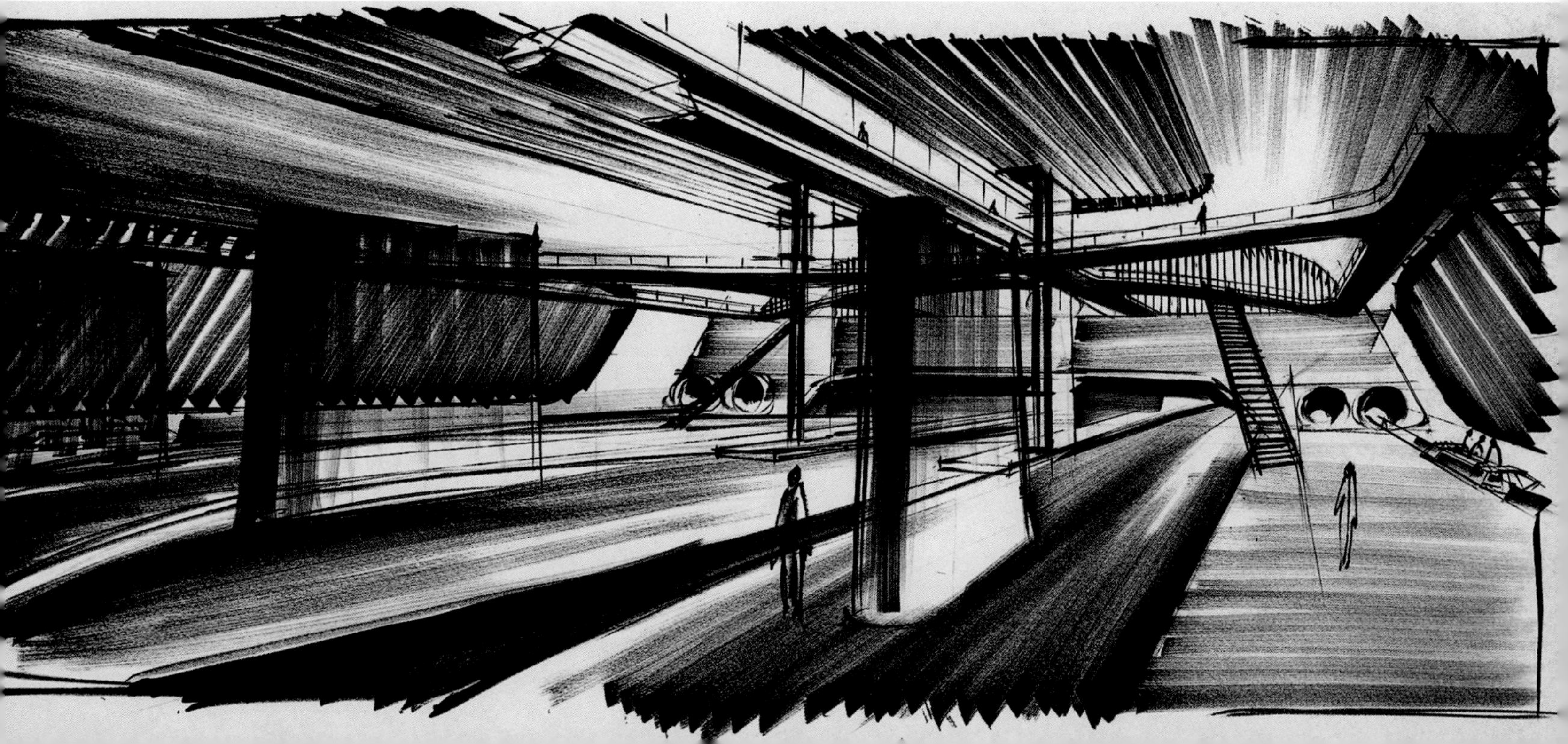

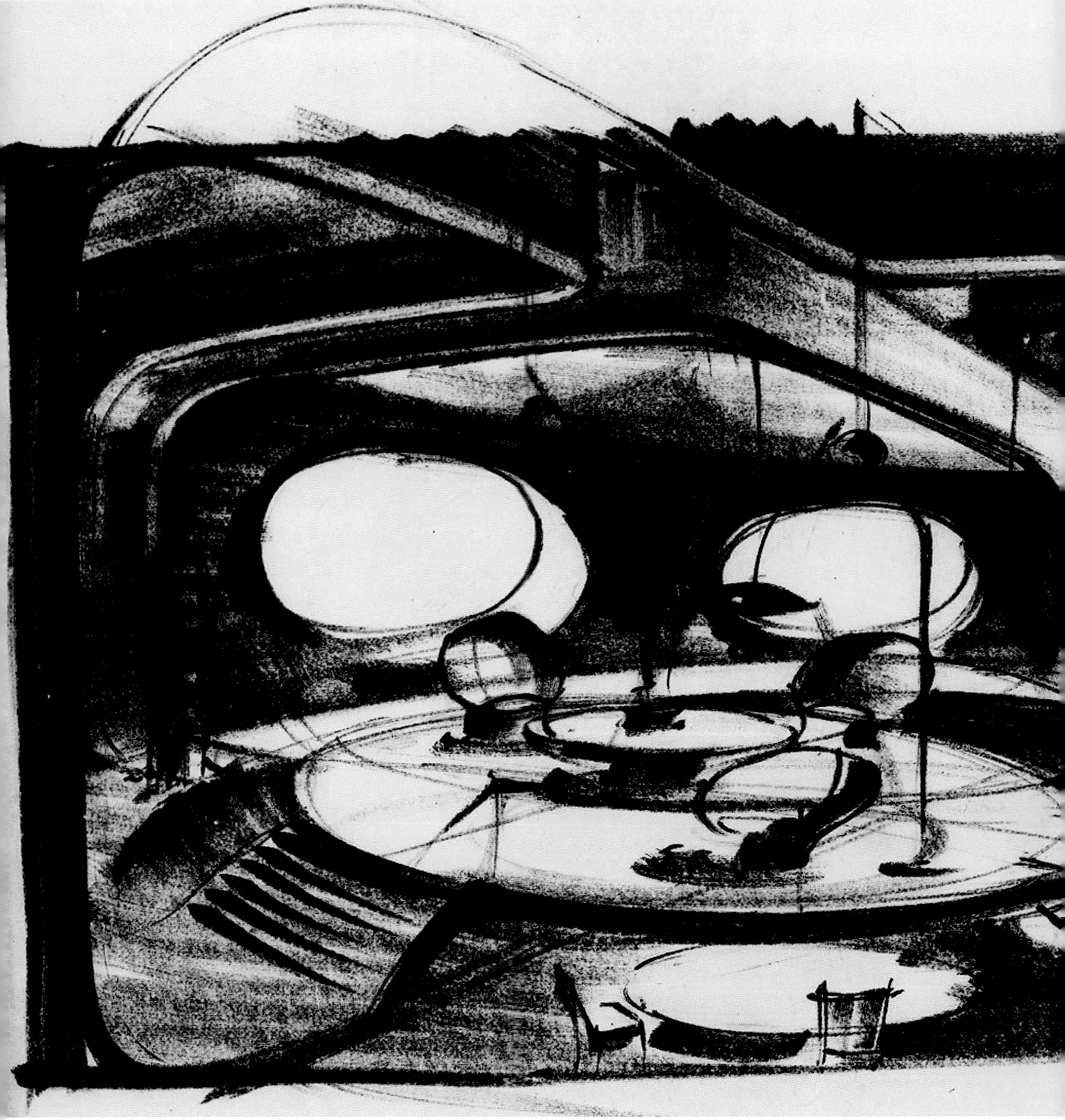

Stromberg's living quarters on Atlantis 1976
Final concept
30 × 59 cm

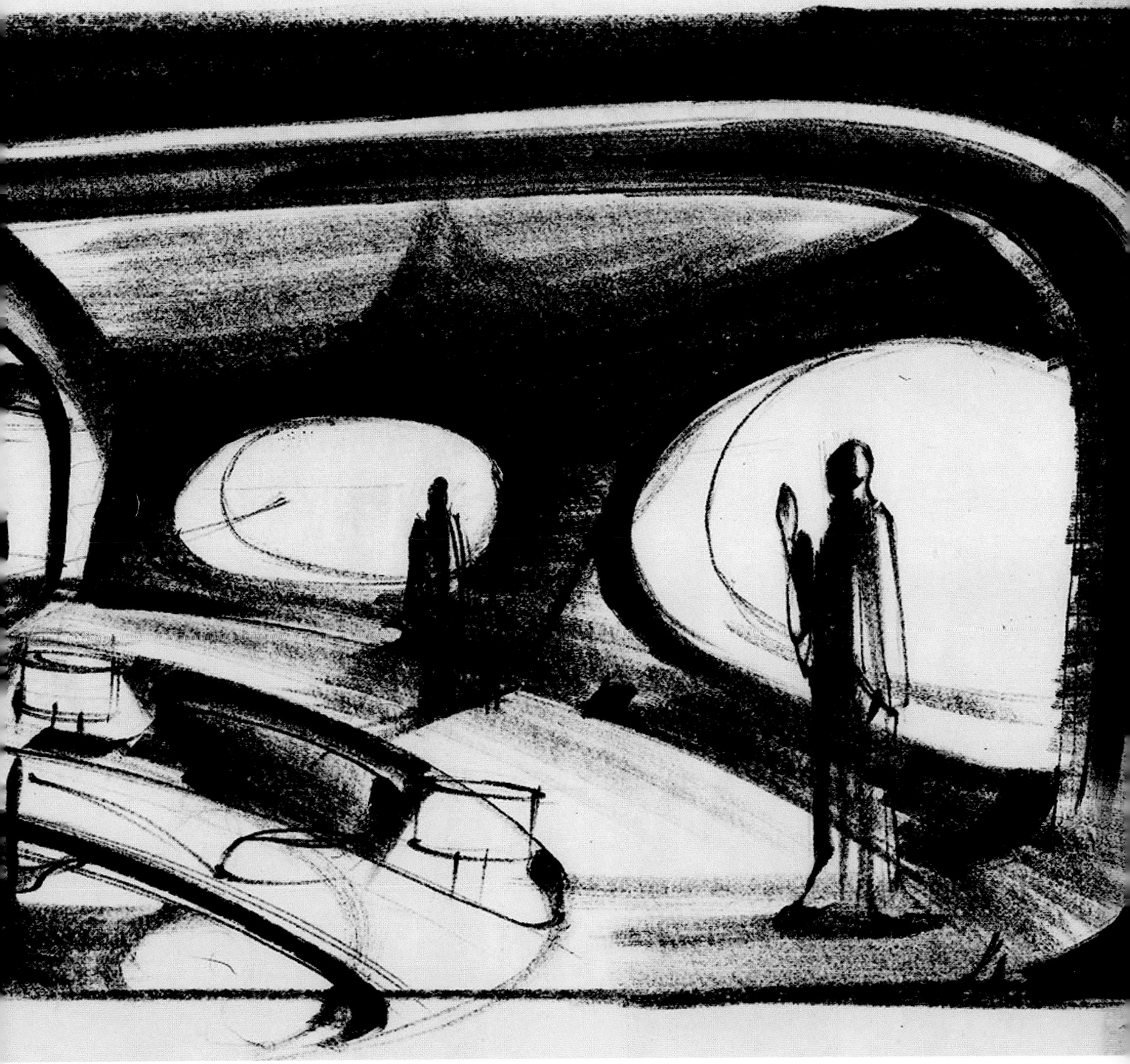

My Bond designs and all my other ahead-of-modern designs were always very linear; simple but efficient, with a bareness of line. But on *Spy* I also went into curved shapes. The combination excited me, and that excitement reflected on some of the other designs I did. Something just clicked, and I knew I'd done it right.

There was more of an overall feel to the picture, reflected in another Oscar nomination following your win for Barry Lyndon *two years before.*

I was functioning not just by creating individual sets, but by having a production-design progression. I did go through a slight insecurity period again, however, because although it's an advantage to get as much freedom as I have in designing the Bond films it's an immense responsibility.

Especially when you're building a sound stage to hold just one set, and that sound stage costs $1,800,000 in 1976 currency.

I had to design and build the inside of a supertanker which would accommodate three submarines and a control room. And having no desire to repeat the workable but ultimately wasteful free-standing set idea we did in *You Only Live Twice*, I designed the supertanker interior in terms of what could remain for use after the film was finished. And that's how the James Bond 007 Stage at Pinewood came into being. Instead of building the set inside an existing stage, none of which were big enough anyway, we built the stage over and around the set.

Everything in Spy *was big. From the reality of the pyramids and temples of Egypt to the villain's submersible lair, Atlantis.*

It was contagious. I even scaled up Anya's bedroom, making it big and palatial to play against the usual concept of Russia. And I did the same thing with Gogol's office – in part inspired by Eisenstein, though no one may have noticed – to counterpoint M's office, which is so typically English. **JD**

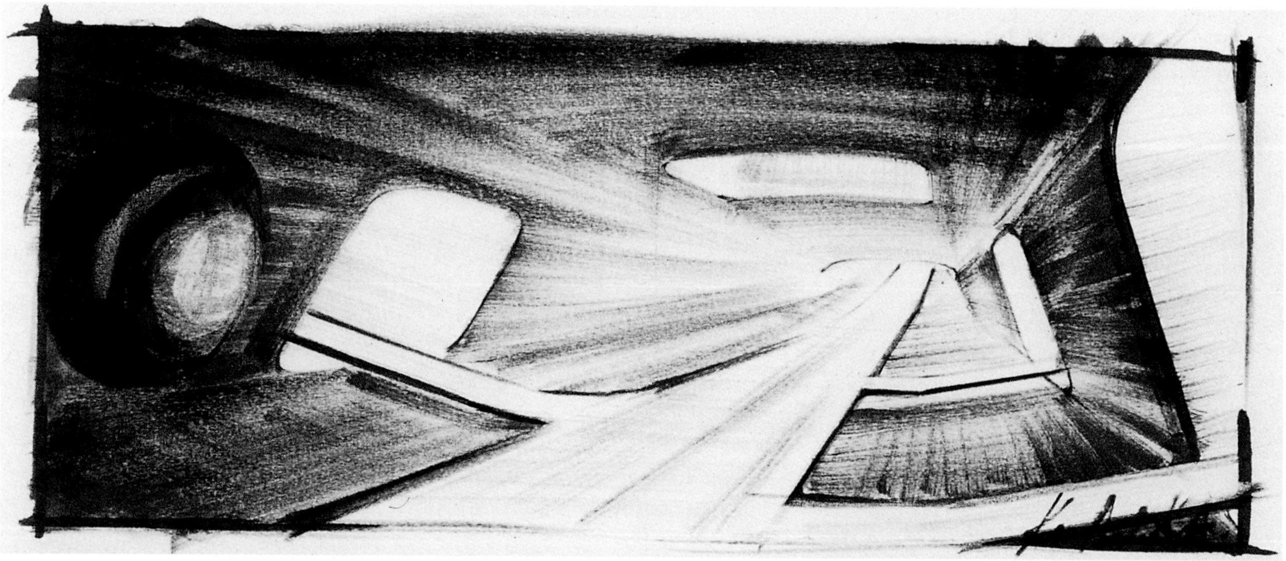

Corridor, Atlantis 1976
Final concept
23 × 54 cm

Locations were used in Sardinia, in Egypt at the Pyramids and Luxor and Aswan, and in Japan at Okinawa, where the footage of fish in the aquaria was shot. The interiors were constructed at Pinewood. **SG**

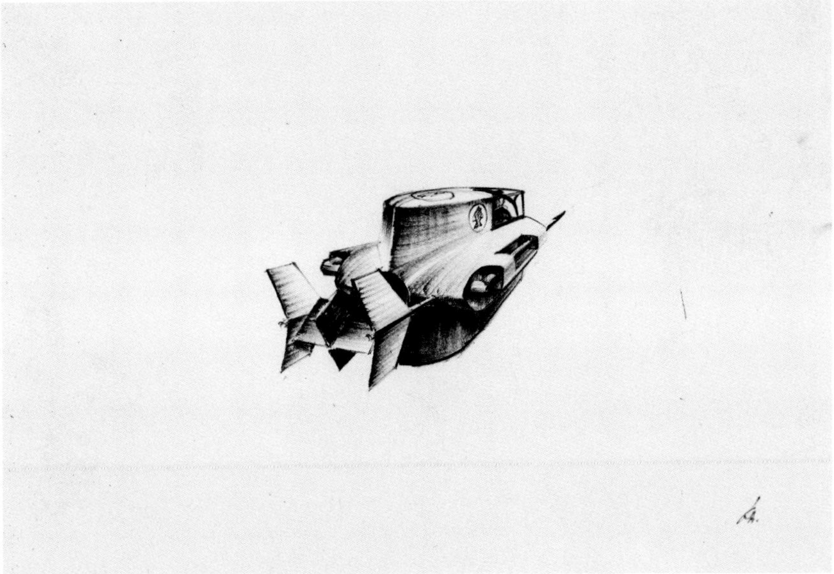

Perry submarine 1976
Final concept
c. 36.5 × 55 cm

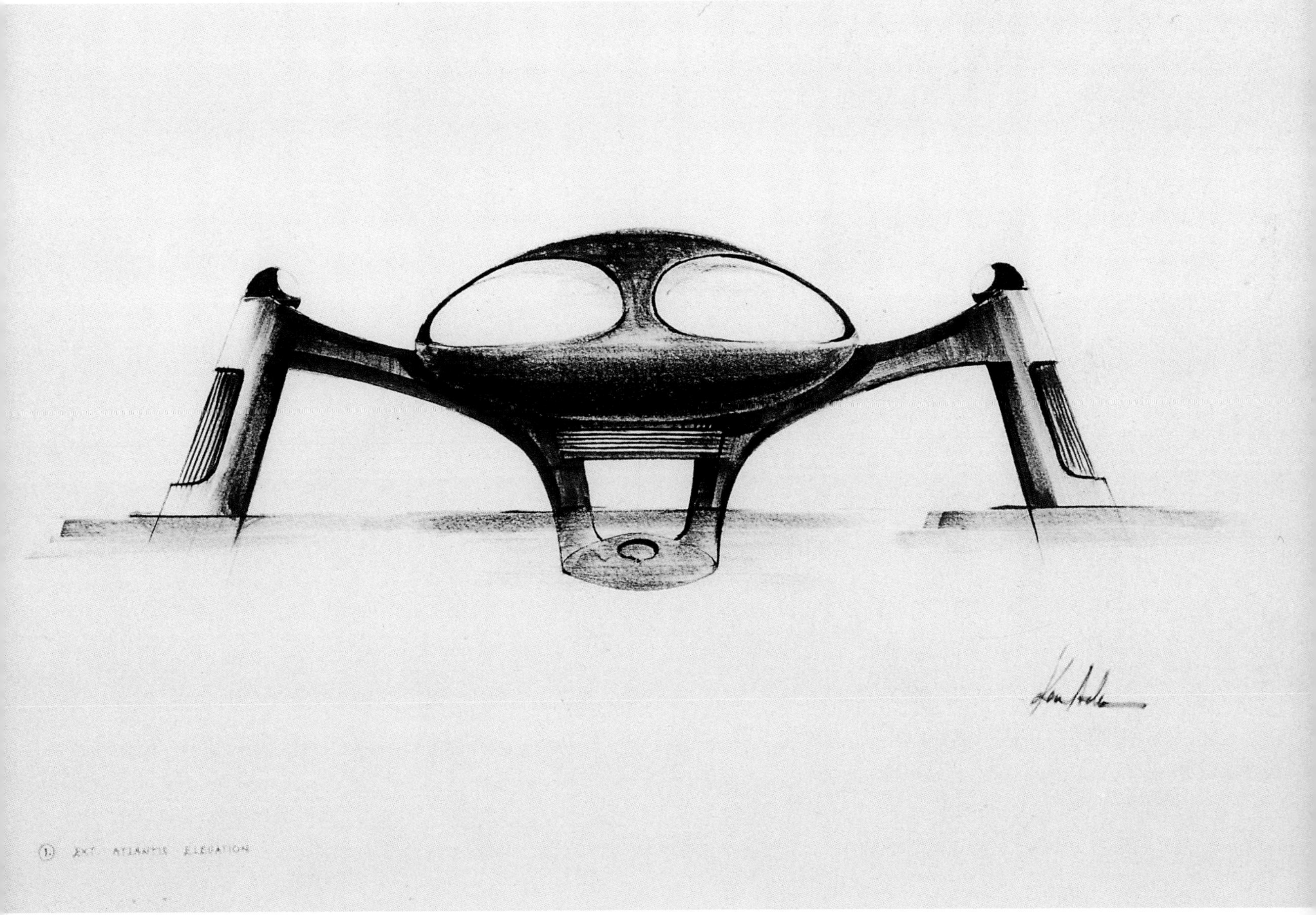

Atlantis 1976
Final concept
c. 30 × 57 cm

Star Trek

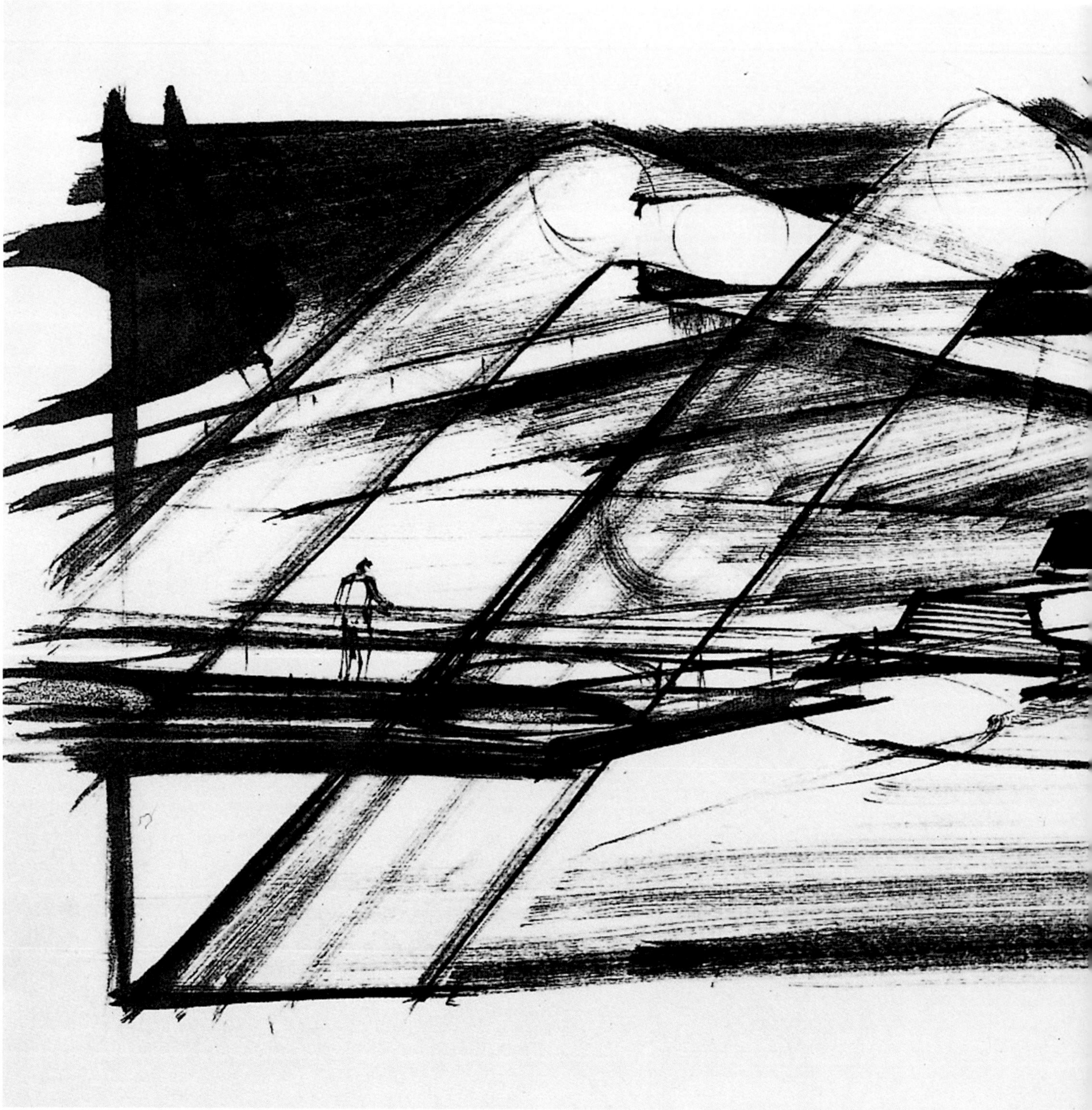

The hangar deck of the S.S. Enterprise 1977
Study
29.5 × 58 cm

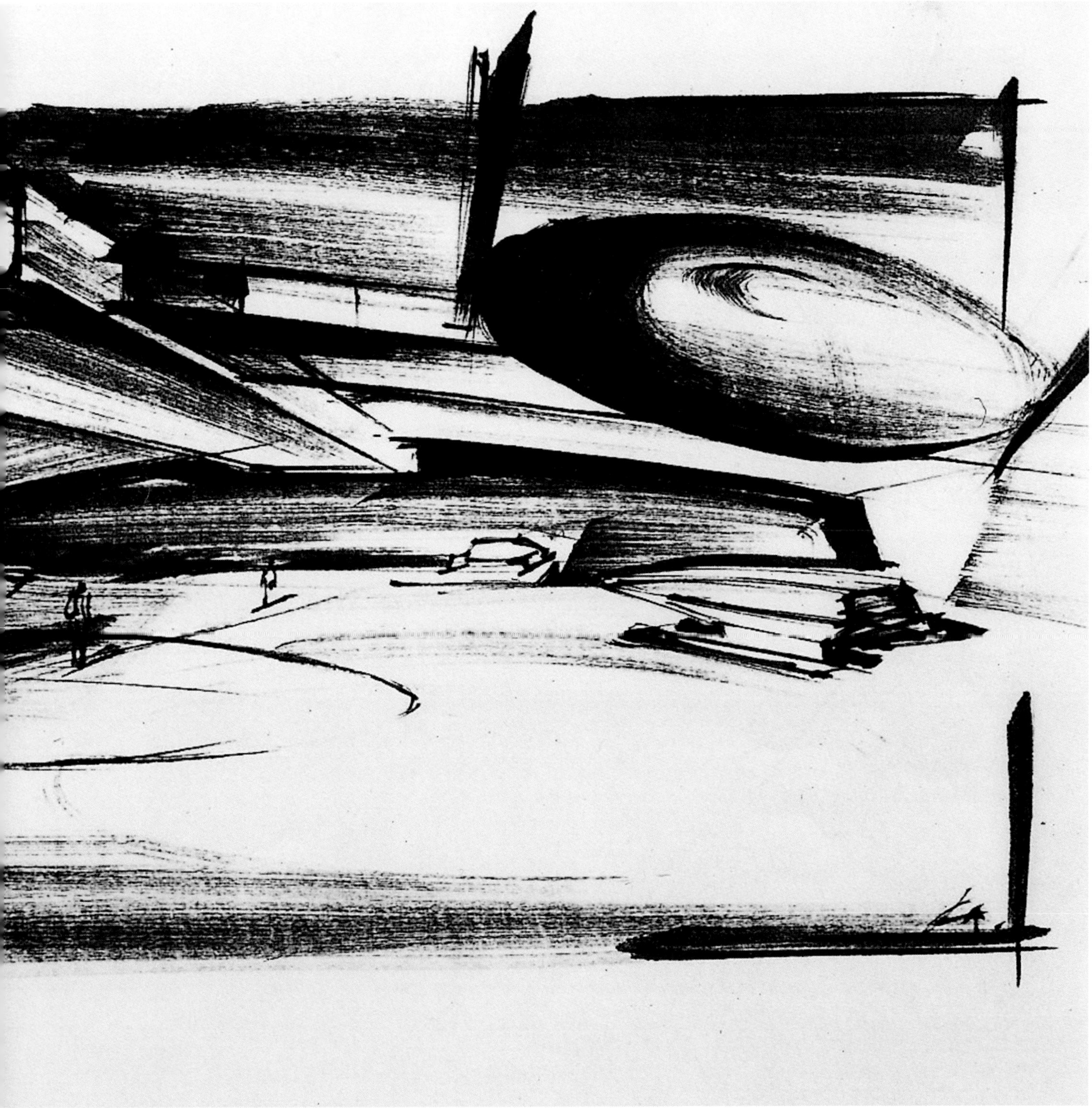

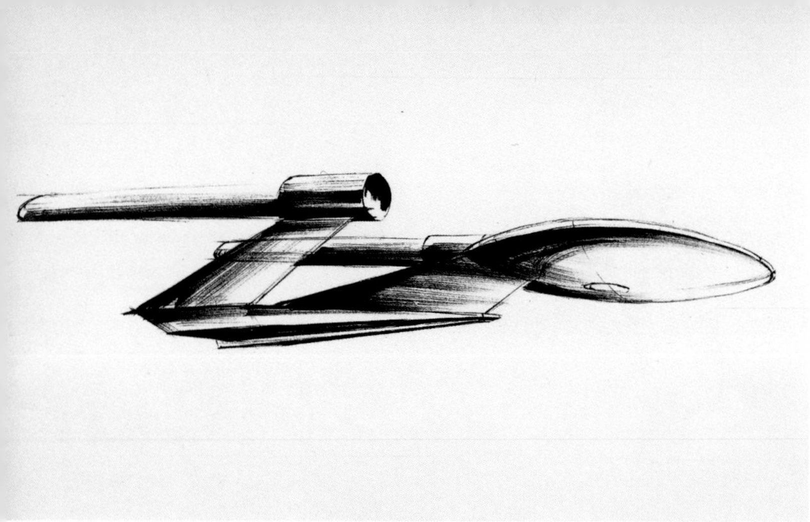

The S.S. Enterprise 1977
Study
36.5 × 56.5 cm

I was involved in the original *Star Trek* film when it was to be directed by Philip Kaufman. I worked on it for three months, then Paramount called it off and revived it about a year and a half later. By that time, we were both working on other things. That was really science fiction and way-out. I had a lot of headaches. I didn't find it difficult to dream up a different planet environment or even what this earth might look like a thousand years from now. What I found almost impossible to design was extraterrestrial beings or forms of life without the whole thing looking ridiculous. You have to start by getting scientists to tell you about the forms of life or what the chemical composition is before you can design anything, because if you start sketching things out, they always look ridiculous with three eyes or one leg. I talked a lot to Kubrick, and he said, 'Forget it.' They tried on *2001*, and they gave it up. You can call in the most brilliant designer – nobody can project that. **VL**

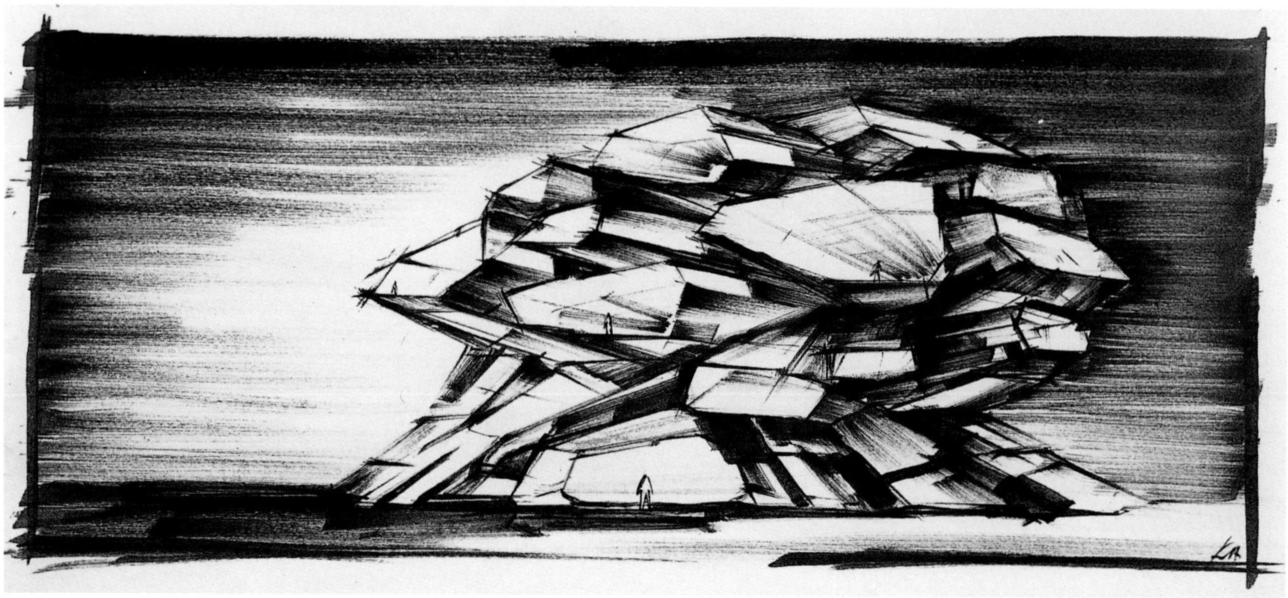

The Super Brain 1977
Study
29 × 57 cm

La Fanciulla del West

I designed this Puccini opera twice – in 1977 at Covent Garden, and then at Charleston, South Carolina, and Spoleto in 1985. I was asked to do the Covent Garden production by John Tooley and Zubin Mehta, and the one at Charleston and Spoleto by Giancarlo Menotti. Initially Menotti hired me to do *Turandot*, but at almost the last minute asked me to do a new version of *Fanciulla*, to be directed by Bruce Beresford. **SG**

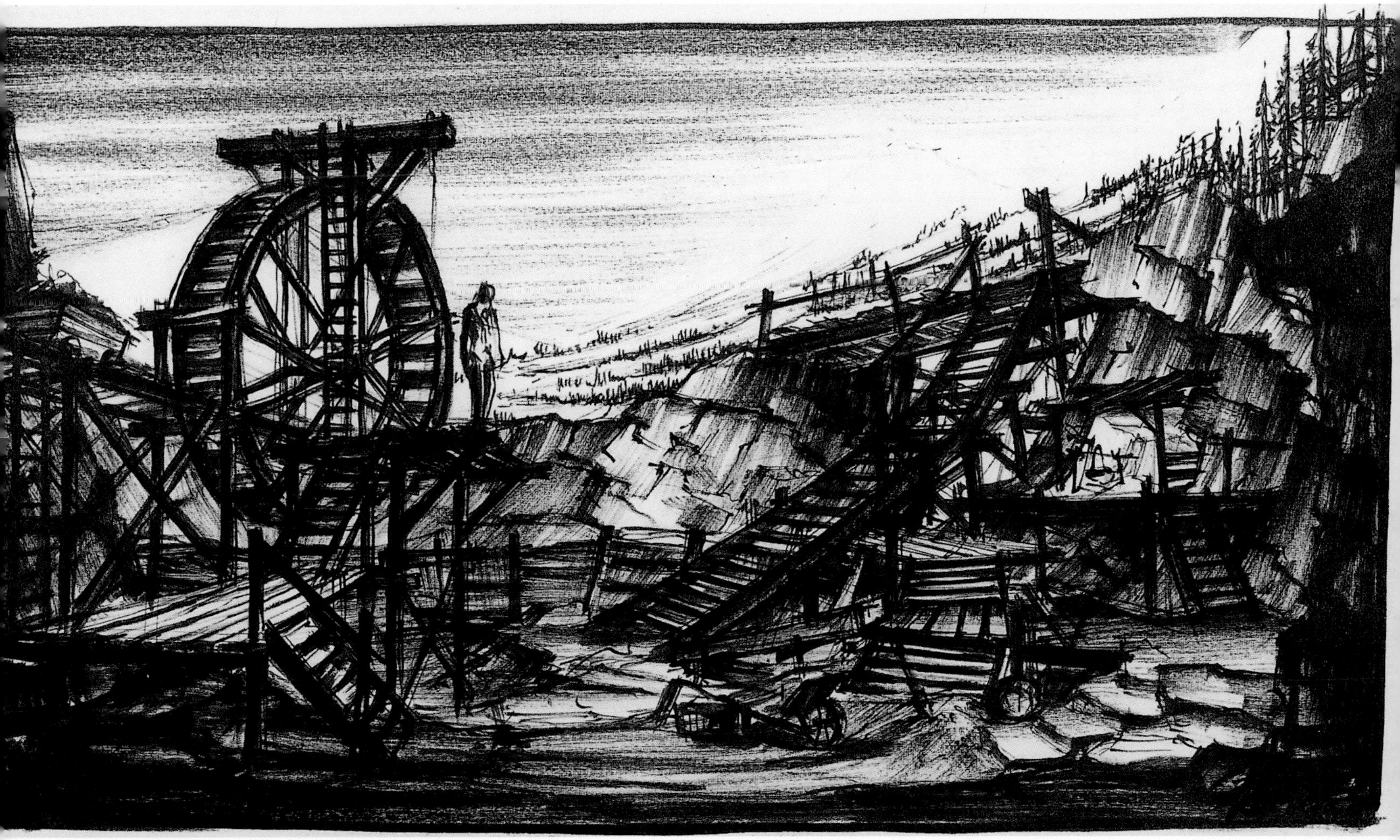

Act III, Covent Garden production 1977
Final concept
Felt-tip pen and watercolour on card
34 × 57 cm

Moonraker

Once again James Bond investigates the disappearance of space hardware. Directed by Lewis Gilbert, he follows the culprit, megalomaniac industrialist Hugo Drax, from California to the Amazon jungle and finally to a space station from which Drax intends to dominate the world.

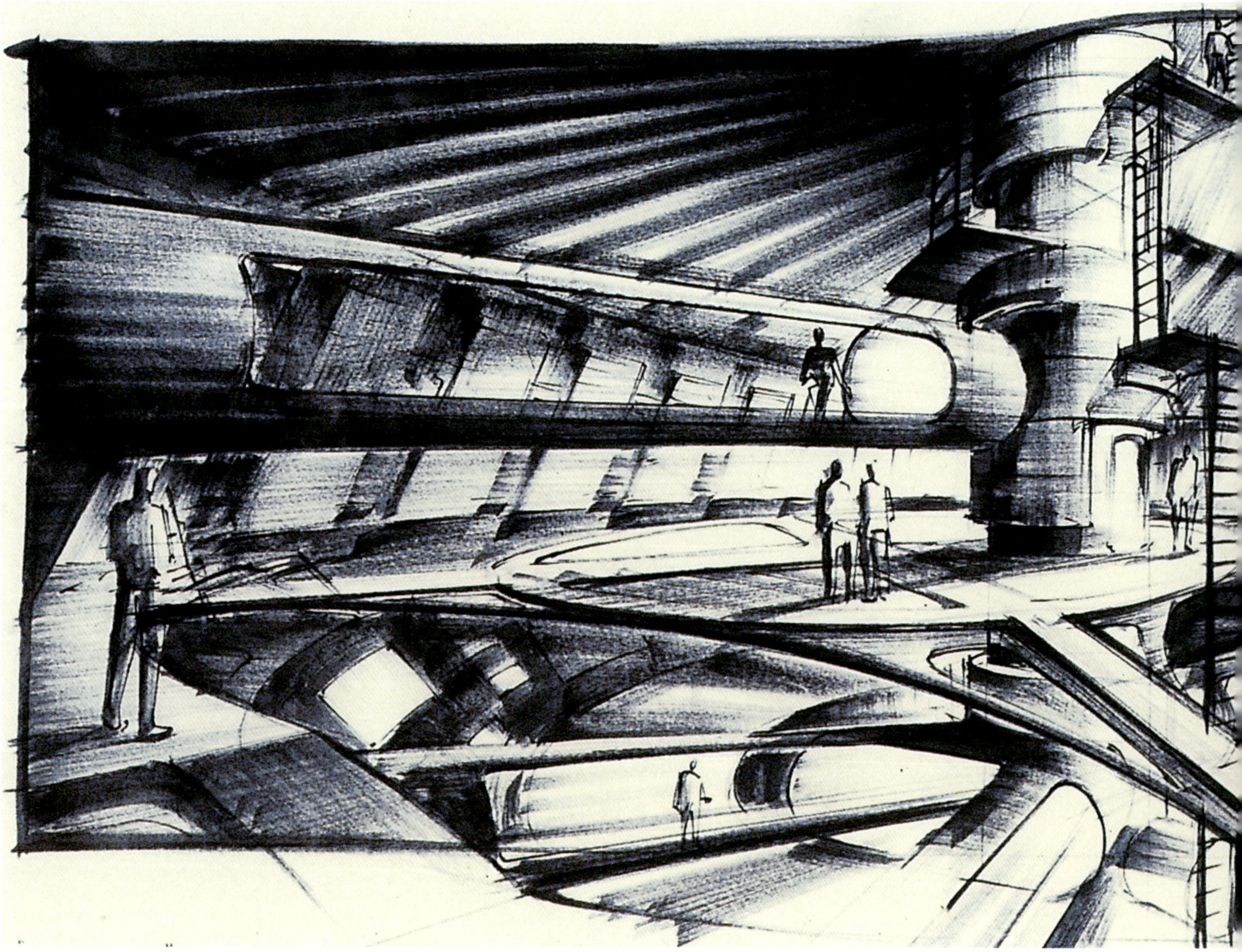

The interior of the space station command centre 1978
Final concept
41.5 × 59 cm

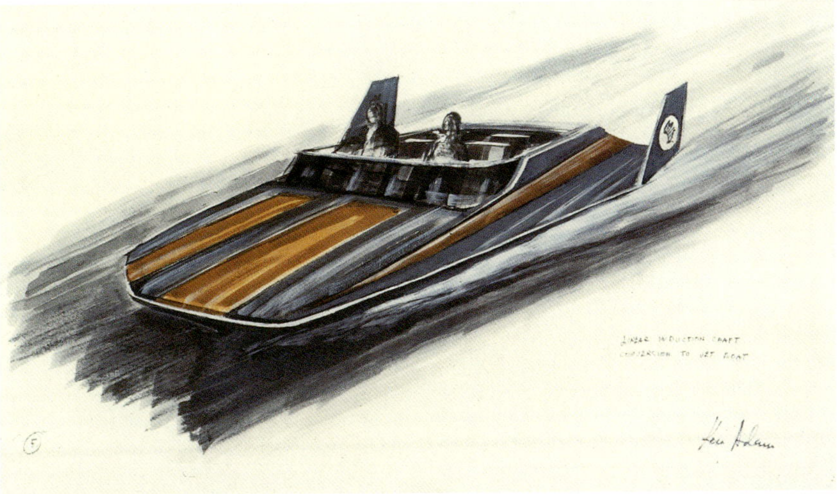

Speedboat 1978. Final concept
Pen and watercolour on paper
c. 38 × 59 cm

Top:
The centrifuge 1978
Final concept
42 × 59.5 cm

Middle:
The Great Chamber 1978
Final concept
41.5 × 59.5 cm

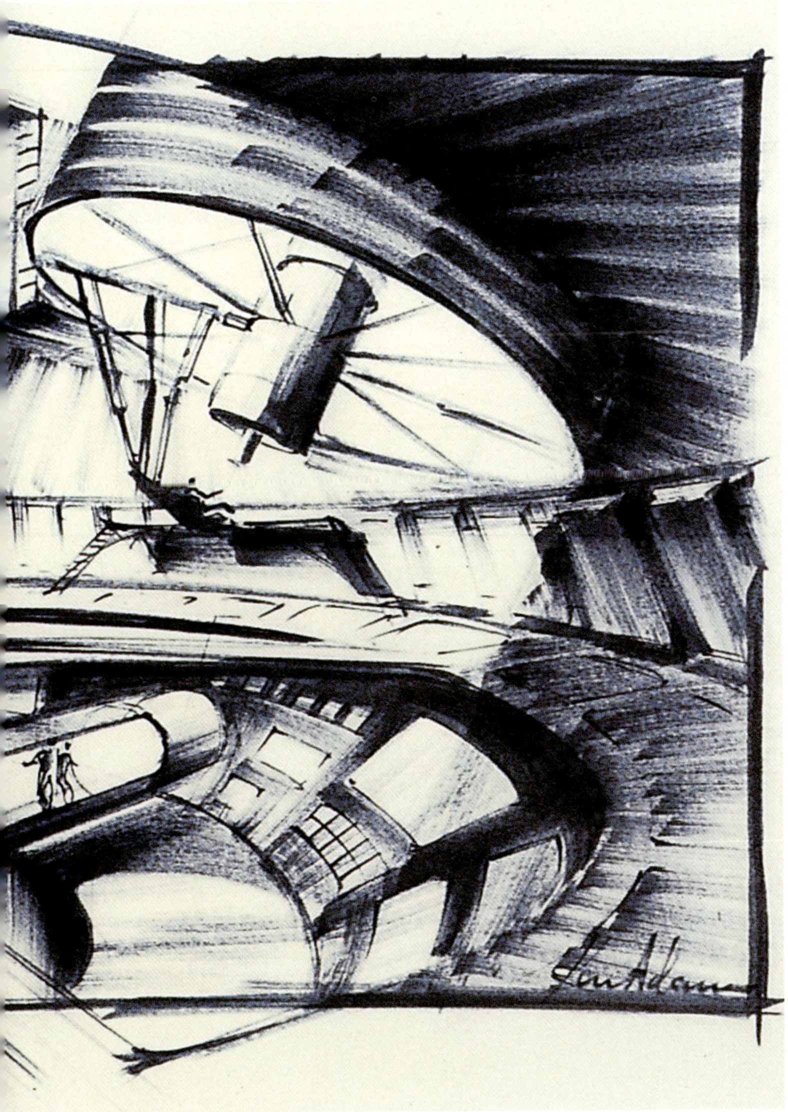

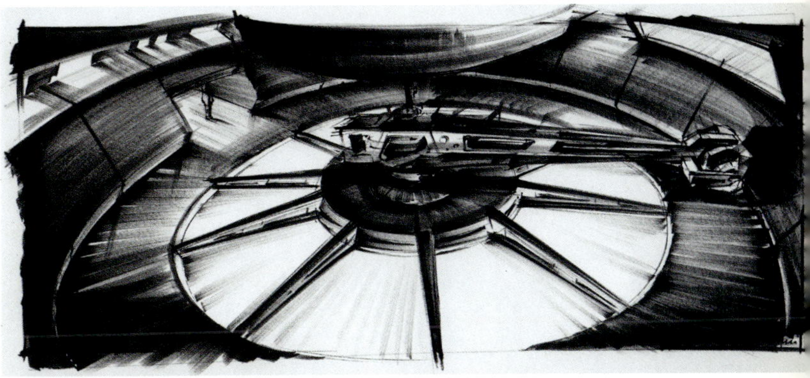

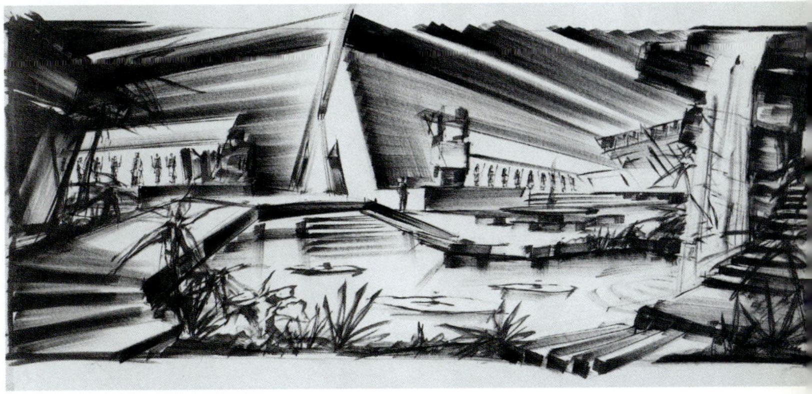

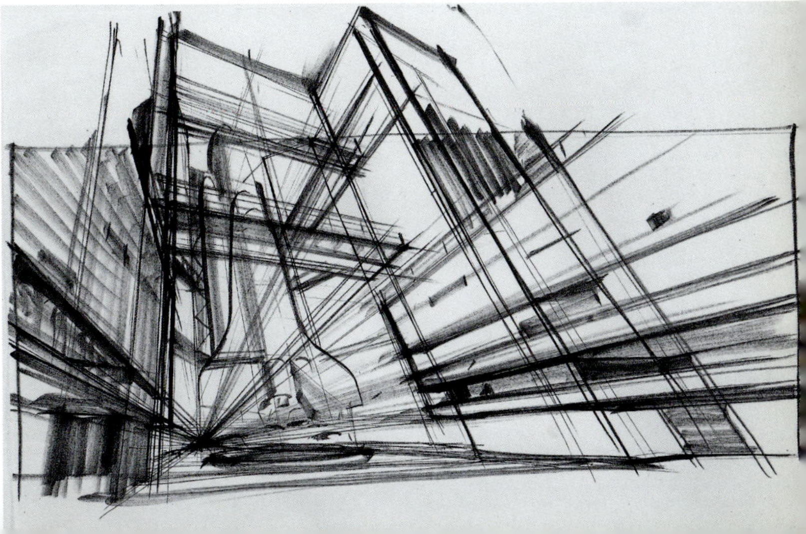

The space shuttle launch pad 1978
Study
42 × 58 cm

Moonraker was the biggest, most complex film I've ever worked on, with up to four separate units shooting all over the world at once, plus all those special effects! We shot combinations of real locations, full-scale mock-ups, partial mockups, and miniatures in a number of sequences, and they cut together quite well. But it was a logistics nightmare. For tax reasons we had to shoot most of our interiors in Paris where there wasn't very much stage space. As soon as we'd finish on a set it would have to be struck and a new one built in its place. This meant having to go on location a lot. In fact on *Moonraker* we shot more location interiors than on any previous Bond.

We found the chateaux in and around Paris, and used the Pompidou Centre for part of the Drax Complex, including Holly's office. We shot locations in Brazil and Venice, where we used various boats and gondolas I designed for the chase through the canals. Interiors for many locations were precise, including the Vennini Glass Museum; but, obviously, the key to the whole picture was the space station.

The copy line everyone was using around the time of Moonraker*'s release was, 'This film isn't science fiction, it's science fact.' How does that apply towards a space station?*

Before I designed our space station, I spent some time at NASA, looking at their conceptual designs for real ones. But when I actually designed our station, I departed sharply from their futuristic concepts, because Stanley Kubrick had already used the wheel in *2001*. I thought it would be a difficult thing for interior settings because it's rather like shooting inside a bicycle tyre. NASA had another concept, a series of cylinders which would be bolted together in space. But that was rather boring, visually. So I compromised. I still used the cylinder idea, but I designed the space station like a mobile, in a completely irregular form, so that once it begins to rotate the audience gets a different composition from each angle. **JD**

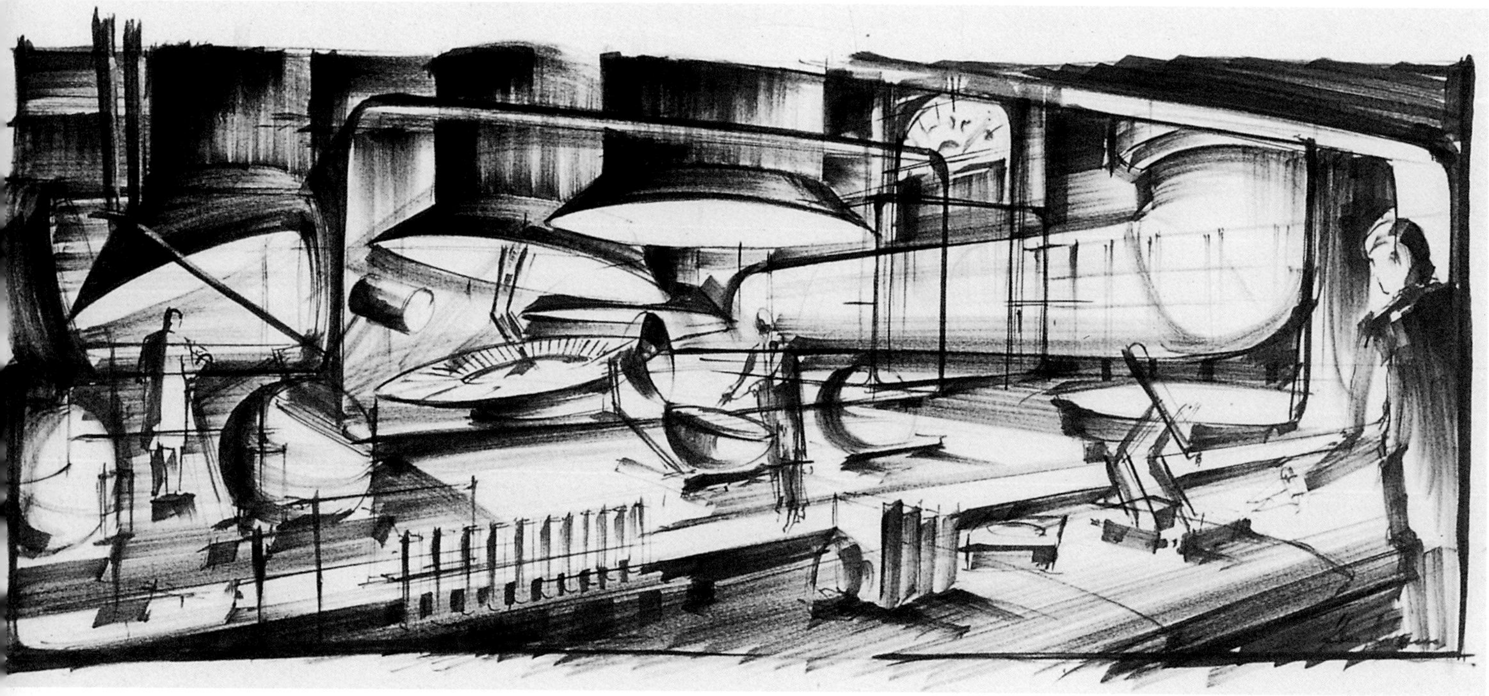

The Drax laboratory in Venice 1978
Final concept
41 × 59.5 cm

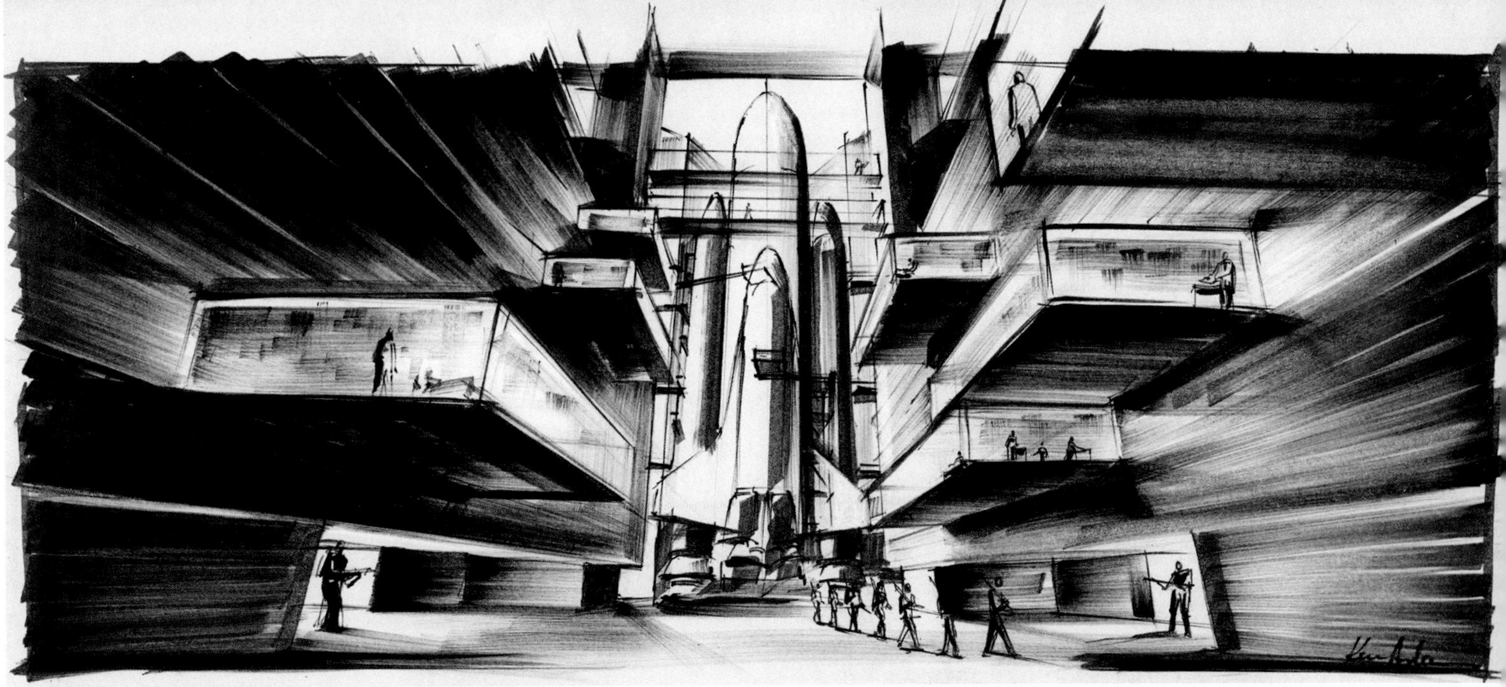

The space shuttle launch pad 1978
Study
32 × 56.5 cm

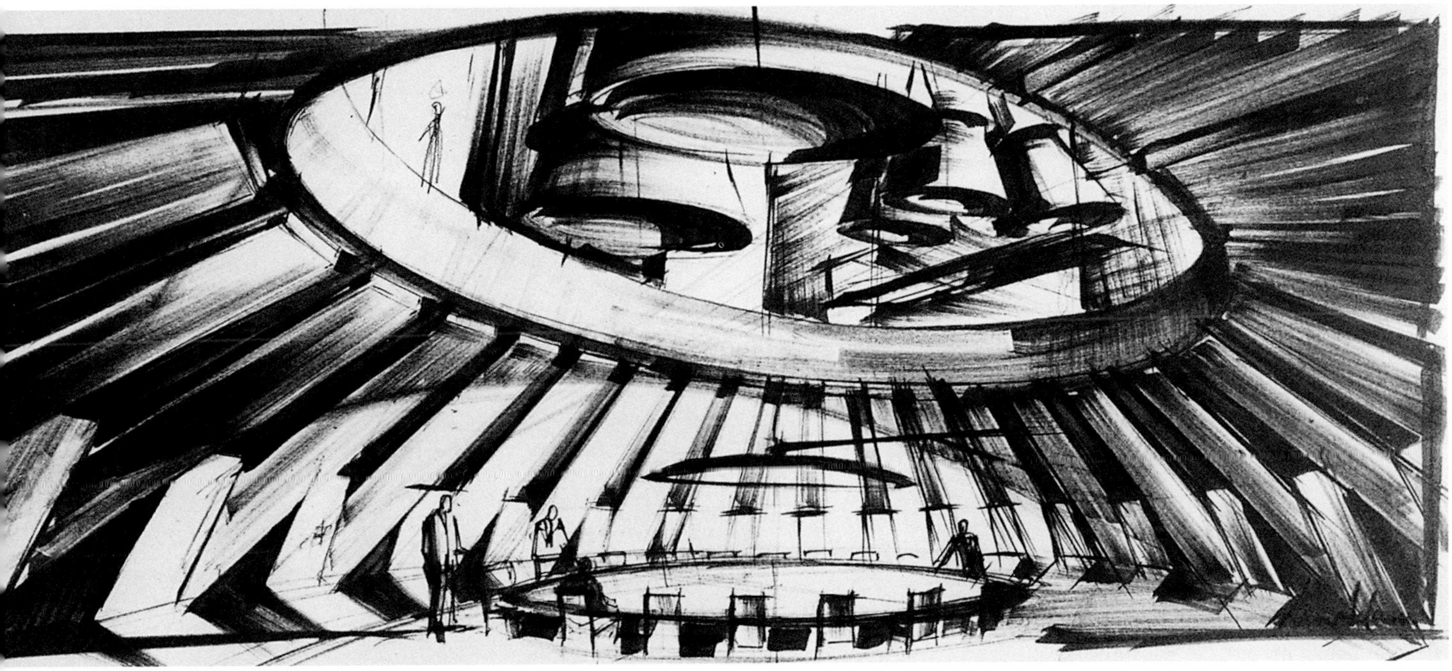

The exhaust chamber
1978
Final concept
c. 35 × 56 cm

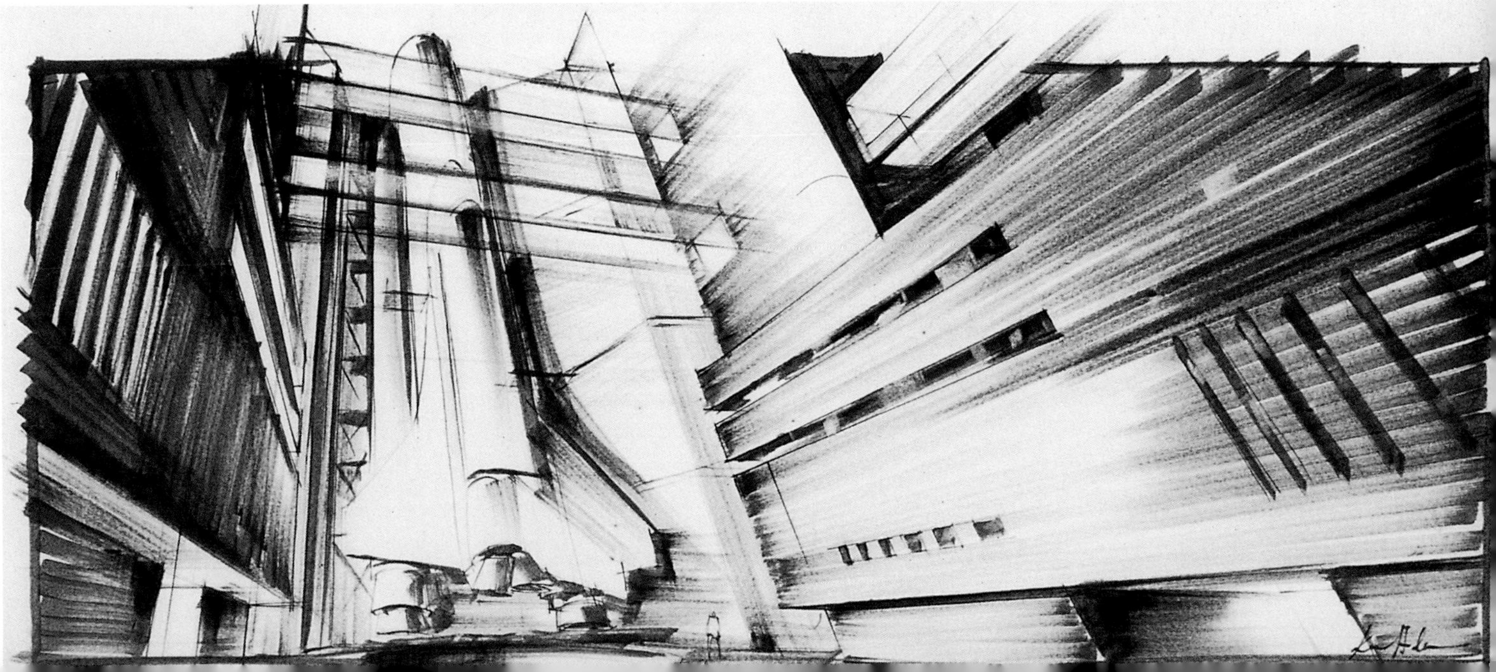

The space shuttle launch pad 1978
Final concept
42 × 58 cm

Pennies from Heaven

Musical drama, directed by Herb Ross, that transports to Chicago Dennis Potter's BBC television series about life in the depressed 1930s, in which the cast mime to period performances of popular songs. An unhappily married sheet-music salesman makes a naïve schoolteacher pregnant. Wrongly accused and convicted of murdering a blind girl, he is executed.

It wasn't originally intended to be shot entirely at the studio, but that's the way it worked out. Because of severe budgetary restrictions, all the scenes we were going to shoot on location in Chicago were brought back to MGM. I built part of the Loop area on a sound stage, and though I questioned having to do that at first, I'm convinced now it was the right choice. In the end, having to shoot everything at Metro was stylistically correct.

We had innumerable battles because I strongly believed all the time that we had to start off with a big number, to set the tone up a few notches from the depressing mood the film sets during the first few minutes. So we start off with a big dance number in the bank, which I think will be wonderful. I think the dance numbers will provide a relief, when we open up the sets both physically and through lighting.

The bank set is Bondian in proportions.

Its size was a big bone of contention. In the BBC series the film is based on, the scene took place in the manager's office of a small provincial bank in England. For the film, the story was re-set in Chicago, though it was still kept in the thirties, so I went there looking for locations and photographed a number of banks from the period. They were enormous, neo-classic palaces. I finally made my point when I showed the photos I had taken to Herb and Dennis Potter (author of both mini-series and film). They agreed that it was the right sort of concept.

I designed a bank, then we had arguments over whether it should be bigger or smaller, but I stuck to my original concept again. I also wanted to introduce an Art Deco element into the film, rather than going for the neo-classic style I had seen. The Board of Trade Building in Chicago has a lovely Art Deco feeling, so I used that for our bank exterior, and the whole thing became a marble cathedral to the power of money. I thought it was important to see the contrast of the Depression and this monument.

There are a number of smaller, more intimate sets in the picture, like the flop house, the movie theatre interior, and the hotel bedroom with its imaginary elevator for lovemaking.

Those were designed for dual purposes, fantasy and reality, as was the major set we built, the 'el' street. We shot a number of scenes there with our characters and planned to do a big hooker number, but the transformation of the el to the hooker street and the number itself were cut for budgetary reasons.

The street looks very real, not as stylised as the rest of the major sets.

That was a major concern to everyone. No one thought it would be possible to obtain a believable exterior feeling on a sound stage. The reality of an actual street was elusive, but with our superb craftsmen and painters I think we managed to get it. The street was designed for interiors and exteriors, and included Arthur's record shop, the *Nighthawks* bar and the cinema. Herb was particularly keen on some of the painters of that period, like Reginald Marsh and Edward Hopper. So I incorporated Marsh's *A Movie Theater* and Hopper's *Nighthawks* bar into the street. The employment agency and the pawnshop came from photographs by Walker Evans, and a second-floor fur shop was also included. It became a jigsaw puzzle of varying artists of the period. **JD**

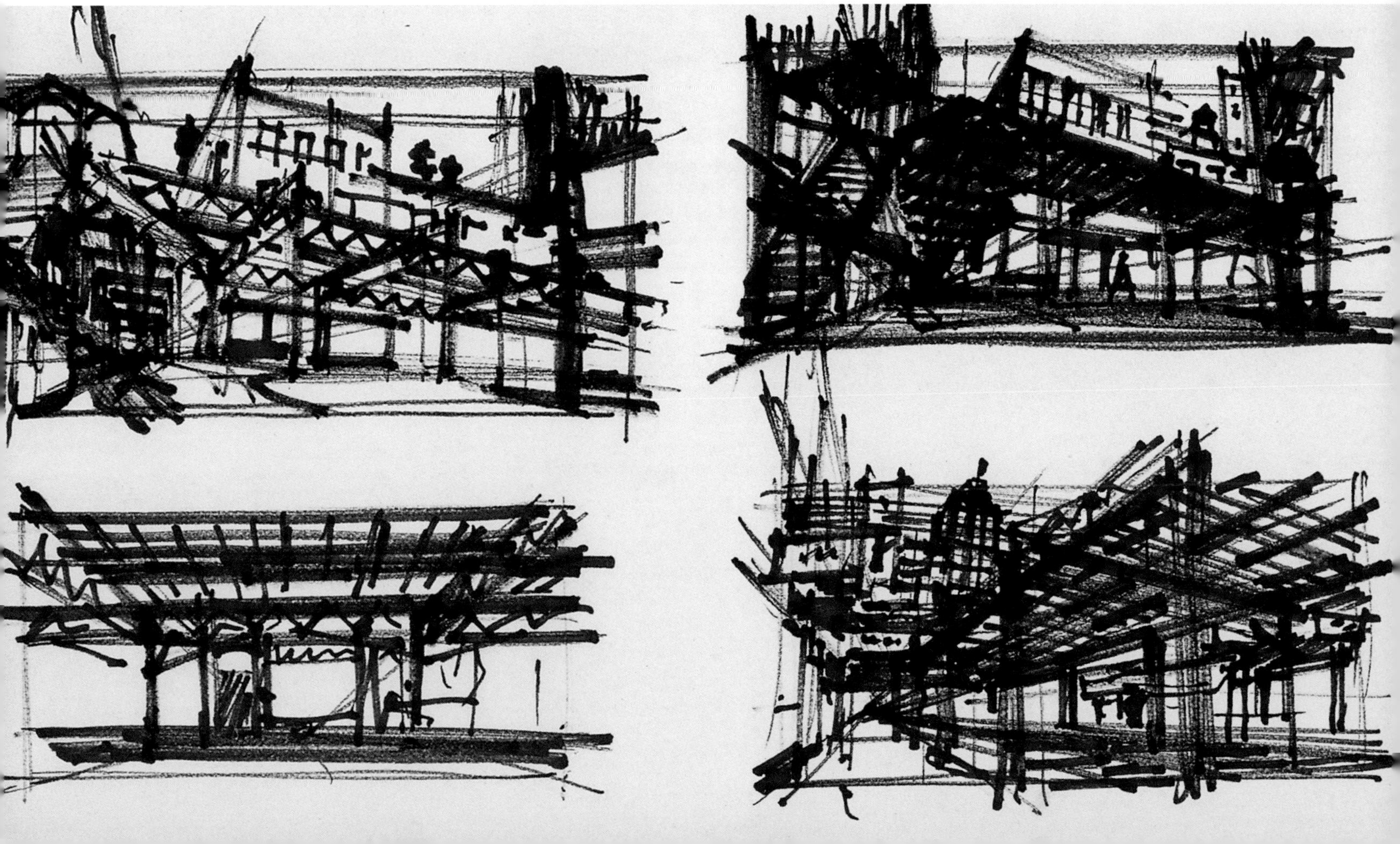

'El' street intersection, Chicago 1980
Studies
21 × 29.5 cm

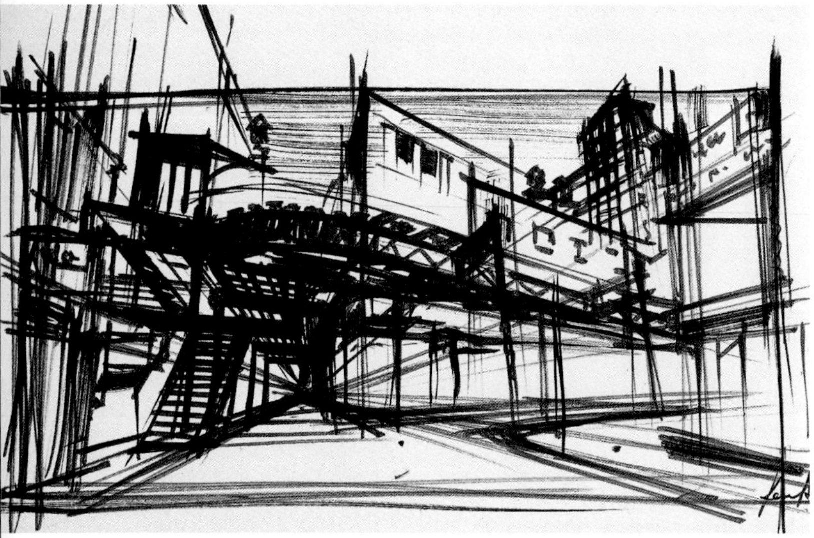

'El' street intersection, Chicago 1980
Study
c. 38 × 55 cm

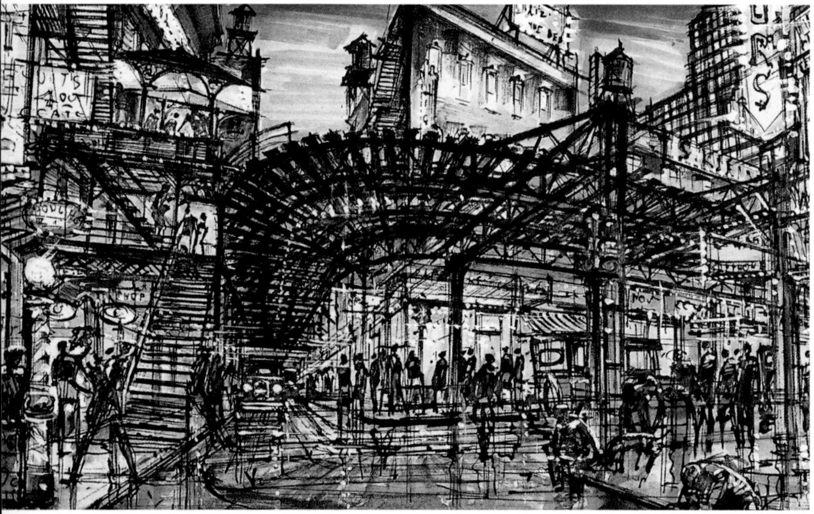

'El' street intersection, Chicago 1980
Final concept
38 × 55 cm

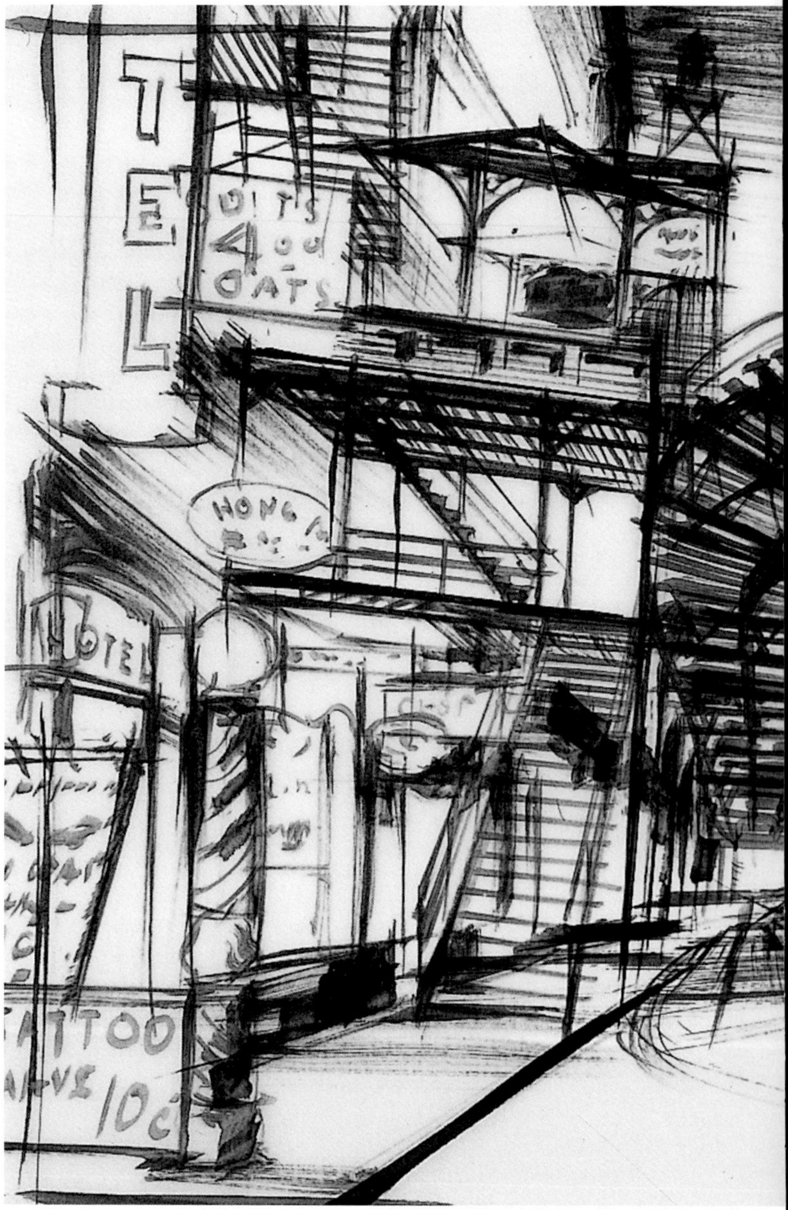

'El' street intersection, Chicago 1980
Final concept
Colour felt-tip pen on paper
20.5 × 40.5 cm

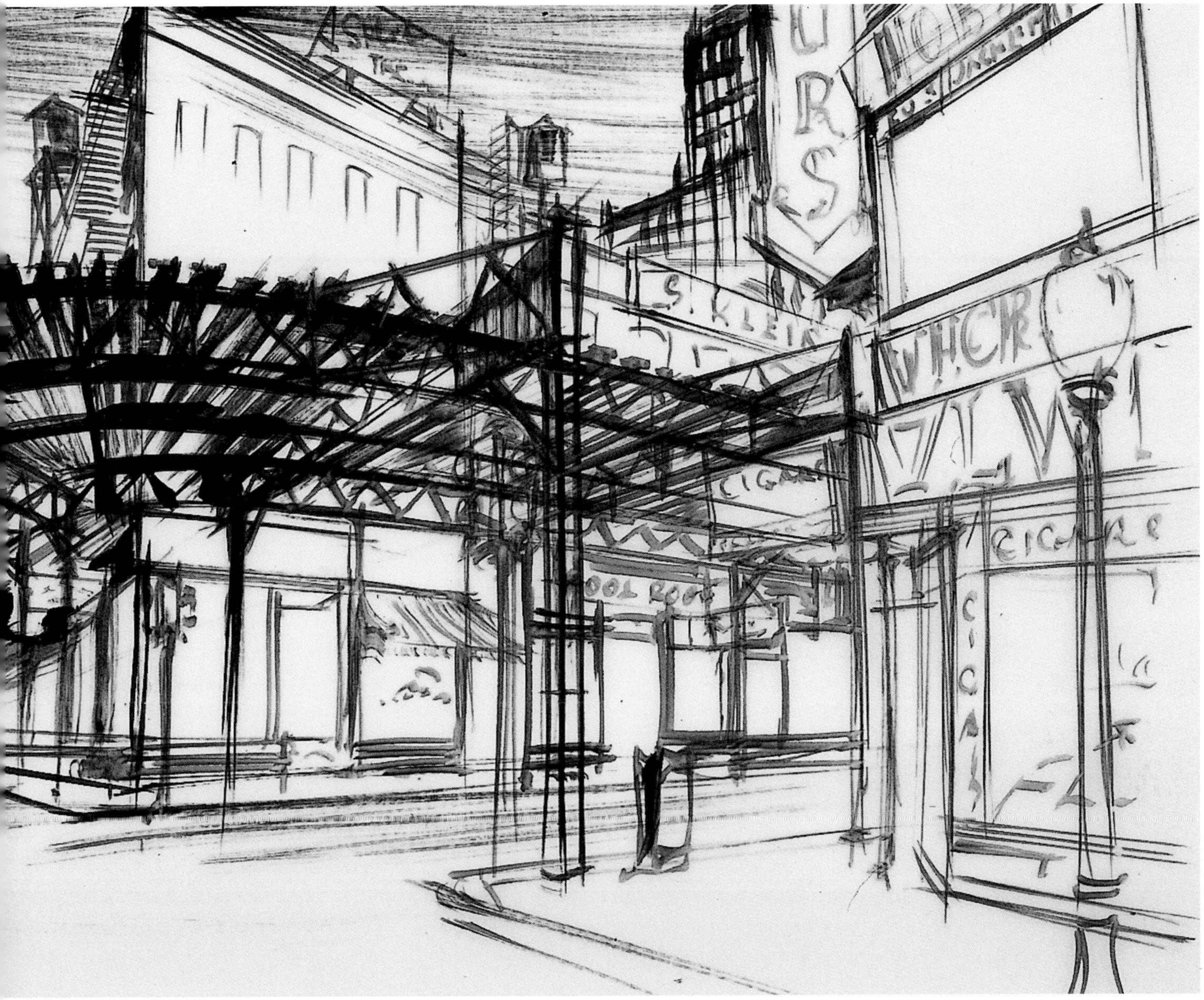

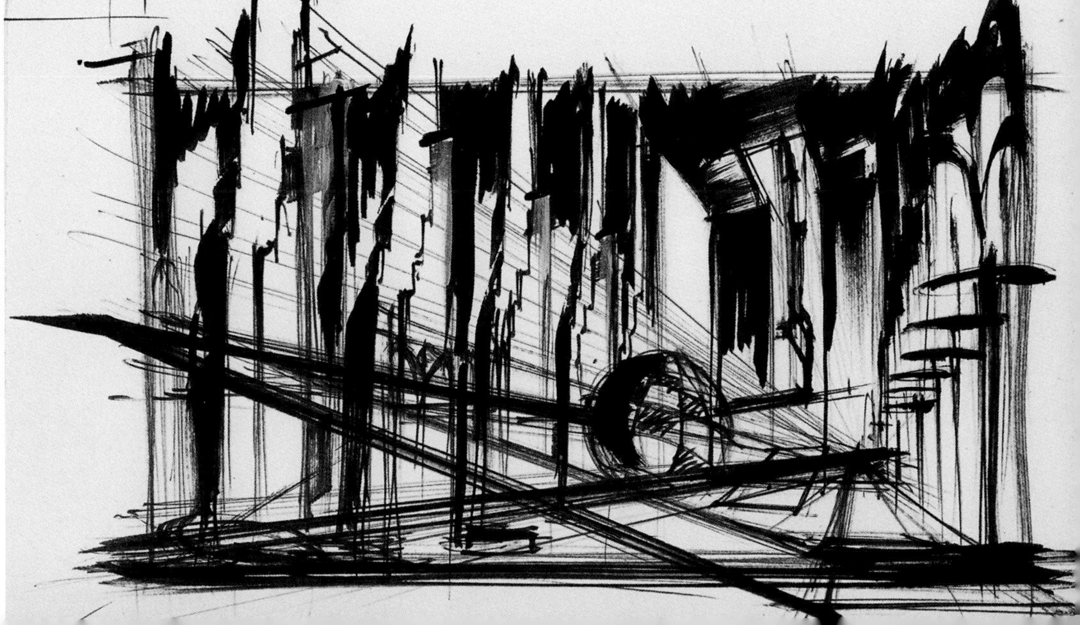

The bank interior 1980
Study
c. 22 × 31.5 cm

1981–82

A Special Project for Twentieth Century-Fox

I worked for I suppose a year at Twentieth Century-Fox in Los Angeles and the idea was to come up with some scheme for a multimedia theatre. Fox were basing the concept on the old movie palaces of the twenties where you had the most flamboyant architecture and decor and you entertained the public not only with one film but sometimes with two films or the famous Wurlitzer organ or even stage acts like a vaudeville. So I finally come up with an inflatable structure which was reasonably economical to build and could be erected quite quickly and all over the United States provided you found an empty lot with a good parking area: the parking area was the key to where these structures would be built.

I also designed the interior of a space station so that the public would go through this before entering the Imax cinema. I did a lot of research with the Canadians, who had invented the Imax, which was already in use at that time and had a fantastic 70mm widescreen process. So that was the main purpose of the Special Project. I also did research with NASA's jet propulsion lab and with Caltech.

Then Dennis Potter was asked to write the first screenplay for this new type of cinema. It was basically about a spaceship sent into the universe and on this spaceship there were, I don't know, 500 or a 1000 embryos because a trip to that new planet would take about twenty years. And then that spaceship on its journey is hit by some electric storm or asteroid or something, and all things are short-circuited and half the embryos turn out to be villains whereas the other half turn out to be good. They finally arrive at a planet which turns out to be our planet at the time of Adam and Eve.

We started taking on staff and it became really the talking point of Los Angeles. The head of Fox was a man called Marvyn Davis and my boss was a film producer called Danny Melnick, a very flamboyant character. There was a disagreement between them which resulted in the shelving of our project. **SG**

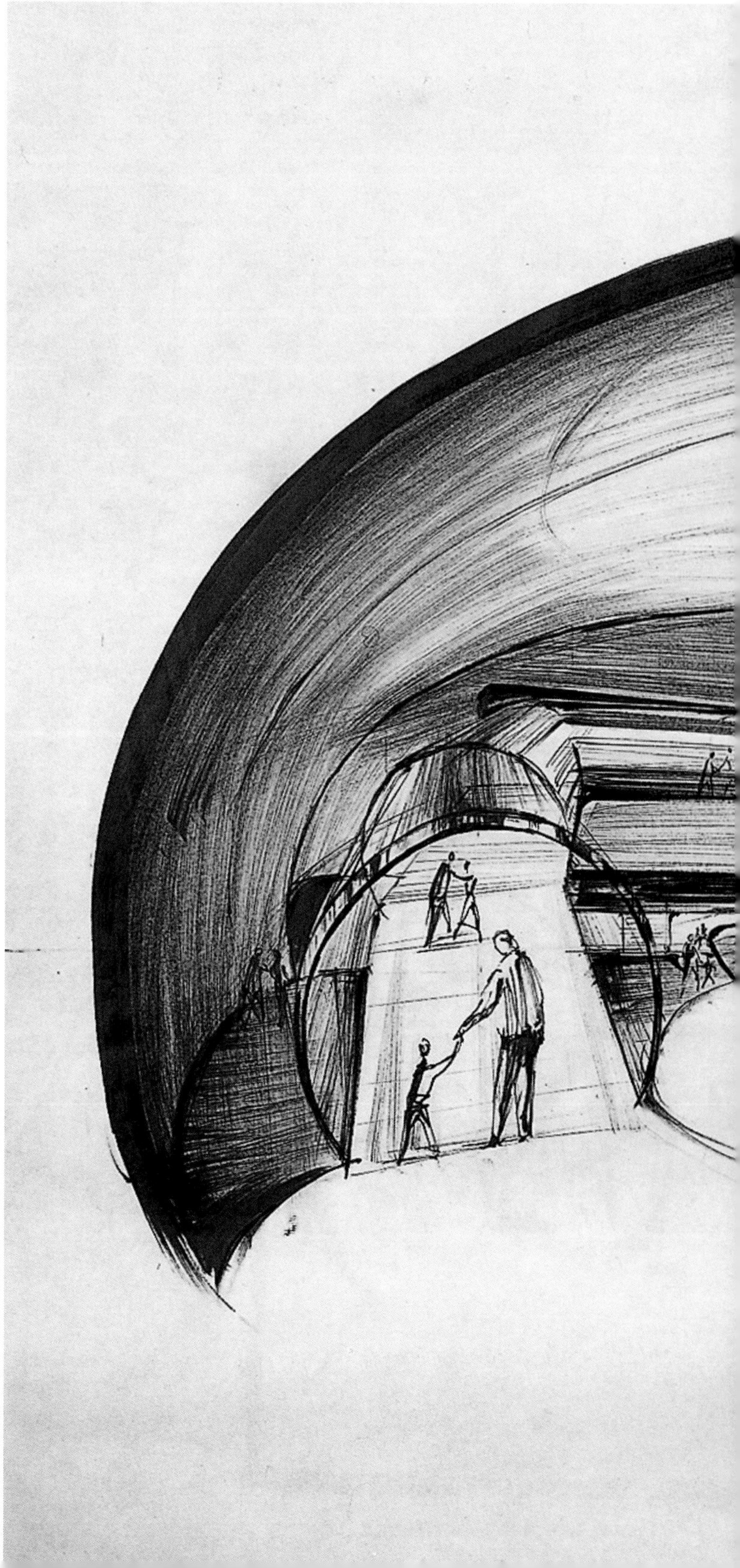

Interior of the lobby in the multimedia complex 1981
Study
48 × 61 cm

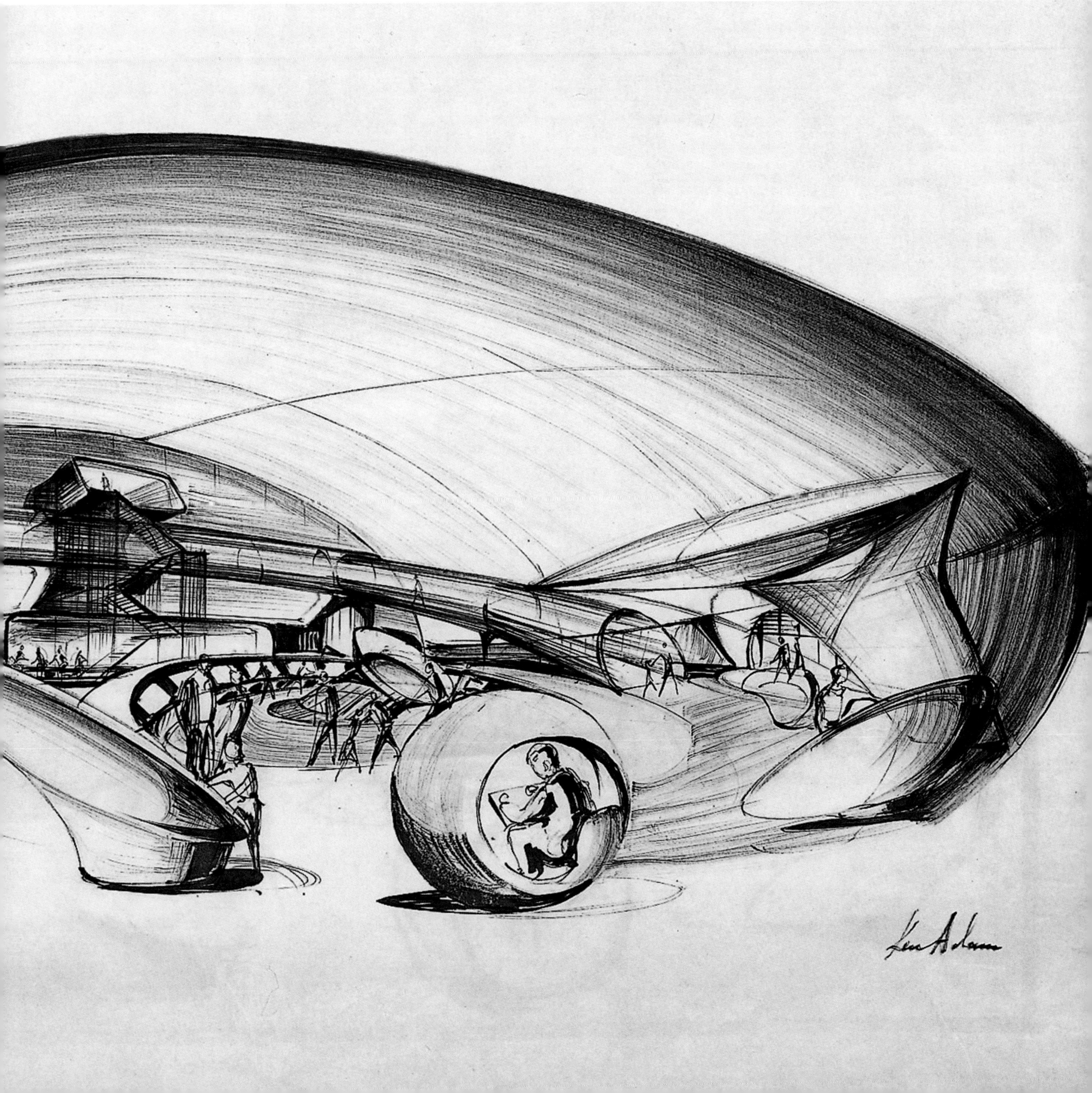

King David

Biblical biopic, made in Italy by Bruce Beresford, tracing the career of David, the shepherd boy who is brought into the court of King Saul, at the insistence of the prophet Samuel, and succeeds him as King of Israel.

Finding the exteriors we needed in Italy, we didn't have to go to Israel or North Africa. I found this incredible town built into a canyon called Matera which Pasolini had used for *The Gospel According to St Matthew*. Matera is reputed to be one of the oldest cities in the world. It goes back five, six thousand years and you can see the varying periods like cave dwellings going through to medieval times. In some places we found beautiful frescoes from the twelfth century and you could have cut them out and taken them home. Nobody cared. I decided to use Matera for Jerusalem and I constructed the walls and tower and the entrance gate to the city. Nearby I found a disused quarry which I then used as one of the other cities. The area around Matera was owned by an oil company and when I scouted it the first time it looked absolutely like a desert. It was in summer and I said, Why go to Tunisia or places like Morocco? We can shoot here. The only problem was they had so much rain during the winter that the next spring when we started filming, there was suddenly an explosion of flora, of every kind of flower you could imagine. I had my painter with a tanker full of brown paint spraying areas by kilometres, you know, to get rid of that thing, I mean it was just unbelievable. The film was an enormous challenge for me and I decided to do it not like a biblical picture that we had been used to with all the glamour. You remember this is around a thousand years before Christ so I wanted to do make it really primitive. **SG**

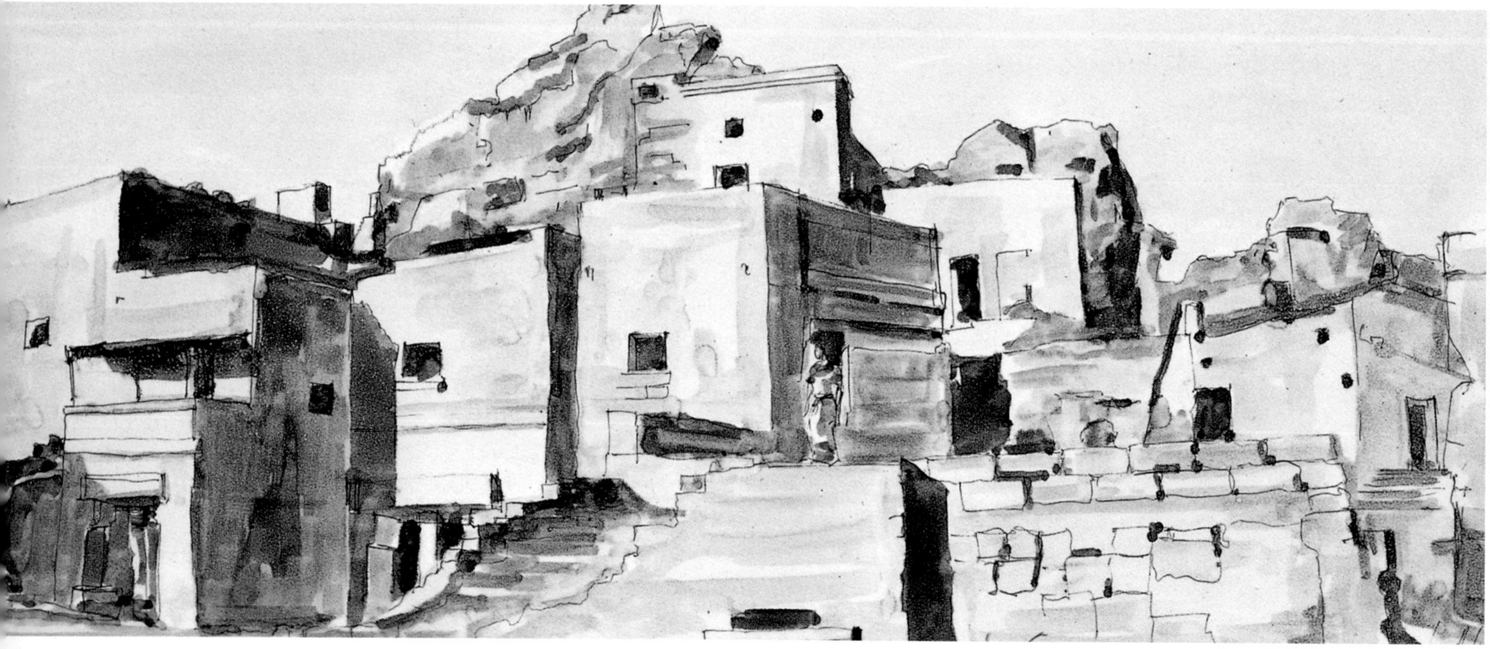

Jerusalem 1984
Study
Felt-tip pen and watercolour on paper
c. 18.5 × 30 cm

Saul's citadel 1984
Final concept
Felt-tip pen and watercolour on paper
c. 18.5 × 30 cm

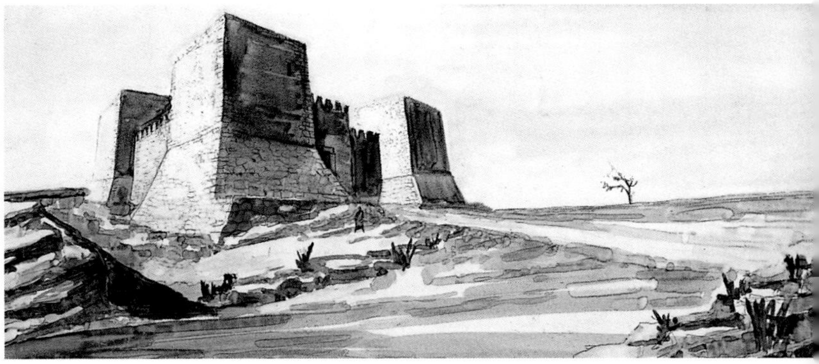

Matera, Italy, and the design for its proposed conversion into Jerusalem
1984
Final concept
Photograph and felt-tip pen and watercolour on paper
18.5 × 40 cm (image size)

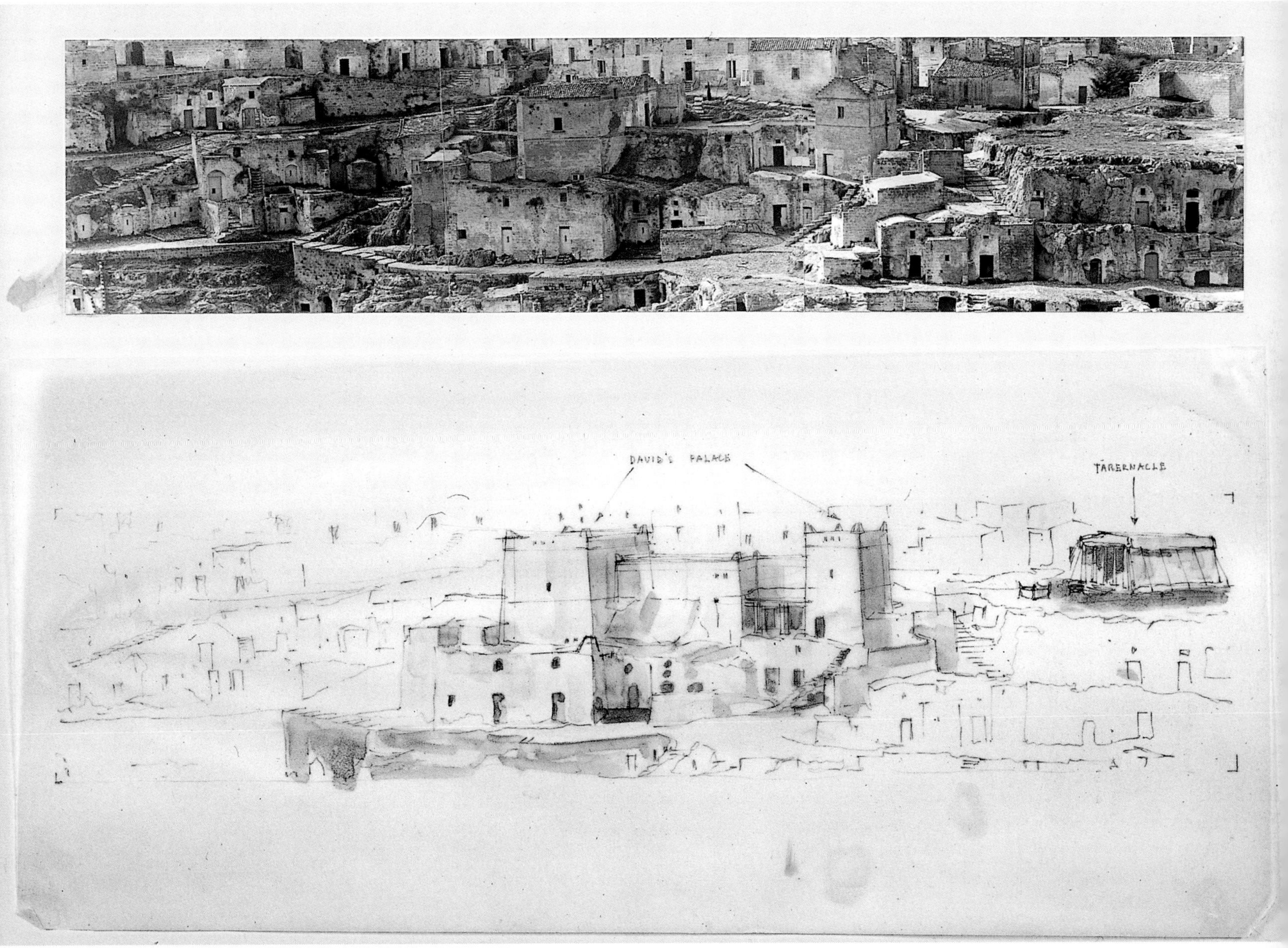

1985

Agnes of God

Religious drama, directed by Norman Jewison. A female psychiatrist – a divorced lapsed Catholic – is appointed by a Quebec court to report on the mental state of a novice, Sister Agnes, accused of strangling her newborn baby in her cell at a Montreal convent. She comes into conflict with the Mother Superior, who tuns out to be Agnes's aunt.

It was an exciting project because we were working with some great actresses: Jane Fonda, who I'd worked with before, Anne Bancroft, with whom I hadn't, and who was a delightful person, and Meg Tilly, who was one of the most charming young actresses I ever worked with. And Jewison was in very good form and everybody was fascinated by the story. What was amazing was that the majority of the actresses who played the nuns finally imagined themselves as nuns and we could not accept them when we met them in normal dress. It was incredible. The liturgical music and the Latin Mass became a part of all of us.

The main site was a disused school near Toronto, to which I had to add a bell tower and cloisters, besides rebuilding interiors. A number of exterior locations were filmed in Montreal, as was the apartment used as Jane Fonda's apartment. The remaining interiors were filmed in sets built in a studio near Toronto.

The sequence in which some of the nuns were skating on an ice rink was something that Norman got me to direct. I was up on a 70-foot tower, and getting there was difficult enough, but asking people to give me extra clothing was too much; I was too proud. Looking through the camera it was incredible to see these women in their black nun cloaks skating. Without the confines of the skating area, you just saw them gliding on white ice that seemed to go on for ever. **SG**

Convent room 1984
Study
20 × 35 cm

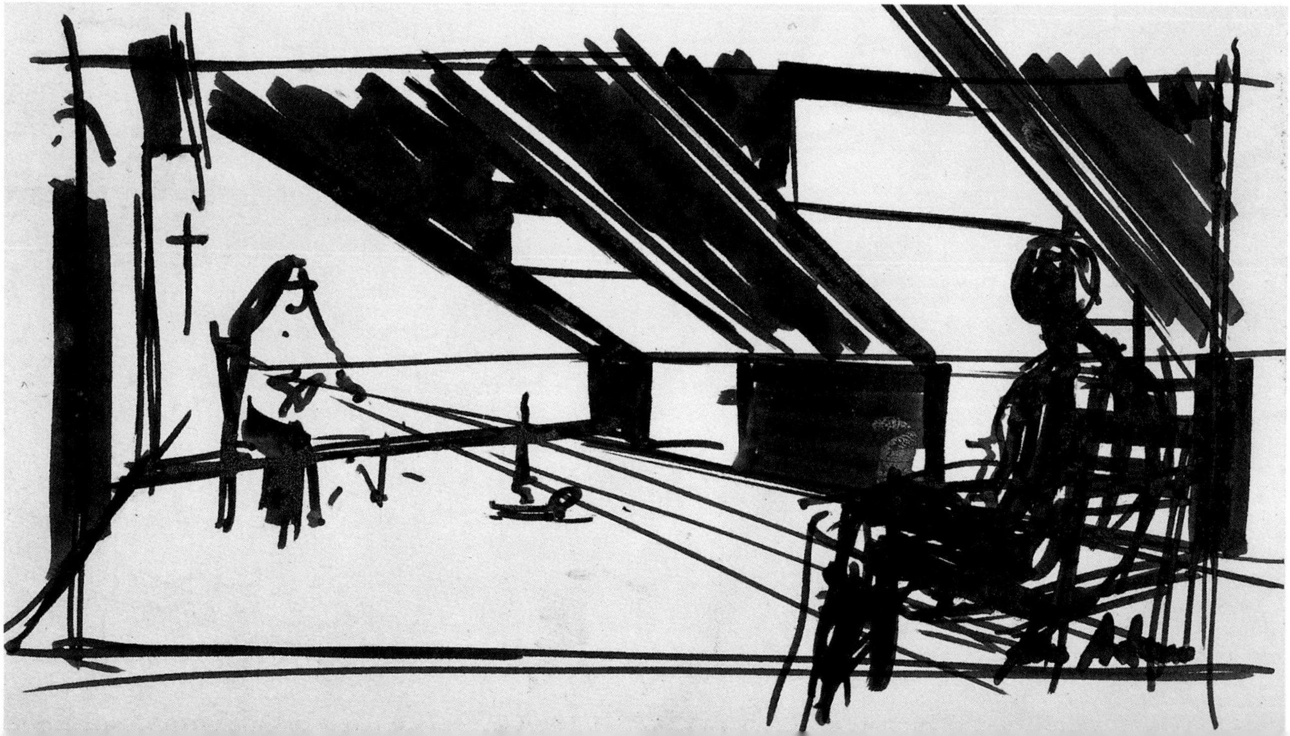

The Last Emperor

I was approached by Jeremy Thomas, the producer, and met Bertolucci and we all got on like a house on fire. I think I worked on the project for nine or ten months. The three of us spent four weeks in China, going through locations. We had a large number of meetings with the authorities in Beijing and we also, in what was quite a dramatic incident, took the Emperor's brother, who had survived him, back to the Forbidden City where he grew up, and hadn't been since he was a little boy. They were pretty receptive and gave permission to shoot in the Forbidden City, which had never happened before. Back in England I started coming up with the conceptual designs and eventually set up an art department in Rome where we were going to do the studio work.

But Jeremy had serious problems in finding finance. He was only coming up with a hundred thousand here and a hundred thousand there. As the future of the project seemed very unsure, I went to New York for 36 hours to discuss another project – after checking with Jeremy. When I got back I found a telex from Bernardo, from Beijing, saying he didn't want me on the picture. And so I packed up all my stuff in Italy and came back to London. It was very unfortunate: it should have never happened and I think all three of us regretted it ever did happen. I got an incredibly nice letter from Bernardo written on a 747 flying back from Beijing, but by this time it was too late. **SG**

Imperial Palace Corridor 1985
Presentation drawing, final concept
Felt-tip pen and coloured ink wash on paper
25 × 42 cm

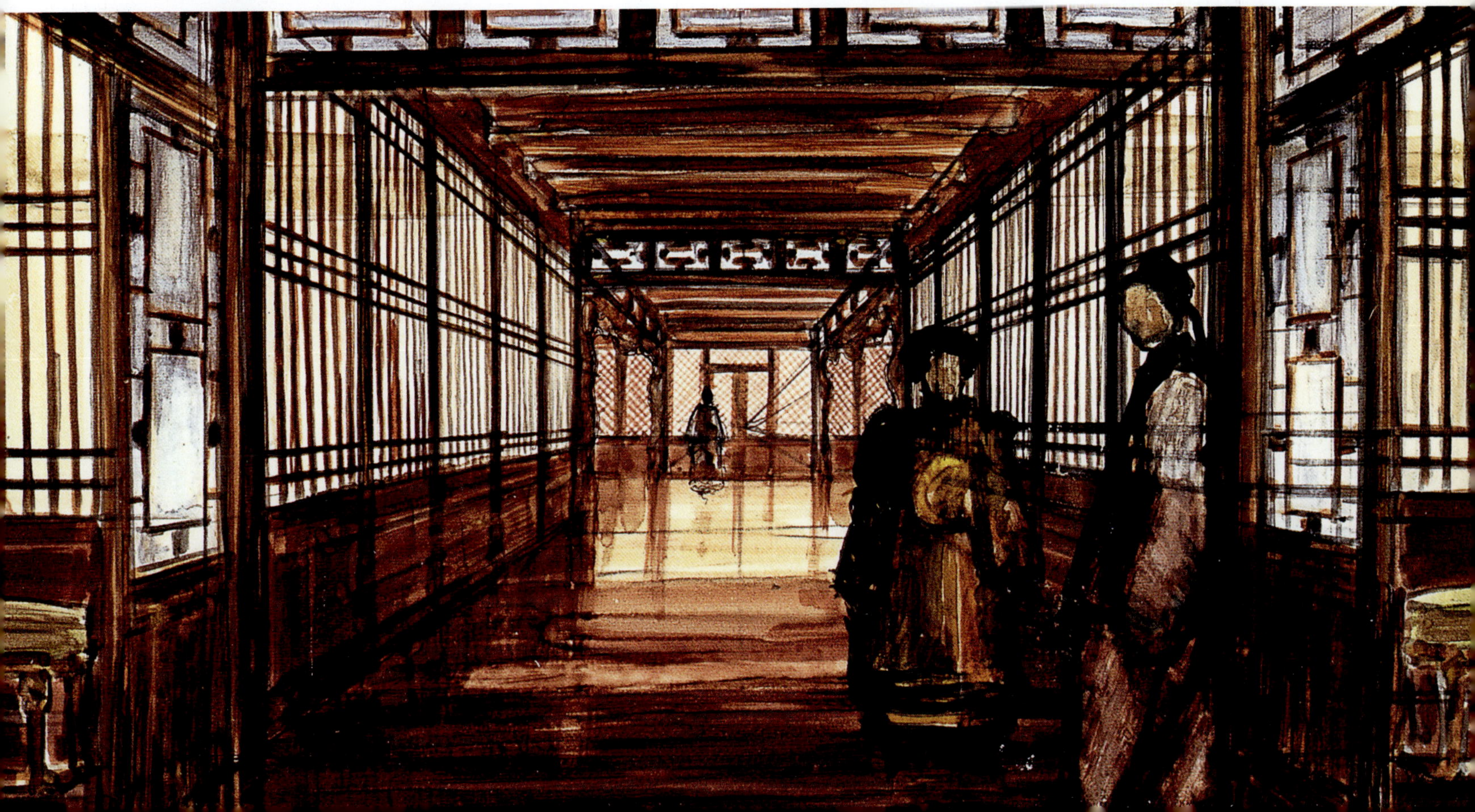

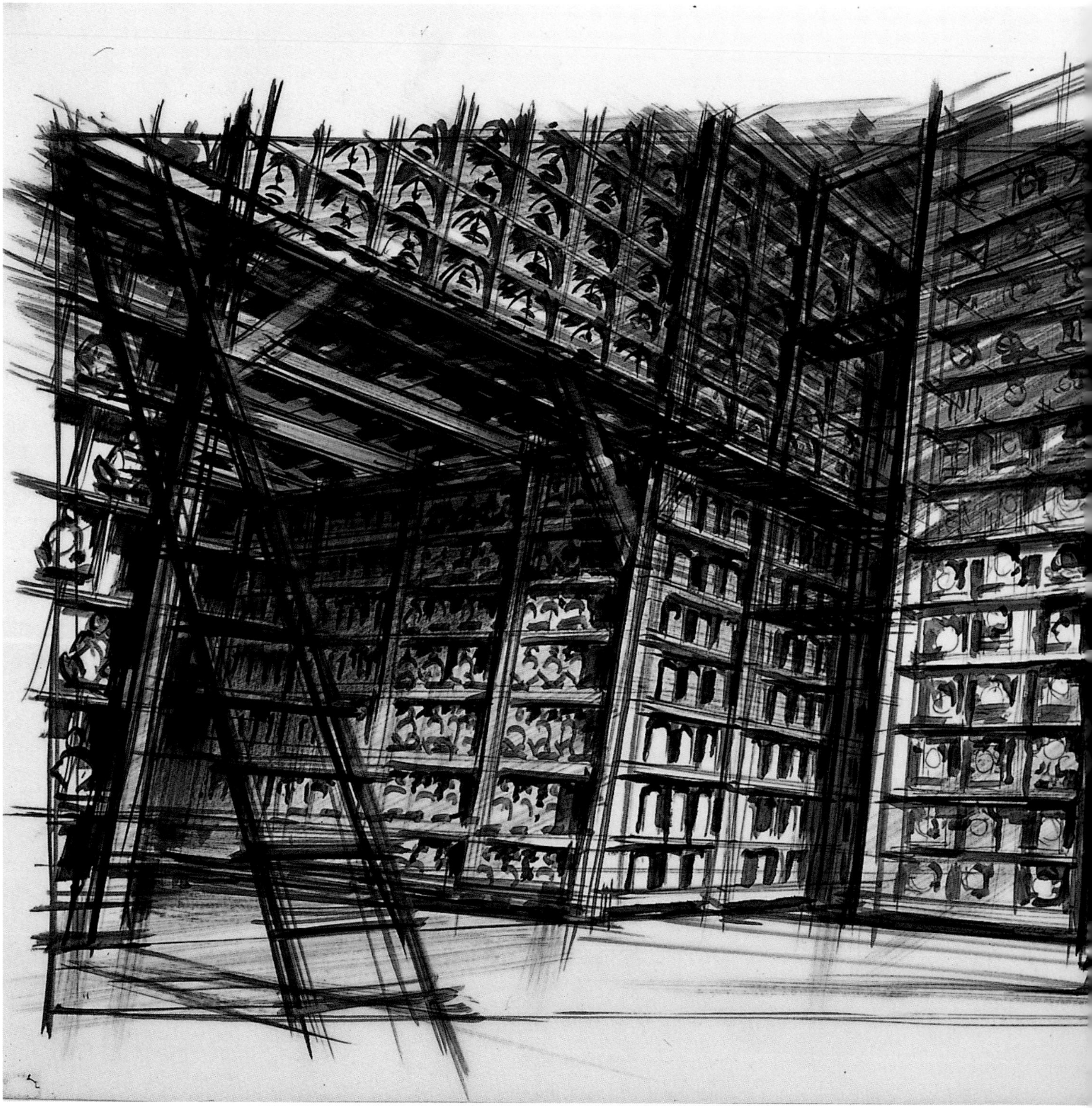

Storage chamber 1985
Final concept
30 × 49 cm

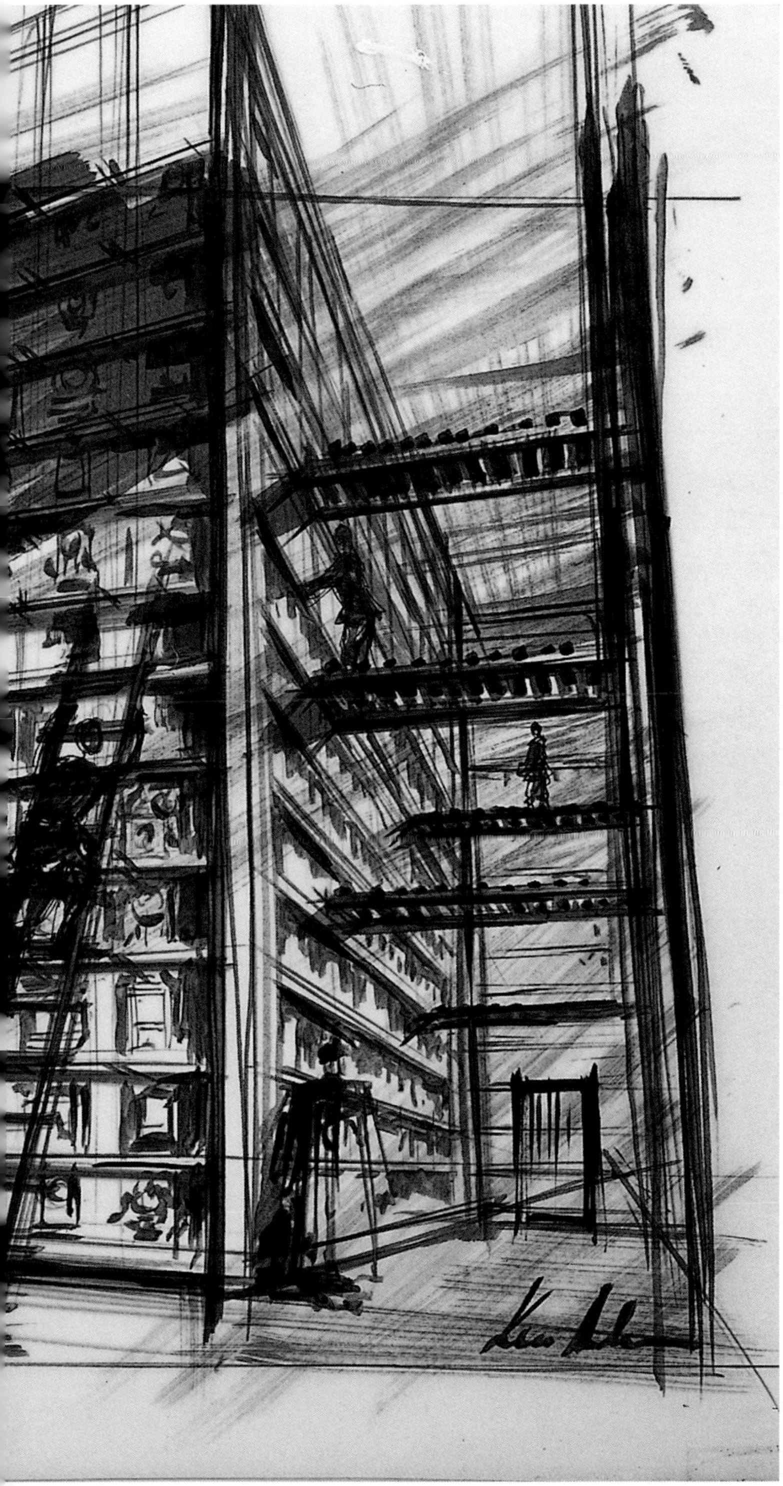

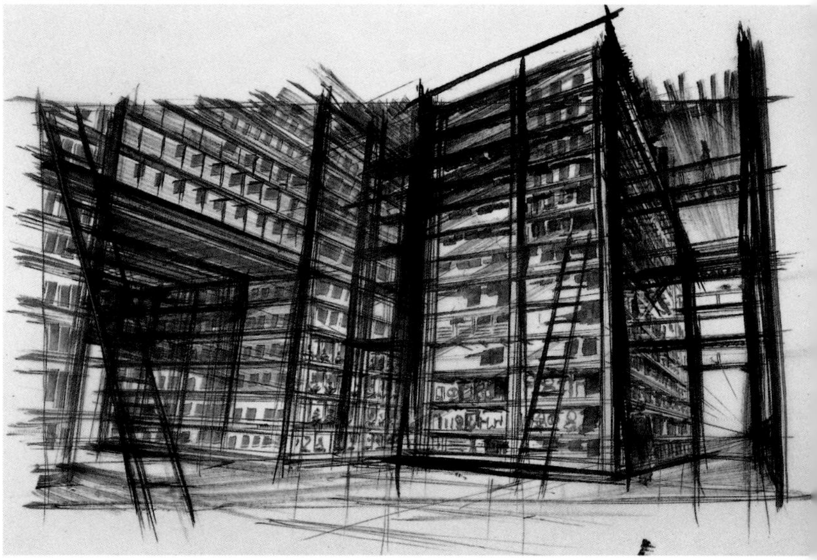

Storage chamber 1985
Initial concept
39.5 × 56 cm

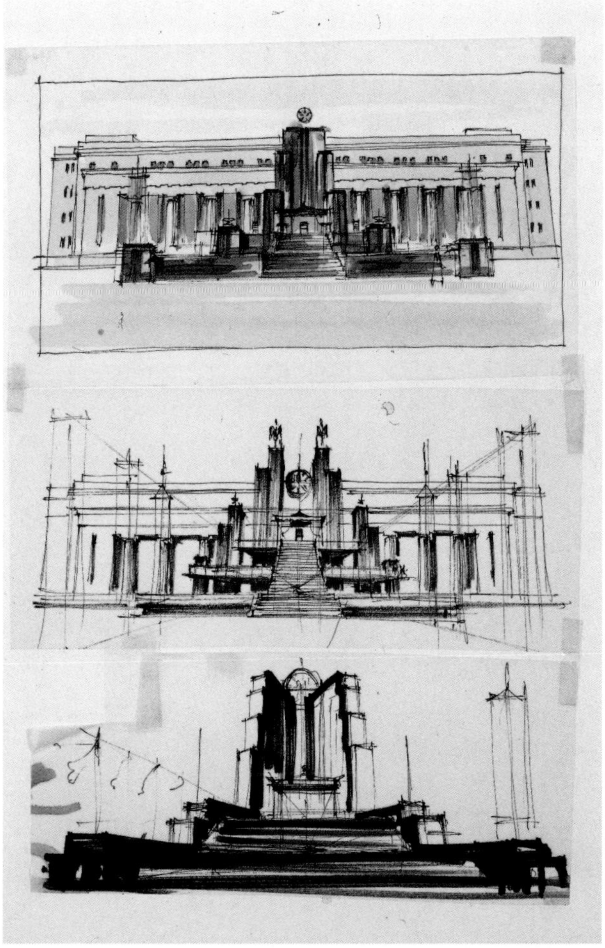

Setting for the puppet coronation in Manchuria 1985
Studies
Felt-tip pen and watercolour on paper
12 × 20.5 cm, 9.5 × 20.5 cm, 8.5 × 19 cm

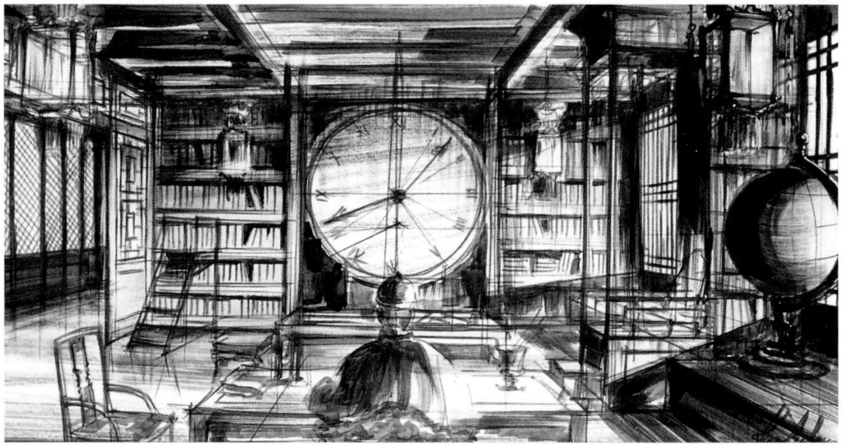

Puji's study 1985
Final concept
29 × 49 cm

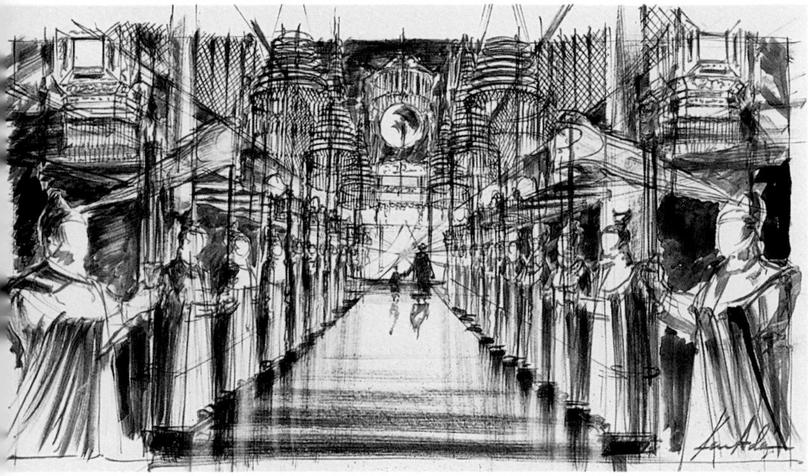

Puji visiting the dying Dowager Empress 1985
Final concept
30 × 50 cm

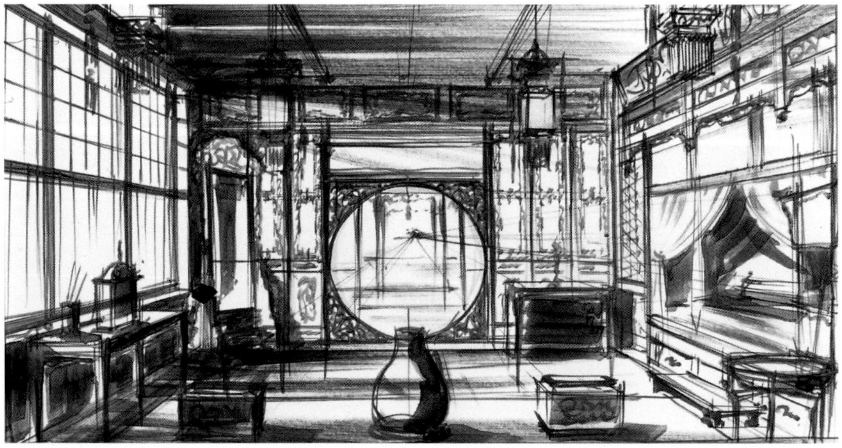

Corridor outside Puji's study 1985
Final concept
30 × 49.5 cm

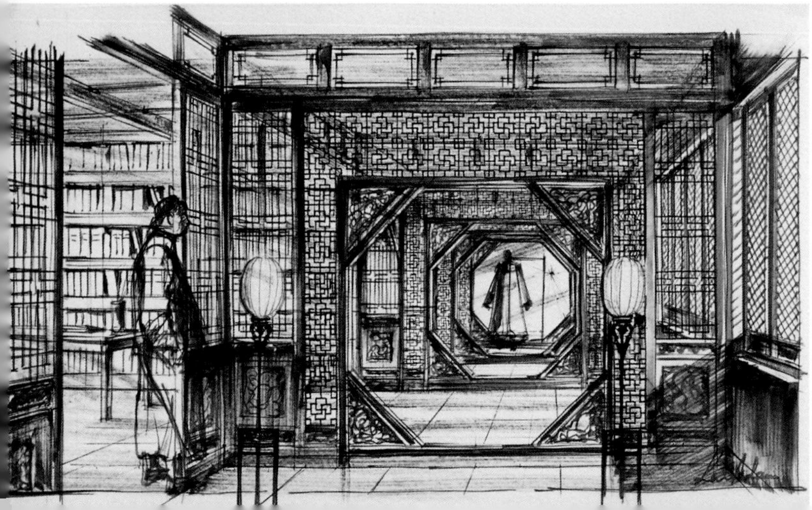

Puji's apartment in the Imperial Palace 1985
Final concept
c. 30 × 50 cm

The Freshman

In Andrew Bergman's comedy, Marlon Brando virtually reprises his Don Corleone from *The Godfather* as a Mafia boss who hires a naïve New York film-school student to run errands for the mob.

The interiors were studio sets in Toronto, apart from a location in an office at NYU, on Washington Square. The exteriors were locations in both New York and Toronto, including the station in Toronto, which was designed by the architect of Grand Central Station. **SG**

The restaurant kitchen 1989
Final concept
48.5 × 61 cm

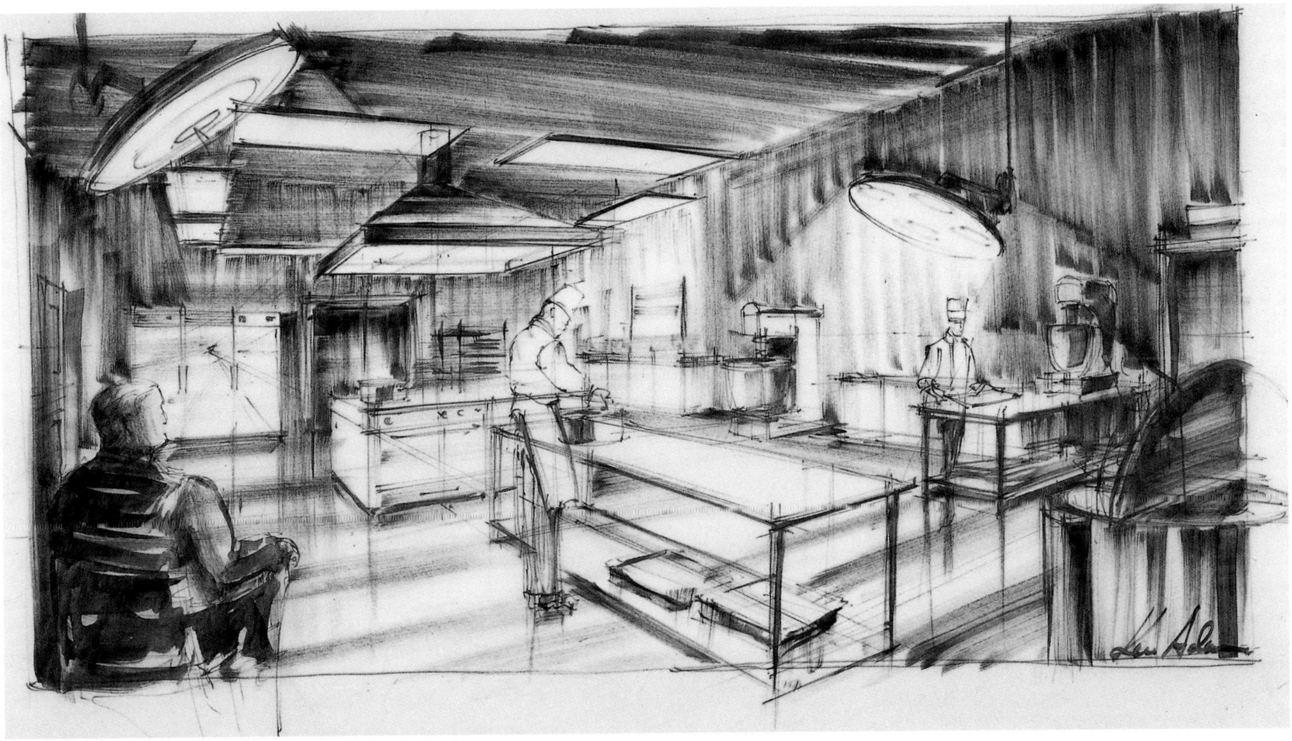

In the back of the set behind Brando, I forced the perspective. Like a theatrical set, I lowered the ceiling and raised the floor up to make him look even bigger. I came up with the idea of putting him against a window. Now what kind of window? It was an industrial window, which you find everywhere in New York. The texture on the walls was really incredible. We papered the walls, repapered them, then painted them, and peeled them off. The ceilings and the wainscoting was that tinned material that is so New York. It was to give *The Godfather* atmosphere to it, but in fact it wasn't anything that we had seen in *The Godfather* except in terms of the lighting. **VL**

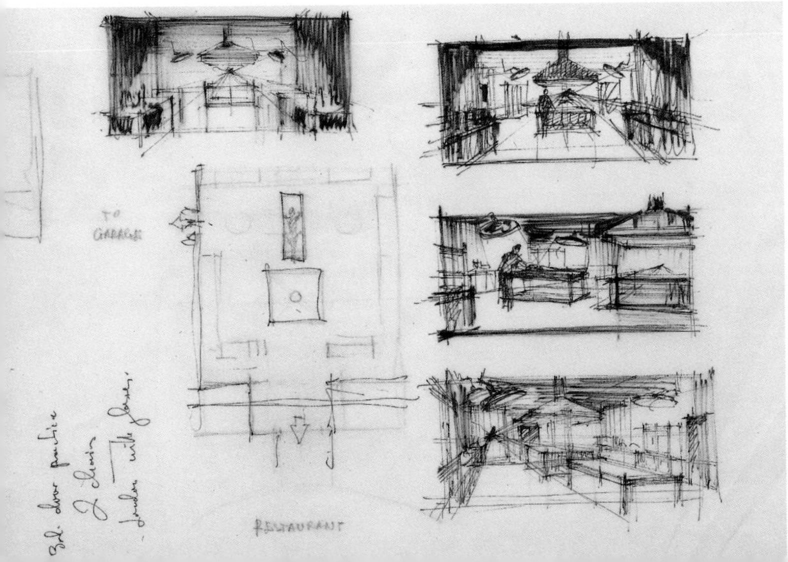

The restaurant kitchen and floorplan 1989
Studies
23 × 30.5 cm

The Doctor

Psychological drama, directed by Randa Haines, starring William Hurt as an aloof, egocentric Los Angeles surgeon who undergoes a lesson in humanity when a malignant throat tumour makes him a patient at his own coldly impersonal hospital.

The hospital sets were constructed in a disused warehouse in Valencia, outside Los Angeles. Exterior locations were filmed in San Francisco and around Los Angeles. The interior of the doctor's house was a location near Malibu.

It was one of those films where I had a very close relationship with the director, in this case Randa Haines. And we had a very pleasant producer, Ed Feldman. It was difficult working for Disney, because they were watching every penny that we spent. It was a new experience for me because Disney in those days had a different attitude from MGM, Warner Bros or Fox. **SG**

The radiation room 1990
Study
36 × 50.5 cm

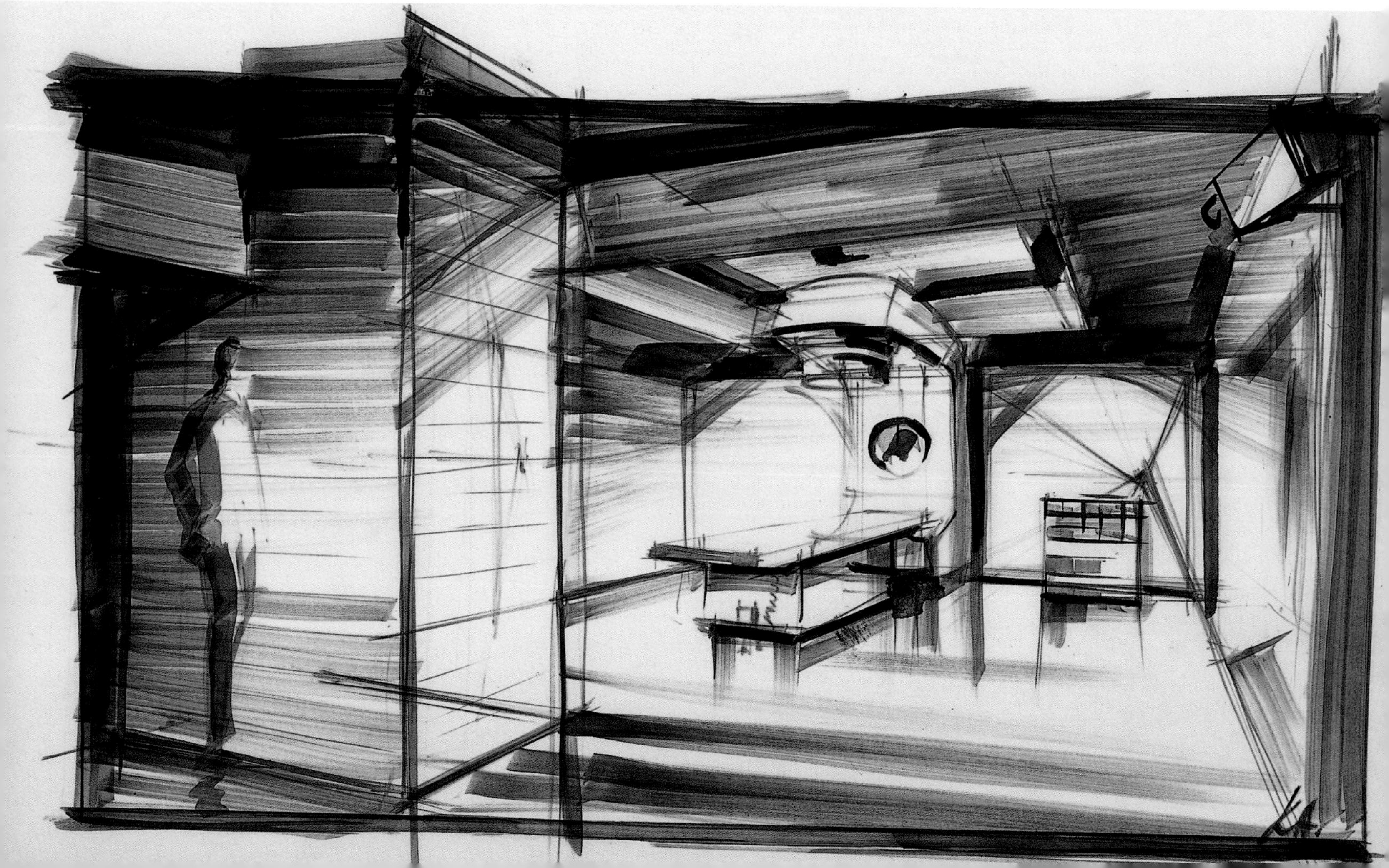

Addams Family Values

Directed by Barry Sonnenfeld, the film is the second of two big-screen comedies featuring the bizarre, topsy-turvy family created by Charles Addams in his *New Yorker* cartoons. In this one Morticia has a baby, her jealous children are sent to summer camp and a new nanny has designs on Uncle Fester.

I was asked to do it by Scott Rudin, but when I arrived in Los Angeles I found a script that they had left me to read by the next morning which was nothing like the script I had seen in England and accepted. So I was up in arms. I called the director, Barry Sondheim, who said, 'What is it you don't like?' and I told him and he said, 'I think you're right. Why don't you fly with me to New York and talk to Scott?' So the next day I was on a plane to New York talking to the producer all day and they changed a lot of things that I didn't like. And then it was a *tour de force* because they wanted to start shooting in eight weeks and that meant designing the picture and building the sets in eight weeks.

The exterior and all the interiors of the Addams House were studio-built simultaneously at Paramount, Warner Bros and Century City. There were several locations in Los Angeles, including the interior and exterior of a private house.

It was difficult for me to find a big enough, capable enough, art department to do all the work and I never finished sketching. I did one sketch after the other. My salvation was that I related so much to Charles Addams and, unlike Richard MacDonald, who had done the first Addams Family film, tried to interpret his cartoons into three-dimensional settings. It was a gigantic undertaking only to be compared with some of the Bonds. **SG**

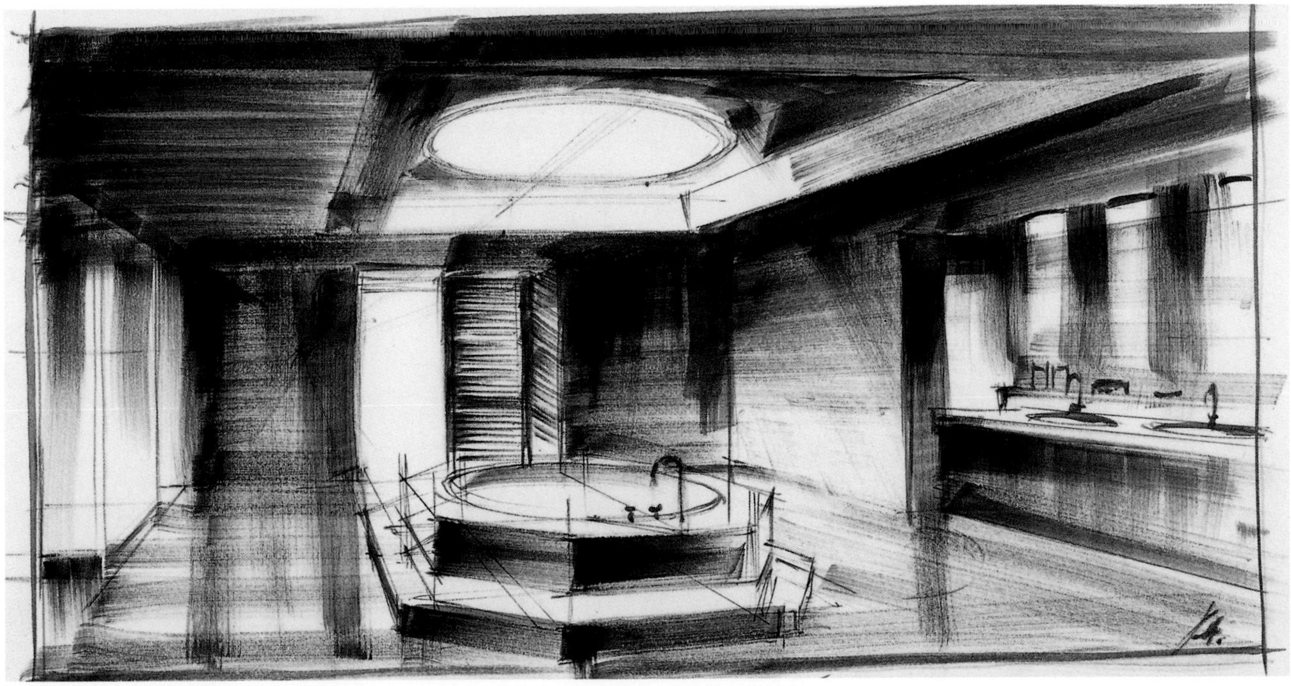

Design for hotel bathroom, Hawaii 1992
Final concept
Felt-tip pen and wash on paper
22.5 × 35 cm

1994

The Madness of King George

Adaptation to the screen by its author, Alan Bennett, and director Nicholas Hytner, of the National Theatre production of the costume comedy drama set in 1788 England with many of the original cast, including Nigel Hawthorne as the king who goes insane, creating a power struggle between his Tory prime minister Pitt and the Whig opposition, but is restored to health by an innovative doctor, so averting a constitutional crisis.

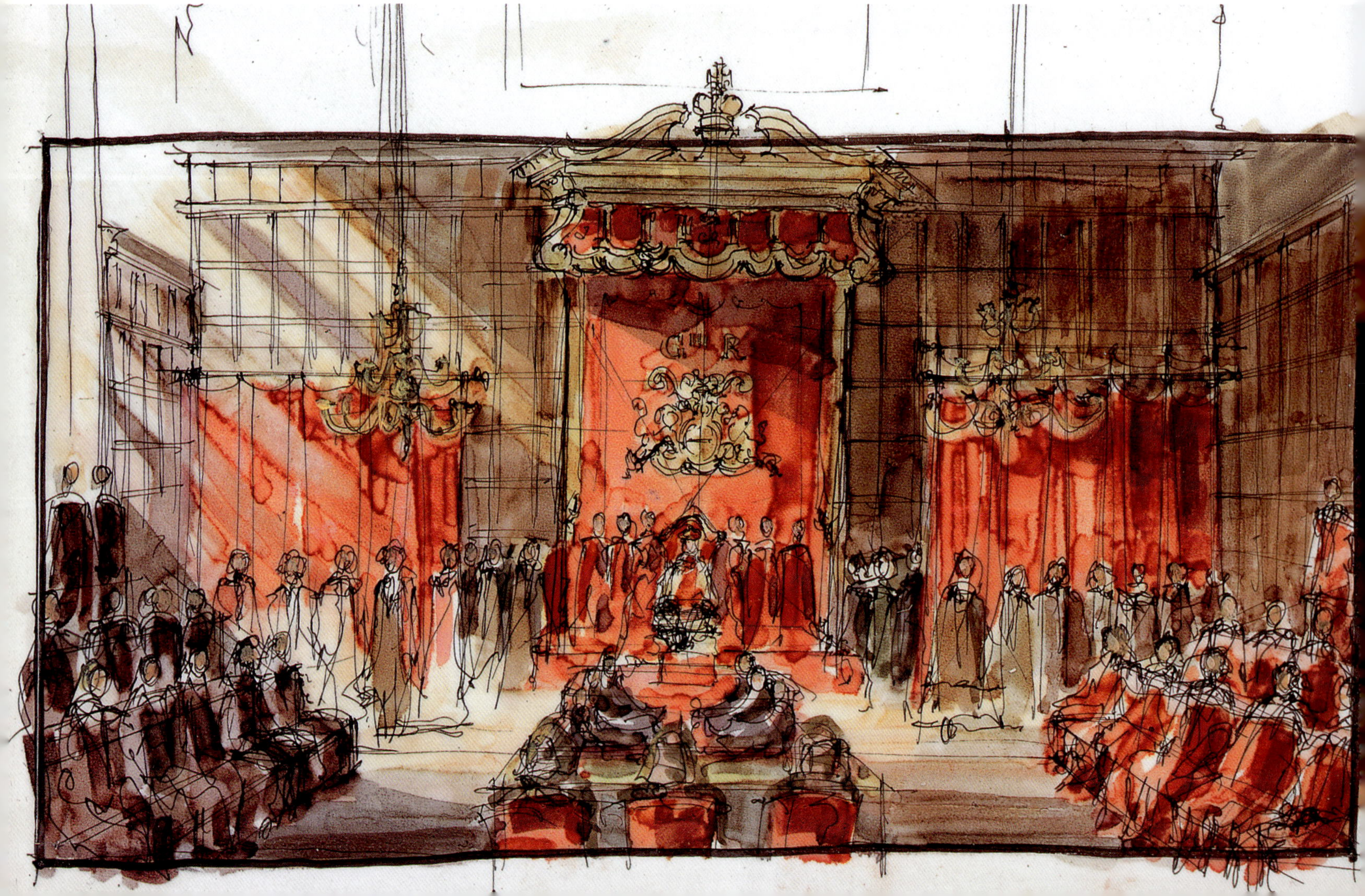

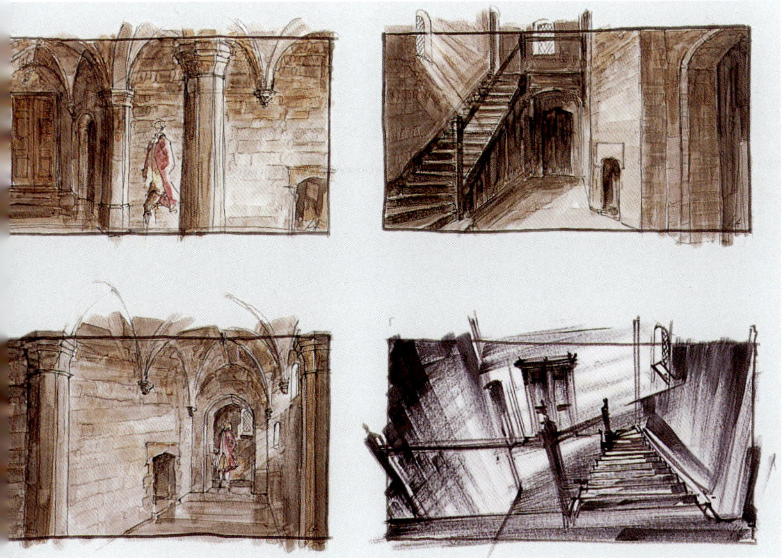

Corridor and stairs outside the Royal Apartment, Windsor 1994
Studies
Felt-tip pen and watercolour on paper
38 × 52 cm

Nicholas Hytner contacted me in New York and brought me the Alan Bennett script, which was incredible. It isn't often that you get a script like that. So the combination of Hytner and Alan Bennett intrigued me and I said to my agent that whatever happened, even if I didn't get paid anything, I wanted to do this film. And in fact I did it for half my normal fee. We did the whole film for US $8million, shooting it in eight weeks. You know, sometimes the chemistry works on films and *King George* was a very good example. Also, I hadn't done films in England for quite a long time, in fact since *King David*, in 1984, so it was exciting for me to work back here again.

We used a mixture of location sets, interior and exterior, and studio sets. The royal apartment was almost entirely built at Shepperton; one of the rooms was the Double Cube Room at Wilton, but otherwise they were studio sets. One of the adaptations I made in exterior locations was on the roof of Arundel Castle. I was fascinated by some very tall chimneys. It almost looked like a Greek temple and so I added a few more chimneys to enhance the effect. **SG**

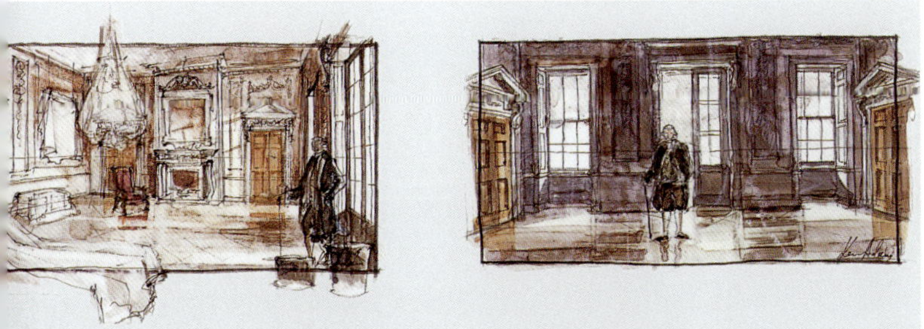

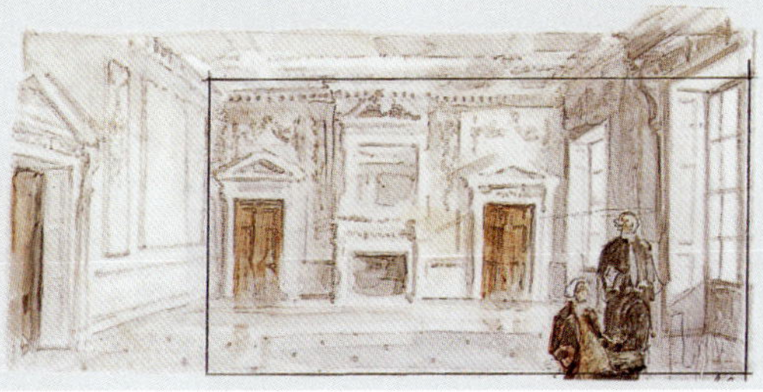

Entrance Hall, Kew 1994
Studies
Felt-tip pen and watercolour on paper
33.5 × 50.2 cm

The House of Lords 1994
Final concept
Felt-tip pen and watercolour on paper
18 × 31 cm

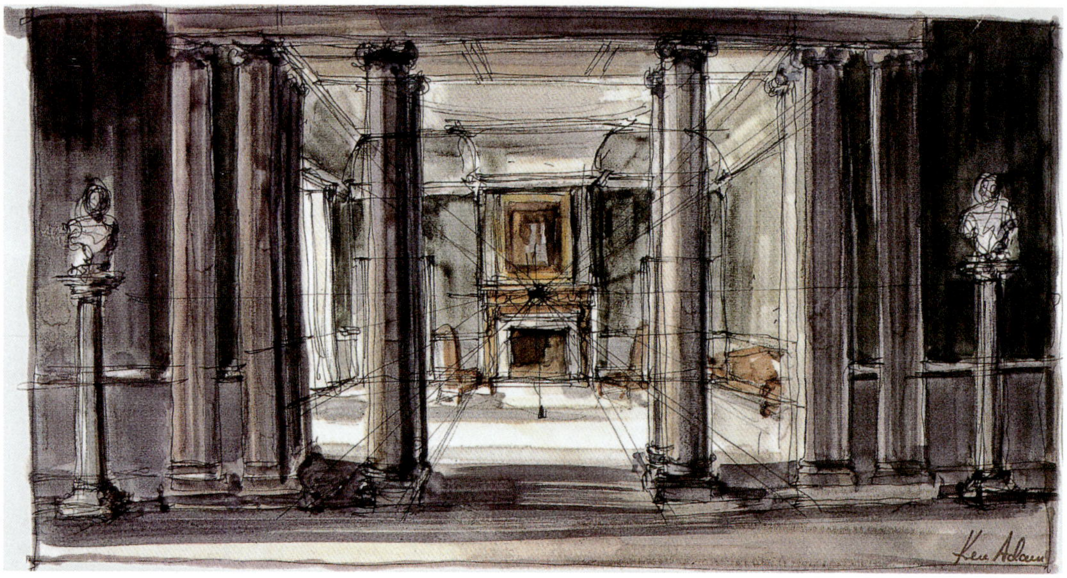

The state room, Kew 1994
Final concept
Felt-tip pen and watercolour on paper
20 × 29.5 cm

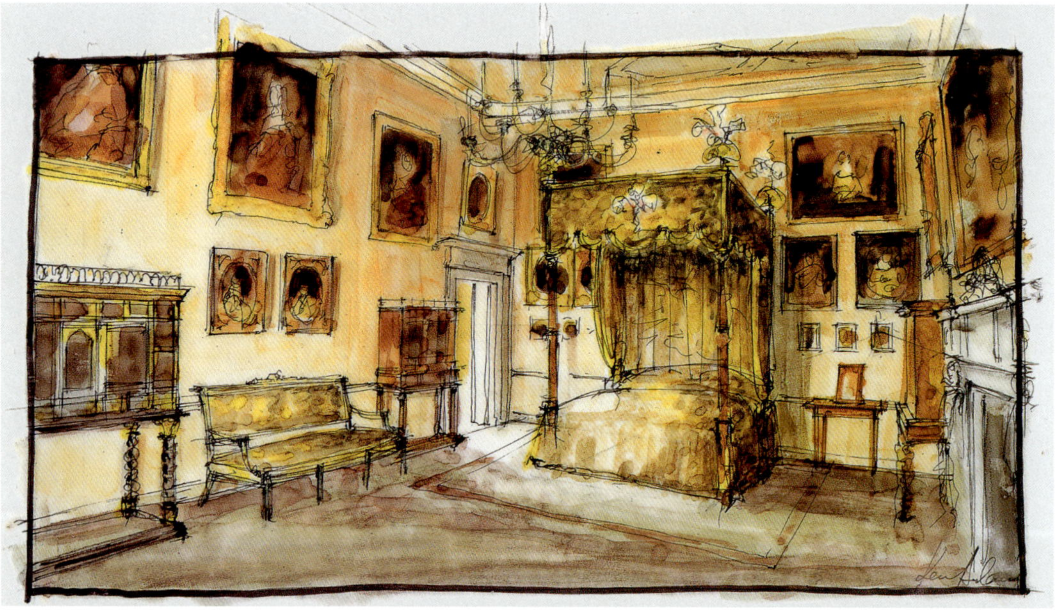

The Prince of Wales' bedroom, Carlton House 1994
Final concept
Felt-tip pen and watercolour on paper
23.5 × 34.5 cm

The King's bedroom at Windsor 1994
Final concept
Felt-tip pen and watercolour on paper
20.5 × 29.5 cm

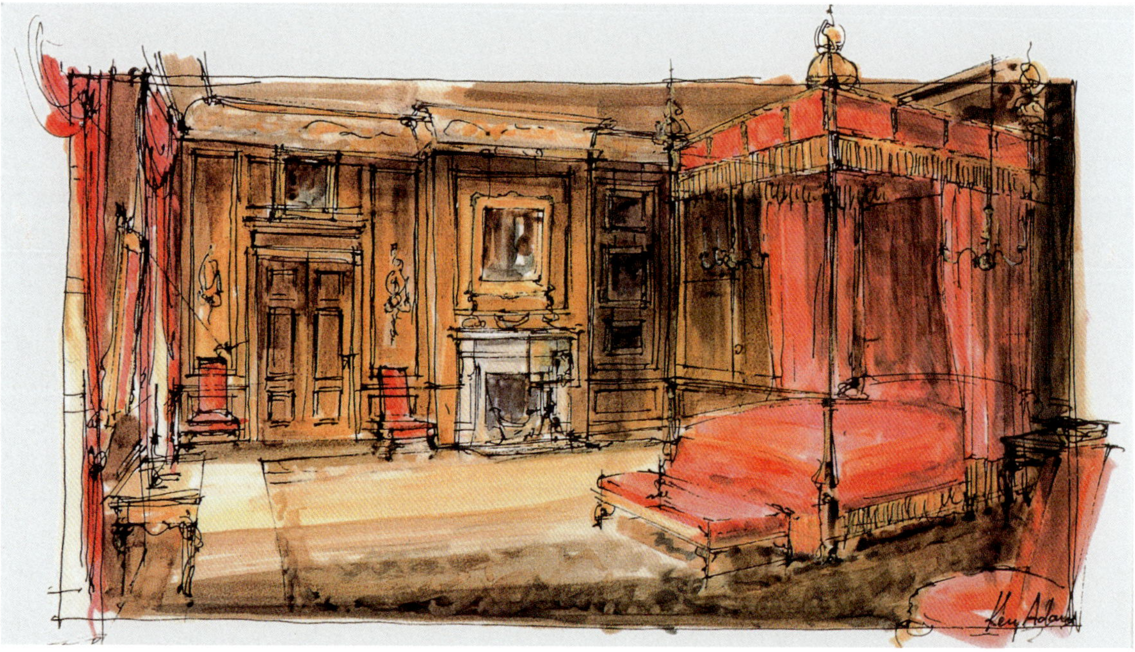

1997

Wozzeck

I was asked to design a production of Alban Berg's opera *Wozzeck* by Bill Friedken at the Maggio Fiorentino in Florence and I made a number of drawings. Sadly my designs were never realised. **SG**

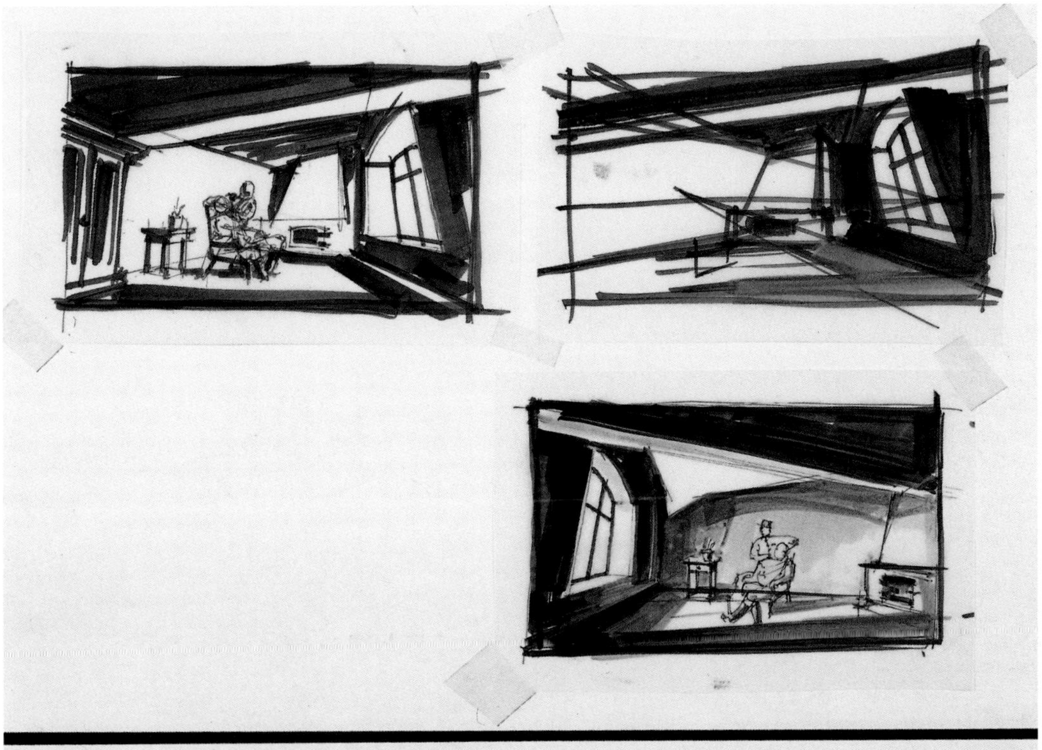

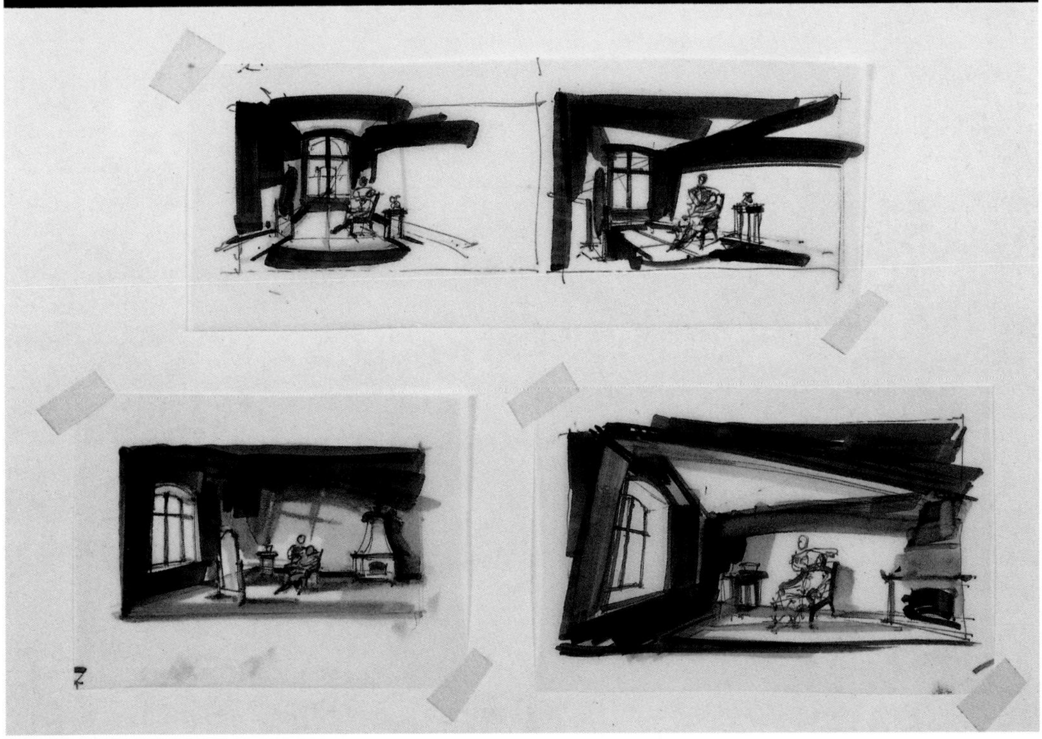

The doctor's appointment
1997
Studies
21 × 29.5 cm each

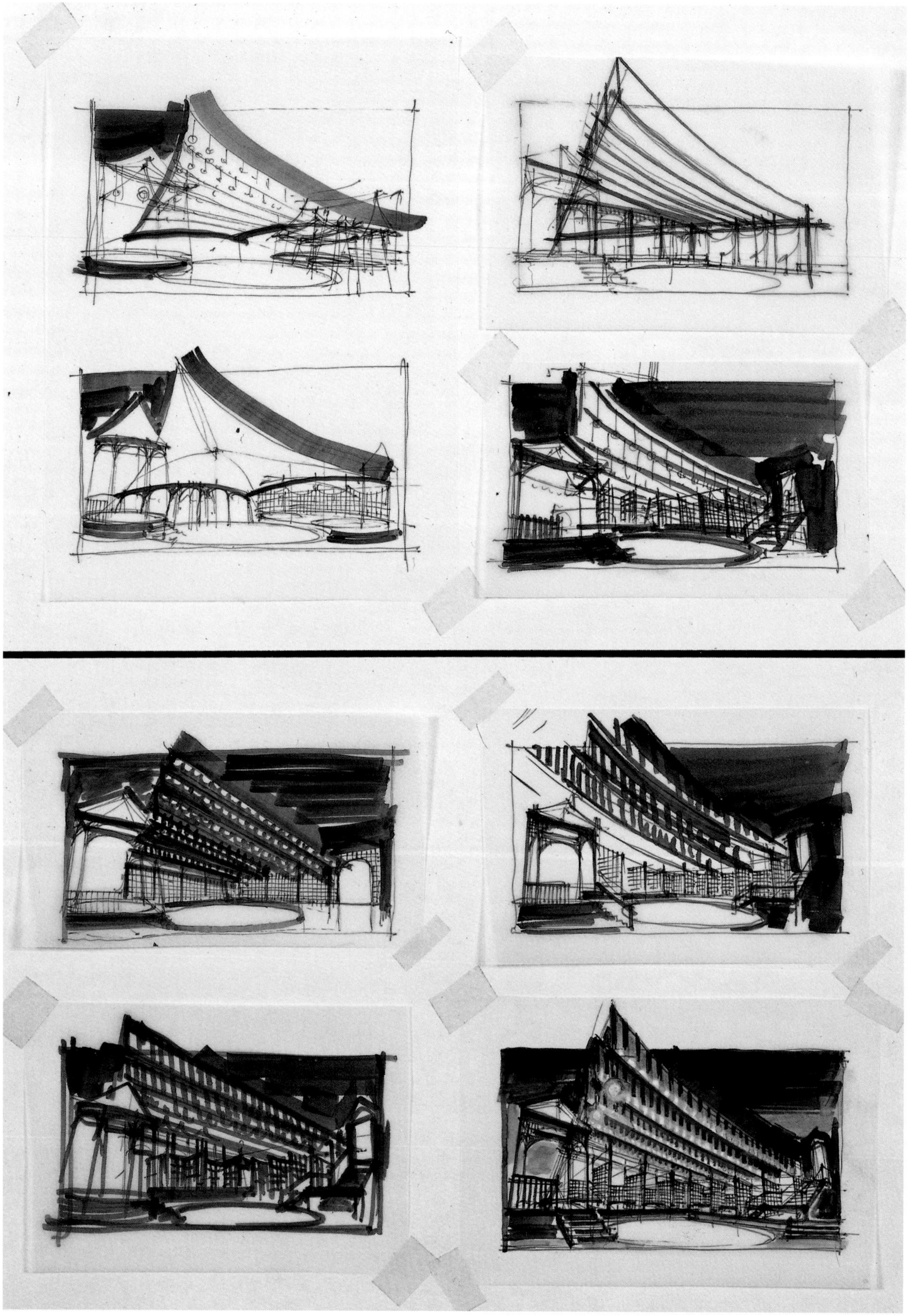

The Garden Festival 1997
Studies
21 × 29.5 cm each

Catherine A. Surowiec

Filmography

Key:

p	producer
	(*co.p* – co-producer)
	(*xp* – executive producer)
	(*ap* – associate producer)
p.c	production company
dist	distributor
d	director
2nd unit d	second unit director
sc	screenplay/script/ screenwriter/writer
ph	photography/director of photography
ed	editor
mus	music composer
p.d	production designer
a.d	art director
	(*sup.a.d* – supervising art director)
	(*assoc.a.d* – associate art director)
	(*asst.a.d* – assistant art director)
set dec	set decorator
cont.sketch	continuity sketches
draught	draughtsman
sfx	special effects
cost	costume designer
dress des	dress designer
wardrobe sup	wardrobe supervisor
cast	cast
Locs	locations

1.
This Was a Woman
GB 1948.
d – Tim Whelan. *p* – Marcel Hellman, *p.c* – Excelsior. *dist* – 20th Century-Fox. *sc* – Val Valentine, from the play by Joan Morgan. *ph* (*b/w*) – Günther Krampf. *cd* – E.B. Jarvis. *mus* – Mischa Spoliansky. *sup.a.d* – Andrew Mazzei. *a.d* – Ivan King. *draught* – Ken Adam.
cast – Sonia Dresdel (*Sylvia Russell*), Barbara White (*Fenella Russell*), Walter Fitzgerald (*Arthur Russell*), Cyril Raymond (*Austin Penrose*), Marjorie Rhodes (*Mrs. Holmes*), Emrys Jones (*Terry Russell*), Celia Lipton (*Effie*), Julian Dallas (*Valentine Christie*), Kynaston Reeves (*Dr Morrison*).
Studio: Riverside.
Year Ken Adam worked on film: 1947.

2.
Brass Monkey (retitled: Lucky Mascot)
GB 1948.
d – Thornton Freeland. *p* – Nat A. Bronsten, *ap* – John R. Sloan, *p.c* – Diadem/Alliance. *dist* – United Artists. *sc* – Alec Coppel, from an original story by Coppel and Thornton Freeland. *ph (b/w)* – Basil Emmott. *ed* – David Hawkins. *mus* – Dr. Bernard Grun. *a.d* – Walter A. Scott. draught – Ken Adam. *ward.sup* – Dorothy Sinclair.
cast – Carroll Levis (*himself*), Carole Landis (*Kay Sheldon*), Herbert Lom (*Peter Hobart*), Avril Angers (*herself*), Ernest Thesiger (*Ryder-Harris*), Henry Edwards (*Inspector Miller*), Edward Underdown (*Max Taylor*), Gwyneth Vaughan (*Miss Hamilton*), Terry-Thomas, Leslie 'Hutch' Hutchinson, Carroll Levis's Discoveries.
Studio: Alliance, Hammersmith; Twickenham.
Year Ken Adam worked on film: 1947.

3.
The Queen of Spades
GB 1948. (released 1949)
d – Thorold Dickinson. *p* – Anatole de Grunwald, *ap* – Jack Clayton, *p.c* – Associated British Picture Corporation/World Screenplays. *dist* – Associated British-Pathé.
sc – Rodney Ackland, Arthur Boys, from the story by Alexander Pushkin. ph (b/w) – Otto Heller. *ed* – Hazel Wilkinson. mus – Georges Auric. *p.d* – Oliver Messel. *a.d* – William Kellner. *asst.a.d.* (*uncredited*) – John Howell, Don Ashton. *chief draught* – Peter Glazier. *draught* – Ken Adam. *set dresser* – Philip Stockford. *cost* – Oliver Messel.
cast – Anton Walbrook (*Herman Suvorin*), Edith Evans (*Countess Ranevskaya*), Ronald Howard (*Andrei*), Mary Jerrold (*Varvarushka*), Yvonne Mitchell (*Lizaveta Ivanovna*), Anthony Dawson (*Fyodor*), Miles Malleson (*Tchybukin*), Athene Seyler (*Princess Ivashin*), Michael Medwin (*Ilovaisky*), Ivor Barnard (*bookseller*), Gibb McLaughlin (*birdseller*).
Studio: Welwyn.
Year Ken Adam worked on film: 1948.

4.
World Premiere (unrealised film)
GB 1948.
A film project to star Luise Rainer. Ken Adam worked with producer Anatole de Grunwald and production designer Georges Wakhévitch to create models for this film. It was never made.
Studio: Teddington.

5.
Third Time Lucky
GB 1949.
d – Gordon Parry. *p* – Mario Zampi, *p.c* – Kenilworth/ Alliance Anglofilm. *dist* – General Film Distributors. *sc* – Gerald Butler, from his novel *They Cracked Her Glass Slipper*. *ph* (*b/w*) – Cedric Williams. *ed* – Giulio Zampi. *mus* – Stanley Black. *a.d* – Ivan King. *draught* – Ken Adam. *construction mgr* – Peter Dukelow.
cast – Glynis Johns (*Joan Burns*), Dermot Walsh (*Lucky*), Charles Goldner (*Flash*), Harcourt Williams (*Doc Harris*), Yvonne Owen (*Peggy*), John Stuart (*Inspector*), Helen Haye (*Old Lady*), Ballard Berkeley (*Bertram*), Sebastian Cabot (*Bennett*).
Studio: Twickenham.
Year Ken Adam worked on film: 1948.

6.
Dick Barton Strikes Back
GB 1949.
d – Godfrey Grayson. *p* – Anthony Hinds, Mae Murray, *p.c* – Exclusive Films/Hammer. *dist* – Exclusive.
sc – Elizabeth Baron, Ambrose Grayson, from the BBC radio serial by Edward J. Mason. *ph* (*b/w*) – Cedric Williams. *ed* – Ray Pitt. *mus* – Frank Spencer, Rupert Grayson. *a.d* – Ivan King. *asst.a.d* – Ken Adam.
cast – Don Stannard (*Dick Barton*), Sebastian Cabot (*Fouracada*), Bruce Walker (*Snowey White*), Jean Lodge (*Tina*), James Raglan (*Lord Armadale*), Humphrey Kent (*Colonel Gardner*), John Harvey (*Major Henderson*).
Studio: Viking Studios, Kensington. *Locs*: Blackpool; London Zoo.
Year Ken Adam worked on film: 1948.

7.
Three Men and a Girl (retitled: Golden Arrow) (US: The Gay Adventure)
GB 1949. (released 1953)
d – Gordon Parry. *p* – Anatole de Grunwald. *dist* – Renown.
sc – Paul Darcy, Sid Colin, from a story by Anatole de Grunwald. *ph* (*b/w*) – Otto Heller. *ed* – Gerald Turney-Smith. mus – Mischa Spoliansky. *a.d* – Tom Goswell [+ Georges Wakhévitch]. *asst. a.d* – Ray Simm. *draught* – Ken Adam.
cast – Burgess Meredith (*Dick*), Jean-Pierre Aumont (*André Marchand*), Richard Murdoch (*David Felton*), Paula Valenska (*Suzy/Sonia/Hedy*), Kathleen Harrison (*Isobel*), Karel Stepanek (*Schroeder*), Edward Lexy (*Colonel*), Natasha Parry (*Betty Felton*).
Studio: Twickenham. Locs: French Riviera.
Year Ken Adam worked on film: 1948.

8.
Obsession (US: The Hidden Room)
GB 1949.
d – Edward Dmytryk. *p* – Nat A. Bronsten, *p.c* – Independent Sovereign. *dist* – GFD.
sc – Alex Coppel, from his play *A Man about a Dog*.
ph (*b/w*) – C.M. Pennington-Richards, Robert Day.
ed – Lito Carruthers. *mus* – Nino Rota. *a.d* – Duncan Sutherland. *asst.a.d* – Ken Adam.
cast – Robert Newton (*Dr Clive Riordan*), Sally Gray (*Storm Riordan*), Phil Brown (*Bill Kronin*), Naunton Wayne (*Superintendent Finsbury*), Olga Lindo (*Mrs Humphreys*).
Studio: Pinewood.
Year Ken Adam worked on film: 1948.

9.
Your Witness (US: Eye Witness)
GB 1950.
d – Robert Montgomery. *p* – David E. Rose, Joan Harrison, *p.c* – Coronado Productions. *dist* – Warner Bros.
sc – Hugo Butler, Ian McLellan Hunter, William Douglas Home, from a story by Hugo Butler. *ph* (*b/w*) – Gerald Gibbs. *ed* – Lito Carruthers. *mus* – Malcolm Arnold.
a.d – Ralph Brinton. *asst.a.d* – Ken Adam. wardrobe sup – Phyllis Dalton.
cast – Robert Montgomery (*Adam Heywood*), Leslie Banks (*Colonel Summerfield*), Patricia Wayne [Cutts] (*Alex Summerfield*), Felix Aylmer (*Judge*), Andrew Cruickshank (*Sir Adrian North KC*), Harcourt Williams (*Beamish*), Michael Ripper (*Sam Baxter*), Jenny Laird (*Mary Baxter*).
Studio: Teddington.
Year Ken Adam worked on film: 1948.

10.
Captain Horatio Hornblower R.N.
GB 1951.
d – Raoul Walsh. *p* – Gerry Mitchell, *p.c/dist* – Warner Bros.
sc – Ivan Goff, Ben Roberts, Aeneas Mackenzie, from the novel by C.S. Forester. *ph* (Technicolor) – Guy Green. *ed* – Jack Harris. *mus* – Robert Farnon.
a.d – Tom Morahan. *asst.a.d* – John Hoesli, Ken Adam.
chief draught – William Holmes. *draught/cont.sketch* – Syd Cain. *shipbuilder* – Bernard Voison. *sfx* – Harry Barndollar, Arthur S. Rhoades, George Blackwell, Cliff Richardson. *cost* – Tom Morahan, Sheila Graham.
cast – Gregory Peck (*Capt Horatio Hornblower*), Virginia Mayo (*Lady Barbara Wellesley*), Robert Beatty (*Lt William Bush*), James Robertson Justice (*Quist*), Denis O'Dea (*Rear-Admiral Sir Rodney Leighton*), Terence Morgan (*Lt Gerard*), Richard Hearne (*Polwheal*), Stanley Baker (*Mr Harrison*), Christopher Lee (*Spanish Captain*), Kynaston Reeves (*Admiral Lord Hood*).
Studios: Denham; Elstree; La Victorine (Nice).
Year Ken Adam worked on film: 1949.

11.
The Crimson Pirate
GB 1952.
d – Robert Siodmak. *p* – Harold Hecht, *p.c* – Norma Productions/Warner Bros. *dist* – Warner Bros.
sc – Roland Kibbee. *ph* (*Technicolor*) – Otto Heller.
ed – Jack Harris. *mus* – William Alwyn. *a.d* – Paul Sheriff. *assoc.a.d* – Ken Adam. *scenic artist* – Olga Lehmann. *cont.sketch* – Stephen Grimes. *draught* – Ray Simm. *sfx* – Russell Shearman. *cost* – Margaret Furse. *Burt Lancaster & Nick Cravat cost* – Marjorie Best.
cast – Burt Lancaster (*Vallo*), Nick Cravat (*Ojo*), Eva Bartok (*Consuelo*), Torin Thatcher (*Humble Bellows*), James Hayter (*Prudence*), Margot Grahame (*Bianca*), Leslie Bradley (*Baron Gruda*), Noel Purcell (*Pablo Murphy*), Eliot Makeham (*Governor*), Frederick Leister (*El Libre*), Frank Pettingell (*Colonel*).
Studios: Teddington; ABPC, Elstree. *Locs*: Ischia.
Year Ken Adam worked on film: 1951.

12.
The Master of Ballantrae
GB 1953.
d – William Keighley. *p.c/dist* – Warner Bros.
sc – Herb Meadow, Harold Medford, Robert Hall, T.J. Morrison, from the novel by Robert Louis Stevenson.
ph (*Technicolor*) – Jack Cardiff. *ed* – Jack Harris.
mus – William Alwyn. *a.d* – Ralph Brinton. *assoc.ad.* – Ken Adam. *asst.a.d* – Edward Marshall. *scenic artist* – Olga Lehmann. *cost* – Margaret Furse.
cost.asst – Letizia Adam.
cast – Errol Flynn (*James Durisdeer*), Roger Livesey (*Col. Francis Burke*), Anthony Steel (*Henry Durisdeer*), Beatrice Campbell (*Lady Alison*),Yvonne Furneaux (*Jessie Brown*), Jacques Berthier (*Arnaud*), Felix Aylmer (*Lord Durisdeer*), Mervyn Johns (*MacKellar*), Charles Goldner (*Mendoza*), Robert Beatty (*narrator*).
Studio: ABPC, Elstree. *Locs*: Palermo, Sicily.
Year Ken Adam worked on film: 1952.

13.
Ah Non, Chérie (unrealised screenplay)
GB 1953.
Screenplay by Ken Adam and Peter Martin, for a romantic comedy based on newlyweds Ken and Letizia Adam, for the British production company Group 3. The film was never made.

14.
The Intruder
GB 1953.
d – Guy Hamilton. *p* – Ivan Foxwell, *p.c* – Ivan Foxwell Productions, British Lion. *dist* – British Lion.
sc – Robin Maugham, John Hunter, Anthony Squire, from the novel *Line on Ginger* by Robin Maugham.
ph (*b/w*) – Ted Scaife. *ed* – Alan Osbiston. *mus* – Francis Chagrin. *a.d* – Joseph Bato. *asst.a.d* – Ken Adam.
cast – Jack Hawkins (*Wolf Merton*), Hugh Williams (*Tim Ross*), Michael Medwin (*Ginger Edwards*), George Cole (*John Summers*), Dennis Price (*Leonard Pirry*), Susan Shaw (*Nina*), Dora Bryan (*Dora Bee*), Edward Chapman (*Walter Lowden*).
Studio: Shepperton.
Year Ken Adam worked on film: 1953.

15.
Star of India
GB/Italy 1954.
d – Arthur Lubin. *p* – Raymond Stross, *p.c* – Raymond Stross Productions/Titanus (Rome). *dist* – Eros (UK); United Artists (US).
sc – Seton I. Miller, C. Denis Freeman, from an orig. story by Herbert Dalmas. *ph* (*Technicolor*) – C.M. Pennington-Richards. *ed* – Russell Lloyd. *mus* – Nino Rota; Muir Mathieson. *a.d* – Cedric Dawe. *asst.a.d* – Ken Adam.
cast – Cornel Wilde (*Pierre St. Laurent*), Jean Wallace (*Katrina*), Herbert Lom (*Vicomte de Narbonne*), Yvonne Sanson (*Madame de Montespan*), Basil Sydney (*Louis XIV*), Walter Rilla (*Van Horst*), John Slater (*Emile*).
Studio: Riverside.
Year Ken Adam worked on film: 1953.

16.
Helen of Troy
USA/Italy 1955.
d – Robert Wise. *p.c/dist* – Warner Bros.
sc – John Twist, Hugh Gray, adapt. from Homer by Hugh Gray and N. Richard Nash. *ph* (*Warnercolor*, CinemaScope) – Harry Stradling. *ed* – Thomas Reilly.
mus – Max Steiner. *a.d* – Edward Carrere. *asst.a.d* – Ken Adam. *cost* – Roger Furse.
cast – Rossana Podestà (*Helen*), Jacques Sernas (*Paris*), Cedric Hardwicke (*Priam*), Stanley Baker (*Achilles*), Niall MacGinnis (*Menelaus*), Nora Swinburne (*Hecuba*), Robert Douglas (*Agamemnon*), Torin Thatcher (*Ulysses*), Harry Andrews (*Hector*), Janette Scott (*Cassandra*), Ronald Lewis (*Aeneas*), Brigitte Bardot (*Andraste*), Maxwell Reed (*Ajax*).
Studio: Cinecittà (*Rome*).
Year Ken Adam worked on film: 1953.

17.
Ben-Hur (pre-production work, 1955)
USA 1959.
d – William Wyler, *p* – Sam Zimbalist, *p.c* – MGM.
a.d – William A. Horning, Edward Carfagno.
**Ken Adam worked on the budget and first planning of this film in spring 1955 for MGM senior production executive Henny Hennickson and art director Edward Carfagno. The film was to be made in Italy.

18.
Soho Incident (US: Spin a Dark Web)
GB 1956.
d – Vernon Sewell. *p* – M.J. Frankovich, George Maynard, *p.c* – Film Locations. *dist* – Columbia.
sc – Ian Stuart Black, from the novel *Wide Boys Never Work* by Robert Westerby. *ph* (*b/w*) – Basil Emmott. *ed* – Peter Rolfe Johnson. *mus* – Robert Sharples. *a.d* – Ken Adam.
cast – Faith Domergue (*Bella Francesi*), Lee Patterson (*Jim Bankley*), Rona Anderson (*Betty Walker*), Martin Benson (*Rico Francesi*), Robert Arden (*Buddy*), Joss Ambler (*Tom Walker*), Peter Hammond (*Bill Walker*), Peter Burton (*Inspector Collis*).
Studio: Walton-on-Thames.
Year Ken Adam worked on film: 1955.

19.
Around the World in Eighty Days
USA 1956.
d – Michael Anderson. *p* – Michael Todd, ap – William Cameron Menzies, *p.c* – The Michael Todd Company, Inc. *dist* – United Artists.
sc – S.J. Perelman, James Poe, John Farrow, from the novel by Jules Verne. *ph* (*Technicolor*, *Todd-AO*) – Lionel Lindon. *ed* – Gene Ruggiero, Howard Epstein.
mus – Victor Young. *a.d* – Ken Adam (British & French studio work and locations), James W. Sullivan (Hollywood studio work & other locations). *set dec* – Ross Dowd. *set-up sketches* (*English sequences*) – Olga Lehmann. *scenic artist* (*England*) – Gilbert Wood. *set construction* – Peter Dukelow, Cyril Graysmark. *sfx* – Lee Zavitz. *cost* – Miles White, Anna Duse (England). *title anim* – Saul Bass.
cast – David Niven (*Phileas Fogg*), Cantinflas (*Passepartout*), Robert Newton (*Inspector Fix*), Shirley MacLaine (*Princess Aouda*). Plus an all-star cast in cameo appearances, including Charles Boyer, John Carradine, Ronald Colman, Noël Coward, Marlene Dietrich, Fernandel, John Gielgud, Hermione Gingold, José Greco, Cedric Hardwicke, Trevor Howard, Buster Keaton, Beatrice Lillie, Peter Lorre, Edmund Lowe, Victor McLaglen, John Mills, Robert Morley, Jack Oakie, George Raft, Cesar Romero,

and Frank Sinatra.
Studios: MGM, Elstree; Billancourt (Paris).
Locs: London; Paris.
** Academy Award nomination, Art Direction (Colour).
Year Ken Adam worked on film: 1955.

20.
Child in the House
GB 1956.
d – C. Raker Endfield, Charles de Lautour. *p* – S. Benjamin Fisz, *p.c* – Laureate/Golden Era. *dist* – Eros.
sc – C. Raker Endfield, Charles de Lautour, from the novel by Janet McNeill. *ph* (*b/w*) – Otto Heller. *ed* – Charles Hasse. *mus* – Mario Nascimbene. *a.d* – Ken Adam. *set construction* – Wally Smith.
cast – Phyllis Calvert (*Evelyn Acheson*), Eric Portman (*Henry Acheson*), Stanley Baker (*Stephen Lorimer*), Mandy Miller (*Elizabeth Lorimer*), Dora Bryan (Cassie), Percy Herbert (*Det. Sgt. Taylor*), Joan Benham (*Vera McNally*).
Studio: Walton-on-Thames.
Year Ken Adam worked on film: 1956.

21.
John Paul Jones (pre-production work, 1956)
USA 1959.
d – John Farrow. *p* – Samuel Bronston, *p.c/dist* – Warner Bros. *a.d* – Franz Bachelin.
**Ken Adam was involved with the pre-production in 1956, when the film was to be directed by William Dieterle, with Boris Leven as production designer. Ken Adam supervised the design of the ships. The project was cancelled owing to financial problems and was only resumed a year and a half later. By that time Ken Adam was already working on another film, but his ship designs were used in the final Technicolor/ Technirama version, which starred Robert Stack and Marisa Pavan.

22.
The Devil's Pass
GB 1957.
p/d/sc – Darcy Conyers. *p.c* – The David Henley Partnership. *dist* – Associated British-Pathé.
ph (*b/w*) – S.D. Onions. *ed* – Helen Wiggins. *mus* – Philip Green. *a.d* – Ken Adam.
cast – John Slater (*Bill Buckle*), Christopher Warbey (*Jim*), Richard George (*Ted Trelawney*), Joan Newell (*Nan Trelawney*), Charles Leno (*Headmaster*).
Studio: Viking, Kensington. *Locs*: Brixham, Devon.
Year Ken Adam worked on film: 1953.

23.
Night of the Demon (US: Curse of the Demon)
GB 1957.
d – Jacques Tourneur. xp – Hal E. Chester, *p* – Frank Bevis, *p.c* – Sabre Film Productions. *dist* – Columbia.
sc – Charles Bennett, Hal E. Chester, from the story *Casting the Runes* by Montague R. James. *ph* (*b/w*) – Ted Scaife. *ed* – Michael Gordon. *mus* – Clifton Parker. *p.d* – Ken Adam. *asst.a.d* – Peter Glazier.
sfx – George Blackwell, Wally Veevers.
cast – Dana Andrews (*Dr John Holden*), Peggy Cummins (*Joanna Harrington*), Niall MacGinnis (*Dr Karswell*), Athene Seyler (*Mrs Karswell*), Maurice Denham (*Professor Harrington*), Liam Redmond (*Professor Mark O'Brien*), Peter Elliott (*Kumar*), Reginald Beckwith (*Mr Meek*).
Studio: ABPC, Elstree.
Year Ken Adam worked on film: 1956–57.

24.
Battle of the V-1 (US: Unseen Heroes)
GB 1958.
d – Vernon Sewell. *p* – George Maynard, Vernon Sewell, *p.c* – Criterion Films. *dist* – Eros.
sc – Jack Hanley, Eryk Wlodek, from the book *They Saved London* by Bernard Newman. *ph* (*b/w*) – Basil Emmott. *ed* – Lito Carruthers. *mus* – Robert Sharples.
p.d – Ken Adam. *a.d* – Bernard Sarron. *set dec* – Freda Pearson. *cost* – Morris Angel.
cast – Michael Rennie (*Stefan*), Patricia Medina (*Zofia*), Milly Vitale (*Anna*), David Knight (*Tadek*), Esmond Knight (*Stricker*), Christopher Lee (*Brunner*), Carl Jaffé (*General*).
Studios: Brighton Studios, Sussex; National Studios, Elstree.
Year Ken Adam worked on film: 1957.

25.
Gideon's Day (US: Gideon of Scotland Yard)
GB 1958.
d – John Ford. *p* – Michael Killanin, *p.c* – Columbia British/A John Ford Production. *dist* – Columbia.
sc – T.E.B. Clarke, from the novel by J.J. Marric (John Creasey). *ph* (*Technicolor*) – Freddie Young.
ed – Raymond Poulton. *mus* – Douglas Gamley.
a.d – Ken Adam. *set construction* – Peter Dukelow.
wardrobe – Jack Dalmane.
cast – Jack Hawkins (*Chief Inspector George Gideon*), Anna Lee (*Kate Gideon*), Anna Massey (*Sally Gideon*), Ronald Howard (*Paul Delafield*), Dianne Foster (*Joanna Delafield*), Cyril Cusack (*Birdy Sparrow*), Andrew Ray (*Simon Farnaby-Green*), James Hayter (*Mason*), Howard Marion-Crawford (*Chief*), Laurence Naismith (*Arthur Sayer*), Derek Bond (*Sgt Kirby*), Frank Lawton (*Sgt Liggott*), John Loder (*Duke Ponsford*), Miles Malleson (*Judge*).
Studio: MGM, Elstree.
Year Ken Adam worked on film: 1957.

26.
Ten Seconds to Hell
GB/USA 1959.
d – Robert Aldrich. *p* – Michael Carreras, *p.c* – Hammer Film Productions/Seven Arts. *dist* – United Artists.
sc – Robert Aldrich, Teddi Sherman, from the novel *The Phoenix* by Lawrence P. Bachmann. *ph* (*b/w*) – Ernest Laszlo. *ed* – James Needs, Harry Richardson.
mus – Kenneth V. Jones. *p.d* – Ken Adam.
cast – Jack Palance (*Eric Koertner*), Jeff Chandler (*Karl Wirtz*), Martine Carol (*Margot Hofer*), Wesley Addy (*Sulke*), Virginia Baker (*Frau Bauer*), Richard Wattis (*Major Haven*).
Studios: Bray; UFA Tempelhof (Berlin).
Year Ken Adam worked on film: 1958.

27.
The Angry Hills
GB 1959.
d – Robert Aldrich. *p* – Raymond Stross, *p.c* – Raymond Stross Productions. *dist* – MGM.
sc – A.I. Bezzerides, from the novel by Leon Uris.
ph (*b/w*) – Stephen Dade. *ed* – Peter Tanner.
mus – Richard Rodney Bennett. *p.d* – Ken Adam.
cast – Robert Mitchum (*Mike Morrison*), Stanley Baker (*Konrad Heisler*), Lisabeth [DG: Elisabeth] Müller (*Lisa Kiriakides*), Gia Scala (*Eleftheria Pirikos*), Theodore Bikel (*Demetrios Tassos*), Sebastian Cabot (*Chesney*), Leslie Phillips (*Ray Taylor*), Donald Wolfit (*Dr Stergiou*), Marius Goring (*Col. Oberg*), Kieron Moore (*Andreas Pirikos*).
Studio: MGM, Elstree. *Locs*: Greece (Athens).
Year Ken Adam worked on film: 1958.

28.
Beyond This Place (US: Web of Evidence)
GB 1959.
d – Jack Cardiff. *xp* – George Minter, *p* – Maxwell Setton, John R. Sloan, *p.c* – Georgefield Productions.
dist – Renown.
sc – Ken Taylor, from the novel by A.J. Cronin.
ph (*b/w*) – Wilkie Cooper. *ed* – Ernest Walter. *mus* – Douglas Gamley. *a.d* – Ken Adam.
cast – Van Johnson (*Paul Mathry*), Vera Miles (*Lena Anderson*), Emlyn Williams (*Enoch Oswald*), Bernard Lee (*Patrick Mathry*), Jean Kent (*Louise Birt*), Leo McKern (*John McEvoy*), Rosalie Crutchley (*Ella Mathry*), Moultrie Kelsall (*Superintendent Dale*), Ralph Truman (*Sir Matthew Sprott, QC*), Geoffrey Keen (*Prison Governor*).
Studios: MGM, Elstree; Riverside; Walton-on-Thames.
Locs: Liverpool.
Year Ken Adam worked on film: 1959.

29.
The Rough and the Smooth (US: Portrait of a Sinner)
GB 1959.
d – Robert Siodmak. *p* – George Minter, p.c/*dist* – Renown.
sc – Audrey Erskine Lindop, Dudley Leslie, from the novel by Robin Maugham. *ph* (*b/w*) – Otto Heller.
ed – Gordon Pilkington. *mus* – Douglas Gamley. *p.d* – Ken Adam. *dress des* – Julie Harris.
cast – Tony Britton (*Mike Thompson*), Nadja Tiller (*Ila Hanssen*), William Bendix (*Reg Barker*), Natasha Parry (*Margaret Goreham*), Norman Wooland (*David Fraser*), Donald Wolfit (*Lord Drewell*), Adrienne Corri (*Jane Buller*), Joyce Carey (*Mrs Thompson*).
Studio: MGM, Elstree.
Year Ken Adam worked on film: 1959.

30.
In the Nick
GB 1959.
d/sc – Ken Hughes. *xp* – Irving Allen, Albert R. Broccoli, *p* – Harold Huth, *p.c* – Warwick Films.
dist – Columbia.
Based on an original story by Frank Norman. *ph* (*b/w, CinemaScope*) – Ted Moore. *ed* – Geoffrey Foot.
mus – Ron Goodwin. *p.d* – Ken Adam.
cast – Anthony Newley (*Dr Newcombe*), James Booth (*Spider Kelly*), Anne Aubrey (*Doll*), Bernie Winters (*Jinx Shortbottom*), Harry Andrews (*Chief Williams*), Al Mulock (*Dancer*), Ian Hendry (*Ted Ross*), Niall MacGinnis (*Prison Governor*).
Studio: MGM, Elstree.
Year Ken Adam worked on film: 1959.

31.
The Hellions (pre-production work, late 1959/early 1960)
GB 1961.
d – Ken Annakin. *p* – Harold Huth, *p.c* – Irving Allen-Jamie Uys, GW Film. *dist* – Columbia.
** Ken Adam was involved in the pre-production for Irving Allen's and Albert R. Broccoli's Warwick Films. He had completely designed the film, a story set in South Africa in 1860, when it was postponed; by the time the project was resumed, he was unable to do the final film owing to other commitments. The design of the finished film was credited to William Constable. Shot in Technicolor and Technirama, it starred Richard Todd, Jamie Uys, Anne Aubrey, Marty Wilde, James Booth, and Lionel Jeffries.

32.
The Long Ships (pre-production work, 1959)
GB/Yugoslavia 1963.
d – Jack Cardiff. *p* – Irving Allen, Denis O'Dell, *p.c* – Warwick Films (London)/Avala (Belgrade). *dist* – Columbia. *a.d* – John Hoesli, Zoran Zorcic, William Constable, Vlastimir Gravik. matte artist – Ivor Beddoes. *cast* – Richard Widmark, Sidney Poitier, Rosanna Schiaffino, Russ Tamblyn, Oscar Homolka. Filmed in *Technicolor* and Technirama.
** Ken Adam researched the locations for this film in Yugoslavia in 1959.

33.
Let's Get Married
GB 1960.
d – Peter Graham Scott. *p* – John R. Sloan, *p.c* – Viceroy Productions. *dist* – Eros.
sc – Ken Taylor, from the novel *Confessions of a Kept Woman* by Gina Klausen. *ph* (*b/w*, *CinemaScope*) – Ted Moore. *ed* – Ernest Walter. *mus* – Edwin Astley. *p.d* – Ken Adam.
cast – Anthony Newley (*Dickie Bird*), Anne Aubrey (*Anne Linton*), Bernie Winters (*Bernie*), Hermione Baddeley (*Mrs O'Grady*), James Booth (*Photographer*), Lionel Jeffries (*Marsh*), John le Mesurier (*Dean*), Joyce Carey (*Miss Finch*).
Studio: MGM, Elstree.
Year Ken Adam worked on film: 1959.

34.
The Trials of Oscar Wilde (US: The Man with the Green Carnation)
GB 1960.
d/sc – Ken Hughes. *xp* – Irving Allen, Albert R. Broccoli, *p* – Harold Huth, *p.c* – Warwick Film Productions/Viceroy Films. *dist* – Eros.
Based on the book by Montgomery Hyde, and the play *The Stringed Lute* by John Fernald. *ph* (*Technicolor*, *Super Technirama-70*) – Ted Moore. *ed* – Geoffrey Foot. *mus* – Ron Goodwin. *p.d* – Ken Adam. *assoc.a.d* – William Constable. *set dresser* – Terence Morgan.
cast – Peter Finch (*Oscar Wilde*), Yvonne Mitchell (*Constance Wilde*), John Fraser (*Lord Alfred Douglas*), James Mason (*Sir Edward Carson*), Nigel Patrick (*Sir Edward Clarke*), Lionel Jeffries (*Marquess of Queensberry*), Emry Jones (*Robbie Ross*), James Booth (*Alfred Wood*), Sonia Dresdel (*Lady Wilde*), Maxine Audley (*Ada Leverson*), Paul Rogers (*Frank Harris*), Laurence Naismith (*Prince of Wales*), Naomi Chance (*Lily Langtry*).
Studio: Associated British, Elstree.
Year Ken Adam worked on film: 1960.
** Moscow Film Festival Prize for Best Art Direction.

35.
[Unrealised project]
GB 1960/61.
Ken Adam and Maurice Binder planned to make a film for Irving Allen, which they would co-direct. This untitled production never materialised.

36.
The Roman Spring of Mrs Stone
(pre-production work)
USA/GB 1961. (rel. 1962)
d – José Quintero. *p* – Louis De Rochemont, *ap* – Lothar Wolff, *p.c* – A.A. Productions/Seven Arts. *dist* – Warner Bros.
**Ken Adam completed the first designs for this Technicolor film version of Tennessee Williams's novella for producer Louis De Rochemont. Director José Quintero, however, had already engaged Roger Furse as the production designer. The film starred Vivien Leigh and Warren Beatty.

37.
Sodoma e Gomorra/Sodom and Gomorrah
USA/Italy/France 1961.
d – Robert Aldrich, Sergio Leone. *xp* – Goffredo Lombardo, Joseph E. Levine, *p* – Goffredo Lombardo, *p.c* – Titanus (Rome)/Société Nouvelle Pathé (Paris)/ Société Générale de Cinématographie (Paris). *dist* – Rank (GB)/20th Century-Fox (US).
2nd unit d – Oscar Rudolph. *sc* – Hugo Butler, Giorgio Prosperi. *ph* (*DeLuxe Color*) – Silvano Ippoliti, Mario Montuori, Cyril Knowles. *ed* – Peter Tanner. *mus* – Miklos Rozsa. *p.d* – Ken Adam. cont.sketch – Scott MacGregor. *set dec* – Gino Brosio. *sfx* – Lee Zavitz, Serse Urbisaglia, Wally Veevers. *travelling matte* – Vic Margutti. *cost* – Giancarlo Bartolini Salimbeni. *titles* – Maurice Binder.
cast – Stewart Granger (*Lot*), Anouk Aimée (*Queen Bera*), Stanley Baker (*Astaroth*), Pier Angeli (*Ildith, Lot's wife*), Rossana Podestà (*Shuah*), Claudia Mori (*Maleb*), Daniele Vargas (*Segur*), Rik Battaglia (*Melchior*), Giacomo Rossi Stuart (*Ishmael*).
Studios: Cinecittà (*Rome*); Shepperton.
Year Ken Adam worked on film: 1960–61.

38.
Dr No
GB 1962.
d – Terence Young. *p* – Harry Saltzman, Albert R. Broccoli, *p.c* – Eon Productions. *dist* – United Artists.
sc – Richard Maibaum, Johanna Harwood, Berkely Mather, from the novel by Ian Fleming. *ph* (*Technicolor*) – Ted Moore. *ed* – Peter Hunt. *mus* – Monty Norman. *p.d* – Ken Adam. *a.d* – Syd Cain. *draught* – Alan Tomkins. *sfx* – Frank George. *titles* – Maurice Binder.
cast – Sean Connery (*James Bond*), Ursula Andress (*Honey Ryder*), Joseph Wiseman (*Dr No*), Jack Lord (*Felix Leiter*), Bernard Lee (*M*), Lois Maxwell (*Miss Moneypenny*), Anthony Dawson (*Professor Dent*), Zena Marshall (*Miss Taro*), John Kitzmiller (*Quarrel*), Eunice Gayson (*Sylvia Trench*).
Studio: Pinewood. *Locs*: Jamaica; Florida.
Year Ken Adam worked on film: 1961–62.

39.
In the Cool of the Day
GB 1962.
d – Robert Stevens. *p* – John Houseman, *p.c* – MGM/ John Houseman Productions. *dist* – MGM.
sc – Meade Roberts, from the novel by Susan Ertz. *ph* (*Metrocolor*, *Panavision*) – Peter Newbrook. *ed* – Thomas Stanford. *mus* – Francis Chagrin. *a.d* – Ken Adam. *sfx* – Tom Howard. *ward.sup* – Ivy Baker. *Jane Fonda's wardrobe des* – Orry-Kelly. *Constance Cummings's wardrobe* – Pierre Balmain.
cast – Jane Fonda (*Christine Bonner*), Peter Finch (*Murray Logan*), Angela Lansbury (*Sybil Logan*), Arthur Hill (*Sam Logan*), Constance Cummings (*Mrs Gellert*), Alexander Knox (*Frederick Bonner*), Nigel Davenport (*Len*).
Studio: MGM, Elstree. *Locs*: Greece.
Year Ken Adam worked on film: 1962.

40.
Dr Strangelove or: How I Learned to Stop Worrying and Love the Bomb
GB 1963. (General release Jan. 1964)
p/d – Stanley Kubrick. *p.c* – Hawk Films.
dist – Columbia.
sc – Stanley Kubrick, Terry Southern, Peter George, from the novel 'Red Alert' by Peter George. *ph* (*b/w*) – Gilbert Taylor. *ed* – Anthony Harvey. *mus* – Laurie Johnson. *p.d* – Ken Adam. *a.d* – Peter Murton. *sfx* – Wally Veevers. *travelling matte* – Vic Margutti. *scenic painter* – Alan Maley. *wardrobe* – Bridget Sellers.
cast – Peter Sellers (*Group Captain Lionel Mandrake/ President Muffley/Dr Strangelove*), George C. Scott (*General 'Buck' Turgidson*), Sterling Hayden (*General Jack D. Ripper*), Keenan Wynn (*Colonel 'Bat' Guano*), Slim Pickens (*Major T.J. 'King' Kong*), Peter Bull (*Ambassador de Sadesky*), Tracy Reed (*Miss Scott*), James Earl Jones (*Lt Lothar Zogg*).
Studio: Shepperton. *Locs*: Heathrow Airport (establishing shot of airbase).
Year Ken Adam worked on film: 1962–63.
** British Film Academy award, Best Art Direction.

41.
Woman of Straw
GB 1964.
d – Basil Dearden. *p* – Michael Relph, *p.c* – Novus Film. *dist* – United Artists.
sc – Robert Muller, Stanley Mann, Michael Relph, from the novel by Catherine Arley. *ph* (*Eastmancolor*) – Otto Heller. *ed* – John D. Gutheridge. *mus* – Beethoven, Berlioz, Mozart, Rimsky-Korsakov, *arr.* Muir Mathieson. *song* – Norman Percival. *p.d* – Ken Adam. *a.d* – Peter Murton. *set dec* – Freda Pearson. *cost* – Beatrice Dawson. *Miss Lollobrigida's clothes* – Christian Dior.
cast – Gina Lollobrigida (*Maria*), Sean Connery (*Anthony Richmond*), Ralph Richardson (*Charles Richmond*), Alexander Knox (*Lomer*), Johnny Sekka (*Thomas*).
Studio: Pinewood. *Locs*: Majorca.
Year Ken Adam worked on film: 1963.

42.
Goldfinger
GB 1964.
d – Guy Hamilton. *p* – Harry Saltzman, Albert R. Broccoli, *p.c* – Eon Productions/Danjaq, SA. *dist* – United Artists.
sc – Richard Maibaum, Paul Dehn, from the novel by Ian Fleming. *ph* (*Technicolor*) – Ted Moore. *ed* – Peter Hunt. *mus* – John Barry.
p.d – Ken Adam. *a.d* – Peter Murton. *asst.a.d* – Michael White, Maurice Pelling. *set dresser* – Freda Pearson. *sfx* – John Stears, Frank George. *set construction* – Ronnie Udell. *title des* – Robert Brownjohn.
cast – Sean Connery (*James Bond*), Honor Blackman (*Pussy Galore*), Gert Fröbe (*Auric Goldfinger*), Harold Sakata (*Oddjob*), Shirley Eaton (*Jill Masterson*), Tania Mallet (*Tilly Masterson*), Bernard Lee (*M*), Martin Benson (*Solo*), Cec Linder (*Felix Leiter*), Lois Maxwell (*Miss Moneypenny*), Desmond Llewelyn (*Q*).
Studio: Pinewood. *Locs*: Fontainebleau Hotel, Miami, Florida; Switzerland; stud farm and Fort Knox, Kentucky.
Year Ken Adam worked on film: 1963-64.
** British Film Academy award nomination, Best Art Direction.

43.
The Ipcress File
GB 1965.
d – Sidney J. Furie. *xp* – Charles Kasher, *p* – Harry Saltzman, *ap* – Ronald Kinnoch, *p.c* – Lowndes Productions/Steven, SA. *dist* – Rank.
sc – Bill Canaway, James Doran, from the novel by Len Deighton. *ph* (*Technicolor*, *Techniscope*) – Otto Heller. *ed* – Peter Hunt. *mus* – John Barry. *p.d* – Ken Adam. *a.d* – Peter Murton. *set dresser* – Michael White.
cast – Michael Caine (*Harry Palmer*), Nigel Green

(*Dalby*), Guy Doleman (*Major Ross*), Sue Lloyd (*Jean Courtney*), Gordon Jackson (*Jock Carswell*), Frank Gatliff (*Eric Grantby*), Aubrey Richards (*Radcliffe*).
Studio: Pinewood. *Locs*: London.
Year Ken Adam worked on film: 1964.
** British Film Academy award, Best Art Direction.

44.
Thunderball
GB 1965.
d – Terence Young. *xp* – Harry Saltzman, Albert R. Broccoli, *p* – Kevin McClory, *p.c* – Eon Productions/ Danjaq, SA. *dist* – United Artists.
sc – Richard Maibaum, John Hopkins, from a story by Kevin McClory, Jack Whittingham, and Ian Fleming, and the novel by Ian Fleming. *ph* (*Technicolor*, *Panavision*) – Ted Moore. *underwater d* – Ricou Browning. *underwater sequences* – Ivan Tors Underwater Studios. *ed* – Peter Hunt. *mus* – John Barry. *p.d* – Ken Adam. *a.d* – Peter Murton. *set dec* – Freda Pearson. *sfx* – John Stears. *cost* – Anthony Mendleson. *titles* – Maurice Binder.
cast – Sean Connery (*James Bond*), Claudine Auger (*Domino*), Adolfo Celi (*Emilio Largo*), Luciana Paluzzi (*Fiona*), Rik Van Nutter (*Felix Leiter*), Bernard Lee (*M*), Martine Beswick (*Paula*), Guy Doleman (*Count Lippe*), Desmond Llewelyn (*Q*), Lois Maxwell (*Miss Moneypenny*), Roland Culver (*Foreign Secretary*), Molly Peters (*Patricia*), Paul Stassino (*Palazzi*) .
Studio: Pinewood. *Locs*: Nassau, the Bahamas.
Year Ken Adam worked on film: 1964–65.

45.
Funeral in Berlin
GB 1966.
d – Guy Hamilton. *p* – Harry Saltzman, Charles Kasher, *p.c* – Lowndes Productions/Jovera, SA. *dist* – Paramount.
sc – Evan Jones, from the novel *The Berlin Memorandum* by Len Deighton. *ph* (*Technicolor*, *Panavision*) – Otto Heller. *ed* – John Bloom. *mus* – Konrad Elfers. *p.d* – Ken Adam. *a.d* – Peter Murton. *set dec* – Vernon Dixon, Michael White.
cast – Michael Caine (*Harry Palmer*), Eva Renzi (*Samantha Steel*), Paul Hubschmid (*Johnny Vulkan*), Oscar Homolka (*Colonel Stok*), Guy Doleman (*Ross*), Hugh Burden (*Hallam*), Heinz Schubert (*Aaron Levine*), Wolfgang Völz (*Werner*), Thomas Holtzmann (*Reinhart*), Günter Meisner (*Kreutzmann*).
Studio: Pinewood. *Locs*: Berlin.
Year Ken Adam worked on film: 1965.

46.
You Only Live Twice
GB 1967.
d – Lewis Gilbert. *p* – Harry Saltzman, Albert R. Broccoli, *p.c* – Eon Productions/Danjaq, SA. *dist* – United Artists.
sc – Roald Dahl, Harry Jack Bloom, from the novel by Ian Fleming. *ph* (*Technicolor*, *Panavision*) – Freddie Young. *ed* – Peter Hunt. *mus* – John Barry. *p.d* – Ken Adam. *a.d* – Harry Pottle. *asst.a.d* – Peter Lamont, Ivor Beddoes. *set dec* – David Ffolkes. *set construction* – Ronnie Udell. *builder* – Bill Brown. *sfx* – John Stears. *wardrobe* – Eileen Sullivan. *titles* – Maurice Binder.
cast – Sean Connery (*James Bond*), Akiko Wakabayashi (*Aki*), Donald Pleasence (*Ernst Blofeld*), Tetsuro Tamba (*Tiger Tanaka*), Mie Hama (*Kissy Suzuki*), Teru Shimada (*Osato*), Karin Dor (*Helga Brandt*), Bernard Lee (*M*), Lois Maxwell (*Miss Moneypenny*), Desmond Llewelyn (Q), Charles Gray (*Henderson*), Alexander Knox (*President*).
Studio: Pinewood. *Locs*: Kyushu Island, Japan.
Year Ken Adam worked on film: 1966.

47.
Chitty Chitty Bang Bang
GB 1968.
d – Ken Hughes. *p* – Albert R. Broccoli, *p.c* – Warfield Productions/Dramatic Features. *dist* – United Artists.
sc – Roald Dahl, Ken Hughes, from stories by Ian Fleming. *ph* (*Technicolor*, *Super Panavision 70*) – Christopher Challis. *ed* – John Shirley. *mus/songs* – Richard M. Sherman, Robert B. Sherman. *p.d* – Ken Adam. *a.d* – Henry Pottle. *inventions* – Rowland Emett. *sfx* – John Stears. *cost* – Elizabeth Haffenden, Joan Bridge.
cast – Dick Van Dyke (*Caractacus Potts*), Sally Ann Howes (*Truly Scrumptious*), Gert Fröbe (*Baron Bomburst*), Lionel Jeffries (*Grandpa Potts*), Heather Ripley (*Jemima Potts*), Adrian Hall (*Jeremy Potts*), Anna Quayle (*Baroness Bomburst*), Benny Hill (*Toymaker*), James Robertson Justice (*Lord Scrumptious*), Robert Helpmann (*Child Catcher*), Davy Kaye (*Admiral*), Max Wall (*Inventor*).
Studio: Pinewood. *Locs*: England; La Bastide Blanche, France; Neuschwanstein Castle, Germany.
Year Ken Adam worked on film: 1967.

48.
Goodbye, Mr Chips
GB 1969.
d – Herbert Ross. *p* – Arthur P. Jacobs, *p.c* – Apjac Productions/ Keep Films/MGM British. *dist* – MGM.
sc – Terence Rattigan, from the novel by James Hilton. *ph* (*Metrocolor*, *Panavision 70*) – Oswald Morris. *ed* – Ralph Kemplen. *songs* – Leslie Bricusse. *p.d* – Ken Adam. *a.d* – Maurice Fowler. *cost* – Julie Harris.
cast – Peter O'Toole (*Arthur Chipping*), Petula Clark (*Katherine Bridges*), Michael Redgrave (*Headmaster*), George Baker (*Lord Sutterwick*), Michael Bryant (*Max Staefel*), Jack Hedley (*William Baxter*), Siân Phillips (*Ursula Mossbank*), Clive Morton (*General Paunceforth*), Barbara Couper (*Mrs Paunceforth*), Elspet Gray (*Lady Sutterwick*), Patricia Hayes (*Miss Honeybun*).
Studio: MGM, Elstree. *Locs*: Sherborne School, Dorset; Pompeii and Paestum, Italy.
Year Ken Adam worked on film: 1968–69.

49.
Peter Pan (unrealised)
GB 1969.
A project for Universal, to be produced by Mel Ferrer and directed by Herbert Ross, to star Mia Farrow. The film was never made.

50.
Lord L (unrealised)
GB 1969.
A joint project with Italian scriptwriter Ennio De Concini, who wanted to direct. Ken Adam was to produce and design the film. De Concini, who had worked with Fellini and Pietro Germi, fashioned a controversial, topical story about God visiting the world of the 1960s, and coming into conflict with the counterculture and political movements; mankind is finally left to deal with its own problems. Universal ended up proposing that this challenging subject be done with another director, on a low budget, and it was shelved.

51.
On Her Majesty's Secret Service (pre-production work, 1968)
GB 1969.
d – Peter Hunt. p: Harry Saltzman, Albert R. Broccoli, *p.c* – Eon Productions/Danjaq, SA. *dist* – United Artists. *p.d* – Syd Cain. *a.d* – Bob Laing.
Based on the novel by Ian Fleming, starring George Lazenby as James Bond, Diana Rigg as Tracy Draco, and Telly Savalas as Ernst Blofeld. Filmed in Technicolor and Panavision. Made at Pinewood Studios, with locations in Switzerland, London and Portugal.
** Ken Adam was involved in the first preparatory phases and researched locations for the film, but withdrew when filming was delayed as he had already accepted the offer to design **The Owl and the Pussycat** for Herbert Ross.

52.
The Owl and the Pussycat
USA 1970.
d – Herbert Ross. *p* – Ray Stark, *p.c* – Rastar Productions. *dist* – Columbia.
sc – Buck Henry, from the play by Bill Manhoff.
ph (*Eastmancolor*, *Panavision*) – Harry Stradling, Andrew Laszlo. *ed* – John F. Burnett. *mus* – Richard Halligan. *design sup* – Ken Adam. *p.d* – John Robert Lloyd. *a.d* – Robert Wightman, Philip Rosenberg. *set dec* – Leif Pedersen. *cost* – Ann Roth. *title des* – Wayne Fitzgerald.
cast – Barbra Streisand (*Doris Wadsworth*), George Segal (*Felix Sherman*), Robert Klein (*Barney*), Allen Garfield (*Dress Shop Proprietor*), Roz Kelly (*Eleanor*), Jacques Sandulescu (*Rapzinsky*), Barbara Anson (*Miss Weyderhaus*), Jack Manning (*Mr Weyderhaus*), Grace Carney (*Mrs Weyderhaus*).
Studio: Fox studio, NYC. *Locs*: Manhattan.
Year Ken Adam worked on film: 1970.
** Ken Adam also played a bit role as one of Barbra Streisand's clients.

53.
Diamonds Are Forever
GB 1971.
d – Guy Hamilton. *p* – Harry Saltzman, Albert R. Broccoli, *p.c* – Eon Productions/Danjaq, SA. *dist* – United Artists.
sc – Richard Maibaum, Tom Mankiewicz, from the novel by Ian Fleming. *ph* (*Technicolor*, Panavision) – Ted Moore. *ed* – Bert Bates, John W. Holmes. *mus* – John Barry. *p.d* – Ken Adam. *a.d* – Jack Maxsted, Bill Kenney. *set dec* – Peter Lamont, John Austin. *sketch artist* – Tom Wright. *special phot. effects/ matte artist* – Albert Whitlock, Wally Veevers. *sfx* – Leslie Hillman, Whitey McMahon.
cast – Sean Connery (*James Bond*), Jill St. John (*Tiffany Case*), Charles Gray (*Blofeld*), Lana Wood (*Plenty O'Toole*), Jimmy Dean (*Willard Whyte*), Bruce Cabot (*Saxby*), Bernard Lee (*M*), Lois Maxwell (*Miss Moneypenny*), Desmond Llewelyn (*M*), Norman Burton (*Felix Leiter*), Joseph Fürst (*Dr Metz*), Putter Smith (*Kidd*), Bruce Glover (*Wint*), Laurence Naismith (*Sir Donald Munger*).
Studio: Universal (Los Angeles); Pinewood. *Locs*: Santa Barbara (oil rig); Las Vegas.
Year Ken Adam worked on film: 1971.

54.
Sleuth
GB 1972.
d – Joseph L. Mankiewicz. *xp* – Edgar J. Scherick, *p* – Morton Gottlieb, *p.c* – Palomar Pictures International. *dist* – 20th Century-Fox/Rank.
sc – Anthony Shaffer, from his play. *ph* (*DeLuxe Color*) – Oswald Morris. *ed* – Richard Marden. *mus* – John Addison. *p.d* – Ken Adam. *a.d* – Peter Lamont. *set dec* – John Jarvis. *set construction* – Mike Redding. *sketch artist/miniature theatre models* – Ivor Beddoes. *cost* – John Furniss.
cast – Laurence Olivier (*Andrew Wyke*), Michael Caine (*Milo Tindle*), Alec Cawthorne (*Inspector Doppler*), Margo Channing (*Marguerite*), John Matthews (*Det Sgt Tarrant*).

Studio: Pinewood. *Locs*: Athelhampton, near Dorchester, Dorset.
Year Ken Adam worked on film: 1972.
** British Film Academy award nomination, Best Art Direction.

55.
The Last of Sheila
USA 1973.
d – Herbert Ross. *xp* – Stanley O'Toole, *p* – Herbert Ross, *p.c* – Warner Bros. *dist* – Columbia-Warner.
sc – Stephen Sondheim, Anthony Perkins. *ph* (*Technicolor*) – Gerry Turpin. *ed* – Edward Warschilka. *mus* – Billy Goldenberg. *p.d* – Ken Adam. *a.d* – Tony Roman. *set dec* – John Jarvis. *gowns* – Halston, Ron Talsky.
cast – Richard Benjamin (*Tom*), Dyan Cannon (*Christine*), James Coburn (*Clinton Greene*), Joan Hackett (*Lee*), James Mason (*Philip*), Ian McShane (*Anthony*), Raquel Welch (*Alice*), Yvonne Romaine (*Sheila Greene*).
Studio: La Victorine (Nice). *Locs*: French Riviera; the Mediterranean.
Year Ken Adam worked on film: 1972.

56.
Barry Lyndon
GB 1975.
d – Stanley Kubrick. *xp* – Jan Harlan, *p* – Stanley Kubrick, *p.c* – Hawk Films/Peregrine Productions. *dist* – Warner Bros.
sc – Stanley Kubrick, from the novel *The Luck of Barry Lyndon* by William Makepeace Thackeray. *ph* (*Eastmancolor*) – John Alcott. *ed* – Tony Lawson. *mus* – Schubert, Vivaldi, Bach, Handel, Mozart, *et al.*, *arr.* Leonard Rosenman; The Chieftains (Irish traditional music). *p.d* – Ken Adam. *a.d* – Roy Walker, (Germany) Jan Schlubach. *set dec* – Vernon Dixon. *cost* – Ulla-Britt Søderlund, Milena Canonero.
cast – Ryan O'Neal (*Barry Lyndon*), Marisa Berenson (*Lady Lyndon*), Patrick Magee (*Chevalier de Balibari*), Hardy Kruger (*Hauptmann Potzdorf*), Steven Berkoff (*Lord Ludd*), Gay Hamilton (*Nora Brady*), Marie Kean (Mrs Barry), Murray Melvin (*Rev. Samuel Runt*), Frank Middlemass (*Sir Charles Lyndon*), André Morell (*Lord Wendover*), Arthur O'Sullivan (*Highwayman*), Godfrey Quigley (*Capt. Grogan*), Leonard Rossiter (*Capt. Quin*), Leon Vitali (*Lord Bullingdon*), Michael Hordern (*narrator*).
Studio: No studio work; filmed entirely on location. *Locs*: Ireland (Waterford and Kilkenny; Interiors: Dublin Castle, Powers Court, Caher Castle, Huntington manor); England (Wilton House, Blenheim, Castle Howard, Corsham Court, Longleat, Petworth); Germany (2nd unit locs., Potsdam).
Year Ken Adam worked on film: 1973–74.
** Academy Award, Best Art Direction.
** British Film Academy award nomination, Best Art Direction.

57.
Salon Kitty (US: Madam Kitty)
Italy/West Germany/France 1976.
d – Giovanni Tinto Brass. *xp* – Carla Cipriani, *p* – Giulio Sbarigia, Ermanno Donati. *p.c* – Coralta Cinematografica (Rome)/Cinema Seven Film (Munich)/ Les Productions Fox Europa (Paris). *dist* – 20th Century-Fox.
sc – Ennio De Concini, Maria Pia Fusco, Giovanni Tinto Brass. *ph* (Eastmancolor) – Silvano Ippoliti. *ed* – Giovanni Tinto Brass. *mus* – Fiorenzo Carpi. *p.d* – Ken Adam. *a.d* – Enrico Fiorentini, Jan Schlubach. *set dec* – Giovanni Checchi. *sfx* – Otello Sisi. *cost* – Ugo Pericoli, Jost Jakob.
cast – Helmut Berger (*Captain Helmut Wallenberg*), Ingrid Thulin (*Kitty Kellermann*), Teresa Ann Savoy (*Margherita*), Bekim Fehmiu (*Captain Hans Reiter*), John Ireland (*Clift*), Tina Aumont (*Herta Wallenberg*).
Studio: Dear (Rome).
Year Ken Adam worked on film: 1975.

58.
The Seven-Per-Cent Solution
USA 1976.
d – Herbert Ross. *xp* – Arlene Sellers, Alex Winitsky, *p* – Herbert Ross, *p.c* – Universal Pictures. *UK dist* – CIC.
sc – Nicholas Meyer, from his novel and characters created by Arthur Conan Doyle. *ph* (*Technicolor*) – Oswald Morris. *ed* – Chris Barnes. *mus* – John Addison. *p.d* – Ken Adam. *a.d* – Peter Lamont. *set dec* – Peter James. *sketch artist* – Ivor Beddoes. *cost* – Alan Barrett. *titles* – Wayne Fitzgerald.
cast – Alan Arkin (*Sigmund Freud*), Vanessa Redgrave (*Lola Deveraux*), Robert Duvall (*Dr Watson*), Nicol Williamson (*Sherlock Holmes*), Laurence Olivier (*Professor Moriarty*), Joel Grey (*James Lowenstein*), Samantha Eggar (*Mary Watson*), Charles Gray (*Mycroft Holmes*), Georgia Brown (*Mrs Freud*), Régine (*Madame*), Jeremy Kemp (*Baron Von Leinsdorf*), Anna Quayle (*Freda*), Jill Townsend (*Mrs Holmes*), Alison Legatt (*Mrs Hudson*).
Studio: Pinewood. *Locs*: Vienna; the Rhine; Severn Valley steam railway.
Year Ken Adam worked on film: 1975.

59.
The Spy Who Loved Me
GB 1977.
d – Lewis Gilbert. *p* – Albert R. Broccoli, *p.c* – Eon Productions. *dist* – United Artists.
sc – Christopher Wood, Richard Maibaum, from the novel by Ian Fleming. *ph* (*Eastmancolor*, *Panavision*) – Claude Renoir. *ed* – John Glen. *mus* – Marvin Hamlisch. *p.d* – Ken Adam. *a.d* – Peter Lamont. *sfx* – Derek Meddings, (studio) John Evans. *spec. phot. effects* – Alan Maley. *fashion consultant* – Ronald Paterson. *titles* – Maurice Binder.
cast – Roger Moore (*James Bond*), Barbara Bach (*Major Anya Amasova*), Curt Jurgens (*Stromberg*), Richard Kiel (*Jaws*), Caroline Munro (*Naomi*), Walter Gotell (*General Gogol*), Geoffrey Keen (*Minister of Defence*), Edward De Souza (*Sheikh Hosein*), Vernon Dobtcheff (*Max Kalba*), George Baker (*Capt. Benson*), Bernard Lee (*M*), Lois Maxwell (*Miss Moneypenny*), Desmond Llewelyn (*Q*), Michael Billington (*Sergei*), Nadim Sawalha (*Fekkesh*), Sydney Tafler (*Liparus Captain*).
Studio: Pinewood. *Locs*: Sardinia; Canada; Egypt (The Pyramids, Luxor and Aswan); the Bahamas; Japan (2nd unit locs., Okinawa).
Year Ken Adam worked on film: 1976.
** Academy Award nomination, Best Art Direction.
** British Film Academy award nomination, Best Art Direction.

60.
Star Trek – The Motion Picture
(pre-production work, 1977)
USA 1979.
d – Robert Wise, *p* – Gene Roddenberry, *p.c* – Paramount. *p.d* – Harold Michelson.
** Ken Adam worked on pre-production planning for the first version of this project in 1977, when it was to be directed by Philip Kaufman for producer Gene Roddenberry, who also hired Ken Adam. Adam spent three months coming up with conceptual ideas for a civilisation *c.* AD 2400, as well as designing the *Starship Enterprise*. Paramount finally put the film on hold, and both Kaufman and Adam left the project. The first film version of the cult TV series was eventually made by a different director and crew.

61.
Moonraker
GB/France 1979.
d – Lewis Gilbert. *xp* – Michael G. Wilson, *p* – Albert R. Broccoli, *p.c* – Eon Productions (London)/Les Productions Artistes Associés (Paris). *dist* – United Artists.
sc – Christopher Wood, from the novel by Ian Fleming. *ph* (*Technicolor*, *Panavision*) – Jean Tournier. *ed* – John Glen. *mus* – John Barry. *p.d* – Ken Adam. *a.d* – Max Douy, Charles Bishop, (visual effects) Peter Lamont, (space) Harry Lange. *set dec* – Peter Howitt, Pierre Charron, André Labussière. *sfx* – John Evans, John Richardson, René Albouze, Serge Ponvianne. *visual effects sup* – Derek Meddings. *cost* – Jacques Fonteray. *titles* – Maurice Binder.
cast – Roger Moore (*James Bond*), Lois Chiles (*Holly Goodhead*), Michel Lonsdale (*Hugo Drax*), Richard Kiel (*Jaws*), Corinne Clery (Corinne Dufour), Emily Bolton (*Manuela*), Toshiro Suga (*Chang*), Geoffrey Keen (*Frederick Gray*), Bernard Lee (*M*), Lois Maxwell (*Miss Moneypenny*), Desmond Llewelyn (*Q*), Walter Gotell (*General Gogol*).
Studios: Epinay, Billancourt, and Boulogne (Paris). *Locs*: California; Florida; Venice (Venini Glass Museum; Palazzo Rezzonico; St. Mark's Square; canals); Brazil (Rio de Janeiro; Ikwasu Falls); France (Vaux-le-Vicomte; Pompidou Centre, Paris).
Year Ken Adam worked on film: 1978.

62.
Destinies (unrealised film)
USA 1979.
A John Frankenheimer project for the production company Lorimar. The story was about a Cuban exile. Ken Adam worked on the film in the summer of 1979, researching locations in Mexico and Miami.

63.
The Aquarius Mission (unrealised film)
USA 1979.
An unrealised project about an underwater civilisation. The project was only in the discussion stage when it was cancelled.

64.
Dress Grey (unrealised film)
USA 1980.
An unrealised Herbert Ross project for Paramount, about the West Point military academy. Ken Adam worked on the project for three or four months, doing research at West Point and preparing most of the designs. The film was to be made on location and at Paramount in Hollywood.

65.
Special Project for 20th Century-Fox
USA 1981–82.
Ken Adam was contracted by 20th Century-Fox for a year to work on a new concept for cinema and multimedia presentation, hoping to create a modern equivalent of the excitement of movie-going in the heyday of the spectacular movie palaces. He worked with Caltech and NASA to devise new technology, drawing up plans and models, and designing an inflatable cinema comparable to a mini-version of today's Millennium Dome. Dennis Potter was commissioned to write a screenplay for a pilot project, and Adam worked out the budgeting, culminating in an official studio presentation. However, owing to a disagreement between studio executives, the whole project was shelved.

66.
Pennies from Heaven
USA 1981.
d – Herbert Ross. *xp* – Richard McCallum, *p* – Nora Kaye, Herbert Ross, *ap* – Ken Adam, *p.c* – MGM/A Hera Production. UK *dist* – United International Pictures.
sc – Dennis Potter, from his BBC TV serial. *ph* (*Metrocolor*) – Gordon Willis. *ed* – Richard Marks. *mus. arr* – Marvin Hamlisch, Billy May. *visual consultant* – Ken Adam. *a.d* – Fred Tuch, Bernie Cutler. *set design* – Christopher Burian-Mohr. *set dec* – Garrett Lewis. *illustrator* – Thomas J. Wright. *sfx* – Glen Robinson. *cost* – Bob Mackie.
cast – Steve Martin (*Arthur Parker*), Bernadette Peters (*Eileen*), Jessica Harper (*Joan*), Christopher Walken (*Tom*), Vernel Bagneris (*Accordion Man*), John McMartin (*Mr Warner*), Tommy Rall (*Ed*).
Studios: MGM (*Culver City*); Goldwyn (*Hollywood*).
Locs: Disney Ranch; Galena, Illinois; Bakersfield, California.
Year Ken Adam worked on film: 1980–81.
** New York Independent Film Critics Award.

67.
The Fantasticks (unrealised film)
USA 1982.
A proposed film of the long-running off-Broadway musical. Ken Adam was engaged as production designer in 1982 by producer Michael Brown. He worked on the project for several months, producing numerous designs. However, the project ran out of money, and the film was postponed and never made.

68.
Mermaid (unrealised film)
USA 1983.
A film project for producer Ray Stark, to be directed by Herbert Ross for Columbia. Ken Adam spent weeks researching locations along the East Coast, from Newport to Miami, and then along the West Coast. He had begun designing the film when the project was shelved owing to differences between Ross and Stark.

69.
King David
USA 1985.
d – Bruce Beresford. *p* – Martin Elfland, *p.c* – Paramount. UK *dist* – United International Pictures.
sc – Andrew Birkin, James Costigan, from the Books of Samuel I and II, Chronicles I, and the Psalms of David. *ph* (*Technicolor*, *Panavision*) – Donald McAlpine. *ed* – William Anderson. *mus* – Carl Davis. *p.d* – Ken Adam. *a.d* – Terry Ackland-Snow, (Italy) Aurelio Crugnola. *set dec* – Peter Howitt, (Italy) Franco Fumagalli. *set dresser* – (Italy) Angelo Santucci. *sketch artist* – Maciek Piotrowski. *sculptor* – Bernard Kramer. *draught* – Peter Childs, Stephen Scott. *sfx sup* – Kit West, (Italy) Dino Galliano. *modellers* – Bernard Kramer, Fred Evans. *cost* – John Mollo. *graphic design* – Maurice Binder.
cast – Richard Gere (*David*), Edward Woodward (*Saul*), Alice Krige (*Bathsheba*), Denis Quilley (*Samuel*), Niall Buggy (*Nathan*), Cherie Lunghi (*Michal*), Hurd Hatfield (*Ahimilech*), Jack Klaff (*Jonathan*), John Castle (*Abner*), Tim Woodward (*Joab*), Jean-Marc Barr (*Absalom*), Jason Carter (*Solomon*).
Studio: Pinewood. *Locs*: Sardinia; Matera, Italy.
Year Ken Adam worked on film: 1983–84.

70.
The Last Emperor (pre-production work, 1985)
Italy/Republic of China 1987.
d – Bernardo Bertolucci. *p* – Jeremy Thomas, *p.c* – TA Films (Rome)/Yanco Films (Beijing)/Recorded Picture Co. *p.d* – Ferdinando Scarfiotti. *cost* – James Acheson.
** Ken Adam was originally engaged as this film's production designer by producer Jeremy Thomas. He worked on the project for nine months, scouting locations and drawing production designs. Shortly before filming began the contract was terminated.

71.
Agnes of God
USA 1985.
d – Norman Jewison. *p* – Patrick Palmer, Norman Jewison, *p.c* – Columbia/Delphi IV Productions. UK *dist* – Columbia-EMI-Warner
sc – John Pielmeier, from his play. *ph* (*Metrocolor*) – Sven Nykvist. *ed* – Antony Gibbs. *mus* – Georges Delerue. *p.d* – Ken Adam. *a.d* – Carol Spier. *set dec* – Jaro Dick. *set dresser* – Dan Conley, Martin Freedman. *sfx co-ord* – Ron Thiessen. *cost* – Renée April.
cast – Jane Fonda (*Dr. Martha Livingston*), Anne Bancroft (*Mother Miriam Ruth*), Meg Tilly (*Sister Agnes*), Anne Pitoniak (*Dr Livingston's Mother*), Winston Rekert (*Detective Langevin*), Gratien Gelinas (*Father Martineau*).
Studio: Toronto. *Locs*: Montreal; locations between Toronto and Montreal, including a disused school.
Year Ken Adam worked on film: 1984–85.

72.
Zorba (unrealised film)
GB 1985.
Ken Adam worked as production designer on this Saul Chaplin musical project for Cannon, which was to be directed by Robert Wise. The script was to be based on the 1964 film starring Anthony Quinn and the Broadway musical of the early 1980s. After preliminary meetings in Britain and location hunting and research in Crete and Israel, the necessary financing was not found and the film was never made.

73.
Crimes of the Heart
USA 1986.
d – Bruce Beresford. *xp* – Burt Sugarman, *p* – Freddie Fields, *p.c* – Crimes of the Heart Productions/De Laurentiis Entertainment Group. *dist* – 20th Century-Fox.
sc – Beth Henley, from her play. *ph* (*Technicolor*) – Dante Spinotti. *ed* – Anne Goursaud. *mus* – Georges Delerue. *p.d* – Ken Adam. *a.d* – Ferdinando Giovannoni. *set dec* – Garrett Lewis. *set dresser* – Tim Pope. *cost* – Albert Wolsky. *title des* – Wayne Fitzgerald.
cast – Diane Keaton (*Lenny Magrath*), Jessica Lange (*Meg Magrath*), Sissy Spacek (*Babe Magrath Botrelle*), Sam Shepard (*Doc Porter*), Tess Harper (*Chick Boyle*), David Carpenter (*Barnette Lloyd*), Hurd Hatfield (*Grandaddy*), Beeson Carroll (*Zackery Botrelle*), Tom Mason (*Uncle Watson*), Gregory Travis (*Willie Jay*).
Locs: Southport and Wilmington, North Carolina.
Year Ken Adam worked on film: 1986.

74.
Conquering Horse (unrealised film)
USA 1987.
A film project by director Michael Cimino, about the North American Plains Indians before their contact with the white man. Ken Adam worked on a feasibility study for Cimino, incorporating a provisional shooting and studio plan for this project, and spending two to three months doing extensive research at Native American reservations and sites in Canada and the USA and museums and collections in the USA and Germany, including copying hundreds of unique ethnographic photographs from the Smithsonian archives in Washington, DC. The film was never made.

75.
The Deceivers
GB 1988.
d – Nicholas Meyer. *xp* – Michael White, *p* – Ismail Merchant, *p.c* – Merchant Ivory/Michael White/ Cinecom/Film Four International. *dist* – Enterprise.
sc – Michael Hirst, from the novel by John Masters.
ph (*Fujicolor*) – Walter Lassally. *ed* – Richard Trevor.
mus – John Scott. *p.d* – Ken Adam. *a.d* – Gianfranco Fumagali, Ram Yedekar. *set dresser* – Letizia Adam.
cost – Jenny Beavan, John Bright. *titles* – Maurice Binder.
cast – Pierce Brosnan (*William Savage*), Saeed Jaffrey (*Hussein*), Shashi Kapoor (*Chandra Singh*), Helena Michell (*Sarah Wilson*), Keith Michell (*Colonel Wilson*), David Robb (*George Angelsmith*), Tariq Yunus (*Feringea*), Neena Gupta (*Widow*).
Locs: India: Jodhpur (Rajasthan); Agra (Uttar Pradesh); Madhya Pradesh.
Year Ken Adam worked on film: 1987.

76.
Dead-Bang
USA 1989.
d – John Frankenheimer. *xp* – Robert L. Rosen, *p* – Steve Roth, *p.c* – Lorimar Film Entertainment. *dist* – Warner Bros.
sc – Robert Foster. *ph* (*Metrocolor*) – Gerry Fisher. *ed* – Robert F. Shugrue. *mus* – Gary Chang, Michael Kamen. *p.d* – Ken Adam. *a.d* – Richard Hudolin, Alan Manzer. *set dec* – Art Parker. *set dresser* – Tedd Kuchera, Janice Blackie. *draught* – Carl Ebner. *illustrator* – John L. Jensen. *sfx* – Clifford P. Wenger. *cost* – Jodie Tillen. *title des* – Burke Mattsson.
cast – Don Johnson (*Jerry Beck*), Penelope Ann Miller (*Linda*), William Forsythe (*Arthur Kressler*), Bob Balaban (*Elliot Webly*), Frank Military (*Bobby Burns*), Michael Jeter (*Dr Krantz*), Tim Reid (*Chief Dixon*), Michael Hibbins (*Rev. Gebhardt*).
Studio: warehouses, Calgary, Canada. *Locs*: Calgary, Alberta, and Rocky Mountains, Canada.
Year Ken Adam worked on film: 1988.

77.
The Freshman
USA 1990.
d/sc – Andrew Bergman. *p* – Mike Lobell, *p.c* – Tri-Star Pictures. *dist* – Columbia Tri-Star.
ph (*Technicolor*) – William A. Fraker. *ed* – Barry Malkin. *mus* – David Newman. *p.d* – Ken Adam. *a.d* – Alicia Keywan, (New York) Dan Davis. *set dec* – Gordon Sim, (NY) Gary J. Brink. *head scenic artist* – Günter Bartlik, (NY) Michael Zansky. *sfx co-ord* – Neil Trifunovich. *cost* – Julie Weiss.
cast – Marlon Brando (*Carmine Sabatini*), Matthew Broderick (*Clark Kellog*), Penelope Ann Miller (*Tina Sabatini*), Maximilian Schell (*Larry London*), Bruno Kirby (*Victor Ray*).
Studio: Toronto. *Locs*: Toronto; New York City (Greenwich Village; Washington Square).
Year Ken Adam worked on film: 1989.

78.
Company Business
USA 1991.
d/sc – Nicholas Meyer. *p* – Charles Jaffe, *p.c* – Steven-Charles Jaffe/Pathé Entertainment. *dist* – MGM. ph (*Technicolor*) – Gerry Fisher. *ed* – Ronald Roose. *mus* – Michael Kamen. *p.d* – Ken Adam. *a.d* – Albrecht Konrad. *cost* – Yvonne Blake.
cast – Gene Hackman (*Sam Boyd*), Mikhail Baryshnikov (*Pyiotr Grushenko*), Kurtwood Smith (*Elliot Jaffe*), Terry O'Quinn (*Col. Grissom*), Oleg Rudnick (*Grigori Golitsin*).
Studio: CCC-Filmstudios (Berlin). *Locs*: Washington, DC; Paris; Berlin.
Year Ken Adam worked on film: 1989–90.

79.
The Doctor
USA 1991.
d – Randa Haines. *xp* – Edward S. Feldman, *p* – Laura Ziskin, *p.c* – Touchstone Pictures/Silver Screen Partners IV. *dist* – Buena Vista.
sc – Robert Caswell, from the book *A Taste of My Own Medicine* by Dr Ed Rosenbaum. *ph* (*Technicolor*) – John Seale. *ed* – Bruce Green, Lisa Fruchtman. *mus* – Michael Convertino. *p.d* – Ken Adam. *a.d* – William J. Durrell, Jr. *set dec* – Gary Fettis. *set dresser* – Ronald Kaeding, Michael Bates, Eric A. Hulett, Kurt V. Hulett. *cost* – Joe I. Tompkins.
cast – William Hurt (*Dr Jack MacKee*), Christine Lahti (*Anne MacKee*), Mandy Patinkin (*Dr Murray Caplan*), Elizabeth Perkins (*June Ellis*), Adam Arkin (*Dr Eli Blumfield*), Wendy Crewson (*Dr Leslie Abbott*), Charlie Korsmo (*Nicky MacKee*), Bill Macy (*Dr Al Cade*).
Studio: converted empty warehouse, Valencia, California. (Note: The whole hospital set was built inside it.) *Locs*: San Francisco; Malibu; Los Angeles.
Year Ken Adam worked on film: 1990–91.

80.
Night Ride Down (unrealised film)
USA 1991.
A film project to star Harrison Ford, which was to be directed by Harold Becker for Paramount. The story dealt with the Pullman attendant revolt in the 1930s, and would have been expensive to make, involving railtracks and steam trains. Ken Adam prepared many designs, but the project was postponed, and eventually shelved.

81.
Undercover Blues
USA 1993.
d – Herbert Ross. *xp* – Herbert Ross, Andrew Bergman, *p* – Mike Lobell, *p.c* – Lobell/Bergman/Hera/MGM. *dist* – MGM.
sc – Ian Abrams. *ph* (*colour*) – Donald E. Thorin. *ed* – Priscilla Nedd-Friendly. *mus* – David Newman. *p.d* – Ken Adam. *a.d* – William J. Durrell, Jr. *set des* – James R. Bayliss. *set dec* – Jeff Haley. *cost* – Wayne Finkelman.
cast – Kathleen Turner (*Jane Blue*), Dennis Quaid (*Jeff Blue*), Fiona Shaw (*Novacek*), Stanley Tucci (*Muerte*), Larry Miller (*Halsey*), Tom Arnold (*Vern Newman*).
Studio: Laird International Studios (old Selznick Studios, Culver City). *Locs*: New York City; New Orleans.
Year Ken Adam worked on film: 1992.

82.
Addams Family Values
USA 1993.
d – Barry Sonnenfeld. *p* – Scott Rudin, *p.c* – Paramount. *dist* – Paramount/UIP.
sc – Paul Rudnick, based on the characters created by Charles Addams. *ph* (*DeLuxe Color*) – Donald Peterman. *ed* – Arthur Schmidt, Jim Miller. *mus* – Marc Shaiman. *p.d* – Ken Adam. *a.d* – William J. Durrell, Jr. *set dec* – Marvin March. *cost* – Theoni V. Aldredge.
cast – Anjelica Huston (*Morticia Addams*), Raul Julia (*Gomez Addams*), Christopher Lloyd (*Uncle Fester*), Joan Cusack (*Debbie Jellinsky*), Christina Ricci (*Wednesday Addams*), Carol Kane (*Granny*), Jimmy Workman (*Pugsley Addams*), Carel Struycken (*Lurch*), Peter MacNicol (*Gary Granger*), Christine Baranski (*Becky Granger*), Kaitlyn and Kristen Hooper (*Pubert Addams*).
Studios: Paramount; Warner Bros.; Studio City. *Locs*: Los Angeles.
Year Ken Adam worked on film: 1992–93.
** Academy Award nomination, Best Art Direction.
** London Film Critics Circle award, Best Technical Achievement of the Year.

83.
Boys on the Side
USA 1994.
d – Herbert Ross. *p* – Arnon Milchan, Steven Reuther, Herbert Ross, *p.c* – New Regency/Hera. *dist* – Warner Bros.
sc – Don Roos. *ph* (*DuArt colour*) – Donald E. Thorin. *ed* – Michael R. Miller. *mus* – David Newman. *p.d* – Ken Adam. *a.d* – William F. O'Brien. *set des* – James R. Bayliss, Jann K. Engel, Stephen Berger. *set dec* – Rick Simpson. *cost* – Gloria Gresham.
cast – Whoopi Goldberg (*Jane*), Mary-Louise Parker (*Robin*), Drew Barrymore (*Holly*), Matthew McConnaughey (*Abe*), James Remar (*Alex*), Billy Wirth (*Nick*), Anita Gillette (*Elaine*).
Studio: Studio City. *Locs*: New York City; Tucson, Arizona.
Year Ken Adam worked on film: 1994.

84.
The Madness of King George
GB 1994.
d – Nicholas Hytner. *p* – Stephen Evans, David Parfitt, *p.c* – Close Call Films/Channel Four. *dist* – Samuel Goldwyn.
sc – Alan Bennett, from his play. *ph* (*Technicolor*) – Andrew Dunn. *ed* – Tariq Anwar. *mus. adapt* – George Fenton. *p.d* – Ken Adam. *a.d* – John Fenner. *set dec* – Carolyn Scott. *cost* – Mark Thompson.
cast – Nigel Hawthorne (*George III*), Helen Mirren (*Queen Charlotte*), Ian Holm (*Dr Willis*), Rupert Everett (*Prince of Wales*), Rupert Graves (*Greville*), John Wood (*Thurlow*), Amanda Donohoe (*Lady Pembroke*), Julian Rhind-Tutt (*Duke of York*).
Studio: Shepperton. *Locs*: Kew Palace; Wilton House; Arundel Castle; Eton College; St. Paul's Cathedral; Westminster Abbey; St George's Chapel, Windsor.
Year Ken Adam worked on film: 1994.
** Academy Award, Best Art Direction.
** British Film Academy award nomination, Best Art Direction.
** London Film Critics Circle award.

85.
Bogus
USA 1996.
d – Norman Jewison. *p* – Norman Jewison, Arnon Milchan, Jeff Rothberg, *p.c* – Yorktown/New Regency. *dist* – Warner Bros.
sc – Alvin Sargent, from a story by Jeff Rothberg and Francis X. McCarthy. *ph* (*DeLuxe Color*, *Panavision*) – David Watkin. *ed* – Stephen Rivkin. *mus* – Marc Shaiman. *p.d* – Ken Adam. *a.d* – Alice Keywan. *visual eff. sup* – Alan Munro. *cost* – Ruth Myers.
cast – Whoopi Goldberg (*Harriet Franklin*), Gérard Depardieu (*Bogus*), Haley Joel Osment (*Albert Franklin*), Denis Mercier (*M. Antoine*), Andrea Martin (*Penny*), Nancy Travis (*Lorraine Franklin*).
Studio: old steel mill, Toronto. *Locs*: New York City; Toronto.
Year Ken Adam worked on film: 1995.

86.
Dr. James Barry (unrealised film)
USA 1995–96.
A film project for director Martha Coolidge, to be produced by Aaron Spelling. The fascinating true story of a woman who lived as a man in the nineteenth century, rising through the ranks in the British army to become the top medical officer in South Africa; her lifelong masquerade was only discovered upon her death. Holly Hunter was to star. Ken Adam worked on this project for several months, researching locations in South Africa and designing exteriors and interiors. Owing to scripting problems the film was postponed.

87.
In & Out
USA 1997.
d – Frank Oz. *p* – Scott Rudin, *p.c* – Spelling Films/Paramount. *dist* – Paramount.
sc – Paul Rudnick. *ph* (*DuArt colour*) – Rob Hahn. *ed* – Dan Hanley, John Jympson. *mus* – Marc Shaiman. *p.d* – Ken Adam. *a.d* – Charles V. Beal. *set dec* – Leslie A. Pope. *scenic artist* – Denise Gurkas. *storyboard artist* – Lorenzo Contessa. *cost* – Ann Roth.
cast – Kevin Kline (*Howard Brackett*), Joan Cusack (*Emily Montgomery*), Tom Selleck (Peter Malloy), Debbie Reynolds (*Berniece Brackett*), Wilford Brimley (*Frank Brackett*), Bob Newhart (*Tom Halliwell*), Matt Dillon (*Cameron Drake*), Glenn Close, Whoopi Goldberg, Jay Leno.
Studio: converted armoury, metropolitan NY area. *Locs*: New York City.
Year Ken Adam worked on film: 1996–97.

88.
The Out-of-Towners
USA 1999.
d – Sam Weisman. *p* – Robert Evans, *p.c* – Cherry Alley Productions/The Cort/Madden Co. *dist* – Paramount.
sc – Marc Lawrence, from the original screenplay by Neil Simon. *ph* (*colour*) – John Bailey. *ed* – Kent Beyda. *mus* – Marc Shaiman. *p.d* – Ken Adam. *a.d* – William F. O'Brien, Charley Beal. *set dec* – Kathryn Peters, Marvin March, George DeTitta. *cost* – Ann Roth.
cast – Steve Martin (*Henry Clark*), Goldie Hawn (*Nancy Clark*), Mark McKinney (*Greg*), John Cleese (*Mr Mersault*), Oliver Hudson (*Alan Clark*).
Studio: Paramount (Los Angeles). *Locs*: New York City; Los Angeles.
Year Ken Adam worked on film: 1997–98.

Leigh Markopoulos

Biographical Note

Ken Adam was born Klaus Adam in Berlin in 1921, one of the four children of Fritz Adam and Lilli, née Saalfeld. Fritz Adam owned the sportswear department store S. Adam, which provided equipment for UFA (Universum Film AG) productions such as *Das Wunder des Schneeschuhs*, *Die weisse Hölle am Piz Palu* and expedition films such as *Silberkondor über Feuerland* (Gunther Plüschow), as well as for Roald Amundsen's various polar expeditions.

As conditions under the recently elected National Socialist regime became increasingly oppressive, the family left for the UK in April 1934. Adam was sent to a boarding school in Edinburgh to learn English and then to a London day prep school before attending St Paul's School.

At the age of seventeen he enrolled for evening classes in the Bartlett School of Architecture, University College London. He also held a day job with C. W. Glover and Partners, an architecture and construction firm.

At the outbreak of World War II, Ken Adam avoided internment as an 'enemy alien' through the intervention of the company director, Captain Glover. In October 1940, Adam interrupted his studies to enlist with the Auxiliary Military Pioneer Corps, a special unit allowing immigrants to pursue active service. He transferred to the Royal Air Force in 1941, and was posted to the USA for training. After his return to the UK he joined 609WR, a famed fighter squadron, in October 1943, flying Hawker Typhoons. He was probably the only German to serve as a fighter pilot with the RAF. In October 1946 he left the RAF with the rank of Acting Flight Lieutenant.

After Adam had tried unsuccessfully to find employment for nine months, his sister Loni, who worked for the American embassy in London and was helping to find props for a film production, introduced him to Andy Massey, the art director of Riverside Studios in Hammersmith, who hired him as a draughtsman on *This Was a Woman* (Tim Wheelan, 1948).

He rose rapidly to art director (*Around the World in Eighty Days*, Michael Anderson, 1956), and then to production designer in the following year (*Night of the Demon*, Jacques Tourneur, 1957). In his forty-two years in the film world Ken Adam has collaborated with such directors as Robert Aldrich (*Ten Seconds to Hell*, 1959; *The Angry Hills*, 1959; *Sodom and Gomorrah*, 1961), Stanley Kubrick (*Dr Strangelove*, 1963; *Barry Lyndon*, 1975), Joseph L. Mankiewicz (*Sleuth*, 1972) and Robert Siodmak (*The Crimson Pirate*, 1951; *The Rough and the Smooth*, 1959) on eighty-eight film projects, seventy-five of which were realised. It was Adam who master-minded the Bond look, creating bold and revolutionary designs for seven films in the series, from the first, *Dr No* (1961), to *Moonraker* (1979). He has also designed sets for two operas, has worked as an interior decorator and designer for private apartments in London, and designed the Harlequin coffee bar in Oxford, as well as coffee bars in London.

In 1952, while filming *The Crimson Pirate* on Ischia, Ken met Letizia Moauro, whom he subsequently married. Letizia Adam has played an active part in her husband's career, often assisting with props acquisition and set dressing. She received a credit as set decorator for *The Deceivers* (Nicholas Meyer, 1988) and a mention as technical adviser on *Agnes of God* (Norman Jewison, 1985).

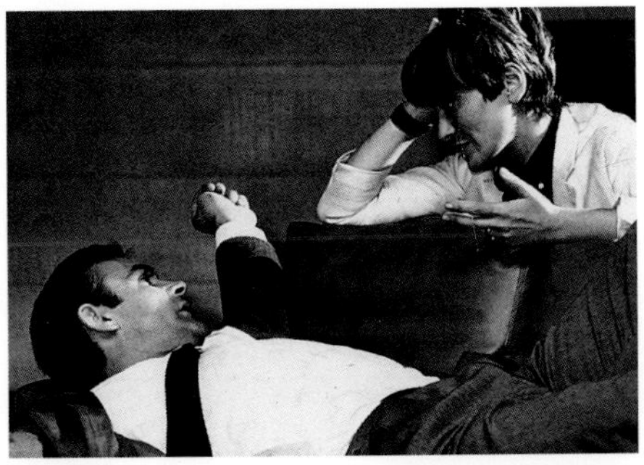

Letizia Adam in conversation with Sean Connery on the set of *You only Live Twice*, 1966

The winner of two Academy Awards for Best Art Direction – on *Barry Lyndon* in 1976 and *The Madness of King George* in 1995 – Ken Adam has also received British Film Academy Awards for Best Art Direction on *Dr Strangelove or: How I Learned to Stop Worrying and Love the Bomb*, in 1964, and *The Ipcress File*, in 1965, and has been nominated for numerous other awards. He was awarded an honorary doctorate by the Royal College of Art in 1995 and received an OBE in the 1996 New Year's honours list.

Ken Adam has recently been the subject of an exhibition organised at the Forum der Technik of the Deutsches Museum in Munich, which opened there in 1994 before touring Germany and travelling to Vienna and Wellington, New Zealand.

He was invited in 1998 to design the core of *Seven Hills: Images and Signs of the 21st Century*, the Berlin millennium exhibition, in the Martin-Gropius-Bau, and is currently working on this project.

Ken Adam continues to be based in London.

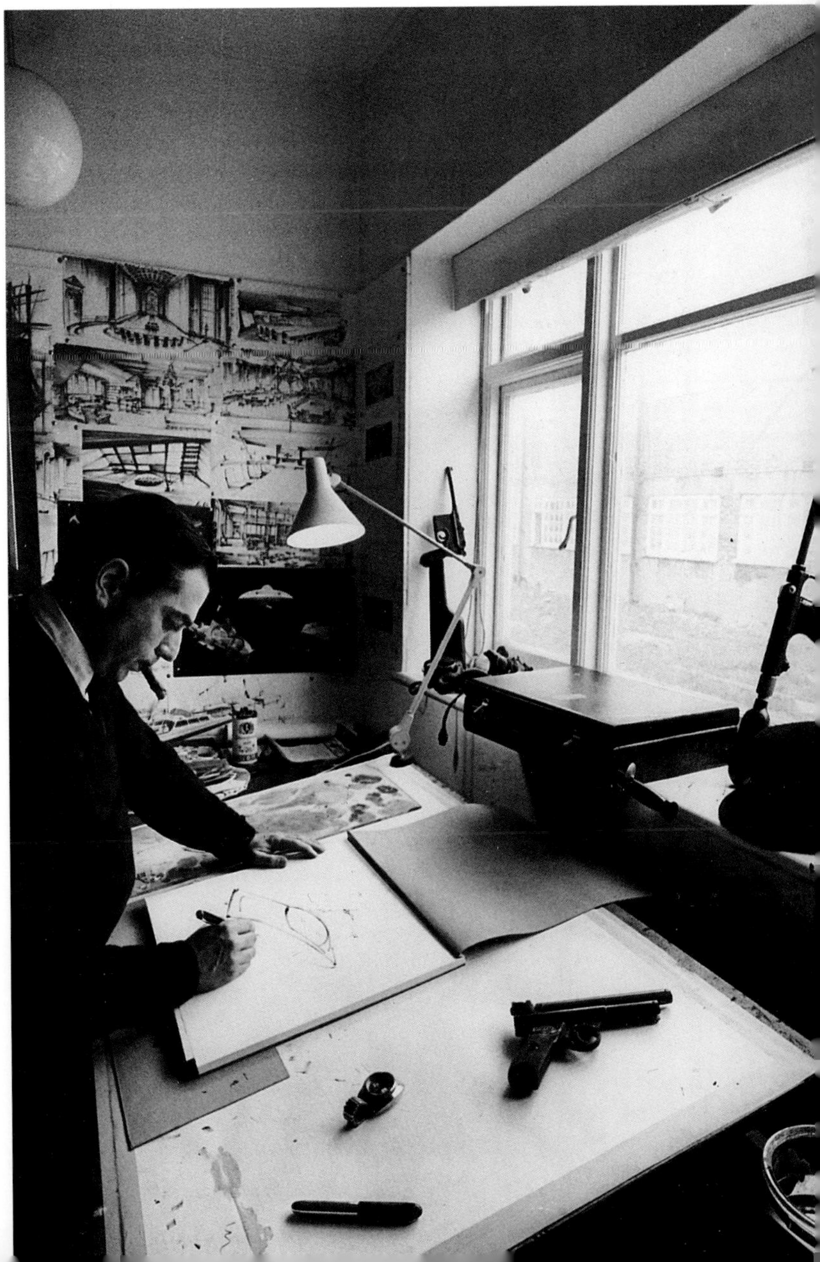

Ken Adam at work in Pinewood Studios, 1964

Catherine A. Surowiec

Bibliography

Adam, Ken, 'Designing Sets for Action', *Films and Filming* (London), Aug 1956.

Adam, Ken, magazine interviews:
Cinéma (Paris), no. 229, Jan 1978, pp. 38–45.
Film Comment (New York), v. 18 no. 1, Jan–Feb 1982, pp. 36–42, 50.
Positif (Paris), no. 191, March 1977, pp. 26–39.
Screen International (London), no. 74, 12 Feb 1977, p. 10.

Albrecht, Donald, *Designing Dreams. Modern Architecture in the Movies* (New York: Harper & Row/The Museum of Modern Art, 1986).

Barsacq, Léon, revised and ed. by Elliott Stein, *Caligari's Cabinet and Other Grand Illusions. A History of Film Design* (Boston: New York Graphic Society, 1976). Originally published as *Le Décor de Film* by Léon Barsacq (Paris: Editions Seghers, 1970).

Baxter, John, *Stanley Kubrick: A Biography* (London: HarperCollins, 1999; orig. publ. 1997).

Berger, Jürgen, ed., *Production Design: Ken Adam. Meisterwerke der Filmarchitektur* (Munich: Kulturreferat der Landeshauptstadt München, 1994). Exhibition catalogue.

Broccoli, Cubby, with Donald Zec, *When the Snow Melts. The Autobiography of Cubby Broccoli* (London: Boxtree, 1998).

Carrick, Edward, *Art and Design in the British Film. A Pictorial Directory of British Art Directors and Their Work* (London: Dennis Dobson, 1948).

Carrick, Edward, *Designing for Films* (London/New York: The Studio Publications, 1949). New, revised edn of his 1941 book *Designing for Moving Pictures*.

Cinématographe (Paris) no. 75, February 1982; no. 76, March 1982. Two special issues on 'Le Décor du Film'.

Contemporary Designers (Detroit/London: St James Press, 2nd edn, 1990): entry on Ken Adam.

Corliss, Mary, and Carlos Clarens, 'Designed for Film. The Hollywood Art Director', *Film Comment* (New York), v. 14, no. 3, May–June 1978. Special 36-page midsection to accompany an exhibition at the Museum of Modern Art, New York, including essays, interviews and filmographies.

The Director's Eye. Drawings and Photographs by European Film-makers (Oxford: Museum of Modern Art, 1996). Exhibition catalogue.

Drawing into Film. Directors' Drawings (New York: The Pace Gallery, 1993). Exhibition catalogue.

Eisner, Lotte H., *The Haunted Screen. Expressionism in the German Cinema and the Influence of Max Reinhardt* (London: Secker & Warburg, 1973).

Ettedgui, Peter, ed., *Screencraft: Production Design and Art Direction* (Hove: RotoVision, forthcoming, 2000).

Film Dope (London), no. 1, Dec 1972, entry 3: Ken Adam. Updates: no. 39, March 1988, p. 3.

Film Dope (London), no. 13, Jan 1978, pp. 1–15: interview with Max Douy, June 1977, by Jean-Pierre Berthomé; p. 14: about Ken Adam and *Thunderball*.

Hambley, John, and Patrick Downing, *The Art of Hollywood. Fifty Years of Art Direction* (London: Thames Television, 1979). Catalogue for exhibition at the Victoria & Albert Museum.

Heisner, Beverly, *Hollywood Art. Art Direction in the Days of the Great Studios* (Jefferson, North Carolina/London: McFarland, 1990).

Hudson, Roger, 'Three Designers', *Sight and Sound* (London), v. 34, no. 1, Winter 1964–65, pp. 29–31: interviews with Ken Adam, Edward Marshall and Richard Macdonald.

LoBrutto, Vincent, *By Design: Interviews with Film Production Designers* (Westport, CT: Praeger, 1992), pp. 35–47: Ken Adam.

LoBrutto, Vincent, *Stanley Kubrick: A Biography* (New York: Da Capo Press, 1999; orig. publ. 1997).

Mandelbaum, Howard, and Eric Myers, Forties Screen Style. *A Celebration of High Pastiche in Hollywood* (New York: St Martin's Press, 1989).

Mandelbaum, Howard, and Eric Myers, *Screen Deco* (New York: St Martin's Press, 1985).

Marner, Terence St John, compiler/ed., with Michael Stringer, *Film Design* (London: Tantivy Press/New York: A. S. Barnes, 1974; Screen Textbook series). Ken Adam is one of the 12 designer contributors.

Monthly Film Bulletin (London), v. 32, no. 372, Jan 1965, pp. 15–16: 'Checklist 21: Ken Adam'.

Myerscough-Walker, Raymond, *Stage and Film Décor* (London: Pitman & Sons, 1940).

Neumann, Dietrich, ed., *Film Architecture: From Metropolis to Blade Runner* (Munich: Prestel, 1996).

Penz, François, and Maureen Thomas, eds., *Cinema and Architecture: Méliès*, Mallet-Stevens, Multimedia (London: British Film Institute, 1997).

Preston, Ward, *What an Art Director Does. An Introduction to Motion Picture Production Design* (Los Angeles: Silman-James Press, 1994).

Sennett, Robert S., Setting the Scene. *The Great Hollywood Art Directors* (New York: Harry N. Abrams, 1994).

Surowiec, Catherine A., *Accent on Design. Four European Art Directors* (London: British Film Institute, 1992).

Vinson, James, ed., *The International Dictionary of Films and Filmmakers: Vol. Iv. Writers and Production Artists* (Chicago/London: St James Press, 1987), pp. 1–2: 'Ken Adam' by Edith C. Lee. Plus revised, updated edn, 1993: *International Dictionary of Films and Filmmakers 4: Writers and Production Artists* (London: St James Press).

Walker, Alexander, *Hollywood England. The British Film Industry in the Sixties* (London: Michael Joseph, 1974), pp. 194–98: 'The Adam Style'.

Serpentine Benefactors and Staff

Serpentine Gallery Benefactors

Simon Bakewell & Cheri Phillips
Tom Bendhem
David & Janice Blackburn
Anthony & Gisela Bloom
John & Frances Garland Bowes
John & Susan Burns
Calvin Klein Inc
Jonathan & Vanessa Cameron
Cheim & Read
Christie's
Michèle Claudel
Dr & Mrs David Cohen
Mr & Mrs Mark Fenwick
Harry & Ruth Fitzgibbons
David & Jane Fletcher
Bruce & Janet Flohr
Forward Publishing
Eric & Louise Franck
James Freedman & Anna Kissin
Albert & Lyn Fuss
Glovers Solicitors
Francesco Grana & Simona Fantinelli
Sir Ronald Grierson
Richard & Odile Grogan
The Bryan Guinness Charitable Trust
Philip Gumuchdjian
Mr & Mrs Rupert Hambro
Mr & Mrs Antony Harbour
Mr & Mrs Rick Hayward
Thomas Healy & Fred Hochberg
Mr & Mrs Michael Hue-Williams
The Montague Hurst Charitable Trust
Nicola Jacobs & Tony Schlesinger
Howard & Linda Karshan
King Sturge & Co
Mickey & Jeanne Klein
Rosemary Kowalski
Ilene Kurtz-Kretzschmar
The Landau Foundation
Stig Larsen
Barbara Lloyd & Judy Collins
Steve & Fran Magee
Karim Manji
Peter & Elena Marano
The Lord & Lady Marks
James & Viviane Mayor
Georgia Oetker
Omni Colour Presentations
Ophiucus SA
Mr & Mrs Nicholas Oppenheim
Linda Pace
Desmond Page & Asun Gelardin
William Palmer
Andrew Partridge
George & Carolyn Pincus
Mathew & Angela Prichard
John & Jill Ritblat
Dr & Mrs Mortimer Sackler
Alan & Joan Smith
Martin & Elise Smith
Sotheby's
Ian & Mercedes Stoutzker
Timothy Taylor Gallery Ltd
Mrs Britt Tidelius
Barry & Laura Townsley
UBS AG
Mr & Mrs Leslie Waddington
Robert & Felicity Waley-Cohen
Anthony Weldon
Lord & Lady John Wellesley
Robin Wight & Anastasia Alexander
Richard & Astrid Wolman
and Benefactors who wish to remain anonymous

Serpentine Gallery Renovation (1996–1997)

The Serpentine Gallery renovation has been generously funded by

The National Lottery through the Arts Council of England
The Baring Foundation
The Bridge House Estates Trust Fund
The Diana, Princess of Wales Memorial Fund
The John Ellerman Foundation
The Esmée Fairbairn Charitable Trust
The Henry Moore Foundation
The Department of Culture, Media and Sport
The Pilgrim Trust
The Foundation for Sport and the Arts
and The Dr Mortimer and Theresa Sackler Foundation

Board of Trustees

Director
Julia Peyton-Jones

Administration
Head of Finance & Administration
Jackie McNerney
Administrator
Wendy Lothian
Finance Officer
Stephen Crampton-Hayward

Bookshop
Bookshop Manager
*Gavin Everall**
Bookshop Manager
*Ben Hillwood-Harris**
Assistant Bookshop Manager
*Sara Ley**

Development
Acting Head of Development
*Anne Vanhaeverbeke**
Development Officer
Clare Oliver
Events Co-ordinator
Natasha Roach

Education
Head of Education
Vivien Ashley
Education Co-ordinator
Andrew Fisher

Exhibitions
Curator
Lisa Corrin
Exhibition Organiser
Leigh Markopoulos
Temporary Exhibition Organiser
Achim Borchardt-Hume

Gallery and Building Management
Building Manager
Mark Robinson
Gallery Manager
Michael Gaughan
Weekend Duty Manager
*Andy Shiel**

Gallery Assistants
*Fiona Boundy**
*Noel Bramley**
Jeanette Cleary
*Lawrence Corby**
*Claire Cousins**
Katherine Green
*Mark Harris**
*Nicola Holloway**
*Katie McKee**
*Charlotte Newman**
*Emmanuel Simpson**
*Rory Snookes**
*Vicky Steer**
*Emma Wilson**

Press
Press & Publicity Officer
Kathy Stephenson
Press Assistant
*Anna Barriball**

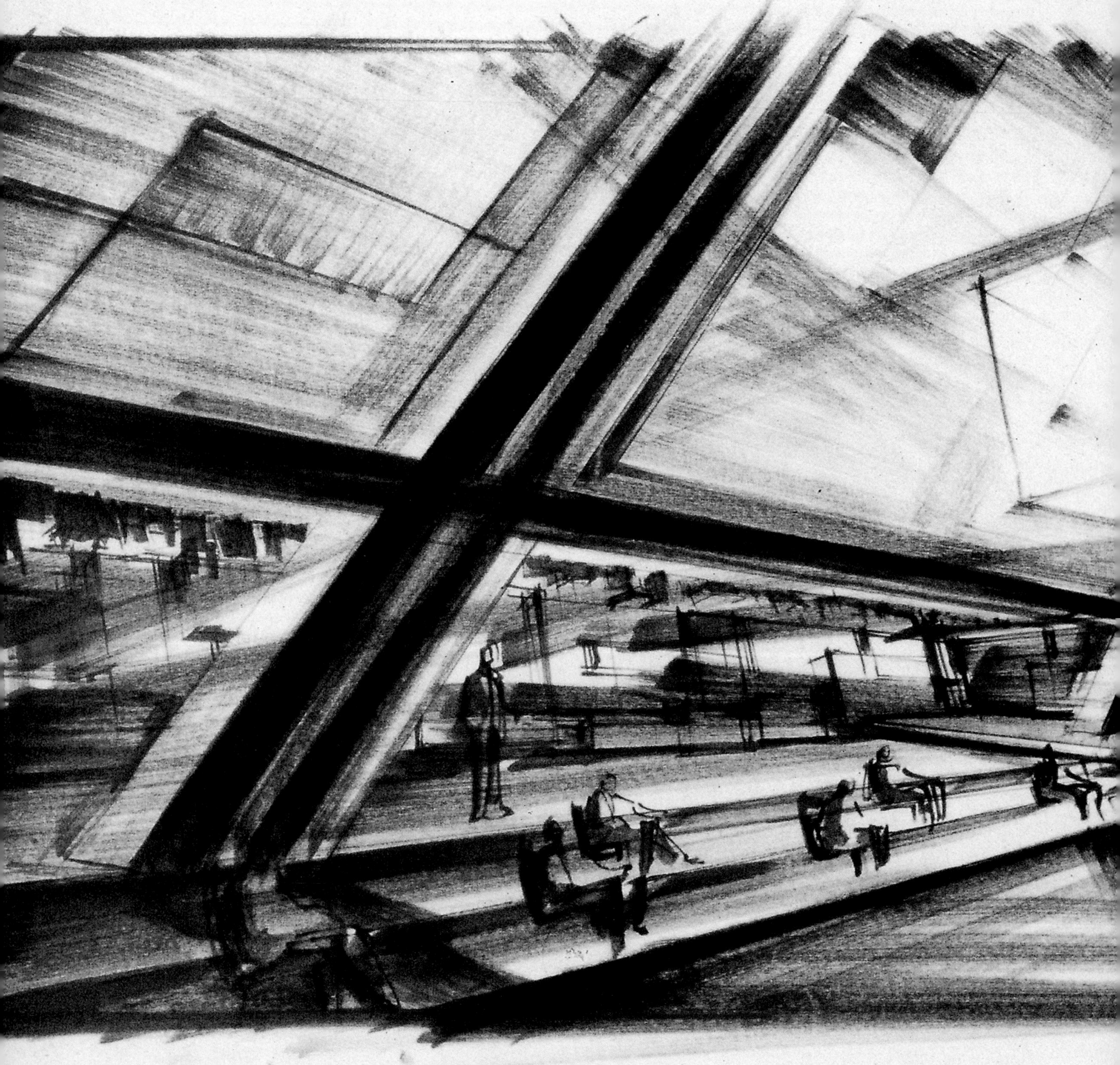